Mastering AWS Security

Strengthen your cloud environment using
AWS security features coupled with proven strategies

Laurent Mathieu

Mastering AWS Security

Group Product Manager: Pavan Ramchandani
Publishing Product Manager: Prachi Rana
Book Project Manager: Ashwin Dinesh Kharwa
Senior Editor: Sujata Tripathi
Technical Editor: Yash Bhanushali
Copy Editor: Safis Editing
Proofreader: Sujata Tripathi
Indexer: Rekha Nair
Production Designer: Nilesh Mohite
DevRel Marketing Coordinator: Marylou De Mello

First edition: October 2017

Second edition: April 2024

Production reference: 1290324

Published by Packt Publishing Ltd.

Grosvenor House

11 St Paul's Square

Birmingham

B3 1RB, UK

ISBN 978-1-80512-544-0

www.packtpub.com

Contributors

About the author

Laurent Mathieu is a seasoned cybersecurity and AWS cloud consultant and instructor with a rich history in cybersecurity spanning two decades and various domains and regions. He holds several professional qualifications, including ISC2 CISSP, ISACA CISM, and CSA CCSK, as well as six AWS certifications. Over the past decade, he has developed a keen interest in cloud computing, particularly in AWS cloud security. As an active member of the AWS Community Builder program since 2020, Laurent is at the forefront of AWS development. He has developed various training materials and led multiple webinars and bootcamps on AWS and security. Besides his instructional work, Laurent provides AWS consulting services, primarily through AWS IQ, to various start-ups and SaaS providers.

About the reviewers

Patrick Hannah is the CTO and co-founder of CloudHesive, an AWS Premier Consulting Partner and Managed Services provider with a SaaS offering, ConnectPath. Patrick is responsible for CloudHesive's product and development strategy as well as the Technology Operations team, which is responsible for delivering managed services, managed security services, and service management to CloudHesive's customers. Before CloudHesive, Patrick was the senior manager of the cloud engineering team at Pegasystems – an enterprise software company located in Cambridge, Massachusetts. Before that, Patrick spent 8 years at Arise Virtual Solutions – a work-at-home BPO in Miramar, Florida, leading the team responsible for their contact center technology platform.

Ayyanar Jeyakrishnan (AJ) is an accomplished professional who holds all 12 AWS certifications and serves as an AWS ML Community Builder. Additionally, he co-organizes the AWS User Group Bengaluru. With over 18 years of IT experience and 50+ industry certifications, AJ excels as an AWS cloud architect, specializing in crafting scalable cloud solutions, machine learning, and data platforms for enterprises. Currently, he is working as executive director and principal engineer at a major financial institution.

Thanks to Ashwin from Packt for making the process seamless. Thanks to my family members, who are my pillars of strength.

Table of Contents

Part 1: Foundations of AWS Security

1

Introduction to AWS Security Concepts and Shared Responsibility Model

2

Infrastructure Security – Keeping Your VPC secure   21

3

Identity and Access Management – Securing Users, Roles, and Policies   49

4

Data Protection – Encryption, Key Management, and Data Storage Best Practices — 79

5

Introduction to AWS Security Services — 105

Part 2: Architecting and Deploying Secure AWS Environments

6

Designing Secure Microservices Architectures in AWS   147

7

Implementing Security for Serverless Deployments   179

8

Secure Design Patterns for Multi-tenancy in Shared Environments   203

9

Automate-Everything to Build Immutable and
Ephemeral Resources   227

Part 3: Monitoring, Automation and Continuous Improvement

10

Advanced Logging, Auditing, and Monitoring in AWS   247

11

Security Compliance with AWS Config, AWS Security Hub, and Automated Remediation   267

12

DevSecOps – Integrating Security into CI/CD Pipelines   287

Preface

Welcome to *Mastering AWS Security, Second Edition*, your comprehensive guide to securing assets in the ever-evolving realm of **Amazon Web Services** (**AWS**). This new edition dives deeper than ever before into the strategies, tools, and best practices essential for safeguarding your AWS cloud environment against modern cyber threats such as **Distributed Denial of Services** (**DDoS**), data exfiltration, and privilege escalation attacks.

With an emphasis on the strategic use of AWS native services, we will embark on a journey that begins with the bedrock of AWS security principles and the shared responsibility model. From there, we will delve into secure architecture design, and advanced protection techniques such as data encryption and identity management, and embrace a DevSecOps mindset for seamlessly integrating security into your workflows. We will discuss cutting-edge security tools and how a commitment to continuous improvement keeps your cloud environment secure in a constantly evolving threat landscape.

Reflecting on my own journey as a security veteran from cloud skepticism to AWS security advocacy, this book encapsulates the insights and strategies honed over years of hands-on experience. Each chapter builds upon the last, ensuring a solid foundation in AWS security mechanisms, best practices, and innovative approaches for securing digital assets. It's not just a book; it's a journey alongside a seasoned practitioner, aimed at demystifying AWS cloud security and arming you with the tools needed for resilience in the face of cyber threats.

With *Mastering AWS Security, Second Edition* as your guide, you will gain the knowledge and skills necessary to design, implement, and maintain secure, resilient, and compliant AWS environments, along with the adaptability needed to face evolving security challenges and ongoing advancements in AWS.

Who this book is for

This book is written for anyone responsible for the security of AWS environments, such as:

- **Cloud Architects and Engineers**: Design and deploy cloud solutions with security woven into their core, not just bolted on after the fact

- **DevOps Professionals**: Learn to integrate security throughout the development and deployment lifecycles for a proactive, preventative approach

- **Cybersecurity Professionals**: Gain a robust understanding of AWS security mechanisms and best practices

- **AWS Enthusiasts**: Enhance your skills and become an advocate for security within your projects and organizations

Whether you are embarking on your AWS security journey or looking to deepen your existing expertise, it provides a comprehensive and practical guide to enhancing your security skills. It is about understanding the *why* behind security measures, enabling informed decisions that align with best practices and organizational objectives.

What this book covers

Chapter 1, Introduction to AWS Security Concepts and the Shared Responsibility Model, establishes the groundwork for securing AWS environments, emphasizing the collaborative model of security responsibilities.

Chapter 2, Infrastructure Security – Keeping Your VPC Secure, offers insights into safeguarding your AWS infrastructure, focusing on VPC configurations, security groups, network access controls, and advanced security measures such as AWS Network Firewall, AWS WAF, and AWS Shield.

Chapter 3, Identity and Access Management – Securing Users, Roles, and Policies, provides a thorough examination of IAM core concepts, detailing best practices for governing identities and managing access to AWS resources securely.

Chapter 4, Data Protection - Encryption, Key Management, and Data Storage Best Practices, explores encryption methods, key management strategies, and best practices for securing data across various AWS storage services.

Chapter 5, Introduction to AWS Security Services, introduces key AWS security services, including Amazon GuardDuty, Amazon Inspector, and AWS Security Hub, and how they can be integrated into a comprehensive security strategy.

Chapter 6, Designing Secure Microservices Architectures in AWS, delves into architectural considerations and security best practices for building microservices using AWS services.

Chapter 7, Implementing Security for Serverless Deployments, addresses the unique security challenges of serverless computing, offering strategies for securing serverless applications in AWS.

Chapter 8, Secure Design Patterns for Multi-Tenancy in Shared Environments, explores multi-tenancy in AWS, discussing design patterns for securely isolating customer data and workloads.

Chapter 9, Automate Everything to Build Immutable and Ephemeral Resources, emphasizes the role of automation in enhancing security by leveraging programmatic management and **Infrastructure as Code (IaC)**.

Chapter 10, Advanced Logging, Auditing, and Monitoring in AWS, covers the tools and techniques for effective logging, auditing, and monitoring of AWS environments.

Chapter 11, Security Compliance with AWS Config, AWS Security Hub, and Automated Remediation, explores achieving and maintaining security compliance through continuous monitoring and automated remediation strategies.

Chapter 12, DevSecOps - Integrating Security into CI/CD Pipelines, introduces the principles of DevSecOps, integrating security practices within development and deployment workflows.

Chapter 13, Keeping Up with Evolving AWS Security Best Practices and the Threat Landscape, discusses strategies to remain well-versed in AWS security evolutions, stay ahead of security trends, adjust to new threats, and apply AWS's newest security capabilities.

Closing Note

To get the most out of this book

This book assumes a good understanding of essential AWS services (such as Amazon S3, AWS Lambda, Amazon EC2, and AWS IAM) and a desire to take your cloud security knowledge to the next level.

Conventions used

There are a number of text conventions used throughout this book.

`Code in text`: Indicates code words in text, database table names, folder names, filenames, file extensions, pathnames, dummy URLs, user input, and Twitter handles. Here is an example: "Apply these universally across AWS services, such as using `aws:MultiFactorAuthPresent` to verify MFA status for resource access."

A block of code is set as follows:

```
from aws_encryption_sdk import KMSMasterKeyProvider, encrypt
key_provider = KMSMasterKeyProvider(key_ids=[
    'arn:aws:kms:us-east-1:012345678912:key/abcd1234-a123-456a-a12b-a123b4cd56ef'
])
plaintext = 'This is a plaintext message.'
ciphertext, encryptor_header = encrypt(
    source=plaintext,
    key_provider=key_provider
)
print(f'Ciphertext: {ciphertext}')
```

> **Tips or important notes**
> Appear like this.

Get in touch

Feedback from our readers is always welcome.

General feedback: If you have questions about any aspect of this book, email us at customercare@packtpub.com and mention the book title in the subject of your message.

Errata: Although we have taken every care to ensure the accuracy of our content, mistakes do happen. If you have found a mistake in this book, we would be grateful if you would report this to us. Please visit www.packtpub.com/support/errata and fill in the form.

Piracy: If you come across any illegal copies of our works in any form on the internet, we would be grateful if you would provide us with the location address or website name. Please contact us at copyright@packt.com with a link to the material.

If you are interested in becoming an author: If there is a topic that you have expertise in and you are interested in either writing or contributing to a book, please visit authors.packtpub.com.

Share Your Thoughts

Once you've read *Mastering AWS Security*, we'd love to hear your thoughts! Scan the QR code below to go straight to the Amazon review page for this book and share your feedback.

https://packt.link/r/1805125443

Your review is important to us and the tech community and will help us make sure we're delivering excellent quality content.

Download a free PDF copy of this book

Thanks for purchasing this book!

Do you like to read on the go but are unable to carry your print books everywhere?

Is your eBook purchase not compatible with the device of your choice?

Don't worry, now with every Packt book you get a DRM-free PDF version of that book at no cost.

Read anywhere, any place, on any device. Search, copy, and paste code from your favorite technical books directly into your application.

The perks don't stop there, you can get exclusive access to discounts, newsletters, and great free content in your inbox daily

Follow these simple steps to get the benefits:

1. Scan the QR code or visit the link below

https://packt.link/free-ebook/978-1-80512-544-0

2. Submit your proof of purchase
3. That's it! We'll send your free PDF and other benefits to your email directly

Part 1: Foundations of AWS Security

Establish your security bedrock: In this part, you will dive into core AWS security principles, lock down your infrastructure, master identity and access management, safeguard your data, and explore essential AWS security services.

This part contains the following chapters:

- *Chapter 1, Introduction to AWS Security Concepts and the Shared Responsibility Model*
- *Chapter 2, Infrastructure Security - Keeping Your VPC secure*
- *Chapter 3, Identity and Access Management - Securing Users, Roles, and Policies*
- *Chapter 4, Data Protection - Encryption, Key Management, and Data Storage Best Practices*
- *Chapter 5, Introduction to AWS Security Services*

Introduction to AWS Security Concepts and the Shared Responsibility Model

Welcome to the initial stage of our deep dive into AWS security. This first chapter serves as an introduction to the complex world of AWS security. We will start by discussing the importance of cloud security and the unique challenges it presents. We will then review the AWS shared responsibility model, a key concept that delineates the security responsibilities of AWS and its customers. We will also examine the AWS global infrastructure, discussing its components and the security considerations associated with each. Finally, we will outline some relevant general AWS security best practices that will be covered in more detail in the successive chapters.

By the end of this chapter, you will have a comprehensive understanding of the AWS security landscape, setting the stage for the more advanced and practical discussions that will follow in the later chapters.

In this chapter, we are going to cover the following main topics:

- Cloud security overview – its importance and challenges
- The shared responsibility model delineating AWS and customer responsibilities
- AWS global infrastructure and security
- AWS security best practices and general guidelines

Cloud security overview – its importance and challenges

As we embark on our journey into AWS security, it is essential to understand the broader landscape of cloud security. This section will set the stage by highlighting the importance of cloud security in our increasingly digital world and the unique challenges it presents.

The significance of cloud security

In the era of digital transformation, the role of cloud security has become paramount. As businesses increasingly shift their operations to the cloud, the need for robust, effective security measures has never been more critical. However, cloud security is not just about protecting data; it is about safeguarding the very foundation of modern businesses. The advent of cloud computing has brought about a paradigm shift in the way businesses operate, offering unprecedented scalability, agility, and cost efficiency. However, this new operational landscape also introduces new considerations and complexities, particularly when it comes to security. Traditional security practices may not be wholly relevant in cloud environments, necessitating a fresh approach and a new mindset.

The cloud model used by providers such as AWS inherently involves entrusting a third-party provider with sensitive data and critical operations. This trust underscores the critical role of cloud security. Organizations must ensure that their cloud provider has robust security controls in place and that they are leveraging all available security features and best practices to protect their data and operations.

However, cloud computing and cloud security are often misunderstood, sometimes even by security professionals. This lack of understanding can lead to security gaps and vulnerabilities, making education and awareness crucial components of effective cloud security.

In essence, cloud security is not just a technical requirement; it is a business imperative. It is about protecting the organization's assets, reputation, and, ultimately, its bottom line. As we dive into the world of AWS security in the subsequent sections and chapters, we will explore how to build and maintain a robust security posture in the AWS cloud, taking into account the unique challenges and opportunities that the cloud presents.

Cloud security challenges

Despite the numerous benefits of cloud computing, it also introduces a unique set of security challenges that organizations must address. These challenges stem from the inherent characteristics of the cloud, such as its shared, on-demand nature, and the fact that it often involves storing and processing sensitive data in third-party data centers.

Responsibility and accountability

In the context of cloud computing, responsibility and accountability are critical aspects that must be clearly defined and understood. This is where the concept of the shared responsibility model comes into play.

The shared responsibility model is a framework that delineates the responsibilities of **cloud service providers** (**CSPs**) and their customers to ensure the security and compliance of cloud computing environments. The model is *shared* because both parties – the CSP and the customer – have responsibilities.

The CSP, such as AWS, is responsible for the security *of* the cloud. This includes all the hardware, software, networking, and facilities that run their cloud services. On the other hand, the customer is responsible for security *in* the cloud. This means the customer is responsible for how they utilize the cloud services provided by the CSP for managing the security of their data and applications.

While responsibilities can be shared, accountability cannot. Regardless of the security measures and services provided by the CSP, the customer always retains ultimate accountability for the security and integrity of their data. This means that even if a security issue arises from a component that is under the responsibility of the CSP, the customer is still accountable for the impact this may have on their business or operations.

Understanding the nuances of this shared responsibility model is vital for customers. It helps them to not only implement their security measures effectively but also to understand and leverage the security controls provided by the CSP. This dual understanding is key to mitigating potential risks and establishing a secure operational environment for their workloads.

The shared responsibility model will be covered in more detail in the *AWS shared responsibility model* section.

Complexity

Cloud environments offered by a leading provider such as AWS are inherently complex. This complexity is multifaceted, stemming from the vast array of services offered, the dynamic and scalable nature of the cloud, and the global reach of the cloud platform.

AWS offers well over 200 fully featured services from data centers globally. These services range from foundational services such as compute (Amazon EC2), storage (Amazon S3), and databases (Amazon RDS), to more advanced solutions such as machine learning, artificial intelligence, data lakes and analytics, and **internet of things (IoT)** solutions. Each of these services has its unique features, configurations, and security considerations, adding to the overall complexity of the environment. The dynamic and scalable nature of the cloud further amplifies this complexity. Resources can be provisioned and decommissioned on-demand and can scale out or in automatically. While this dynamism is one of the cloud's key benefits, it also introduces additional layers of complexity in managing and securing these environments. The state of the environment can change rapidly, and keeping track of these changes can be a challenging task. Moreover, the global reach of cloud platforms adds another dimension to this complexity. AWS spans around 100 **availability zones (AZs)** over 25 geographic regions around the world, frequently announcing plans for additional regional expansion. Managing and securing resources across these geographically dispersed regions can be a daunting task, requiring a deep understanding of different regional regulations and compliance requirements.

This complexity, while offering unmatched flexibility and capabilities, also presents significant challenges. It can make cloud environments difficult to understand and manage, even for seasoned security professionals. The multitude of services, the rapid pace of change, and the global nature of the cloud can be overwhelming. It can be challenging to keep up with the latest services and features, understand their security implications, and implement the necessary controls to secure them while maintaining a consistent security posture. This complexity can easily lead to misconfigurations, which are a leading cause of security incidents in the cloud. With so many services and configurations to manage, it is easy to overlook a setting or make a mistake that could expose the environment to potential threats.

However, it is important to note that this complexity is not insurmountable. With a strong understanding of AWS security, the right strategies, and the effective use of automation and cloud management tools, organizations can navigate this complexity and secure their AWS environments effectively. In the following sections, we will delve deeper into these aspects and provide you with the knowledge and skills to manage and secure complex AWS environments.

Visibility and control

In the realm of cloud security, visibility and control are critical aspects. Unlike traditional on-premises environments where infrastructure is physically accessible and operations are often static, the cloud introduces a dynamic, scalable, and distributed environment that necessitates a different approach to maintaining visibility and control. Visibility in the cloud is about having a clear, detailed, and real-time view of all activities, resources, and users within your cloud environment. This is crucial for several reasons. Firstly, it allows for the detection of anomalies and potential security threats. Secondly, it enables compliance with various regulations, which often require detailed logging and monitoring of activities. Lastly, visibility is key to understanding the state of your cloud environment, which is essential for effective management and decision-making.

The sheer scale of operations, the multitude of services, and the rapid pace of changes all contribute to great complexity when it comes to achieving comprehensive visibility in the cloud. For instance, a single AWS account can have hundreds of instances and containers running across multiple regions, each with its own set of logs and metrics. Keeping track of all these resources and their activities can be a daunting task.

Control in the cloud, on the other hand, is about having the ability to manage, manipulate, and secure your cloud environment effectively. This includes the ability to enforce policies, manage resources, respond to events, and mitigate risks. However, the shared responsibility model of cloud security adds another layer of complexity to this task. Understanding where the responsibility of the cloud provider ends and where the user's responsibility begins is crucial for maintaining control in the cloud.

AWS provides a wide range of services and features to enhance visibility and control in the cloud. AWS CloudTrail, AWS Config, and AWS Security Hub are just a few examples of the tools available for this purpose. These tools provide detailed audit logging, configuration management, and centralized security alerting, respectively. Yet, these tools are only as effective as the policies and practices that guide their use. Proper configuration, continuous monitoring, and regular audits are key to maintaining visibility and control in the cloud. It is also important to leverage automation wherever possible to manage the scale and complexity of cloud operations.

In the next few sections and chapters, we will delve deeper into these aspects and provide you with the knowledge and skills to enhance visibility and control in your AWS environments. We will also discuss specific strategies and best practices for overcoming the challenges associated with visibility and control in the cloud.

Compliance

Ensuring compliance in the cloud means that your operations and workloads running in the cloud align with various regulatory standards and requirements. These could range from industry-specific regulations such as HIPAA for healthcare or PCI DSS for payment card information, to broader regulations such as GDPR for data protection in the **European Union** (**EU**). It also means following best practices for cloud security and operations, such as those outlined in the AWS Well-Architected Framework.

Achieving and maintaining compliance in the cloud can be complicated due to the ever-changing nature of the cloud, the shared responsibility model, and the global reach of cloud platforms. For instance, data residency requirements that dictate where data can be stored and processed can pose challenges when operating in a global cloud environment across multiple regions.

AWS offers a suite of services and features designed to assist customers in meeting their compliance needs. AWS Artifact, for example, provides on-demand access to AWS compliance reports, while AWS Config allows you to audit the configurations of your AWS resources. AWS also upholds a comprehensive compliance program, boasting certifications and attestations for a wide array of global and regional regulations.

It is crucial to remember that while AWS provides tools to facilitate compliance, the ultimate responsibility for ensuring compliance rests with the customer. Grasping the shared responsibility model and effectively utilizing AWS compliance features are key to maintaining compliance in the cloud. For instance, while AWS Artifact helps with compliance, it only reflects the compliance status of AWS's infrastructure and services, and does not extend to the infrastructures or services deployed and configured by customers. Therefore, even if AWS is SOC2-compliant, it doesn't automatically mean that the applications and workloads you deploy will be as well. In subsequent sections and chapters, we will explore these aspects in greater depth, equipping you with the knowledge and skills to traverse the intricate landscape of cloud compliance. We will also discuss specific strategies and best practices for achieving and maintaining compliance in the cloud.

Speed of innovation

The speed of innovation in the cloud is both a boon and a challenge when it comes to security. On one hand, rapid innovation allows for the quick deployment of new features and services that can enhance security. On the other hand, it can also introduce new vulnerabilities and complexities that need to be managed.

In the cloud, new services, features, and updates are rolled out regularly. This constant evolution can provide organizations with powerful new tools to secure their environments.

Yet, the rapid pace of innovation can also introduce new security considerations. Each new service or feature may come with its own set of security controls and configurations that need to be understood and managed. Furthermore, the use of these new services may alter the security posture of an organization's cloud environment, requiring adjustments to existing security strategies and controls.

Moreover, the speed of innovation can put pressure on organizations to adopt new services quickly, sometimes at the expense of thorough security assessments. Organizations must balance the need for innovation with the need for security. This involves conducting comprehensive security assessments of new services before adoption, continuously monitoring the security impact of new services, and adjusting security controls as needed.

In the upcoming sections, we will delve deeper into these aspects and provide you with the knowledge and skills to manage the security implications of rapid innovation in the cloud. We will also discuss specific strategies and best practices for balancing the need for innovation with the need for security.

AWS shared responsibility model

The shared responsibility model is a fundamental principle that underpins the security architecture and operation of AWS services. It delineates the security responsibilities between AWS and the customer, ensuring that both parties understand their respective roles in maintaining a secure environment.

Security "of" the cloud

AWS is responsible for securing the underlying infrastructure that runs all of the services offered in the AWS cloud. This includes fundamental infrastructure components, such as the hardware, software, networking, and facilities that house AWS cloud services. AWS's responsibility *of* the cloud includes a wide range of security measures, such as physical security of data centers, server infrastructure, and network and virtualization security. These are tasks that AWS is uniquely positioned to perform, given its scale and expertise.

Security "in" the cloud

On the other hand, the customer is responsible for security *in* the cloud. This means that customers have control and ownership over their data, platforms, applications, systems, and networks, and they must protect them accordingly. This includes managing and controlling user access, protecting data through encryption, maintaining the security of their guest **operating systems** (**OSs**), applications, and data, and configuring their use of AWS services securely.

IaaS, PaaS, SaaS – different levels of responsibility

The shared responsibility model varies depending on the type of service – **Infrastructure-as-a-Service (IaaS)**, **Platform-as-a-Service (PaaS)**, or **Software-as-a-Service (SaaS)**. AWS offers a wide range of services that fall under these categories, each with its unique features and benefits:

- **IaaS**: AWS provides the fundamental cloud-provider infrastructure, such as the **virtual machine (VM)** (EC2) service, and **virtual private cloud (VPC)** networking components. The customer is responsible for everything else, including the OS, middleware, application, runtime, data, as well as any customer-deployed infrastructure components.

- **PaaS**: This includes additional layers of managed services. AWS handles the runtime, middleware, and OS, allowing developers to focus solely on their applications and data. Services such as RDS, S3, and AWS Elastic Beanstalk are examples of PaaS.

- **SaaS**: AWS is responsible for the entire stack, and the customer only interacts with the application with its data. Services such as Amazon Connect and Amazon Quicksight are examples of SaaS.

The following figure (*Figure 1.1*) illustrates where the responsibility domain lies for each service type:

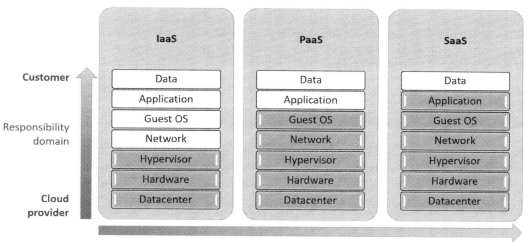

Figure 1.1 – High-level responsibility domain defined for each cloud service model

Now that we have a clear understanding of the shared responsibility model across different service models, let's take a closer look at how this model is implemented in the real world, particularly in the context of a particular category of AWS services.

Shared responsibility in practice – a closer look at AWS compute

The shared responsibility model extends across AWS compute services, but the specific breakdown varies based on the level of abstraction. Here is how it applies to different options:

- **Amazon EC2 (IaaS)**: AWS secures the underlying infrastructure – the hypervisor, physical hardware, and data center security. This grants you full control over the guest OS, applications, data, and network configuration. This flexibility comes with the onus of managing these layers for optimal security.

- **AWS Fargate (PaaS)**: AWS extends its management to include the guest OS, patching and maintaining it for you. You focus on developing and deploying your containerized applications, along with data security and essential network configurations (such as security groups). This reduces operational overhead without sacrificing security control.

- **AWS Lambda (PaaS)**: AWS takes on the responsibility for the infrastructure and the environment your functions run in. Your primary concern is ensuring your code is secure and that it manages any sensitive data appropriately. Additionally, if your Lambda function interacts with resources within a VPC, you may also need to configure network security elements (such as security groups).

The following figure (*Figure 1.2*) illustrates the division of responsibilities among those options:

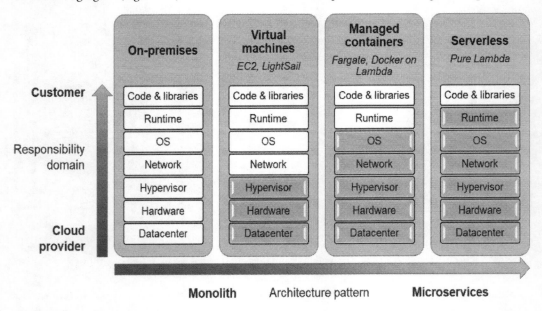

Figure 1.2 – Responsibility domain defined per compute type

It is worth noting that modern applications, especially those based on microservices architectures, frequently opt for managed cloud-native services (PaaS) such as Fargate or Lambda. These services provide more agility and ease of use, eliminating the need for customers to manage things the underlying operating system and networking. For example, a microservices-based eCommerce application could use Lambda for order processing, Fargate for inventory management, and S3 for storing product images, all without worrying about the underlying infrastructure. This means that the responsibility tends to shift more toward the CSP. This allows customers to focus more on their core business, leaving the heavy lifting of infrastructure management and security to AWS.

The importance of understanding the shared responsibility model

Understanding the shared responsibility model is crucial for customers to ensure they are adequately managing their part of the security responsibilities. It is not just a theoretical concept; it has practical implications for how customers use and secure AWS services.

Misunderstandings about the model can not only lead to gaps in security but also foster a false sense of security. Customers may incorrectly assume that certain aspects are managed by AWS when in reality, these remain the customer's responsibility, which may lead to neglecting essential security measures.

By fully understanding and adhering to the shared responsibility model, customers can better secure their AWS environments and ensure they are making the most of the security features and services offered by AWS.

AWS global infrastructure and security

The AWS global infrastructure is a cornerstone of the cloud services provided by AWS. It is designed to provide robust, secure, and scalable services to customers around the globe. The infrastructure is divided into **regions**, **AZs**, and **edge locations**, each playing a crucial role in delivering cloud services.

Regions

Regions represent the broadest geographical division in the AWS infrastructure. Each region is a separate geographic area, and AWS promises no data replication between regions unless initiated by the user. This isolation is crucial for disaster recovery and to comply with data residency requirements.

When selecting a region, several security considerations come into play:

- **Data sovereignty and regulatory compliance**: Various countries and industries have specific laws and regulations that dictate where and how data must be stored. For instance, some countries require certain types of data to remain within their borders, necessitating the selection of a specific region. Similarly, industries such as healthcare in the US must adhere to HIPAA regulations, which have specific requirements for data storage, including in the cloud. Understanding these legal and compliance factors is essential when selecting a region.

- **Latency**: The physical distance between the user and the data center can impact the latency of the service. For applications where latency is a critical factor, selecting a region closer to the end users can improve performance.

- **Service availability**: Not all AWS services are available in every region. When architecting your solution, ensure that the services you plan to use are available in the selected region.

- **Cost**: Pricing for AWS services can vary between regions. Cost should be considered during the planning phase as it can impact the overall budget for security controls and influence the decisions made on risk mitigation.

- **Regional resilience**: Some organizations prefer to architect their applications across multiple regions to achieve higher levels of resilience. This strategy can protect against large-scale events such as natural disasters that might simultaneously impact all AZs within the same region.

Understanding these factors can help you make an informed decision when selecting a region. It is important to note that AWS maintains a high standard of security across all regions, but not all security services may be immediately available in newly released Regions. Therefore, selecting a region could potentially impact your security operations.

AZs

Every region is composed of multiple isolated sites, referred to as AZs. Each AZ houses one or more data centers, all of which are equipped with redundant power, networking, and cooling facilities. These AZs are strategically placed at a considerable distance from each other, spanning several kilometers, but are still within 100 kilometers (60 miles) proximity.

AZs offer a way to build applications that are resilient to individual data center failures, a key consideration for security and business continuity. By distributing instances across multiple AZs within a region, you can protect your applications from the failure of a single location.

However, It is important to note that the selection of AZs should not be done randomly or excessively. While AWS does provide high availability through multiple AZs, the architecture of your application is under your responsibility and plays a crucial role in determining its resilience. For example, if different components of your application stack are spread across different AZs without proper planning, it can create more points of failure rather than improving the overall availability of the stack. When architecting your application, it is advisable to consider the interdependencies of your application components and aim to minimize the impact of a single AZ failure on your overall application. This might involve replicating critical components across multiple AZs or designing your application to degrade gracefully in the event of a component failure.

Furthermore, the level of built-in resiliency can vary depending on the AWS service you choose. For instance, more managed services, such as Lambda, provide multi-AZ resilience out of the box, reducing the need for manual configuration. On the other hand, services such as RDS for MySQL or EC2 require more manual configuration and additional costs to achieve a similar level of resilience.

Understanding these factors can help you make informed decisions when selecting and configuring AZs, ultimately improving the security and resilience of your applications running in the AWS cloud.

Edge locations

Edge locations are sites that are deployed in major cities and highly populated areas worldwide to deliver content to end users with lower latency. While edge locations don't host AWS services, they play a crucial role in the security and performance of services such as Amazon CloudFront, AWS WAF, and AWS Shield.

Edge locations are the endpoints for CloudFront, the **content delivery network (CDN)** of AWS. They are designed to cache content, reducing the load on your application and improving the user experience by delivering content from locations closer to the end user. But beyond performance and latency, edge locations also play a significant role in security, and in particular in mitigating **distributed denial of service (DDoS)** attacks. By using CloudFront, traffic to your application is routed through the edge locations, where the traffic can be inspected before reaching the application. Any sudden surge in traffic can be absorbed and distributed across the entire network of edge locations. This means that even during a DDoS attack, your application remains mostly available to your users.

However, for more advanced and larger-scale DDoS protection, the paid option, AWS Shield Advanced, can be used to provide more enhanced rate limiting and anomaly detection algorithms to detect and mitigate DDoS attacks.

In conclusion, while edge locations are primarily designed for performance, they also provide significant security benefits. By understanding and leveraging these benefits, you can enhance the security and resilience of your AWS applications.

AWS security best practices – general guidelines

When it comes to securing your AWS environment, there are several best practices that you should consider following to help you protect your resources, data, and applications in the AWS cloud. By following them, you can significantly enhance the security of your AWS environment. However, remember that security best practices can vary depending on the specific AWS services you are using and the unique requirements of your applications and workloads.

Understand the shared responsibility model

As discussed earlier, security in the AWS cloud is a shared responsibility between AWS and the customer. AWS is responsible for the security *of* the cloud, while customers are responsible for security *in* the cloud. Understanding this model is crucial to ensuring that you are doing your part to secure your resources.

Use AWS security services and features

AWS offers a wide range of security services and features that can significantly enhance the security posture of your cloud environment. These services are designed to provide robust protection for your resources, data, and applications.

Amazon GuardDuty functions as a vigilant sentinel, constantly scanning for harmful or unauthorized activities that could pose a threat to your AWS accounts and workloads. By harnessing the power of machine learning, anomaly detection, and integrated threat intelligence, it can discern and prioritize potential threats.

Amazon Detective acts as your personal investigator, simplifying the task of analyzing and investigating potential security issues or suspicious activities. It autonomously gathers log data from your AWS resources and applies advanced techniques such as machine learning, statistical analysis, and graph theory to create interactive visualizations.

AWS Security Hub serves as your security command center, providing a comprehensive snapshot of your security posture and compliance status across your AWS accounts. It consolidates and prioritizes security alerts from multiple AWS services and AWS Partner solutions.

AWS Config acts as your configuration auditor, allowing you to assess, audit, and evaluate the configurations of your AWS resources. It continuously monitors and records your AWS resource configurations and allows you to automate the evaluation of recorded configurations against customized target configurations.

AWS Organizations and AWS Control Tower serve as your central governance and management platform across your fleet of AWS accounts and their underlying resources. With AWS Organizations, you can centrally manage policies across multiple accounts, while you can also use AWS Control Tower to set up shared services and govern a secure, multi-account AWS environment.

AWS Secrets Manager is your key to safeguarding access to your confidential data, as well as any secrets and credentials needed to operate your applications, services, and resources without the upfront investment and ongoing maintenance costs of operating your own infrastructure.

These services form the backbone of AWS security offerings. More details on how to use them and other AWS security services will be covered in *Chapter 5*.

Implement a strong identity and access management strategy

Developing a solid strategy for identity and access management is a fundamental aspect of securing your AWS environment. It is about having precise control over who can interact with your AWS resources and in what manner.

AWS **Identity and Access Management** (**IAM**) plays a pivotal role in this strategy. It allows you to manage access to your AWS resources by enabling the creation of users, groups, and roles, each with specific permissions tailored to their responsibilities.

Adhering to the principle of least privilege is a key aspect of this strategy. This principle involves granting only the minimum access necessary for a user, group, or role to perform their tasks. This approach minimizes potential risks associated with misuse of permissions or unauthorized access.

Regularly reviewing and updating these permissions is also crucial. As your AWS environment evolves, the access requirements of your users, groups, and roles may change. Regular audits can help ensure that access permissions remain appropriate and secure.

A thorough understanding and effective implementation of IAM is vital for securing your AWS resources. More details on how to develop a solid identity and access management strategy using AWS IAM will be covered in *Chapter 3*.

Protect your data

Safeguarding your data in the AWS cloud is a critical aspect of your security strategy. This involves multiple facets, including data classification, encryption, and secure data handling practices.

Data classification is an important first step in data protection. Services such as Amazon Macie can be used to discover and classify sensitive data across your AWS environment. By understanding what data you have and its sensitivity, you can apply appropriate protection measures.

Encryption plays a vital role in protecting your data. AWS provides services such as AWS **Key Management Service** (**KMS**) and AWS Certificate Manager to help you manage cryptographic keys and digital certificates used for data encryption. Encrypting your data, both at rest and in transit, can significantly reduce the risk of unauthorized access or exposure.

Secure data handling practices are also essential. This includes secure data storage, backup, and recovery procedures, as well as secure data disposal when data is no longer needed.

Understanding and implementing these data protection measures is crucial for maintaining the confidentiality, integrity, and availability of your data in the AWS cloud. More details on how to protect your data, including encryption, key management, and data storage best practices, will be covered in *Chapter 4*.

Ensure network security

Ensuring the security of your network is a key aspect of protecting your AWS environment. The way you define your VPC and subnets can significantly impact the security of your applications and resources. Proper network segregation can help avoid unnecessary exposure and potential security risks.

AWS provides a variety of services, features, and techniques to help you secure your VPC. For instance, security groups act as virtual firewalls for your instances to control inbound and outbound traffic. **Network access control lists** (**NACLs**) provide a layer of security for your VPC by controlling traffic in and out of one or more subnets.

For more advanced protection, AWS Network Firewall offers flexible, high-performance firewall protection for your AWS resources. It enables you to use familiar firewall rule syntax, threat intelligence feeds, and other features to help protect your VPCs against threats.

Understanding and implementing these network security measures is crucial for maintaining the security of your AWS environment. More details on how to keep your VPC secure, including best practices for infrastructure security, will be covered in *Chapter 2*.

Integrate security into your development life cycle

Incorporating security into the development life cycle is a crucial aspect of maintaining a secure AWS environment. This approach, often referred to as DevSecOps, involves weaving security practices into your DevOps processes.

The principle of *shifting security left* is a core principle of DevSecOps. This concept encourages the integration of security early in the development life cycle. Addressing security issues during the development phase, rather than post-deployment, allows for more effective and efficient identification and mitigation of security risks.

Automation is another key element of DevSecOps. Security tasks such as code analysis, configuration management, and vulnerability scanning should be automated to ensure consistent application of security policies and to minimize the risk of human error.

Continuous monitoring and improvement are essential in a DevSecOps approach. Applications and infrastructure should be continuously monitored for security issues. Tools such as AWS CloudTrail and Amazon CloudWatch can be used to log and monitor activity in your AWS environment. Regular reviews and updates of security practices based on these insights are recommended.

The concept of *security as code* is also integral to DevSecOps. This involves defining security controls and requirements in code files that are versioned and reviewed as part of the software development life cycle. This approach allows for consistency, repeatability, and auditability of security policies.

Finally, fostering a culture of shared responsibility for security within your organization is crucial. Collaboration between development, operations, and security teams should be encouraged to ensure that everyone understands their role in maintaining security.

By integrating security into the development life cycle, security becomes a continuous focus, rather than an afterthought. More details on how to integrate security into your CI/CD pipelines will be explored in *Chapter 12*.

Monitor and audit your environment

Implementing effective monitoring and auditing practices is essential for maintaining the security of your AWS environment. These practices enable you to detect potential security incidents and respond promptly, reducing the potential impact of any security breaches.

AWS CloudTrail is a service that assists with governance, compliance, operational monitoring, and risk auditing of your AWS account. It provides the ability to record, monitor continuously, and retain all account activity associated with actions across your AWS account. This service provides critical insight into user behavior, which is crucial for security analysis and troubleshooting.

Amazon CloudWatch is another robust service that enables the collection and tracking of metrics, log file monitoring, and alarm setting. It delivers data and actionable insights to monitor your applications, understand and respond to performance issues, optimize resource utilization, and gain a comprehensive view of operational health.

Understanding and fully leveraging the potential of these monitoring and auditing tools is crucial for maintaining security in your AWS environment. More details on how to best use AWS CloudTrail, CloudWatch, and Athena for logging, auditing, and monitoring will be covered in *Chapter 10*.

Continuously improve your security posture

Pursuing continuous improvement in your security posture is a vital aspect of maintaining a secure AWS environment. Security is not a one-time task, but an ongoing process that requires regular review and adjustment.

Staying informed about the latest AWS security features, threats, and mitigation techniques is crucial. AWS is constantly evolving, and new security features and services are regularly introduced. Keeping up-to-date with these developments can help you leverage the latest security capabilities to protect your AWS resources.

In addition, the threat landscape is continuously changing. New threats emerge, and existing threats evolve. Staying informed about these threats and the techniques to mitigate them can help you proactively protect your AWS environment.

Regularly reviewing and updating your security settings and configurations is also essential. As your AWS environment evolves, your security requirements may change. Regular audits can help ensure that your security settings and configurations remain appropriate and effective.

Pursuing continuous security improvement involves both proactive measures, such as staying informed and regularly reviewing your security settings, and reactive measures, such as responding to security incidents and adjusting your security posture based on lessons learned.

More details on how to keep up with evolving AWS security best practices and the threat landscape, as well as how to maintain security compliance with AWS Config, Security Hub, and automated remediation, will be covered in *Chapters 13* and *11*, respectively.

Summary

This initial chapter has served as a comprehensive introduction to the world of AWS security, laying the groundwork for the more advanced and practical discussions that will follow. We began by discussing the importance of cloud security, emphasizing the unique challenges it presents and the need for a thorough understanding of these challenges. We then explored the AWS shared responsibility model, a key concept that defines the security responsibilities of AWS and its customers. This understanding is essential as it underpins all security considerations in the AWS cloud. We also examined the AWS global infrastructure, discussing its various components and the security considerations associated with each. Finally, we outlined some general AWS security best practices, providing a set of guidelines that will inform our more detailed discussions in the subsequent chapters.

As we progress into the next chapter and beyond, we will shift from these broad concepts to more specific, practical applications, starting with an in-depth look at infrastructure security. This transition will enable us to apply the principles and concepts we have discussed in this chapter in a more practical manner, deepening our understanding of AWS security.

Questions

Answer the following questions to test your knowledge of this chapter:

1. What is the difference between responsibility and accountability in the shared responsibility model?

2. Can you explain the division of security responsibilities between AWS and its customers in IaaS, PaaS, and SaaS environments?

3. How does the shared responsibility model apply to these two different AWS compute services: EC2 and Lambda?

4. What is the role of edge locations in AWS security?

Answers

Here are the answers to this chapter's questions:

1. While responsibilities can be shared between AWS and the customer, accountability cannot. Regardless of the shared model, the customer always retains ultimate accountability for their data and for ensuring their part of the responsibilities is adequately addressed.

2. The shared responsibility model's significance in terms of IaaS, PaaS, and SaaS lies in the delineation of security responsibilities. For IaaS, AWS is responsible for the security of the underlying infrastructure while the customer is responsible for the security of the OS, application, and data. For PaaS, AWS extends its responsibility to include the runtime and middleware, while the customer is responsible for the applications and data. For SaaS, AWS is responsible for the entire stack, and the customer is only responsible for user-related settings and data.

3. The shared responsibility model applies differently to various AWS compute services. For EC2 instances, the customer is responsible for the guest OS, applications, and data, while AWS is responsible for the underlying infrastructure. For Lambda, AWS extends its responsibility to include the OS and runtime, and the customer is only responsible for the application code and data.

4. Edge locations play a role in AWS security by mitigating DDoS attacks. They are strategically located in major cities around the world and serve requests for CloudFront, improving performance and reducing latency.

Further reading

To learn more about the topics that were covered in this chapter, take a look at the following resources:

- *AWS Shared Responsibility Model*: `https://aws.amazon.com/compliance/shared-responsibility-model/`

- *AWS Security Predictions in 2023 and Beyond*, by CJ Moses (2022): `https://aws.amazon.com/blogs/security/new-ebook-cj-moses-security-predictions-in-2023-and-beyond/`

- *AWS Security & Compliance Quick Reference Guide*: `http://d1.awsstatic.com/whitepapers/compliance/AWS_Compliance_Quick_Reference.pdf`

2

Infrastructure Security – Keeping Your VPC secure

Welcome to the second chapter of our comprehensive journey into AWS security. This chapter focuses on the critical aspects of AWS infrastructure security, with a particular emphasis on creating and maintaining secure **virtual private clouds** (**VPCs**). First, we will guide you through the process of designing secure VPCs tailored to specific use cases. Next, we will navigate through the implementation of security groups, **network access control lists** (**NACLs**), and AWS Network Firewall, ensuring a robust defense mechanism is in place. Finally, we will examine advanced security offerings such as AWS Shield and AWS WAF to augment the protection of your VPC resources.

By the end of this chapter, you will be equipped with comprehensive skills in VPC security, ready to implement robust security frameworks and advanced protective measures, ensuring a resilient VPC environment.

In this chapter, we are going to cover the following main topics:

- Crafting and securing VPCs
- Strategic implementation of security groups, NACLs, and AWS Network Firewall
- Advanced defenses with AWS Shield and AWS WAF

Designing secure VPCs

Our first stop in this chapter is designing secure VPCs. A VPC is a virtual network dedicated to your AWS account, and its design plays a crucial role in the overall security of your AWS resources. In this section, we will walk you through key security considerations and best practices to ensure your VPCs are securely designed.

Understanding VPCs and their importance

VPCs mark a paradigm shift in network architecture within cloud computing, largely enabled by **software-defined networking (SDN)**. SDN overcomes traditional networking's physical constraints, such as limited ports and connections, by virtualizing the network stack and separating it from the physical infrastructure. This advancement facilitates granular access control and the creation of numerous subnets for detailed network segmentation. A VPC mimics a conventional network you might operate in a data center but benefits from AWS's scalable infrastructure and SDN's flexibility. This adaptability is crucial for tailoring the VPC to your business needs and enhancing the security of your AWS resources. Poor VPC design can lead to security vulnerabilities, such as insufficient subnet isolation or misconfigured access controls, exposing sensitive resources.

Consider a real-world example that is all too common. A developer, new to AWS, is tasked with setting up a VPC for a web application. Focused on functionality, the developer overlooks the importance of proper subnet segregation and security groups configuration. As a result, the database storing sensitive customer data and the web application end up in the same publicly accessible subnet. An attacker, scanning for vulnerabilities, identifies that the database is directly accessible from the internet. They exploit this misconfiguration to gain unauthorized access to the database, compromising sensitive customer data. This situation underscores the importance of a well-designed VPC in maintaining the security of your AWS resources.

In summary, a deep understanding of VPCs and their strategic deployment is essential for securing any AWS environment. In this section, we will delve into designing secure VPCs, emphasizing best practices and security measures to mitigate risks and protect your resources.

Key components of a VPC

Before we explore security strategies, let's briefly revisit the building blocks of a VPC to understand their role in enhancing your AWS environment's security.

Subnets

A subnet, also known as a subnetwork, is a logical partition of a larger network – in this case, your VPC. Each subnet is associated with a specific **availability zone (AZ)** and is allocated a unique range of IP addresses. This allocation allows for precise control over network communication and resource distribution, thereby enhancing the security and efficiency of your network operations. Subnets are differentiated into two main types:

- **Public subnets**: They are characterized by their ability to facilitate resources that require direct internet connectivity. Resources within a public subnet are assigned public IP addresses, making them accessible over the internet. The defining feature of a public subnet is its association with a route table that includes a route to the **internet gateway (IGW)**, enabling both outbound and inbound internet traffic.

- **Private subnets**: These are reserved for resources that should remain inaccessible from the internet, such as backend systems or databases. These resources are assigned a private IP address, preventing direct Internet access.

A fundamental aspect of network security lies in the distinction between public and private subnets, which minimizes the attack surface by segregating resources based on their connectivity needs. This segregation is governed by the subnet's route table, which directs network traffic within the VPC and beyond, including with the internet.

Route tables

Route tables define the network traffic flow within your VPC. They consist of a set of rules, known as routes, which define where network traffic is directed. By carefully configuring your route tables, you can control the traffic flow in your VPC and enforce a strong network security posture. For example, you can ensure that traffic from your public subnet can reach the internet, while traffic from your private subnet cannot, thereby protecting your sensitive resources from direct internet exposure.

NAT gateways

An IGW serves as the bridge that enables communication between your VPC and the internet, allowing resources with public IP addresses to send and receive traffic. A **network address translation (NAT)** gateway, on the other hand, is a NAT component that enables resources in private subnets to initiate outbound internet traffic without enabling inbound internet connections to those resources. Unlike direct internet access, which requires public IP addresses for each resource in a public subnet, the NAT gateway uses a single public IP address to manage all outbound traffic. This design means that individual resources in private subnets do not require their own public IP addresses; instead, they utilize the NAT gateway's public IP for all outbound internet communications.

In essence, the NAT gateway acts as a representative on the internet for private subnet resources, negating the need to assign public IP addresses to these resources directly. This architecture allows for secure internet access, enabling critical updates and service connectivity while maintaining the privacy and security of the subnet's resources.

Elastic load balancers (ELBs)

ELBs play a crucial role in enhancing application availability and security within VPCs by efficiently distributing incoming network traffic across multiple targets located in various AZs. ELBs should typically be deployed in public subnets and redirect traffic to targets within private subnets, thus eliminating the need for these resources to be directly accessible via the internet. They serve as endpoints for TLS termination, ensuring that all connections from clients are securely encrypted. There are different types of ELBs:

- **Application load balancer (ALB)**: Ideal for managing HTTP/HTTPS traffic, offering advanced request routing capabilities

- **Network load balancer** (**NLB**): Optimized for high-performance TCP traffic with ultra-low latency
- **Classic load balancer** (**CLB**): Legacy ELB type that should be avoided
- **Gateway load balancer** (**GLB**): Facilitates the deployment of third-party virtual appliances such as firewalls and **intrusion prevention systems** (**IPSs**)

ELBs are essential for managing application load, ensuring security through TLS termination, and providing scalability. They must be properly configured with security groups and possibly integrated with AWS Shield and AWS WAF to protect against **distributed denial of service** (**DDoS**) attacks and web exploits.

Elastic network interfaces (ENIs)

Acting as the virtual equivalent of a physical network card, ENIs provide your AWS resources, such as EC2 instances, with network connectivity within your VPC. Each ENI is equipped with attributes such as a primary private IP address, optional secondary IP addresses, Elastic IP addresses (if assigned), and a MAC address. They are secured using security groups, allowing granular control over inbound and outbound traffic to the resources they are associated with.

Security groups, NACLs, and AWS Network Firewall

Security groups, NACLs, and AWS Network Firewall are distinct and complementary mechanisms that filter network traffic at different levels of your VPC. In the *Implementing security groups, NACLs, and AWS Network Firewall* section, we will dive into these three mechanisms and provide practical insights and guidance on how to leverage them for maximum security.

VPC endpoints

VPC endpoints allow private connectivity between VPC-attached resources and supported AWS services. This means that VPC resources can access these AWS services without exposing network traffic to the public internet. VPC endpoints come in two varieties:

- **Interface endpoints**: These act as ENIs with private IP addresses from your subnet's IP range, serving as the access point for traffic to AWS services. Utilizing AWS **PrivateLink** as the underlying technology, interface endpoints ensure private connectivity, enhancing security by allowing traffic to stay within the AWS network and supporting endpoint policies for granular IAM access control.
- **Gateway endpoints**: Created for specific AWS services such as Amazon S3 and Amazon DynamoDB, gateway endpoints integrate directly with your VPC's route tables, facilitating direct service access. They are region-specific, cost-free, and offer similar security features as interface endpoints.

In both cases, traffic between your VPC and the AWS service does not leave the AWS network, providing a secure and efficient method of accessing services. In addition, IAM-based endpoint policies can be used to control which resources can use a VPC endpoint to access the AWS service. This provides an additional and more granular level of access control beyond traditional network security rules.

VPC peering

VPC peering allows for the establishment of a direct, private connection between two VPCs, enabling resources in either VPC to communicate with each other as if they were in the same network. This method bypasses the internet, enhancing security and reducing latency. It is beneficial for scenarios where two separate VPCs need to share resources without exposing data to the internet. However, it is important to note that VPC peering traffic is not encrypted within the same region, but it is for inter-region traffic.

While it is possible to establish multiple VPC peering connections for a single VPC, AWS does not support the creation of transitive peering relationships, meaning that indirect connectivity between VPCs through a common peered VPC is not possible. If you have a large number of VPCs that need to communicate with each other, managing individual VPC peering connections can become complex and difficult to manage. In such a case, using a transit gateway might be more appropriate.

Transit gateways

Transit gateways act as hubs that allow multiple VPCs and on-premises networks to connect through a central point, simplifying network management and enhancing scalability. This centralized connection model streamlines operations and enables seamless network expansion as business needs grow.

The use cases for transit gateways are diverse. It is particularly useful for building, deploying, and managing applications across hundreds or even thousands of VPCs without having to manage peering connections or update routing tables for every new connection. Additionally, a transit gateway can be used to screen all traffic passing through the central hub. This can be achieved by setting up an AWS Network Firewall in the central hub, which inspects and filters traffic based on predefined security policies.

Virtual private networks (VPNs)

VPNs are essential for creating secure communication channels over the internet and connecting VPCs to on-premises networks or other external networks. There are two types of VPNs:

- **Site-to-site VPN**: This type of VPN provides a secure connection between an external network and a VPC using the **internet protocol security** (**IPsec**) protocol. It is facilitated through an encrypted tunnel between a virtual private gateway on the AWS side and a customer gateway on the external network's side. Its primary application is to extend your network into AWS, effectively making AWS an extension of your data center or environments hosted with other cloud providers. For example, applications running in your VPC that require access to databases or resources in your on-premises data center can benefit from a site-to-site VPN. Moreover, for complex environments that require connectivity between multiple remote networks via VPN, AWS VPN CloudHub offers a more centralized solution. Acting like a transit gateway, it simplifies connectivity but is exclusive to VPN connections.

- **Client VPN**: AWS Client VPN is a managed service that offers secure and scalable remote access to resources within your VPC from any location using an OpenVPN-based client. This service is particularly beneficial for providing developers secure access to resources in private subnets, mitigating the need to expose these resources to the Internet. For example, if you need to perform SQL queries, a client VPN offers a far safer way to interact with your database compared to leaving it open to internet traffic.

Integrating key VPC components

The following diagram (*Figure 2.1*) presents a standard VPC structure featuring two private subnets across two AZs. It highlights how outbound traffic from these resources is channeled through NAT gateways (indicated by red arrows), while inbound traffic navigates from the internet to the resources via the ELB, as shown by blue arrows:

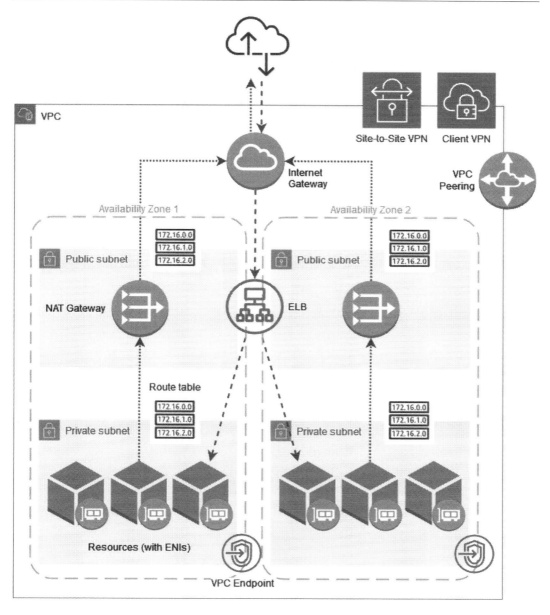

Figure 2.1 – VPC architecture

With the fundamentals in place, let's focus on securing our VPC designs.

Best practices for designing secure VPCs

This section will guide you through a series of best practices that can guide you in designing a skeleton for your VPCs that is not only functional but also secure. These practices are not exhaustive, but they provide a solid foundation for building secure VPCs.

Use subnet segregation heavily

One of the most effective ways to enhance security within a VPC is through heavy subnet segregation. The flexibility offered by VPCs, with virtually no limitation in the number of subnets, allows for granular micro-segmentation. This is a significant advantage over traditional networking, where the number of subnets is limited by physical constraints.

Micro-segmentation involves dividing a VPC into many small, isolated subnets, each hosting a limited number of resources. This approach can significantly improve resources segregation and reduce the attack surface. If a resource in one subnet is compromised, the impact is contained within that subnet and does not affect resources in other subnets. This is a fundamental principle of the zero-trust approach, where each micro-segment of the network is considered a separate trust zone and is secured accordingly. It is a stark contrast to traditional flat network designs where attackers can easily move laterally and jeopardize other systems once they have infiltrated the network.

When designing your VPCs, consider creating separate subnets for different types of resources based on their function and sensitivity. For example, web servers, application servers, and databases should each be placed in separate subnets. Furthermore, you can apply different security controls to each subnet based on the sensitivity and function of the resources within it.

The following figure (*Figure 2.2*) compares traditional segmentation using a limited number of subnets (on the left) with micro-segmentation using a large number of isolated subnets (on the right):

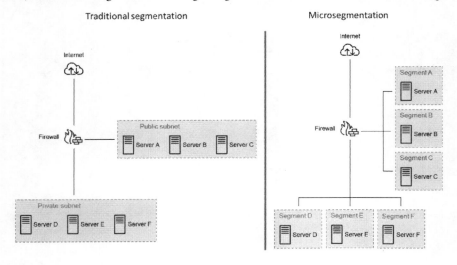

Figure 2.2 – Traditional segmentation and micro-segmentation comparison

Use separate VPCs for different environments

One of the best practices for enhancing the security of your AWS resources is to use separate VPCs and even separate AWS accounts for different environments. This approach ensures that, unlike subnet segregation within a single VPC, where routing between all subnets is inherently allowed, routing across different VPCs is restricted by default. This inherent lack of inter-VPC routing without explicit, connectivity mechanisms provides a stronger segregation level and reduces the risk of potential cross-contamination between environments.

In a typical application life cycle, you have different environments, such as development, testing, and production. Each of these environments has different requirements and risk profiles. For instance, the development environment is where new code is written and tested, and it may be more prone to vulnerabilities and bugs. On the other hand, the production environment hosts the live application and is expected to be stable and secure. This deployment allows for more granular control over permissions and security controls for each environment based on their specific needs. You can have stricter security group rules and NACLs in the production environment to protect your live application while allowing more flexibility in development for testing and debugging purposes.

Separating VPCs for different stages of the application life cycle is just one example of how this strategy can be applied. In architectures such as microservices, you might find different services operating within distinct VPCs, and even across different AWS accounts, especially if they are managed by different teams. By using VPC peering, you can ensure that these services can communicate with each other securely and efficiently, on an as-needed basis.

Use multiple AZs for high availability

For high availability and to ensure resilience against the failure of a single location, AWS resources should be spread across multiple AZs within a region.

However, the use of multiple AZs should be done judiciously. Once an AZ has been assigned to a subnet, this assignment cannot be altered. Consequently, if a change in AZ assignment is necessary, you will need to establish a new subnet in the desired AZ and migrate or recreate the resources associated with the old subnet.

While distributing resources across AZs is beneficial, the architecture of your application should also be taken into account. For instance, if you have a multi-tier application with one tier running in a single AZ and another tier running in a different AZ, a failure in any of the two AZs could render the entire application unavailable. This is due to the interdependencies between the tiers for the application to function correctly.

In terms of practical guidelines, if high availability is a requirement for your application, implementing at least two AZs is recommended. This allows for failover and redundancy in case one AZ experiences an issue. If cost is a primary concern and high availability is not a requirement, you might choose to place all resources in a single AZ. However, be aware that this increases the risk of application downtime if the AZ experiences an issue. For applications with very high availability requirements, you might consider using three or more different AZs to further reduce the risk of downtime. Remember, the choice of how many AZs to use should be based on a careful analysis of your specific availability requirements and cost constraints.

The following table (*Table 2.1*) simulates the availability of a three-tier application spread across different AZs with different deployment options. Note that the application's availability is calculated solely based on the likelihood of AZ failures for this simulation:

Deployment Option	Individual AZ Availability (IAZA)	Availability for the Application (A)	Calculation	Explanation
Simple deployment in a single AZ	99%	99%	A = IAZA = 99%	Each tier is deployed within the same AZ. The application will have the same availability as the AZ.
Simple deployment spread in three AZs	99%	97%	A = (IAZA)^3 = 99%*99%*99%	Each tier is deployed in a different AZ. The application will have a degraded availability because a failure of any single AZ will make the application unavailable.
Redundant deployment in two AZs	99%	99.99%	A = 1-(1-IAZA)^2 = 1-[(1-99%)*(1-99%)] = 1-[0.01*0.01] = 1-0.0001	All tiers are duplicated across two AZs. The application will have a greater availability because the two AZs need to fail simultaneously for the application to become unavailable.
Redundant in three AZs	99%	99.9999%	A = 1-(1-IAZA)^3 = 1-[(1-99%)*(1-99%)*(1-99%)] = 1-[0.01*0.01*0.01] = 1-0.000001	All tiers are duplicated across three AZs. The application will have a greater availability because the three AZs need to fail simultaneously for the application to become unavailable.

Table 2.1 – Availability calculation of a three-tier application spread across different AZs

Minimize exposure of resources to the internet

A common mistake in VPC design is the unnecessary exposure of resources to the internet. This is often due to a misunderstanding of how AWS services work together, or a lack of awareness of the security risks involved. Exposing resources to the internet increases the attack surface and can lead to security breaches if not properly managed.

For instance, it is a common misconception that web servers need to be placed in a public subnet to be accessible from the internet. If you are using an ELB, the ELB itself should be in the public subnet, while the web servers can reside in a private subnet. The ELB handles incoming internet traffic and forwards it to the web servers, keeping them shielded from direct internet access.

Another common error is placing EC2 instances in a public subnet for management purposes, such as SSH or RDP access. While this may seem convenient, it exposes these instances to potential threats from the Internet. Instead, consider the following alternatives:

- **Bastion host**: Deploy a bastion host as a fortified, singular entry point within a VPC for secure management of instances. This method minimizes direct exposure but requires diligent security practices, including applying the principle of least privilege, routine updates and patches, and comprehensive monitoring and logging.

- **AWS Systems Manager (SSM) Session Manager**: This enables secure instance management via a browser-based shell or CLI, facilitated by an agent. This approach eliminates the need for open SSH/RDP ports and the management of SSH keys or Windows credentials, thereby reducing the attack surface and simplifying instance management.

- **EC2 Instance Connect endpoint**: This offers secure instance management without requiring an agent on the instance. It is based on VPC endpoints and leverages IAM-based permissions for improved security, effectively serving as a managed bastion service without the associated vulnerabilities.

- **VPN access**: This establishes a secure, encrypted VPN tunnel to manage instances, shielding your activities from internet threats and offering enhanced privacy and security.

Consider the use of NAT gateways for internet access

NAT gateways enable resources within the private subnet to access the internet or other AWS services securely.

When considering NAT gateways, assess the necessity of internet access for your VPC resources carefully. Workloads that can withstand delayed software updates may find the occasional unavailability of a NAT gateway manageable, allowing for cost-effective deployment in a single AZ. Conversely, applications requiring real-time access to external APIs need consistent internet connectivity. To guarantee high availability, deploy a NAT gateway in every AZ that hosts private subnets needing internet access, ensuring seamless operation despite potential AZ disruptions.

While discussing NAT solutions, it is worth mentioning alternatives such as EC2-based NAT instances. Although capable of similar functionality, EC2-based NAT instances are typically not recommended due to their increased complexity, management demands, and the risk of security vulnerabilities if not correctly configured. NAT gateways, being fully managed, offer better scalability, availability, and security features, making them a more suitable choice for most scenarios.

Nonetheless, the use of NAT gateways should not be indiscriminate. If there are significant security considerations or no essential need for internet access, reconsidering the deployment of NAT gateways may be wise. In cases where only specific AWS services need to be accessed, VPC endpoints offer a secure, efficient, and direct connectivity option, eliminating the necessity for broad internet access and embodying a security-first strategy in VPC configuration.

Use VPC endpoints strategically

Incorporating VPC endpoints into your VPC design can significantly enhance the security posture of your AWS environment. By facilitating private connections between your VPCs and AWS services, VPC endpoints help keep your network traffic within the AWS backbone, eliminating the need to expose your VPC resources to the public internet. This minimizes the attack surface and aligns with best practices for securing cloud-based architectures.

However, it is important to select and implement VPC endpoints judiciously:

- **Cost considerations**: While VPC endpoints offer security benefits, they can introduce significant costs, especially in large-scale AWS deployments. To mitigate these costs without sacrificing security, prioritize gateway endpoints over interface endpoints whenever possible as they are free and provide direct, secure connections to supported AWS services. Additionally, sharing VPC endpoints across your organization can allow you to yield the benefits of using VPC endpoints while significantly reducing overhead. By centralizing VPC endpoints, organizations can realize cost savings and simplify network management across multiple accounts and VPCs.

- **Strategic deployment**: Determine which AWS services are essential for your VPC's operations and deploy VPC endpoints specifically for these services. Prioritize services that handle sensitive data or are critical to your application's functionality. For instance, services such as Amazon S3 for storage, Amazon DynamoDB for database, and AWS Systems Manager for system management are common candidates. This targeted approach ensures you are investing in endpoints that deliver maximum utility and security.

- **Policy management**: Assign IAM roles to VPC resources requiring endpoint connectivity. Craft VPC endpoint policies that specify which IAM roles have access rights, ensuring that only authorized entities can access them.

Ensure proper route table configuration

While setting the right rules in security groups or NACLs is a good practice, it is equally important to ban unwanted connectivity using properly defined route tables. This is because route tables provide an additional layer of security controls. For instance, even if a security group ends up being misconfigured, a well-configured route table can still prevent unwanted network access. This highlights the importance of route tables as a critical security control within your VPCs.

One of the fundamental principles in security is the principle of least privilege. This principle asserts that a system should be granted the bare minimum levels of access necessary to perform its tasks. This principle is crucial when configuring route tables in your VPC. For example, if a subnet does not require internet communication, it should not possess a route to an IGW or a NAT gateway. The same approach applies to connectivity outside of your VPC, such as VPC peering or VPN connection. If a specific subnet does not require access to these external networks, no route should be established to access them from that particular subnet.

Centralize network traffic management in multi-VPC environments

In complex environments featuring multiple VPCs and accounts, centralizing network traffic management becomes paramount for maintaining robust security and simplifying operational demands. Using a transit gateway emerges as a pivotal solution, serving as a centralized hub through which all inter-VPC traffic is routed. This consolidation facilitates several critical security practices:

- **Streamlined connectivity control**: Centralizing network traffic via the transit gateway enables organizations to ensure that all inbound and outbound communications from VPCs pass through this single point.

- **Traffic inspection and filtering**: Integrating AWS Network Firewall along with additional services, such as AWS Shield and AWS WAF, through the transit gateway allows organizations to inspect and filter all traffic traversing the central hub. This setup enforces uniform security policies, ensuring that only authorized and clean traffic flows between VPCs, thereby offering a strong defense against potential threats and malicious activities.

- **Regulated access with route tables**: To further enhance security, modifying the route tables in each VPC to direct all traffic (0.0.0.0/0) to the transit gateway ensures comprehensive routing through the transit gateway. This measure prevents any direct access between VPCs or from VPCs to the internet that bypasses centralized security controls.

- **Compliance and policy enforcement**: In multi-account environments, the centralized management model supports compliance and security policy enforcement across the organization. The combination of **service control policies (SCPs)** and AWS Config plays a crucial role in ensuring and monitoring that the applied route tables consistently redirect all the network traffic via the transit gateway, providing an additional layer of security governance.

- **Centralized VPC endpoint deployment**: This involves deploying VPC endpoints in the central hub, rather than in individual VPCs, to enhance secure communications with AWS services. This strategy avoids public internet exposure and leverages the transit gateway for efficient and centralized access control.

The following diagram (*Figure 2.3*) illustrates a setup where multiple VPCs are interconnected through a central hub VPC via the transit gateway, facilitating centralized internet access and access to AWS services through VPC endpoints. This hub employs AWS Network Firewall, among other services, to screen all passing traffic:

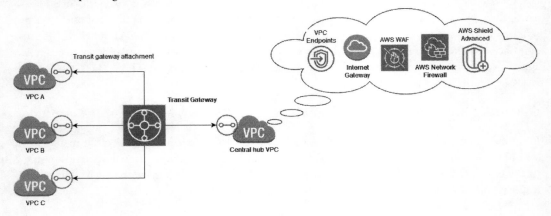

Figure 2.3 – Centralized multi-VPC network architecture

Regularly review and update your configuration

Maintaining secure VPCs is not a one-time task but an ongoing process. As your business needs evolve, so will your configuration. Moreover, the threat landscape is constantly evolving with new vulnerabilities and attack vectors. Therefore, it is crucial to continuously monitor and update your configuration to ensure it remains aligned with your security requirements and the evolving threat landscape.

Regular audits of your configuration should be conducted to identify any potential security gaps. These audits should include checking the security groups and NACLs for any overly permissive rules, reviewing the route tables for any unnecessary routes, and verifying that all resources are in the correct subnets. Any misconfigurations identified during these audits should be corrected promptly to minimize the risk of a security breach. In addition to manual audits, consider leveraging other services. AWS Config, for instance, can be used to continuously monitor the configuration of your VPC resources and evaluate them against desired states.

Finally, remember that security is a shared responsibility. While AWS provides a variety of tools and services to help secure your VPCs, it is ultimately up to you to use these tools effectively.

Shifting from VPC design to its armor, it is time to delve into the essential security mechanisms for network traffic filtering.

Implementing security groups, NACLs, and AWS Network Firewall

Continuing our journey through this chapter, let's focus on the effective implementation of security groups, NACLs, and AWS Network Firewall. These three components are pivotal in ensuring robust protection of your resources within your VPCs, each playing a distinct role in managing and filtering network traffic. In this section, we will clarify their roles, interactions, differences, and overlaps, and provide guidelines for their effective implementation.

First, let's demystify these three mechanisms:

- **Security groups**: These act as virtual firewalls at the ENI level for AWS resources within a VPC, managing both inbound and outbound traffic. Unlike traditional host-based firewalls that are implemented within the **operating system** (**OS**), security groups are managed through the AWS management plane, providing enhanced security by being less susceptible to compromise. Security groups are stateful, allowing automatic inbound response to outbound requests based on rule-defined criteria.

- **NACLs**: These function at the subnet level to control inbound and outbound traffic for all resources within a subnet. NACLs are stateless, requiring explicit allowance of both request and response traffic in the rules for two-way communication.

- **AWS Network Firewall**: This is a paid feature for VPCs that offers a more granular level of traffic control. It enables the creation of detailed rules for inspecting and filtering traffic based on attributes such as domain names and IP addresses. The firewall not only analyzes packet metadata but also its contents, offering advanced decision-making capabilities for allowing or denying traffic. This provides a powerful tool for managing your VPC traffic and enhancing its security to meet the most advanced requirements.

The following table (*Table 2.2*) offers a side-by-side comparison of the aforementioned components, along with their respective use cases:

	Cost	Attachment	Behavior	Default Policy	Use Cases
Security groups	Free	Individual AWS resources (for example, EC2 instances, RDS databases, and Lambda functions)	Stateful, allow rules (whitelist)	Block incoming traffic, allow outgoing traffic	Protection of individual VPC-attached resources; zero-trust approach
NACLs	Free	Every VPC's subnet (private or public)	Stateless, both allow (whitelist) and deny (blacklist) rules	Allow everything	Defense-in-depth approach to complement security groups; rapid blocking of suspicious public IP addresses
AWS Network Firewall	Pay per-hour and per-traffic usage	Selected VPC's subnets	Supports both stateful and stateless rules, with advanced capabilities	No default rules, fully customizable	Advanced control over network traffic; web filtering, intrusion prevention, encrypted traffic inspection; centralized multi-VPC environments

Table 2.2 – Security groups, NACLs, and AWS Network Firewall comparison

The following diagram (*Figure 2.4*) depicts how a VPC's security infrastructure is established, showcasing security groups linked to each ENI and NACLs applied across subnets. It highlights the necessity for AWS Network Firewall to have endpoints in dedicated public subnets for each AZ, directing all traffic through these endpoints for comprehensive screening before reaching its destination, including private subnets, public subnets, or internet access. Note that the NAT gateways are no longer present in this VPC architecture as their function is now performed by AWS Network Firewall for all outbound traffic:

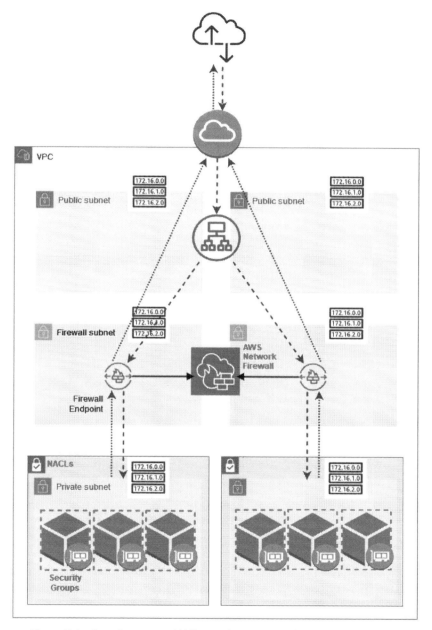

Figure 2.4 – Security groups, NACLs, and AWS Network Firewall integration

Building on this introduction, it is time to dig into the practicalities of working with each of these three essential security components.

Using security groups

Security groups control both inbound and outbound traffic, offering a robust line of defense against unauthorized access or unwanted traffic. In this section, we will delve into some of their most pertinent aspects for advanced AWS users and highlight some common pitfalls to steer clear of.

Significant aspects

Let's explore some of the key functionalities that characterize security groups:

- **Implicit deny rule**: All security groups in AWS come with an implicit deny rule. This means that unless you explicitly allow a type of traffic, it will be automatically denied. This feature enforces the principle of least privilege, ensuring that only necessary traffic is allowed.

- **Multiple security groups assignment**: AWS allows you to assign multiple security groups to a single resource. This capability enables you to create and assign security groups based on specific categories, such as Linux, Windows, web servers, FTP servers, and so on. For instance, if you have an EC2 instance that functions as a Linux-based web server, you can assign it to both the *Linux* and *Web Server* security groups. This approach simplifies the management of your security groups and makes it easier to control access.

- **Trusting other security groups as a source**: Security groups can trust other security groups instead of individual IP addresses. This feature is particularly useful in dynamic environments where IP addresses can change frequently. For example, you could have a security group named *Web Server* and another one named *Database Server*. Instead of allowing access from specific IP addresses, the *Database Server* security group's rules can be configured to allow access from the *Web Server* security group. This ensures continuous access, even if the web server's IP address varies. Furthermore, when using VPC peering, this method's utility extends as you can reference security groups belonging to a peered VPC, adding an extra layer of flexibility. Managing access between VPCs becomes more straightforward, eliminating the need to track and update specific IP addresses. This method not only simplifies access management but also enhances security by ensuring that traffic between services is limited to authorized entities, independent of IP address changes.

Common mistakes

While security groups are a powerful tool, they can lead to security vulnerabilities if they are not used correctly. Here are some common mistakes and how to avoid them:

- **Over-reliance on the default security group**: AWS provides a default security group that permits all local traffic within the group and allows all outbound traffic. This group is frequently used as a catch-all for most resources. However, continuously adding new rules to this group can lead to an overly permissive security posture. Instead, create separate security groups with the minimum necessary access for each type of resource.

- **Creating a unique security group for every new resource**: While it is important to have separate security groups for different types of resources, creating a new security group for every resource can lead to a large number of security groups that are difficult to manage. Instead, try to reuse security groups for similar resources and give them meaningful names and descriptions.

- **Unrestricted web server access**: If your web server is behind an ELB, there is no need to allow access from anywhere. However, the EC2 instance launch wizard suggests allowing HTTP or HTTPS, which can lead to this mistake. Instead, only allow access from the ELB.

- **Overly permissive SSH or RDP access**: The instance wizard generally suggests default SSH or RDP access from anywhere, which can inadvertently lead to overly permissive access and potential security risks. It is advisable to restrict this access from specific IP addresses. Furthermore, consider using alternative methods for remote management, as mentioned in the previous section.

- **Granting excessive access for troubleshooting**: It is not uncommon for users to grant overly permissive access for troubleshooting purposes. This might even involve direct access to the admin interface of a backend system or direct access to databases for developers from the internet. While these rules are often intended to be temporary, it is easy to forget to delete them, leading to potential security vulnerabilities. A more secure alternative is to use a client VPN for secure access. Furthermore, to efficiently track temporary rules, consider creating them in temporary security groups. These can be attached and detached from resources as needed, rather than adding temporary rules to permanent security groups. This approach ensures that temporary access is revoked when it is no longer needed and helps maintain the integrity of your security posture.

- **Not regularly reviewing security group rules**: Security requirements can evolve, and once-essential rules may become obsolete or overly permissive. It is crucial to conduct regular reviews of your security group rules to ensure they align with your current needs and are not inadvertently allowing more access than necessary. Tools such as AWS Config can be instrumental in this process as it continuously monitors and records your AWS resource configurations and can detect and alert you to any changes that deviate from your desired configurations.

- **Neglecting description fields and default names**: Security group rules offer description fields that serve as documentation tools for the rationale behind a rule's creation. Ignoring these fields can lead to confusion and potential errors when it comes to modifying or deleting rules as the original intent behind the rule may be forgotten. Similarly, not changing the default names of security groups can lead to a lack of clarity. It is recommended to use meaningful names and descriptions that reflect the purpose and function of each security group and rule, enhancing the manageability of your security infrastructure.

In conclusion, security groups are a key element of AWS security, providing granular control over network traffic. However, their effectiveness depends on correct usage and management. By leveraging their full potential and avoiding common mistakes, you can greatly improve your VPC's security posture.

Using NACLs

NACLs are an important, yet often overlooked, part of VPC security. While security groups tend to be the focus of most AWS users due to their versatility and ease of use, NACLs provide an additional layer of security and should be considered in a defense-in-depth approach. They operate at the subnet level, providing a rule-based system for controlling inbound and outbound traffic across all AWS resources within a subnet. In this section, we will delve into some of the significant aspects of NACLs that are particularly relevant for advanced AWS users and highlight some common mistakes to avoid.

Significant aspects

Let's explore some of the features that distinguish NACLs:

- **Stateless filtering**: Unlike security groups, which are stateful, NACLs are stateless. This means that they evaluate both the request and the response traffic independently against the rule set. Therefore, for two-way communication, both the request and the response traffic must be explicitly allowed in the NACL rules. This differs from security groups where an allowed outbound request automatically allows the inbound response.

- **Rule numbering**: NACLs use rule numbers to identify rules. These numbers are important because they determine the order in which rules are evaluated, with lower-numbered rules evaluated before higher-numbered rules. This allows you to create granular rules that can override broader ones, a feature not available in security groups where rules are evaluated collectively.

- **Rule action**: NACLs offer a distinct advantage over security groups in terms of rule actions. While security groups only support `allow` rules, NACLs can accommodate both `allow` and `deny` rules. This dual functionality provides a greater degree of control over resource access. Given that NACLs affect an entire subnet, they become an optimal tool for swiftly blocking traffic from a specific IP address. This can be particularly useful in automated response scenarios where you need to programmatically block an IP address exhibiting suspicious activity.

Common mistakes

While NACLs offer an extra layer of security, they can also introduce risks if misused:

- **Not using NACLs in addition to security groups**: While security groups can provide robust security at the instance level, NACLs add an additional layer of security at the subnet level. Not using NACLs in addition to security groups can leave your resources more vulnerable. Furthermore, some compliance benchmarks, such as the CIS AWS Foundations Benchmark, recommend the use of NACLs in addition to security groups.

- **Forgetting the existence of blocking NACL rules**: Since NACLs are not as commonly used as security groups, their existence is often forgotten when troubleshooting connectivity issues. This can lead to confusion and wasted time if a connectivity issue is due to a blocking rule in an NACL that was created long ago or by another user in the same AWS account.

- **Overly permissive rules**: One common mistake for any firewall-like security mechanism is to create overly permissive rules that allow more access than necessary. This can expose your resources to unnecessary risks. Always follow the principle of least privilege when creating NACL rules, just as you would with security groups.

- **Not considering rule order**: The order of rules in an NACL is important because rules are evaluated in order starting with the lowest numbered rule. Not considering rule order can lead to unexpected results. For example, if you have a rule numbered 100 that allows all traffic and a rule numbered 200 that denies traffic from a specific IP address, the deny rule will never be evaluated because the allow rule will match first.

- **Ignoring ephemeral ports**: When creating rules for outbound response traffic, it is important to consider ephemeral ports. These are temporary ports that are assigned by the client's OS for TCP and UDP responses. If these ports are not allowed in your outbound rules, response traffic will be blocked. This is a consideration unique to NACLs due to their stateless nature.

- **Not regularly reviewing NACL rules**: Just like with security groups, it is important to regularly review your NACL rules to ensure they still meet your needs. AWS Config can be used to monitor your NACLs and alert you to any changes.

In conclusion, while NACLs may not be as commonly used as security groups, they are an important part of a comprehensive security strategy. By understanding their significant aspects and avoiding common mistakes, you can use NACLs effectively to enhance the security of your network traffic in your VPCs.

Using AWS Network Firewall

AWS Network Firewall is a stateful, managed service that provides a high level of control over network traffic, allowing advanced traffic filtering capabilities at the perimeter of your VPCs and optionally between subnets. This includes traffic going to and coming from an IGW, NAT gateway, VPN, or between VPC's subnets.

Significant aspects

Let's take a closer look at the advanced features that make AWS Network Firewall a compelling option for enhancing VPC security:

- **Internet content screening**: AWS Network Firewall offers internet content screening for both incoming and outgoing traffic, including encrypted web traffic. For HTTPS, it utilizes the unencrypted **server name indication** (**SNI**) extension of TLS to identify and scrutinize the destination **fully qualified domain name** (**FQDN**) a client is trying to access.

- **Active threat mitigation**: AWS Network Firewall incorporates active threat mitigation capabilities, functioning similarly to an IPS. This helps in identifying harmful network traffic that matches known threat signatures. AWS offers various managed rules that can be activated either in a monitor-only mode or a blocking mode. These rules encompass a broad spectrum of threats, including botnets, DoS attacks, and web attacks, and are continuously updated by AWS.

- **Inspection of encrypted traffic**: A notable feature of AWS Network Firewall is its capability to inspect inbound encrypted traffic. Coupled with threat mitigation capability, this feature enables the inspection of encrypted traffic getting into your VPCs by decrypting TLS traffic to block malicious content on the fly.

Use cases

AWS Network Firewall shines in environments that require precise control over network traffic. It is capable of filtering traffic based on complex rules and can scrutinize traffic entering or leaving your VPCs through deep packet inspection. This level of scrutiny enables identifying and blocking sophisticated threats that may not be detected through standard header-based inspection methods.

The decision to use AWS Network Firewall in conjunction with or as a replacement for NACLs and security groups hinges on your unique needs and the complexity of your network traffic. NACLs and security groups offer a fundamental level of security, but AWS Network Firewall provides a more nuanced control level and advanced features like encrypted traffic inspection. However, managing three security layers can be complex and may not be necessary for all use cases. Hence, it is generally considered suitable to substitute NACLs with AWS Network Firewall, while concurrently ensuring that security groups are kept stringent for adequate protection at the individual resource level.

For environments with straightforward, predictable network traffic where security needs are met with NACLs and security groups, incorporating AWS Network Firewall may not yield significant additional benefits. However, for environments with complex network traffic, a need to inspect encrypted traffic, or a requirement for high-level network traffic control, AWS Network Firewall can be a valuable enhancement to your security infrastructure.

Furthermore, AWS Network Firewall is engineered to scale automatically with your network traffic, making it particularly suitable for large environments with multiple VPCs and accounts. AWS Network Firewall integrates with AWS Firewall Manager, enabling you to manage security policies centrally and automatically enforce mandatory security policies across existing and new AWS accounts and VPCs.

In conclusion, AWS Network Firewall is a potent tool for managing and tightly controlling network traffic in your VPCs. It offers a high level of control and a range of advanced features, making it a valuable addition to infrastructures requiring an advanced level of network security.

Shifting from foundational security mechanisms to advanced shields, let's explore AWS Shield and AWS **Web Application Firewall** (**WAF**) implementation.

Configuring AWS Shield and AWS WAF for advanced protection

Moving forward in this chapter, this section explores the role and practicalities of AWS Shield and AWS WAF to ensure your applications and data in your VPCs are well-protected. AWS Shield specializes in mitigating DDoS attacks, offering automatic detection and response capabilities that scale with your traffic, ensuring continuous protection. AWS WAF complements this by guarding web applications from exploits such as SQL injection and **cross-site scripting** (**XSS**) attacks through customizable security rules. Utilizing both services together enhances your security posture, shielding your applications and data from volumetric attacks and targeted web vulnerabilities with minimal manual intervention. By deploying these services in tandem, you can fortify your applications and data against a broad spectrum of threats. First, let's dive into the capabilities offered by AWS Shield in more detail.

Enabling AWS Shield for DDoS protection

AWS Shield offers two tiers of security:

- **Standard**: Automatically activated across all AWS accounts at no additional cost, it protects against the most common types of network-oriented DDoS attacks.

- **Advanced**: Designed for customers who need a higher level of protection against attacks targeting their applications, AWS Shield Advanced provides enhanced protection with advanced detection and mitigation capabilities against larger and more sophisticated DDoS attacks, including those targeting the application layer. Customers with Business or Enterprise support plans also gain access to the **AWS Shield Response Team** (**SRT**) for expert assistance during DDoS incidents. Additionally, AWS Shield Advanced includes DDoS cost protection to mitigate unexpected expenses from scaling due to traffic spikes and integrates seamlessly with AWS WAF for comprehensive security coverage.

Choosing AWS Shield Advanced is particularly relevant in the following situations:

- **High-risk industries**: Industries such as finance, healthcare, or eCommerce are frequently targeted by sophisticated DDoS attacks. The advanced tier offers enhanced detection and mitigation capabilities, making it essential for these sectors to protect their critical operations and sensitive data.

- **Complex network architectures**: For organizations with intricate network setups that manage high volumes of traffic, the advanced tier's advanced detection and mitigation strategies are crucial. It enables these organizations to maintain operational integrity despite complex security challenges.

- **High-value applications**: Organizations operating applications where downtime equates to significant financial losses or reputational damage can particularly benefit from the advanced tier. It provides robust protection measures to ensure application availability and continuity.

- **Multi-account AWS environments**: The advanced tier facilitates centralized protection management through AWS Firewall Manager, which is ideal for organizations using multiple VPCs and AWS accounts. This feature simplifies its configuration across an organization's AWS landscape.

- **Cost concerns related to DDoS attacks**: Financial safeguards against DDoS-related costs due to traffic spikes act as a form of insurance against such risks.

Switching to AWS Shield Advanced requires an annual commitment, which is automatically renewed. The subscription covers the entire organization, not just a single AWS account, meaning the monthly fee is paid once for all accounts. However, if any account within the organization activates the advanced tier, the entire organization incurs the cost.

In conclusion, AWS Shield offers a comprehensive DDoS protection solution for your applications and resources hosted on your VPC with two levels to cater to different needs. The choice between the two depends on your specific needs, the complexity of your network, the associated costs, and the level of risk your organization faces.

Now, let's turn our attention to our next topic – AWS WAF.

Configuring AWS WAF for web application protection

AWS WAF is a crucial tool in the AWS security suite that provides a line of defense against web-based threats. It monitors HTTP and HTTPS requests forwarded to your web applications and allows you to control access to your content based on the criteria you specify. This could be anything from the originating IP addresses of requests to the values of query strings. Depending on your rules, the service associated with your protected resource responds to requests either with the requested content, with a forbidden response (HTTP 403 status), or with a custom response, such as a captcha verification.

The importance of having a WAF in place cannot be overstated. Often, web applications are launched without a WAF, leaving them vulnerable to a variety of threats. These vulnerabilities can lead to unauthorized access to data, loss of data, and even a complete system compromise. By implementing AWS WAF, you add an additional layer of security that can help protect your applications from these threats.

When it comes to selecting the right rules for your environment, consider the specific threats your application is most likely to face. AWS WAF enables the creation of custom rules to block specific web exploits relevant to your environment. Additionally, it offers managed rule groups for pervasive web threats such as bot traffic and account takeover fraud, among others.

These managed rule groups can be used alongside your custom rules to provide comprehensive protection for your applications. The choice between using free and paid managed rules depends on your specific needs and budget. Free rules offer basic protection against common threats, while paid rules provide more advanced features and greater flexibility. It is also important to understand which managed rules apply to your environment. For instance, the **SQL database** managed rule group is only applicable if your web application uses a relational database but would not protect the application in case it only uses a NoSQL database, such as DynamoDB. Selecting unwanted rules unnecessarily increases the number of **web ACL capacity units (WCUs)** used, leading to higher costs and limiting the capacity for more relevant rules.

Custom rules offer the greatest level of flexibility and control. They allow you to define conditions based on IP addresses, HTTP headers, methods, URI strings, and HTTP bodies that you want to allow or block. This can be particularly useful if your application has unique security requirements or if you need to address specific threats that are not covered by the preconfigured rules. However, it can be very time-consuming to fine-tune the right custom rules for your environment. It is generally a good idea to select appropriately managed rules as a basis and to complement them with custom rules if deemed relevant.

AWS WAF can protect a variety of AWS resources, including Amazon CloudFront distributions, Amazon API Gateway REST APIs, ALBs, AWS AppSync GraphQL APIs, Amazon Cognito user pools, and more.

Here is a step-by-step guide on how to configure AWS WAF for web application protection:

1. **Create a web ACL**: The first step in configuring AWS WAF is to create a web ACL. This is essentially a container for your rules and acts as a standard ACL. It allows you to group and manage related rules.

2. **Define rules**: Once you have a web ACL, you can start defining rules. The rules specify the conditions under which AWS WAF should allow, block, or count web requests. AWS WAF evaluates rules in the order they are set. Be mindful of the WCU count associated with each rule to keep costs under control and stay within the capacity limit per web ACL (at the time of writing, this is 5,000 WCUs).

3. **Add conditions to rules**: Each rule contains a set of conditions that specify the parts of web requests to inspect. You can also specify whether to allow, block, or count web requests that match these conditions.

4. **Associate the web ACL with a resource**: After you have defined your web ACL and rules, you need to associate the web ACL with the AWS resource that you want to protect, such as an Amazon CloudFront distribution or an ALB.

5. **Validate and test**: Once your web ACL is associated with a resource, AWS WAF starts inspecting web requests to that resource and performs the corresponding action for each rule that a web request matches. You can then validate and test your rules to ensure they are working as expected, which can be done by generating test traffic that matches the conditions of your rules and monitoring the response. You can use common web application security testing tools to perform these tests. AWS WAF provides real-time metrics and captures raw requests, which can be used to verify that your rules are correctly identifying and responding to threats.

6. **Monitor and adjust**: Once you have implemented AWS WAF, you can monitor the requests that AWS WAF inspects and blocks using Amazon CloudWatch and AWS WAF reports. Based on this information, you can adjust your rules and conditions as needed to address new threats and to ensure they continue to meet your security needs.

> **Important note**
>
> AWS has a policy for penetration testing that allows you to carry out penetration tests against or from resources on your AWS account without needing approval from AWS. Before stress-testing your network, review the AWS policy regarding the use of security assessment tools and services.

In conclusion, AWS WAF provides a robust and flexible framework for protecting your web applications from a variety of common exploits. By carefully configuring your web ACLs and rules, you can ensure that your applications are well-protected against potential threats.

Summary

This chapter delved into the intricacies of infrastructure security, focusing on the design and implementation of secure VPCs in AWS. We began by discussing the importance of VPCs and their role in AWS security, highlighting the shift from on-premises traditional physical networking to SDN in the cloud. Then, we explored the key components of a VPC and best practices for designing secure VPCs, emphasizing the importance of subnet segregation, separate VPCs for different environments, and proper route table configuration. After, we discussed the effective implementation of security groups, NACLs, and AWS Network Firewall, clarifying their roles, interactions, and guidelines for their appropriate use in building a strong security posture for your VPCs. Finally, we focused on the use of AWS Shield and AWS WAF, which both provide advanced protection for your VPC resources.

Having covered network-related access management in the VPC, the next chapter will take us deeper into the cloud-native access management approach using AWS **Identity and Access Management (IAM)**.

Questions

Answer the following questions to test your knowledge of this chapter:

1. What is the principle of least privilege and how does it apply to the configuration of route tables in a VPC?

2. Why is it recommended to use separate VPCs for different environments?

3. You have decided to use a bastion host for EC2 instance management. Can you explain how this enhances your security and what potential weaknesses you should be aware of?

Answers

Here are the answers to this chapter's questions:

1. The principle of least privilege asserts that a system should be granted the minimum levels of access necessary to perform its tasks. In the context of route tables in a VPC, this principle implies that if a subnet does not require certain connectivity (for example, internet communication or access to external networks), it should not possess a route to an IGW, NAT gateway, or an external network.

2. Using separate VPCs for different environments provides an additional layer of isolation and reduces the risk of potential cross-contamination between environments. It also allows for more granular control over permissions and security controls for each environment based on their specific needs.

3. A bastion host acts as a proxy to control access to other EC2 instances, reducing the attack surface by only exposing the bastion host to the internet. However, the security of the bastion host depends largely on your efforts to harden it against attacks, as it introduces a single point of failure. If compromised, it could allow an attacker access to all connected instances within the VPC. Alternatively, adopting managed services such as AWS Systems Manager Session Manager or EC2 Instance Connect Endpoint transfers the burden of security hardening to AWS.

Further reading

The following resources offer further insights and best practices for VPC security:

- *AWS Whitepaper – Amazon Virtual Private Cloud Connectivity Options*: `https://docs.aws.amazon.com/whitepapers/latest/aws-vpc-connectivity-options`

- *AWS Whitepaper – Building a Scalable and Secure Multi-VPC AWS Network Infrastructure*: `https://docs.aws.amazon.com/whitepapers/latest/building-scalable-secure-multi-vpc-network-infrastructure`

- *Best practice rules for Amazon Virtual Private Cloud (VPC)*, by TrendMicro: `https://www.trendmicro.com/cloudoneconformity-staging/knowledge-base/aws/VPC/`

- *Best practices for securely configuring Amazon VPC*, by Jordan Obey (2022): `https://www.datadoghq.com/blog/vpc-components/`

Identity and Access Management – Securing Users, Roles, and Policies

Welcome to the third chapter of our deep dive into AWS security. In this chapter, we will focus on AWS **Identity and Access Management** (**IAM**), which is the backbone of AWS security. We will embark on a journey where we will cover the foundational access control models, such as RBAC and ABAC, and their pivotal role in AWS. Transitioning from there, we will explore the vast landscape of IAM identities, shedding light on both human and non-human identities, the nuances of various credential types, and the detailed workings of IAM users, groups, roles, and externally managed identities. As we progress, IAM policies will come to the forefront, where we will discuss everything from their basic structure to advanced use cases and efficient management techniques. Toward the end, we will tackle the challenges posed by IAM in expansive, multi-account AWS deployments, emphasizing the value of centralized IAM management and the indispensable role of automation in a DevOps-centric world.

By the conclusion of this chapter, you will possess a comprehensive understanding of AWS IAM, its components, and best practices. You will be equipped with the knowledge to manage IAM identities effectively, craft and manage IAM policies with precision, and navigate the challenges of large-scale IAM deployments.

In this chapter, our exploration will encompass the following key areas:

- Exploring access control models
- Managing identities via IAM users, groups, roles, and external identities
- Mastering IAM policies management from creation to advanced use cases
- Challenges and solutions for IAM in multi-account environments

Access control models

In the realm of AWS IAM, understanding access control models is fundamental. These models provide a structured approach to defining how users (or roles) interact with resources within your AWS environment. The two most commonly used models in AWS are **role-based access control** (**RBAC**) and **attribute-based access control** (**ABAC**), but others may also be relevant, depending on your specific use case.

Access control models overview

Access control models are essentially frameworks that dictate who can access what within a system. They define how permissions are granted and how different identities (users, roles, and others) can interact with resources. The choice of an access control model can significantly impact the security posture of your AWS environment, so it is crucial to understand the different options available and their implications.

In AWS IAM, the primary access control models are RBAC and ABAC. However, there are also other models, such as **discretionary access control** (**DAC**), **mandatory access control** (**MAC**), and others, that might be used in specific scenarios. Each model has its strengths and weaknesses, and the choice between them depends on your specific requirements and the nature of your AWS environment.

Understanding RBAC

RBAC is a prevalent model for managing permissions within a system. It regulates access to computer or network resources by leveraging the concept of user roles within an organization. Such roles include a set of permissions indicating allowed actions within the system. Users are given roles that permit them to perform designated functions, thereby regulating access to system resources. This model greatly simplifies access management, particularly in large organizations, by allowing administrators to manage users and permissions in terms of roles rather than on an individual basis.

In the context of AWS, IAM groups and policies facilitate the implementation of RBAC. It is important to note that the concept of roles in RBAC is different from AWS IAM roles. In RBAC, roles are more about job functions within an organization, such as developer, auditor, or network engineer, and the access permissions that these job functions require.

RBAC is not without its limitations. One of the main challenges of RBAC is the potential for role explosion, where the number of roles can grow exponentially with the complexity of the system, making it difficult to manage. Additionally, RBAC does not consider the context of a request, such as the current time, the location of the user, or the tags applied to resources, which can be a significant limitation for certain applications. Furthermore, RBAC can become complex and difficult to manage in highly dynamic environments where access control requirements change frequently.

Despite these limitations, RBAC remains a powerful model for managing access control, providing a balance between security and usability.

Understanding ABAC

ABAC is a flexible and granular access control model that uses attributes as building blocks in access control decisions. These attributes can be associated with a user, a resource, an environment, or a combination of these.

In the context of AWS, ABAC is particularly useful because it allows you to simplify permission management at scale. You can create policies that are narrowly tailored to allow only the necessary access instead of managing permissions for each user. For example, you might have a policy that allows developers in your organization to modify resources, but only in the development environment. This policy could be based on attributes such as `user.Role=Developer` and `resource.Environment=development`.

The following figure (*Figure 3.1*) shows an example of ABAC implementation based on tags assigned to users and resources. In this example, only users with the `Team` tag associated with the `Blue` value attached to them can access resources that have the same tag. The same logic applies to users with other tag values who can access their respective resources:

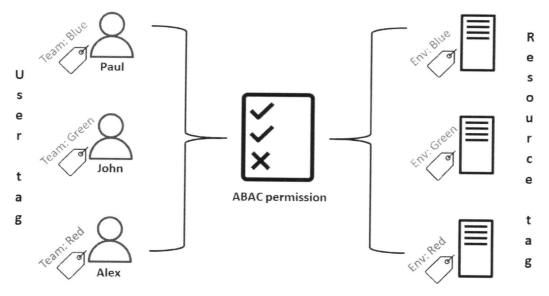

Figure 3.1 – ABAC example using tags

In addition, Amazon Cognito, an identity management solution for application users, simplifies managing end user identities and attributes. In tandem with IAM, it enables the creation of attribute-referencing policies, facilitating fine-grained access control in your applications running on AWS through ABAC. More details on integrating Cognito with IAM for ABAC will be covered in *Chapter 8*.

ABAC is also useful in scenarios where you need to grant access based on conditions that are evaluated at runtime. For example, you might have a policy that allows access to a resource only if the request comes from a specific IP address range.

Remember, when implementing ABAC, it is important to carefully manage your attributes and regularly review your policies to ensure they are granting the appropriate level of access.

Other access control models for multi-account environments

While RBAC and ABAC are the most commonly used models, other access control models are worth mentioning when handling multiple resource owners and AWS accounts. They are as follows:

- **DAC**: In this model, the owner of the resource has the discretion to decide who can access a specific resource and what operations they can perform on it. This model is flexible and intuitive, but it can be risky if the owner is not careful about granting permissions. Using separate AWS accounts with decentralized IAM can help achieve this model. Each AWS account owner is responsible for managing access to the resources created in his account.

- **MAC**: This model is more rigid and is often used in environments that require a high level of security. In MAC, access to resources is controlled by a central authority, not by the owner of the resource. This can be achieved by utilizing AWS Organizations, IAM Identity Center, and **service control policies** (SCPs) to centrally control permissions in a multi-account environment.

Choosing the right access control model

Each of these models has its strengths and weaknesses, and the choice of model depends on the specific requirements of an organization. In practice, many organizations use a combination of different models to achieve a balance between security and usability.

The following table (*Table 3.1*) compares different access control models mentioned in this section, helping to understand their characteristics and to choose the most suitable models for your specific requirements:

Criteria/Model	RBAC	ABAC	DAC	MAC
Definition	Based on roles within an enterprise. Users are assigned roles, and roles have permissions.	Uses attributes (user, resource, environment) to make access decisions.	Resource owners decide who can access their resources.	Central authority controls access, not the resource owner.

Criteria/Model	RBAC	ABAC	DAC	MAC
Granularity	Medium: Based on roles.	High: Can be very specific based on multiple attributes.	High: Based on the owner's discretion.	Based on central policies.
Flexibility	Moderate: Can be tailored to organizational roles.	High: Can adapt to dynamic conditions.	High: Entirely up to the resource owner.	Low: Rigid, defined by central authority.
Complexity	Can become complex with role explosion.	Complex due to multiple attributes but offers fine-grained control.	Moderate: Depends on the owner's management.	Moderate to High: Centralized policies can be intricate.
Best for	Organizations with defined roles.	Dynamic environments that need fine-grained access control.	Scenarios where resource owners should have full control.	High-security environments that need centralized control at scale.
Potential Limitations	Role explosion; does not consider context	Complexity in managing multiple attributes	Risky if owners are not careful	Rigid, might not adapt quickly to changes

Table 3.1 – Comparison of the different types of access control models

Building on the understanding of key access control models, let's advance to the practical management of IAM identities, also known as principals, to apply these models effectively.

Managing IAM identities

In AWS, managing identities is a crucial aspect of maintaining secure and efficient access to your environment. In the following subsections, we will delve deeper into the types of identities and credentials used in AWS, review IAM users, groups, and roles, and explore the concept of external identities and federations in AWS. This integration allows you to align AWS IAM with external identity systems. We will also discuss best practices for managing IAM identities.

Managing both human and non-human identities

Human identities typically represent individual users having access to your environment. These users might be system administrators, developers, or business users who need access to AWS resources. Each human user is typically represented in AWS IAM as an IAM user. IAM users can be grouped into IAM groups for easier management. Each IAM user can be assigned individual security credentials, such as passwords and access keys.

Non-human identities, on the other hand, represent applications or services that need to interact with AWS resources, such as objects stored in an S3 bucket, or a DynamoDB table. These identities could be applications running on EC2 instances, AWS Lambda functions, or even on-premises. Non-human identities are typically represented as IAM roles.

Managing both human and non-human identities effectively is key to maintaining a secure and efficient AWS environment. This involves not only creating and configuring IAM users and roles but also regularly reviewing and updating their permissions to ensure that they have the least privilege necessary to perform their tasks. This principle of least privilege reduces the risk of unauthorized or unintended actions in your AWS environment.

Types of credentials and their use cases

In AWS IAM, there are two types of credentials: long-term and temporary.

Long-term credentials

Long-term credentials are typically associated with IAM users and can be used to directly access AWS services until they are manually revoked. These credentials include passwords and access keys. Their security can be enhanced by leveraging **multi-factor authentication** (**MFA**) devices.

Passwords

Passwords are used by IAM users to sign into the AWS Management Console, as well as other AWS web pages, such as the AWS Discussion Forums and the AWS Support Center. AWS allows you to enforce custom password policies that can specify password length, require specific character types, and mandate password rotation. It is crucial to enforce strong password policies to reduce the risk of unauthorized access.

However, it is important to note that passwords are based on a single factor of authentication, something the user knows, and are very commonly compromised. Therefore, they cannot be considered as a strong means of authentication on their own and are not enough to protect critical access to sensitive data and resources.

MFA

MFA adds an extra layer of protection by combining two different kinds of authentication factors: something the user knows (the password) and something he owns (an MFA device). With MFA, users have an MFA device that generates a **one-time password** (**OTP**) that they must provide when signing in. AWS supports both virtual MFA and physical MFA devices. A virtual MFA device runs in an application on a mobile device such as a smartphone, while a physical MFA device runs on dedicated hardware. Note that MFA can only be used for human users. This is because non-human users, such as applications and services, cannot *own* an MFA token.

MFA is a must for high-privilege human users, including those with broad permissions, access to sensitive data and resources, and of course the root user. It is also a good practice to enforce MFA for all human users, regardless of their privilege level. This is because any compromised account can potentially be escalated to higher privileges due to misconfigurations or other weaknesses.

Access keys

Access keys consist of an access key ID and a secret access key, which are used to sign programmatic requests made on AWS by IAM users. These programmatic requests include access to the AWS CLI, the AWS SDKs, and the AWS API.

Access keys should be handled carefully. They should not be stored in the clear in any configuration file, or environment variable, embedded in code, or shared publicly. There have been real-world incidents where access keys were accidentally committed to public code repositories, leading to significant data breaches. Therefore, it is crucial to ensure access keys are securely managed. It is also crucial to regularly rotate old access keys and revoke unused keys to ensure the security of your AWS account.

Also, note that access keys alone cannot be considered a strong means of authentication. It is also strongly recommended that you enforce MFA for AWS CLI access from human users, which needs a specific IAM policy to be explicitly required.

Temporary credentials

Unlike long-term credentials, temporary security credentials in AWS are designed to be short-lived. They are dynamically generated and automatically expire after a certain period, ranging from a few minutes to several hours. This way, temporary credentials provide an added layer of security because they are not permanently stored with the user (human or non-human) and are automatically revoked when they expire. This means that even if they were to be accidentally exposed, they could not be used beyond their configured lifetime.

Temporary credentials are used in several scenarios, including identity federation, cross-account access, and roles assigned to EC2 instances, Lambda functions, or other resources.

In identity federation, temporary credentials are used to grant external identities (such as users in your corporate directory) permissions to access resources without having to create an IAM user for each identity. In cross-account access, temporary credentials allow users from one AWS account to access resources in another account.

When running an application on an EC2 instance, you can provide temporary security credentials to your instance by attaching an IAM role to it. These temporary credentials are available to all applications running on the instance, eliminating the need to store long-term credentials such as access keys locally on that instance. The same applies to Lambda functions, where using an IAM role also eliminates the need to store access keys in environment variables, or worse, within the code of the function. This approach is the most secure way to manage non-human identities in an AWS environment.

IAM Roles Anywhere further extends the versatility of temporary credentials by enabling applications running outside of AWS, such as on-premises servers, to securely assume IAM roles. However, enabling IAM Roles Anywhere outside AWS involves a more complex setup as it requires a *trust anchor* between your **public-key infrastructure** (**PKI**) and AWS to establish trust.

Security implications

In conclusion, the type of credentials you choose to use in AWS depends on your specific use case and security requirements. Long-term credentials are suitable for persistent access but require careful management and regular rotation. On the other hand, temporary credentials offer a high level of security due to their short lifespan and are ideal for scenarios that require temporary, limited access, or access from non-human identities hosted in AWS.

The following table (*Table 3.2*) compares the different types of credentials mentioned in this sub-section, including their use case, the types of users, and their level of security:

Credentials Type	Use Cases	User Types	Security Level
Passwords	AWS Management Console	Human	Low (single factor)
MFA	AWS Management Console and CLI	Human	High (two factors)
Access keys	AWS CLI, AWS SDKs, and AWS API	Human, non-human	Low (single factor)
Temporary credentials	Identity federation, cross-account access, IAM roles assigned to non-human identities	Human, non-human	High (short lifespan, automatically revoked)

Table 3.2 – Comparison of the different types of credentials

Remember, the security of your AWS environment is only as strong as the weakest link. Therefore, it is crucial to enforce strong security practices across all types of credentials regardless of their security level. As we wrap up our discussion on the types of credentials and their use cases, let's transition to the foundational elements of AWS IAM identities: users, groups, and roles. Understanding these elements is essential for implementing robust access control measures.

IAM users, groups, and roles

In the vast ecosystem of AWS IAM, the concepts of users, groups, and roles are foundational. These components are the building blocks that allow for fine-grained access control, ensuring that only authorized identities can access your AWS resources. Let's delve deeper into each of these components, understanding their significance, use cases, and best practices.

Users

An IAM user is an individual identity with specific permissions that determine what it can and cannot access in AWS. Each IAM user is associated with a single AWS account. While each AWS account starts with a single IAM user, the root user, it is essential to differentiate between human and non-human users.

Use cases for IAM users

IAM users are mostly suitable in the following situations:

- **Human users**: These are individuals such as developers, system administrators, or any other personnel who interact with AWS services via the console or the CLI. They typically require credentials to access services and resources.

- **Non-human users**: These are applications, scripts, or tools that make programmatic calls to AWS services. Examples include a SaaS application that needs to read a file from your S3 bucket or a script running on-premises that periodically starts and stops certain instances.

Best practices for IAM users

Here are some guidelines to ensure secure and efficient management of IAM users:

- *Distinguish between human and non-human users*: Recognize that applications or scripts might not need the same level of access as human users. Tailor permissions accordingly, and do not use the same IAM user for both types of access. A common mistake is developers using their own IAM users (human access) to grant access keys to an application (non-human access). This situation leads to too broad permissions granted to the application, and it may cause the application to stop working when the developer leaves the organization, and their user account is deleted.

- *Prefer IAM roles for non-human identities*: When dealing with non-human identities, especially those running within the AWS environment such as EC2 instances, Lambda functions, or ECS tasks, it is best to use IAM roles instead of IAM users to access other AWS resources. Roles automatically provide temporary credentials, eliminating the risks associated with managing long-term credentials.

- *Avoid using the root user*: It is strongly recommended to avoid using the root user for everyday tasks.

- *Enable MFA*: For an added layer of security, enable MFA for all IAM users, especially for users with extensive permissions or access to sensitive data.

- *Restrict IP addresses*: Further, enhance security by limiting access based on network location using conditions such as *SourceIP* or *SourceVPC* within the IAM policies associated with IAM users. This ensures they can only access AWS resources from trusted and specified network ranges or VPCs, effectively whitelisting corporate network ranges or specific VPCs.

- *Regularly rotate credentials*: Regularly rotate security credentials for IAM users. If an access key is compromised, the potential impact is reduced if the keys are changed regularly. Therefore, it is recommended to rotate access keys at least every 90 days to 365 days, depending on your security requirements.

- *Utilize tags for efficient management*: When dealing with a large number of IAM users, using tags can be invaluable. Tags allow for categorization based on department, role, project, or any other criteria, making it easier to manage, audit, and control access.

- *Regularly review and audit*: Periodically review IAM user access, permissions, and activity. Remove or modify any outdated permissions and delete users who no longer need access.

Groups

An IAM group acts as a bridge between individual users and the permissions they need. Instead of being a standalone identity, an group is essentially a container that holds a set of users. It is a mechanism to bundle users under a common umbrella of permissions, streamlining the management process. For example, you could have a group called **Network administrator** and grant that group the necessary permissions to administer resources in AWS VPCs. This approach aligns well with the concept of RBAC, which was discussed earlier, where permissions are granted based on roles rather than individual user identities.

Use cases for IAM groups

IAM groups can be leveraged in various scenarios, both for human and non-human users:

- **Departmental or functional roles**: For instance, you might have a group named **Developers** where all members need access to certain development tools and resources. Similarly, a **Finance** group might need access to billing information but not to development resources.

- **Application-based grouping**: Consider a scenario where multiple applications (non-human users) require similar access to a set of AWS resources. Instead of assigning permissions to each application's IAM user, you can group these users under one group and assign the necessary permissions to that group.

- **Multi-role users**: Sometimes, a user might wear multiple hats. For instance, a user might be part of both the **Developers** and **QA** groups, inheriting permissions from both. This flexibility can be particularly useful in dynamic environments where roles and responsibilities might overlap.

Best practices for IAM groups

Here are some guidelines for managing IAM groups effectively:

- **Groups as a management tool**: It is not uncommon to see AWS setups with numerous IAM users but sparse usage of groups. Using groups effectively can significantly simplify permission management, especially when managing a large number of IAM users in a single AWS account.

- **Role-based grouping**: Align your groups with the RBAC model. This ensures that permissions are granted based on roles, making the system more intuitive and manageable.

- **Regularly audit group memberships**: Ensure that the members of a group are still relevant. As roles change or employees transition, it is essential to keep group memberships up-to-date.

- **Use descriptive naming and tagging**: Group names should be self-explanatory. For example, *S3-FullAccess* immediately indicates that members have full access to S3 resources. Just as with IAM users, using tags can be invaluable when dealing with a large number of groups.

- **Avoid broad permissions**: It is tempting to create a *catch-all* group, but it is safer to have multiple groups with specific, narrow permissions. This minimizes potential risks and aligns with the principle of least privilege.

Roles

An IAM role represents a unique and dynamic approach to handling permissions within AWS. Unlike traditional IAM users, roles don't have a fixed identity tied to them. Instead, they act as containers for permissions that can be assumed by other identities such as IAM users and roles. This mechanism provides a flexible way to grant temporary access.

How IAM roles work

At the heart of IAM roles is the AWS **Security Token Service (STS)**, which is instrumental in the dynamic issuance of temporary credentials. When an identity assumes a role, STS provides temporary credentials for use within a limited session duration. These credentials, which are time-bound and automatically rotated by STS, significantly bolster security by reducing the risk of compromise.

The operation of STS, while integral, typically occurs behind the scenes thanks to its seamless integration with IAM. This integration often negates the need for users to directly interact with STS. Central to utilizing IAM roles is the *Assume Role* action. This action is initiated when an identity (be it a human user, an application, or another AWS service) requires specific permissions to perform an action. To assume a role, the identity must satisfy the conditions defined in the role's **trust policy**, which specifies who can assume the role and under what conditions. Once the trust policy conditions are met and the role is assumed, the identity is endowed with the permissions associated with that role for the duration of the session.

The following diagram (*Figure 3.2*) illustrates the following role assumption workflow:

1. **Assume Role request**: A successfully authenticated identity submits an **Assume Role** request to STS.

2. **Temporary credentials**: If the request complies with the associated IAM permissions and the requested role's trust policy, STS grants the assumed role to the requesting identity and issues the associated temporary credentials.

3. **Resource access request**: The requesting identity uses the provided temporary credentials associated with the assumed role to request access to AWS resources.

4. **Authorization check**: IAM then evaluates the access request against the permissions linked to the assumed role, the requested resource, and the actions specified in the request. If authorized, IAM grants access to the resource:

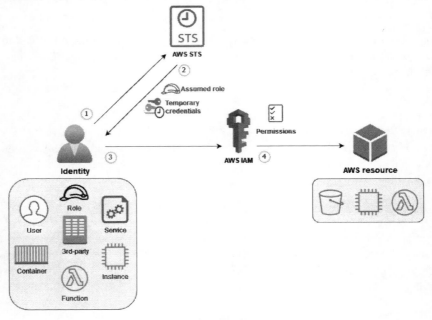

Figure 3.2 – The Assume Role workflow

By understanding how IAM roles work, you can leverage the benefits of secure, temporary access and fine-grained control within your AWS environment.

Use cases for IAM roles

Roles are designed to provide temporary access to AWS resources, ensuring that permissions are only granted when needed and for the duration they are required. Here are some common scenarios where roles are invaluable:

- **Cross-account access**: Roles are invaluable when working with multiple AWS accounts. Instead of creating duplicate IAM users in each account, you can define roles in the target account and allow identities from the source account to assume them.

- **Applications in and beyond the AWS cloud**: For AWS services such as EC2 or Lambda, roles provide a secure way to grant permissions to AWS resources without embedding long-term credentials. For instance, an EC2 instance can assume a role to access S3 buckets without needing to store access keys on the instance. Extending this capability, IAM Roles Anywhere allows for the secure assumption of IAM roles outside of AWS.

- **Service-linked roles for AWS services**: They allow AWS services to perform actions on your behalf in your AWS account. These roles are usually pre-defined by AWS and include all the permissions the service needs to call other AWS services on your behalf, simplifying setup and providing a secure way to manage permissions for services that need to access resources in your account.

- **Identity federation**: For organizations using an **identity provider** (**IdP**) outside of AWS, roles offer a way to grant AWS access to external identities. After authenticating with the IdP, users receive a token or an assertion that they can exchange for temporary AWS credentials by assuming a role.

- **Temporary elevated access**: In situations where a user needs temporary access to additional resources, roles can be used to grant these permissions without altering the user's original permissions.

Best practices for IAM roles

IAM roles are a powerful tool, but they require careful management to ensure security:

- **Enforce short-lived sessions**: Limit the duration of sessions to the minimum required for the task. This reduces the window of opportunity for any potential misuse of the role's permissions.

- **Limit trust**: Be selective about which identities are allowed to assume a role. Use trust policies to define these identities explicitly.

- **Enforce mandatory MFA**: For high-privilege roles granting access to sensitive or critical AWS resources that can be assumed by human users, enforce the use of MFA. This adds an additional layer of security, ensuring that even if a user's primary credentials are compromised0, the role remains protected.

- **Use roles over user access keys**: When granting permissions to AWS resources, prefer using roles over IAM user's access keys. Roles provide temporary credentials, reducing the risk associated with long-term credentials. By using roles, you eliminate the need to share or embed permanent AWS access keys, thereby enhancing security. This approach ensures that permissions are only granted for the duration they are required, minimizing potential exposure.

- **Limit service-link roles**: Ensure service-linked roles are assumed only by the AWS service they are designed for, not by IAM users or other roles. Assign each service-linked role to a single AWS service and avoid granting additional permissions beyond what is necessary for the service's operation, maintaining the principle of least privilege.

- **Use descriptive naming and tagging**: Ensure role names indicate their purpose and use tags to categorize them. Most AWS accounts end up with a lot of roles created, so this is particularly important here.

- **Regularly review and audit roles**: While roles can be used to grant temporary access for specific tasks, it is crucial to monitor and log such accesses. This ensures that the permissions are not misused and provides an audit trail for any actions performed during these sessions. Regularly assess the roles in your AWS environment, removing obsolete ones and adjusting permissions as necessary, ensuring they adhere to the principle of least privilege.

Having explored the roles of IAM users, groups, and roles in detail, let's turn our attention to how AWS accommodates external identities and federations, further expanding the horizons of identity management.

External identities and federation in AWS

In the realm of AWS IAM, the ability to integrate external identities and establish federation is a powerful feature that facilitates seamless and secure access to AWS resources. This integration allows organizations to leverage their existing identity solutions, such as corporate directories or social identity providers, to grant access to AWS without the need to create a separate IAM user for each individual. To better grasp this concept, let's delve into the role and mechanics of external identities in AWS.

Understanding external identities

External identities refer to identities that are managed outside of AWS. These can be identities from a corporate directory such as Microsoft **Active Directory** (**AD**), IdPs such as Okta or Auth0, or other IdPs compatible with **OpenID Connect** (**OIDC**) or SAML 2.0. The primary advantage of using external identities is that organizations can maintain a centralized identity source, making user management, authentication, and authorization more streamlined and consistent.

Federation in AWS

Federation, in the context of AWS, is the process of delegating authentication and, potentially, authorization to an external system. Instead of directly authenticating against AWS, the user authenticates against the external identity provider. Once authenticated, the user is granted temporary access to AWS resources based on the permissions mapped to their external identity.

How federation works

Federation in AWS involves a series of steps that authenticate, validate, and grant access to users from an external IdP. Here are the steps that are followed in case of a SAML-based IdP:

1. **Authentication**: First, the user authenticates with the IdP, typically through a corporate login portal or another SAML-based authentication system.

2. **SAML assertion issuance**: Upon successful authentication, the IdP issues a SAML assertion. This assertion contains information about the user's identity and attributes, along with a digital signature to ensure its authenticity.

3. **SAML assertion exchange**: The user or application then sends the SAML assertion to AWS STS.

4. **Temporary credentials**: STS validates the SAML assertion with the IdP and, if successful, issues temporary AWS credentials to the user. These credentials allow the user to access AWS resources based on the IAM permissions defined for their identity.

Benefits of federation

Federation streamlines identity management in AWS, offering several benefits:

*   **Centralized management**: Organizations can manage users and their permissions from a single, centralized location, reducing administrative overhead.

*   **Reduced IAM users**: There is no need to create individual IAM users for everyone in the organization. This not only simplifies management but also enhances security by reducing the number of long-term credentials.

*   **Consistent security policies**: By leveraging external identity providers, organizations can enforce consistent security policies, such as password policies or MFA, across all applications, including those running in AWS.

*   **Seamless user experience**: For end users, federation provides a seamless experience. They can use their existing corporate credentials to access AWS resources, eliminating the need for multiple logins.

Best practices for federation

Adopting these best practices ensures a secure and efficient federation integration:

- **Prioritize federation over IAM users**: Shift toward federated identities as the primary method for authentication, leveraging external identity providers to minimize the use of IAM users. This method offers the dual benefits of enhanced security through temporary credentials and simplified account management.

- **Implement session timeout**: Set a strict session timeout for federated users. If a user is inactive for a specified duration, their session should automatically expire, requiring re-authentication.

- **Enforce strong authentication**: Ensure that the external identity provider enforces strong authentication mechanisms, such as MFA, especially for high-privilege roles or access to sensitive applications.

- **Integrate with Cognito**: When federating with mobile or web applications, consider integrating with Amazon Cognito to streamline the authentication and authorization process, benefiting from its built-in security features.

- **Monitor and audit**: Use AWS CloudTrail and other logging mechanisms to monitor and audit federated access. Regularly review logs to detect any unusual or unauthorized activities.

- **Regularly review trust relationships**: Periodically review and update the trust relationships between AWS and your external identity providers. Remove any outdated or unnecessary relationships.

With a clear understanding of external identities, we can now compare the different IAM identity types, which will help us appreciate the nuances and applications of each within the AWS security landscape.

Comparing IAM identity types

The following table (*Table 3.3*) compares the different types of IAM identities mentioned in this sub-section, including their use case and the type of credentials they can be used with:

Identity Type	Use Cases	Credentials
Users	- Human users such as developers and system administrators who interact with AWS - Non-human users such as applications running outside AWS that make programmatic calls to AWS services	Long-term credentials: passwords, access keys, MFA devices
Groups	- Departmental or functional roles - Application-based grouping where multiple applications require similar AWS access	None (groups don't have credentials but hold users who do)

Identity Type	Use Cases	Credentials
Roles	- Cross-account access between AWS accounts - AWS services such as Lambda accessing other resources - Applications outside AWS via IAM Roles Anywhere - Identity federation with external identity providers - Temporary elevated access for specific tasks	Temporary credentials provided by STS
External Identities	- SSO for users to access AWS resources after logging into a corporate portal - Web and mobile applications using federation for user authentication - Temporary access based on external identity	Tokens or assertions issued by an external IdP, which are exchanged for temporary credentials via STS

Table 3.3 – Comparison of the different types of IAM identities

It is important to note that AWS strongly discourages the use of IAM users for both human and non-human entities due to the security vulnerabilities associated with long-term credentials, even when enhanced with MFA. Instead, it is recommended to employ federation with identity providers for human users, granting access via temporary credentials. For non-human users or systems, leveraging IAM roles or integrating with third-party security vaults that issue temporary credentials is advised. IAM users should be considered only as a last resort when no other secure method is feasible. In such a situation, it is crucial to enhance their security by applying the best practices discussed in this section.

Transitioning from IAM identities, let's pivot to the equally vital aspect of IAM policies.

Managing IAM policies

IAM policies play a pivotal role in defining permissions within AWS. They dictate who can do what and where. As AWS environments grow in complexity, the need for fine-grained control and understanding of IAM policies becomes paramount. Misconfigured policies can introduce significant security risks, emphasizing the importance of getting them right. In this section, we will delve deep into the intricacies of IAM policies, their types, how they are evaluated, and best practices for creating and managing them.

Understanding IAM policies

Understanding the nuances of IAM policies becomes indispensable. This subsection explores the different types of policies and delves into how AWS IAM evaluates them.

Identity-based versus resource-based policies

IAM policies can be broadly classified into two categories – identity-based and resource-based:

- **Identity-based policies** are attached directly to an identity, such as an IAM user, group, or role. These policies define the permissions for the identity, specifying what actions they can perform, on which resources, and under what conditions. For example, an identity-based policy might grant an IAM user permission to launch specific EC2 instances or read objects from a designated S3 bucket.

- **Resource-based policies**, conversely, are attached directly to resources. A classic example of this is an S3 bucket policy or an SQS queue policy. These policies dictate which identities can or cannot perform actions on that particular resource. For instance, a resource-based policy on an S3 bucket might allow an IAM role from a different AWS account to read objects.

Customer-managed versus AWS-managed policies

AWS provides two distinct types of managed policies – customer-managed and AWS-managed:

- **Customer-managed policies** are those crafted and maintained by AWS users. They offer the flexibility to be tailored to specific organizational needs, allowing for more granular control over permissions. For instance, an organization might have a customer-managed policy that restricts access to a specific S3 bucket, allowing only designated departments or teams to upload or download content.

- **AWS-managed policies**, on the other hand, are predefined by AWS. They are designed to provide permissions for common use cases, ensuring that users don't have to start from scratch. For example, AWS offers a managed policy named `AWSLambda_ReadOnlyAccess` that grants read-only access to AWS Lambda functions. It is important to bear in mind that AWS-managed policies can be automatically updated by AWS to reflect new services or features. While this ensures policies are up-to-date, administrators need to stay informed about these changes to avoid unexpected permission alterations.

Inline policies

Apart from managed policies, AWS also offers inline policies. An inline policy is a policy that is directly embedded in a single user, group, or role. They are not standalone like managed policies and exist solely for the identity to which they are attached. While inline policies can be useful for one-off permission requirements, they can become challenging to manage at scale. If multiple identities require the same permissions, you would have to replicate the inline policy for each identity, leading to redundancy and potential inconsistencies. Hence, the use of inline policies is generally not advised, especially in larger or complex environments.

IAM policy evaluation logic

AWS employs a specific logic when evaluating IAM policies to determine whether a request should be permitted or denied. Understanding this evaluation logic is crucial. It ensures that administrators can predict the outcome of policy changes and troubleshoot access issues effectively. Here is a brief rundown of the process:

- **Default deny**: All requests are denied by default unless explicitly allowed by a policy.

- **Explicit deny**: If a policy explicitly denies a particular action, it takes precedence over any allow statement. This ensures that security administrators can enforce stringent restrictions when necessary.

- **Explicit allow**: If no explicit deny is found, AWS checks for explicit allow statements. If one is found that matches the request, the action is permitted.

As reflected in the following diagram (*Figure 3.3*), AWS evaluates both identity-based and resource-based policies associated with the request. If any of these policies have an explicit deny, the request is denied. If there is an explicit allow and no corresponding explicit deny, the request is allowed:

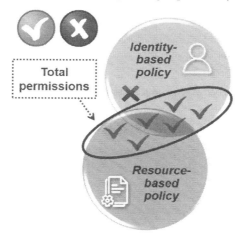

Figure 3.3 – Identity-based and resource-based policies evaluation

To illustrate, imagine an IAM user trying to access an S3 bucket. If the user's attached identity-based policies or the bucket's resource-based policies have an explicit deny for the user's action, the request will be denied. If there is no deny but an explicit allow, the user will gain access. If neither is present, the default deny principle will apply, and the user's request will be denied.

With IAM policies clarified, let's learn how to craft and oversee them effectively.

Creating and managing IAM policies

Crafting and managing IAM policies is an art that requires precision, understanding, and continuous monitoring. As AWS environments evolve, so do the requirements for permissions. In this subsection, we will explore the process of writing IAM policies, delve into advanced conditions, and discuss best practices for testing, versioning, and troubleshooting policies.

Writing IAM policies

IAM policies are structured documents written in JSON format, embodying the principles of the CEDAR policy language, as illustrated in the following diagram (*Figure 3.4*). Each policy comprises one or more statements, with each statement defining a single permission. A statement encompasses elements such as `Effect` (allow or deny), `Action` (the operations you are allowing or denying), `Resource` (the object the action is performed on), and, when necessary, `Condition` (the circumstances under which the policy is in effect):

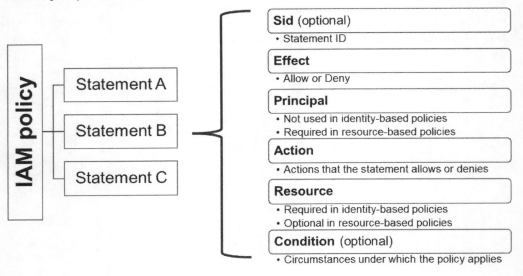

Figure 3.4 – IAM policy structure

It is essential to avoid creating overly permissive policies. Always adhere to the principle of least privilege to ensure that identities only have the permissions they need.

As an example, consider a scenario where you want to grant an IAM identity permission to read objects from a particular S3 bucket. The policy might look something like this:

```
{
    "Version": "2012-10-17",
    "Statement": [
```

```
    {
      "Effect": "Allow",
      "Action": "s3:GetObject",
      "Resource": "arn:aws:s3:::example-bucket/*",
    }
  ]
}
```

This is a straightforward policy, but as AWS environments grow and requirements change, policies can become more complex.

Advanced IAM policy conditions

Conditions provide the granular control that many organizations need. They allow you to specify the circumstances under which the policy statement is in effect. These conditions can be:

- **Global conditions**: Apply these universally across AWS services, such as using `aws:MultiFactorAuthPresent` to verify MFA status for resource access
- **Service-specific conditions**: These are unique to certain AWS services, such as `s3:prefix`, to restrict access to specific folders (prefixes) in an S3 bucket
- **Conditions based on tags**: Utilize resource tags, such as restricting actions to EC2 instances tagged with `"Environment:Production"`

Building on our previous example, let's say you want the IAM user to access the S3 bucket only if they are logging in from a specific IP address, during business hours, and have MFA enabled. Here, the policy might evolve into the following:

```
{
  "Version": "2012-10-17",
  "Statement": [
    {
      "Effect": "Allow",
      "Action": "s3:GetObject",
      "Resource": "arn:aws:s3:::example-bucket/*",
      "Condition": {
        "IpAddress": {"aws:SourceIp": "22.3.111.9/32"},
        "DateGreaterThan": {"aws:CurrentTime": "09:00:00Z"},
        "DateLessThan": {"aws:CurrentTime": "17:00:00Z"},
        "Bool": {"aws:MultiFactorAuthPresent": "true"}
      }
    }
  ]
}
```

This policy uses global conditions (`aws:SourceIp`, `aws:CurrentTime`, and `aws:MultiFactorAuthPresent`) to restrict access based on the user's IP address, the time of their request, and whether they have used MFA for authentication.

Testing IAM policies

Once you have crafted an IAM policy, it is imperative to test it to ensure it behaves as expected. AWS's IAM policy simulator is a valuable tool for this purpose, allowing you to validate your policies' effects without making actual AWS service calls. However, while the simulator is a great starting point, real-world testing in a controlled environment, such as a development or staging setup, is also invaluable. This hands-on approach ensures that the policy works as intended in all scenarios, capturing nuances that the simulator might miss.

IAM policy versions and rollbacks

As AWS environments evolve, IAM policies may need adjustments. AWS facilitates this by allowing policies to have versions. When you modify a customer-managed policy, AWS automatically creates a new version, enabling you to roll back to previous policy versions if required. Periodically reviewing policy versions and retaining only necessary ones helps maintain a clean policy environment and facilitates quick rollbacks during emergencies. It is worth noting that inline policies do not support versioning, which is another reason to avoid using them altogether.

Troubleshooting and debugging IAM policies

Despite meticulous planning, there will be times when IAM policies don't behave as anticipated. AWS CloudTrail is invaluable in these situations. It logs all AWS API calls, providing insights into the caller identity, the time of the call, request parameters, and response elements. Analyzing CloudTrail logs can help pinpoint the exact policy or statement causing issues. Another common challenge is understanding the policy evaluation order, especially when juggling both identity-based and resource-based policies. Remembering the evaluation logic can significantly aid in debugging such challenges. Lastly, always ensure that the policy JSON is formatted correctly. Simple syntax errors can lead to policies not being applied as expected.

Reviewing IAM policies

Regularly reviewing IAM policies is a crucial best practice that ensures security configurations remain aligned with the organization's evolving requirements. AWS IAM offers several tools to aid with managing and refining policies:

- **Generating a policy based on CloudTrail events**: Available at the user or role level, this tool allows you to review and tighten the permissions assigned to an identity based on the actual usage patterns observed in CloudTrail events within a chosen period.

- **Access Advisor**: Available in both identity and policy configuration, this tool provides insights into the services allowed by the permissions and indicates when those services were last accessed by the associated. Such data is invaluable for identifying permissions that may no longer be necessary, reinforcing the principle of least privilege.

- **Access Analyzer**: Identify and mitigate excessive permissions by generating actionable reports on external and unused access. These reports pinpoint policies that allow public or cross-account access and highlight unused permissions like write access to S3 buckets that have not been accessed in months, allowing you to take targeted action and tighten policies effectively.

As we transition from IAM policy creation and management, we will focus on exploring their application in more complex, real-world situations.

Advanced IAM policy use cases

While AWS provides a plethora of built-in policies and templates, understanding how to tailor policies for specific scenarios can make all the difference. In this subsection, we will explore four advanced IAM policy use cases that address challenges commonly faced by organizations. The following examples will illustrate the depth and breadth of possibilities when it comes to IAM policy conditions.

Enforcing MFA for AWS CLI access

One of the foundational security practices in AWS is to enforce MFA for all human IAM users, especially for the ones with the most permissive access. While MFA is commonly associated with AWS Management Console access, it is equally important for **CLI** operations. However, this is not enforced by default. Here is a policy that denies all actions if the request is made from the CLI without MFA:

```
{
    "Version": "2012-10-17",
    "Statement": {
      "Effect": "Deny",
            "NotAction": [
      "iam:CreateVirtualMFADevice",
      "iam:DeleteVirtualMFADevice",
      "iam:ListVirtualMFADevices",
      "iam:EnableMFADevice",
      "iam:ResyncMFADevice",
      "iam:ListAccountAliases",
      "iam:ListUsers",
      "iam:ListSSHPublicKeys",
      "iam:ListAccessKeys",
      "iam:ListServiceSpecificCredentials",
      "iam:ListMFADevices",
      "iam:GetAccountSummary",
```

```
        "sts:GetSessionToken"
    ],
            "Resource": "*",
    "Condition": {
        "Bool": {
        "aws:MultiFactorAuthPresent": "false",
        "aws:ViaAWSService": "false"
        }
        }
    }
}
```

Restricting Lambda function invocation based on the VPC endpoint

To ensure that Lambda functions are only invoked from within a specific VPC, you can craft a policy that checks that the function is invoked from a particular VPC endpoint:

```
{
    "Version": "2012-10-17",
    "Statement": {
        "Effect": "Allow",
        "Action": "lambda:InvokeFunction",
        "Resource": "arn:aws:lambda:region:account-id:function:function-
name",
        "Condition": {
            "StringEquals": {
                "aws:sourceVpce": "vpce-0abcd1234efgh5678"
            }
        }
    }
}
```

Dynamically allowing access based on tags

AWS resources can be tagged with key-value pairs, which can then be used in IAM policies to grant or deny access dynamically. Imagine a scenario where you want to allow developers to start or stop EC2 instances, but only if the instance has an Owner tag that specifies their IAM username:

```
{
    "Version": "2012-10-17",
    "Statement": {
        "Effect": "Allow",
        "Action": ["ec2:StartInstances", "ec2:StopInstances"],
        "Resource": "*",
        "Condition": {
```

```
      "StringEquals": {
        "ec2:ResourceTag/Owner": "${aws:username}"
      }
    }
  }
}
```

Forcing encryption with a specified KMS key

Imagine that you are managing a multi-tenant AWS environment. Each IAM user represents a tenant and has a `tenant` tag indicating their tenant ID. Each KMS key is named according to the tenant it belongs to. You want to ensure that when a tenant launches an EC2 instance, any attached EBS volume is encrypted using the KMS key that matches their tenant ID. Here is an IAM policy that enforces this:

```
{
   "Version": "2012-10-17",
   "Statement": [
     {
       "Effect": "Allow",
       "Action": "ec2:RunInstances",
       "Resource": [
         "arn:aws:ec2:region:account-id:instance/*",
         "arn:aws:ec2:region:account-id:volume/*"
       ],
       "Condition": {
         "StringEquals": {
           "ec2:Encrypted": "true",
           "ec2:KmsKeyId": "arn:aws:kms:region:account-
  id:key/${aws:PrincipalTag/tenant}"
         }
       }
     }
   ]
}
```

These advanced use cases demonstrate the flexibility and depth of IAM policies in AWS. By understanding the various condition keys and their applications, organizations can craft precise and effective policies that cater to their unique security requirements.

With a solid understanding of IAM policies in hand, let's turn our attention to the complexities of managing IAM at scale and across multiple AWS accounts.

IAM in multi-account deployments

Managing IAM in a multi-account environment is a complex endeavor, especially when dealing with large-scale deployments. AWS provides a suite of tools to streamline this process, but understanding how they fit in the picture is crucial. In this section, we will delve deeper into the challenges, solutions, and best practices for managing IAM in such environments.

Challenges with managing large-scale IAM deployments

IAM management in expansive environments brings forth a myriad of challenges:

- **Scalability**: As organizations grow, so does the need for more AWS resources and accounts. This ensures that IAM policies scale effectively without becoming unwieldy is a challenge.

- **Granularity versus manageability**: As the number of IAM identities grows, administrators face the dilemma of granularity versus manageability. While it is tempting to create highly specific permissions for each identity, this can lead to an administrative nightmare.

- **Policy overlaps**: With multiple policies and permissions, there is a risk of overlaps or contradictions, which can lead to security vulnerabilities.

- **Consistency across accounts**: Ensuring that IAM policies remain consistent across multiple AWS accounts is a significant challenge. This is especially true when different teams manage different accounts, each with its own set of requirements.

- **Audit and compliance**: Auditing multiple accounts, each with numerous IAM identities, is a complex task. Ensuring compliance with both internal and external standards adds another layer of complexity.

- **Delegation and trust**: In a multi-account setup, determining which accounts can assume roles in other accounts and establishing trust relationships is a delicate process that requires careful planning.

Centralized IAM management

For expansive organizations with numerous AWS accounts, centralizing IAM management is not just beneficial – it is essential. It fosters consistency, trims administrative tasks, and bolsters security. With AWS Organizations providing the structural backbone, we now turn to the mechanisms of IAM Identity Center and SCPs to enhance the management of access across multiple accounts.

Managing access to multiple accounts

IAM Identity Center (formerly AWS SSO) offers a consolidated management of all identity-centric data spanning multiple AWS accounts. This centralized platform empowers administrators with insights into IAM role usage patterns, frequently accessed permissions, and unused permissions. By discerning active permissions, administrators can fine-tune IAM policies, ensuring they are both robust and efficient.

Users can be integrated into IAM Identity Center from an external IdP, such as Microsoft AD or any SAML 2.0 compliant IdP, or they can be defined within the Identity Center directory itself. This flexibility allows organizations to leverage their existing identity management infrastructure or to use IAM Identity Center as a standalone solution for managing access to AWS resources across multiple accounts.

Unlike traditional IAM federation, which requires setting up trust relationships in each account, IAM Identity Center offers a centralized solution with features such as SSO. For users, the experience is significantly simplified. Once authenticated through IAM Identity Center, they gain the ability to seamlessly navigate across accounts, accessing the necessary resources without the need for repeated logins. The SSO mechanism not only improves user productivity but also strengthens security by minimizing the need for multiple credentials and reducing the potential attack surface.

Restricting permissions across the organization

SCPs are a powerful feature of AWS Organizations. They allow administrators to set permission restrictions that apply to all or a selected set of accounts within an organization. Unlike IAM policies, which grant permissions, SCPs primarily function to deny specific actions, setting the upper bounds of what IAM identities are not allowed to do, thereby ensuring uniform security postures across all accounts. This capability is crucial in maintaining a controlled environment where SCPs, by design, override any locally defined IAM policies with more permissive settings. The hierarchical structure of SCPs allows for the mitigation of overly permissive policies in individual accounts through SCP-imposed restrictions. A prime example includes universally blocking the deletion of S3 buckets and objects to protect data integrity. This framework highlights the significance of a strategically layered IAM architecture, where SCPs enforce organization-wide restrictions and local policies tailor finer-grained access controls.

Cross-account access

In the AWS multi-account ecosystem, IAM identities in one account often require access to resources in another. AWS addresses this through role-based cross-account access. Here, the *trusting account* stipulates which external accounts can tap into its resources. Conversely, the *trusted account* designates which entities are permitted to assume specific roles. This mechanism eliminates the need to share access keys between accounts, enhancing security. For example, a developer in a development AWS account might need to access a database in a production AWS account. Instead of granting direct access, a role with the necessary permissions can be assumed.

Sharing resources at scale

Managing IAM in large-scale deployments can be challenging, but efficient resource sharing across multiple accounts is equally important. AWS **Resource Access Manager** (**RAM**) addresses this need by simplifying the sharing of resources such as subnets, transit gateways, or RDS Aurora clusters across multiple accounts. This service is particularly valuable in scenarios where, for instance, a shared Aurora cluster is accessed by various development teams using different accounts. Traditionally, managing access for each team would require individual configurations, risking inconsistencies and security gaps. RAM, however, streamlines this process by enabling the creation of *resource shares* that define which accounts can access the *shared resources*, along with precise control over their permissions. Under the hood, RAM creates specific resource-based policies, even for resource types that typically do not support such policies directly through IAM. RAM plays a crucial role in helping large organizations avoid resource duplication and manage who has access to those resources centrally.

Automating IAM implementation in a DevOps world

In the age of DevOps, automation is king. The same holds true for IAM. **Infrastructure as code (IaC)** tools, such as CloudFormation and Terraform, allow for the automated provisioning of AWS resources, including IAM configurations. This automation ensures that IAM configurations are consistent, version-controlled, and replicable across environments. Such automation is especially crucial in large-scale and multi-account settings, where manual configurations can become untenable. AWS Config complements this by continuously monitoring AWS resource configurations, ensuring they comply with desired setups. For instance, if an IAM policy that is too permissive is detected, AWS Config can automatically rectify it.

Best practices for multi-account IAM

Managing IAM across multiple AWS accounts requires a strategic approach. Here are some important best practices to consider:

- **Clear account structure**: Organize AWS accounts based on function or organizational structure. This not only simplifies management but also reduces the blast radius in case of issues.

- **Use IAM Identity Center**: Leverage IAM Identity Center to centralize access management across multiple AWS accounts. It is also recommended to use SCPs tailored to prevent the creation of IAM users and groups in each account.

- **Limit root user access**: A root user has unrestricted access to all resources within its AWS account. It is crucial to use SCPs to prevent its usage.

- **Regular audits**: Tools such as IAM Access Analyzer can be instrumental in analyzing policies and ascertaining which resources can be accessed publicly or from other accounts. Regular audits ensure that policies remain tight and secure.

In conclusion, while managing IAM in large-scale, multi-account AWS deployments can be challenging, AWS provides the tools and methodologies to navigate this complex landscape. By centralizing, automating, and adhering to best practices, even organizations with the most complex environments can ensure a secure, efficient, and manageable IAM landscape.

Summary

In this chapter, we navigated the multifaceted world of AWS IAM. Starting with a thorough understanding of access control models, such as RBAC and ABAC, we shifted gears to managing IAM identities, covering the spectrum from human and non-human identities and credential types to the intricacies of IAM users, groups, roles, and externally managed identities. Then, IAM policies took center stage, with discussions ranging from basic concepts to advanced use cases and policy management techniques. This chapter wrapped up by addressing the challenges of IAM in large-scale environments, the merits of centralized IAM management, and the importance of automation in today's DevOps-driven landscape.

As we transition to the next chapter, we will focus on data protection in AWS, diving into encryption methods, key management techniques, and best practices for data storage.

Questions

Answer the following questions to test your knowledge of this chapter:

1. Which two access control models are primarily discussed in the context of AWS IAM, and how do they fundamentally differ in their approach to permissions?

2. What is the primary purpose of SCPs in AWS Organizations, and how do they interact with local IAM policies?

3. In a multi-account AWS setup, what mechanism allows IAM identities in one account to access resources in another account without sharing access keys, and what are the benefits associated with it?

4. In the era of DevOps, why is automating IAM implementation considered crucial, especially in large-scale and multi-account AWS environments?

Answers

Here are the answers to this chapter's questions:

1. The two primary access control models are RBAC and ABAC. RBAC regulates access based on predefined roles assigned to users, where each role has a specific set of permissions. In contrast, ABAC uses attributes (associated with users, resources, or the environment) as building blocks in access control decisions, allowing for more granular and dynamic permissions.

2. SCPs in AWS Organizations set permission restrictions for all accounts in an organization. They define the maximum permissions that IAM identities can have. SCPs take precedence over any locally defined IAM policies, meaning if an account has a permissive policy, the SCPs can still restrict it, ensuring centralized control.

3. Role-based cross-account access allows IAM identities in one AWS account to access resources in another account without sharing access keys. The trusting account specifies which external accounts can access its resources, while the trusted account designates which of its entities can assume specific roles. This mechanism reduces the risk associated with sharing access keys and ensures a more secure way of granting cross-account access.

4. Automation ensures that IAM configurations are consistent, version-controlled, and replicable across different environments. In large-scale and multi-account settings, manual configurations can become challenging to manage and prone to errors. Tools such as AWS CloudFormation and Terraform allow for automated provisioning of AWS resources, including IAM configurations, ensuring a more secure and efficient setup.

Further reading

To learn more about the topics that were covered in this chapter, take a look at the following resources:

- *Best practice rules for AWS Identity and Access Management (IAM)*, by TrendMicro: `https://www.trendmicro.com/cloudoneconformity-staging/knowledge-base/aws/IAM/`

- *An introduction to AWS IAM best practices*, by Stephen J. Bigelow (2021): `https://www.techtarget.com/searchcloudcomputing/tip/An-introduction-to-AWS-IAM-best-practices`

- *12 AWS IAM Security Best Practices*, by Tobias Schmidt (2023): `https://spacelift.io/blog/aws-iam-best-practices`

- *AWS re:Post - How can I require MFA authentication for IAM users that use the AWS CLI*: `https://repost.aws/knowledge-center/mfa-iam-user-aws-cli`

4

Data Protection – Encryption, Key Management, and Data Storage Best Practices

Welcome to the fourth chapter of our in-depth exploration of AWS security. This chapter is dedicated to the critical subject of data protection within AWS, a topic that is indispensable for any organization aiming to secure its assets in the cloud. We will kick off this chapter by delving into AWS encryption mechanisms, focusing on how AWS approaches data-at-rest and data-in-transit encryption. This first part will pave the way for a comprehensive understanding of the types of encryption supported by AWS. We will discuss envelope encryption, symmetric versus asymmetric encryption, and the options of using bring-your-own or AWS-managed keys. As we move forward, the spotlight will turn to the management of cryptographic keys. We will explore AWS **Key Management Service** (**KMS**) in detail, covering the types of keys, their life cycles, and best practices for key policies and access management. We will also touch upon its seamless integration with AWS CloudHSM, ensuring you grasp the full spectrum of AWS cryptographic offerings. Finally, we will shift our focus to the data protection strategies that are employed across pivotal data storage and database AWS services. We will guide you through the best practices encompassing backup, encryption, and access control, ensuring your data remains safe at all times.

By the end of this chapter, you will have a holistic understanding of AWS data protection strategies. You will be equipped with the knowledge to implement robust encryption mechanisms, manage cryptographic keys efficiently, and ensure data protection across a myriad of AWS services.

In this chapter, we will cover the following key areas:

- Deciphering AWS encryption mechanisms and services
- Managing cryptographic keys using KMS and CloudHSM
- Implementing data protection best practices in key AWS services

AWS encryption mechanisms and services

In an era marked by escalating cyber threats, encryption emerges as a robust shield in the arsenal of cloud security. It is more than just the science of code-making; it is a critical layer in a multi-tiered defense strategy that includes other controls such as access control and network security. As data volumes swell in the cloud, the imperative for securing this data through encryption and other means has never been more significant. AWS offers a multitude of encryption mechanisms that not only secure your data but also help you meet compliance mandates. This section delves into the multifaceted encryption services provided by AWS, shedding light on their functionalities and best use cases.

AWS approach to encryption

The AWS approach to encryption is holistic, ensuring data protection both when it is at rest and in transit, thanks to a comprehensive suite of encryption tools and features. This approach allows organizations to enforce end-to-end encryption from the point of entry to the point of exit within their environment, further bolstering their security posture. Now, let's examine the key aspects of AWS encryption capabilities.

Data at rest

Data at rest refers to data that is not actively moving through networks. This could be data stored in databases, filesystems, or object storage such as Amazon S3. AWS ensures that this data remains confidential and tamper-proof by providing encryption solutions. When data is encrypted at rest, even if physical storage is compromised, the data remains unintelligible without the corresponding decryption keys.

AWS offers several services that support the encryption of data at rest. For instance, S3 provides server-side encryption, where data is automatically encrypted before it is stored. Similarly, Amazon RDS supports the encryption of databases using keys you manage through AWS KMS. AWS also provides options to use **hardware security modules** (**HSMs**) for encryption, ensuring that even the most sensitive data meets stringent compliance requirements.

Data in transit

Data in transit, or data in transport, refers to data actively moving between devices, be it between user locations and AWS or between AWS services. Given the potential vulnerabilities associated with data transmission, especially over the internet, AWS emphasizes the importance of using secure protocols to protect data as it travels.

AWS employs industry-standard **transport layer security** (**TLS**) to encrypt data in transit. AWS uses TLS to secure data when it is moving between AWS service endpoints both via the Internet and within VPCs when using VPC endpoints. Beyond just TLS, AWS also supports **virtual private networks** (**VPNs**) to provide an additional layer of security, especially for data traversing over public networks. VPNs create a secure, encrypted tunnel, ensuring data remains confidential and protected from potential eavesdroppers.

Integration

AWS encryption approach is not just about providing tools; it is about integrating these tools seamlessly into the AWS ecosystem. This ensures that as developers and architects build and deploy on AWS, they can do so with the confidence that their data – one of the most valuable assets – remains secure against both external threats and inadvertent internal mishaps.

However, it is crucial to note that while AWS provides the tools and mechanisms, users bear the responsibility of implementing encryption correctly. As mentioned earlier, AWS operates on a shared responsibility model, meaning that while AWS manages the security of the cloud, users are responsible for security *in* the cloud. This underscores the importance for AWS users to be vigilant, informed, and proactive in their encryption choices and implementations.

Types of encryption supported by AWS

AWS offers a range of encryption options, each tailored to address specific operational, security, and compliance requirements in various situations. This section delves into the various encryption methodologies supported by AWS, providing insights into their mechanics, advantages, and potential use cases.

Envelope encryption

Envelope encryption is a sophisticated encryption strategy that involves two layers of encryption keys. The primary data, or the **payload**, is encrypted using a unique data key. This data key, instead of being stored plainly, is then encrypted using another key, known as the master key. The encrypted data key is stored alongside the encrypted data. When decryption is required, the master key is used to decrypt the data key, which, in turn, decrypts the primary data. This dual-layered approach ensures that even if the encrypted data and its associated encrypted data key are accessed, the data remains secure without the master key. Another advantage of envelope encryption is the ease of key rotation. By rotating the master key, the security of data remains intact without the need to re-encrypt all the data. Instead, only the data key, which is considerably smaller and faster to process, needs to be re-encrypted.

AWS's implementation of envelope encryption is both robust and efficient. AWS services such as S3 use envelope encryption to provide an added layer of security. The advantage of this approach is that it allows for the secure distribution and storage of data keys, as the master key, which remains securely stored in services such as KMS, is never directly exposed.

Figure 4.1 represents the envelope encryption workflow that's used in AWS:

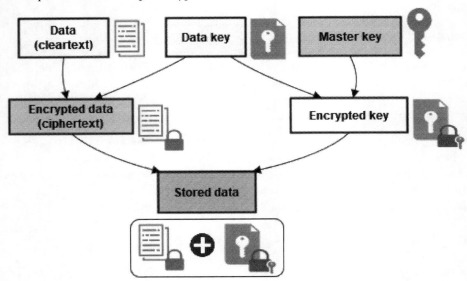

Figure 4.1 – Envelope encryption workflow

Symmetric versus asymmetric encryption

At its core, encryption relies on keys to encrypt and decrypt data. Encryption methods differ based on the keys they use, leading to two primary encryption mechanisms:

- **Symmetric encryption**: This type of encryption employs a single key for both encryption and decryption. This simplicity promotes efficiency, but it is crucial to ensure the key's security. Symmetric encryption is ideal for encrypting large volumes of data due to its speed and efficiency. It is particularly suited for services such as S3, where data is stored in bulk, or RDS, where databases need to be encrypted. AWS services such as KMS primarily use symmetric encryption with AES 256.

- **Asymmetric encryption**: This type of encryption employs a pair of mathematically related keys – a public key for encryption and a private key for decryption. Asymmetric encryption is best suited for securing sensitive operations in AWS, such as establishing secure TLS connections or generating digital signatures for code or documents. It is beneficial when setting up secure communication channels between components and applications, where the public key can be shared without compromising security. AWS supports asymmetric encryption in services such as KMS, allowing users to create RSA and **elliptic curve cryptography** (**ECC**) key pairs.

Bring-your-own versus AWS-managed keys

Key management is a critical aspect of encryption, and AWS offers flexibility in this domain:

- **Bring-your-own keys (BYOKs)**: This allows users to generate and use their own encryption keys. This is particularly useful for organizations that have specific regulatory or compliance requirements dictating key management practices or those that want to maintain a consistent key management strategy across both on-premises and cloud environments.

- **AWS-managed keys**: These are generated, managed, and stored by AWS. This option is suitable for users who prefer to offload the complexities of key management and leverage the benefits of seamless integration with AWS services. AWS ensures the security and availability of these keys, rotating them as necessary and providing robust logging and monitoring through services such as AWS CloudTrail.

For organizations using BYOK, it is essential to have a strategy in place for key rotation. While AWS-managed keys come with the convenience of automatic rotations, BYOKs might necessitate manual intervention or the development of a custom solution to ensure keys are rotated regularly, maintaining the security posture.

Server-side encryption (SSE) versus client-side encryption (CSE)

The location and control of the encryption process can significantly impact data security and operational efficiency. It can also play a key role in meeting specific regulatory standards and other compliance requirements:

- **SSE**: AWS manages the encryption process. When data is uploaded to a service, AWS encrypts it before storing it. During retrieval, AWS decrypts the data before transmitting it back to the user. This approach offloads the encryption overhead from the user, ensuring a seamless experience. AWS services such as S3 offer SSE, where users can choose between AWS-managed keys or customer-provided keys (BYOKs) for encryption.

- **CSE**: This involves encrypting data on the user's side before uploading it to the AWS cloud. This approach gives users more control over the encryption process and keys but comes at the cost of much more complexity, as well as additional latency due to the encryption process being executed on the client's side before the data is transferred. AWS SDKs provide libraries to facilitate CSE, allowing users to maintain complete control over their encryption keys and the encryption process.

SSE offers hassle-free encryption and seamless integration with AWS services, making it perfect for businesses wanting a straightforward security solution. CSE, on the other hand, is ideal for organizations with stringent data security requirements, where they prefer to have complete control over the encryption keys and process.

For instance, when considering the choice between SSE and CSE, a financial institution might prioritize CSE for sensitive transactions to ensure maximum control. However, a media company streaming large video files might prioritize SSE to minimize latency and ensure smooth playback for end-users.

Comparison

To provide a clearer perspective on the choices available, the following table (*Table 4.1*) compares SSE and CSE side-by-side with BYOK and AWS-managed keys options, highlighting the benefits and limitations of each possibility:

	BYOKs	**AWS-Managed Keys**
SSE	Users provide their encryption keys. AWS handles the encryption process. Benefits: Full control over encryption keys and flexibility to manage. Limitations: Increased responsibility for key management.	AWS manages both the keys and the encryption process. Benefits: Simplified key management. Limitations: Less control over the key life cycle.
CSE	Users manage both the encryption keys and the encryption process. Benefits: Data is encrypted before it reaches AWS, ensuring end-to-end security. Limitations: Complexity in managing the encryption process.	AWS provides the keys, but users handle the encryption on their premises. This choice is less common due to the complexities of CSE while having reduced control over the key life cycle.

Table 4.1 – Comparison of the different encryption processes and keys

Choosing the right encryption method is key for robust cloud data security. AWS offers flexible options such as envelope encryption's added protection, symmetric encryption's speed, or CSE's granular control. Organizations should evaluate their specific needs, compliance requirements, and operational factors to select the best fit, ensuring their data remains secure and protected.

The AWS Encryption SDK

In the vast ecosystem of AWS encryption services, the AWS Encryption SDK stands out as a powerful tool that simplifies CSE implementation for developers. This client-side library offers streamlined encryption for data at rest and in transit, working seamlessly across AWS services and even outside the AWS environment. With language-specific versions (Java, Python, C, and JavaScript), the SDK empowers developers to integrate robust encryption directly into their applications.

Key features

Here are some of the most relevant features of the AWS Encryption SDK:

- **Data key caching**: One of the standout features of the SDK is its ability to cache data keys. This means that once a data key is used, it can be reused for subsequent encryption tasks without the need to make repeated calls to the KMS service. This not only improves performance but also reduces the cost associated with frequent KMS requests.

- **Algorithm suite**: The SDK offers a suite of robust encryption algorithms and options, including AES-GCM with a 256-bit key, ensuring that developers have the flexibility to choose an encryption method that aligns with their security and performance requirements.

- **Message protection**: The SDK ensures that encrypted messages are protected against tampering, providing an added layer of security.

Advantages

The AWS Encryption SDK offers several benefits that make it a relevant option to consider for developers and organizations. They are as follows:

- **Flexibility**: One of the primary advantages of the AWS Encryption SDK is its flexibility. It is not tied to any specific AWS service, meaning developers can use it for a wide range of applications, both within and outside the AWS ecosystem.

- **Performance**: With features such as data key caching, the SDK is optimized for high-performance scenarios. By reducing the need for frequent KMS calls, applications can encrypt data faster, leading to improved application responsiveness.

- **Enhanced security**: The SDK provides a holistic approach to security. Beyond just encryption, it ensures that encrypted data is also protected against tampering. This multi-faceted approach ensures that data remains confidential and maintains its integrity.

- **Developer-centric**: The AWS Encryption SDK is designed with developers in mind. Its language-specific versions, comprehensive documentation, and integration with popular development tools make it a developer-friendly tool.

- **Cost-efficiency**: By reducing the number of calls to KMS through features such as data key caching, the SDK can lead to cost savings. Fewer KMS requests translate to reduced costs, especially in applications that require frequent encryption.

- **Integration with AWS services**: While the SDK is versatile enough to be used outside AWS, it is deeply integrated with AWS services. This means developers can leverage the full power of AWS, from monitoring with AWS CloudTrail to management via the AWS Management Console.

Example

Imagine a healthcare application that stores patient records. Given the sensitive nature of health data, it is imperative to ensure that this data is encrypted both when stored and when transmitted between the application and other systems.

Using the AWS Encryption SDK, developers can seamlessly integrate encryption into the application. When a new patient record is added, the data can be encrypted on the client side before being sent to the server for storage. This ensures that even if there is a breach and the data is intercepted during transmission, it remains unreadable without the decryption key. Here is a simplified Python code snippet example to encrypt data using a KMS key specified as a key provider:

```python
from aws_encryption_sdk import KMSMasterKeyProvider, encrypt
key_provider = KMSMasterKeyProvider(key_ids=[
    'arn:aws:kms:us-east-1:012345678912:key/abcd1234-a123-456a-a12b-a123b4cd56ef'
])
plaintext = 'This is a plaintext message.'
ciphertext, encryptor_header = encrypt(
    source=plaintext,
    key_provider=key_provider
)
print(f'Ciphertext: {ciphertext}')
```

When the application retrieves a patient record, it decrypts the data on the client side, ensuring that the server never sees the unencrypted data. This adds an additional layer of security, which is especially important given the stringent regulations around health data. You can use the following code snippet to decrypt data using the same KMS key specified:

```python
from aws_encryption_sdk import KMSMasterKeyProvider, decrypt
key_provider = KMSMasterKeyProvider(key_ids=[
    'arn:aws:kms:us-east-1:012345678912:key/abcd1234-a123-456a-a12b-a123b4cd56ef'
])
decrypted, decryptor_header = decrypt(
    source=ciphertext,
    key_provider=key_provider
)
print(f'Decrypted: {decrypted.decode("utf-8")}')
```

This practical example underscores the importance and utility of the AWS Encryption SDK in real-world scenarios, especially when dealing with sensitive information.

Use cases

Given its features and advantages, the AWS Encryption SDK can be employed in a variety of scenarios:

- **Large-scale data processing**: For applications that process large volumes of data, such as big data analytics platforms, the SDK's performance optimizations can be invaluable.

- **Sensitive data storage**: For applications that store sensitive data, such as personal information or financial data, the SDK's robust encryption and tampering protection ensure that this data remains secure.

- **Multi-platform development**: Organizations that develop applications across multiple languages can leverage the SDK's language-specific versions to maintain a consistent encryption strategy across all their platforms.

- **Hybrid cloud environments**: Businesses operating with a mix of on-premises, AWS, and other cloud infrastructures can use the AWS Encryption SDK to ensure consistent encryption practices across their overall landscape. This uniformity is crucial for maintaining data security standards, irrespective of where the data resides or is processed.

- **Regulatory compliance**: For businesses that operate in highly regulated industries, the SDK can help meet compliance requirements related to data encryption and protection.

The AWS Encryption SDK simplifies data security with its combination of powerful encryption and developer-friendly design. This makes it easier for organizations to protect sensitive data without sacrificing efficiency. With the ever-growing focus on data security, tools like this are essential. Now that we have explored encryption strategies, let's turn our attention to AWS tools and best practices for securing and managing cryptographic keys.

Managing cryptographic keys

While encryption is the process of converting data into a code to prevent unauthorized access, the keys used in this process are the linchpin. Without secure and efficient key management, even the most robust encryption can be rendered ineffective, giving a false sense of security.

Key management services in AWS

AWS offers a robust set of services and features for key management that go beyond mere storage and retrieval. These services are designed to integrate seamlessly with AWS encryption offerings, providing a holistic security solution that aligns with the most stringent compliance requirements. AWS global infrastructure and data centers across multiple regions allow organizations to easily address data residency requirements when selecting AWS for key management.

AWS KMS is often the first stop for organizations looking to manage cryptographic keys. However, AWS also offers AWS CloudHSM for those who require a dedicated HSM. Additionally, **AWS Certificate Manager** (**ACM**) is available for TLS certificate management, which is crucial for secure web communications.

AWS also supports a hybrid approach, allowing you to integrate your on-premises key management solutions with AWS services. This is particularly useful for organizations transitioning to the cloud or operating in a multi-cloud environment. AWS key management services are designed to work in tandem with its encryption services, providing not just a secure place to store keys but also a set of controls for key usage, rotation, and auditing.

The real value comes from the deep integration of these key management services with other AWS offerings. For example, you can use KMS keys to encrypt data in S3 buckets, RDS databases, and even within custom applications developed using AWS SDKs. This level of integration simplifies the key management process, allowing you to focus on application development rather than security plumbing.

KMS in-depth overview

KMS is a fully managed service that makes it easy to create and control cryptographic keys within AWS, which can then be used to encrypt and decrypt data and sign and verify messages.

Types of keys

KMS offers different types of keys to cater to various security needs:

- **Customer master keys** (**CMKs**): These are the primary types of keys you interact with in KMS. CMKs can be either symmetric or asymmetric and are used to encrypt/decrypt up to 4 KB of data directly or to encrypt generated data keys. They are often used in scenarios requiring direct control over the key material, such as regulatory compliance.

- **Data keys**: These are symmetric keys that you can use to encrypt and decrypt data outside of KMS in your applications. They are generated by a CMK and can be either plain (unencrypted) or encrypted. Data keys are best suited for encrypting large volumes of data at the application layer.

- **AWS managed keys**: These are keys that are automatically created by AWS services on your behalf. They are designed to simplify the encryption process for AWS-managed services such as S3 and RDS. You can see AWS-managed keys in KMS, but you cannot manage them. They are often used in situations where the focus is more on ease of use rather than granular control.

- **Custom key stores**: For those who require more control over their cryptographic keys, KMS allows you to create CMKs using custom key stores backed by CloudHSM clusters or third-party key managers outside AWS.

Key life cycle

Understanding the life cycle of a KMS key is crucial for effective key management:

- **Creation**: When creating a CMK, you can choose to either generate a new key or import your key material (BYOK). You can also tailor your key configuration by selecting its type (symmetric or asymmetric) and encryption algorithm. Alongside these options, it is crucial to define the key's administrative and usage permissions by defining a key policy. This involves specifying who can administer the key and what cryptographic operations can be performed with it.

- **Rotation**: Key rotation is not just a best practice; it is a must for robust cryptography. Failing to regularly rotate keys can expose your organization to various security risks, including the increased likelihood of successful brute-force attacks. KMS supports automatic key rotation for CMKs, where a new key material is generated every year. However, you also have the option to manually rotate keys. When a key is rotated, the key material changes, but the key ID remains the same. Previous versions of the key are retained to ensure that data encrypted with an older version can still be decrypted. This dual approach to key rotation – automatic and manual – provides organizations with the flexibility to align their key management practices with their specific security policies.

- **Deletion**: Deleting a key is a process that demands careful consideration. Before a CMK can be deleted, it must be scheduled for deletion, which initiates a waiting period, defaulting to 30 days. This waiting period serves as a safety net, preventing accidental deletion of crucial keys. Once the waiting period is over and the key is deleted, any data that's encrypted becomes irretrievable, emphasizing the need for a well-thought-out key archival and deletion strategy.

Key policies and access management

Key policies in KMS are JSON documents that define who has what kind of access to a specific key. Let's explore some advanced access management techniques.

Cross-account access

KMS allows for cross-account access to CMKs, enabling scenarios where resources in one AWS account might need to decrypt data that's been encrypted by another account. This is often used in multi-account AWS architectures, facilitating secure data sharing across different parts of an organization.

Here is a key policy example that restricts access to an encryption key in a local AWS account, 11111111111, to a specific user in another AWS account, 22222222222:

```
{
  "Version": "2012-10-17",
  "Statement": [
    {
      "Sid": "AllowEncryptDecryptCrossAccount",
      "Effect": "Allow",
```

```
      "Principal": {"AWS": "arn:aws:iam::222222222222:user/user1"},
      "Action": [
        "kms:Encrypt",
        "kms:Decrypt"
      ],
      "Resource": "arn:aws:kms:us-east-1:111111111111:key/MyKey"
    }
  ]
}
```

While cross-account access is beneficial for resource sharing, it comes with its own set of risks. For instance, if the external account is compromised, it could lead to unauthorized access to your resources. Therefore, it is crucial to implement additional security measures, such as requiring MFA, for cross-account access.

ABAC policies

As discussed in *Chapter 3*, **attribute-based access control** (**ABAC**) is an access control model that allows you to grant permissions based on both identities and resource attributes. This strategy can also be implemented in KMS to control access to encryption keys. This allows for more granular control by enabling permissions based on attributes. For example, you can set up a key policy that only allows users or roles with a specific tag value to decrypt data using the key with the same tag value:

```
{
  "Version": "2012-10-17",
  "Statement": [
    {
      "Sid": "AllowEncryptDecryptWithTagMatch",
      "Effect": "Allow",
      "Principal": "*",
      "Action": [
        "kms:Encrypt",
        "kms:Decrypt"
      ],
      "Resource": "*",
      "Condition": {
        "StringEqualsIfExists": {
          "aws:RequestTag/Department": "${aws:PrincipalTag/
Department}"
        }
      }
    }
  ]
}
```

Best practices for KMS

Here are some guidelines to maximize the security and efficiency of using KMS:

- **Access control**: Adhere to the principle of least privilege. Limit access to keys to only those who need it, and use policies to enforce these restrictions.

- **Audit logging**: Enable CloudTrail to log all API requests made on your KMS keys. This is crucial for compliance and for investigating any security incidents.

- **Key rotation**: KMS supports automatic key rotation for CMKs, but it is also advisable to periodically review and manually rotate keys when necessary. This ensures that your encryption remains robust against potential vulnerabilities.

- **Multi-region replication**: For applications that are globally distributed, consider replicating your keys in multiple regions to reduce latency and improve availability.

- **Use aliases and tagging**: Rather than directly referencing keys by their key ID, employ aliases and tags for easier key management. Aliases simplify the process of switching between keys without altering your application code, while tags facilitate better organization and tracking of your keys and allow for ABAC.

- **Encryption context**: Use the encryption context for additional authenticated data to ensure that the ciphertext and the encryption context are not changed.

With these practices in place, organizations can ensure efficient and secure key management using KMS. Now, let's focus our attention on the more advanced AWS alternative that organizations can utilize to manage their keys: AWS CloudHSM.

CloudHSM integration and use cases

CloudHSM is an HSM that's designed for generating and using your cryptographic keys within AWS. While KMS offers a multi-tenant, managed service for cryptographic operations, CloudHSM provides a dedicated physical device in a single-tenant environment. This ensures a higher level of isolation for your most sensitive cryptographic operations and compliance with stringent regulatory requirements as it is FIPS 140-2 Level 3 validated. CloudHSM is particularly valuable in scenarios where specific use cases necessitate this level of isolation and control beyond the capabilities of the standard KMS environment.

Integration with KMS

One of the most compelling features of CloudHSM is its seamless integration with KMS, which allows you to create a custom key store backed by your CloudHSM cluster. This integration enables you to use KMS APIs for cryptographic operations while ensuring that the actual cryptographic material is generated and stored in CloudHSM. This is a powerful combination that brings together the ease of use of KMS with the robust security features of CloudHSM.

To integrate CloudHSM with KMS, you will need to create a CloudHSM cluster and then initialize at least one HSM instance within that cluster. Once the cluster is active, you can create a custom key store in KMS and associate it with your CloudHSM cluster. This process involves specifying the cluster ID and providing credentials for an HSM user that has sufficient permissions to manage keys.

Use cases

Understanding when to leverage CloudHSM over KMS is crucial. Some primary use cases are as follows:

- **Regulatory compliance**: For organizations that are subject to rigorous compliance requirements, CloudHSM provides a level of security that is often mandated by regulatory bodies. For example, financial institutions dealing with the **Payment Card Industry Data Security Standard** (**PCI DSS**) or healthcare organizations subject to the **Health Insurance Portability and Accountability Act** (**HIPAA**) can benefit from the dedicated and tamper-evident hardware provided by CloudHSM.

- **High-value transactions**: In scenarios where extremely sensitive data is being transmitted, such as high-value financial transactions or confidential government communications, the additional security layer provided by CloudHSM can be invaluable. The dedicated, single-tenant environment ensures that cryptographic operations are isolated, reducing the risk of unauthorized access or data leakage.

- **Root of trust**: Organizations that require a root of trust that is entirely under their control can use CloudHSM to generate and store root keys. These keys can then be used to derive other keys for various purposes, ensuring a secure key hierarchy that is isolated from multi-tenant environments.

- **Secure key export and import**: CloudHSM allows for secure key export and import using mechanisms such as PKCS#11, **Java Cryptography Extensions** (**JCE**), and Microsoft's **Cryptographic API Next Generation** (**CNG**). This is particularly useful for organizations that have hybrid cloud or multi-cloud architectures and need to move keys securely between different environments.

Best practices for CloudHSM

Here are some guidelines to ensure the security and efficiency of CloudHSM:

- **Access control**: Just as with KMS, implement the principle of least privilege. Ensure that only authorized personnel can perform cryptographic operations in CloudHSM.

- **Audit logging**: Enable audit logging both in CloudHSM and KMS to keep a record of all cryptographic operations.

- **High availability**: Always configure your CloudHSM clusters across multiple **availability zones** (**AZs**) to ensure high availability. KMS, by default, is designed to be highly available, but when integrating with CloudHSM, the onus is on you to ensure that the HSMs are also fault-tolerant.

- **Key rotation**: While KMS supports automatic key rotation, CloudHSM does not. You will need to implement your own key rotation logic when using CloudHSM, either manually or by using custom automation scripts.

- **Disaster recovery**: Given the critical nature of cryptographic keys, it is essential to have a backup strategy in place. While AWS provides high availability, having a disaster recovery plan specifically for your cryptographic keys is crucial.

Compliance in AWS key management

KMS and CloudHSM allow organizations to align with a range of industry standards and certifications, which are particularly crucial for organizations operating in regulated sectors. Here are some key standards:

- **FIPS 140-2**: Both KMS and CloudHSM are FIPS 140-2 validated, ensuring that they meet US federal standards for secure cryptographic modules. However, KMS is validated at Level 2, while CloudHSM offers Level 3 validation. This higher level provides tamper-evident hardware and stricter security requirements, which might be mandated by specific compliance regulations.

- **PCI DSS**: While KMS and CloudHSM can aid in PCI DSS compliance, AWS Payment Cryptography has been more recently added to AWS's service offering to provide focused features tailored to organizations handling cardholder data.

- **HIPAA**: Healthcare organizations can leverage AWS key management services to meet HIPAA requirements for protecting sensitive patient data.

- **General Data Protection Regulation (GDPR)**: Both services are designed to help you meet the GDPR requirements, particularly concerning data encryption and pseudonymization.

While AWS provides the tools and services to facilitate compliance, organizations must adopt best practices to ensure they fully meet regulatory requirements:

- **Regular audits**: Periodically review your key policies, access controls, and usage logs in CloudTrail to ensure ongoing compliance with evolving regulations.

- **Data classification**: Not all data is created equal. Classify your data based on sensitivity and apply encryption and key management practices accordingly. For instance, **personally identifiable information (PII)** might require more stringent controls than other types of data.

- **Key rotation**: Regularly rotating cryptographic keys is a staple of many compliance standards. Ensure that you have processes in place, whether manual or automated, to rotate keys in both KMS and CloudHSM.

- **Access control**: Restrict access to cryptographic keys based on the principle of least privilege. Regularly review policies to ensure that only authorized entities can access and manage keys.

- **Documentation**: Maintain comprehensive documentation of all cryptographic operations, policies, and procedures, including key creation, rotation, and deletion procedures. This not only aids in audits but also ensures that key management practices are transparent and reproducible.

AWS key management services are not just about providing robust security; they are about building a framework that enables organizations to meet compliance requirements. Transitioning from the realm of key management, let's explore the critical aspect of data protection in essential AWS services.

Data protection in key AWS services

In this section, we will delve into the various mechanisms and strategies for data protection across key AWS services, showing how encryption and key management are just pieces of a larger puzzle that also includes backups and access control.

S3 buckets

While S3's ease of use and scalability make it popular, securing data stored in buckets is essential. Let's dive into data protection features in S3, focusing on versioning, encryption, and access control.

Versioning and MFA Delete

Versioning is an often-underestimated feature that can serve as a first line of defense against both accidental deletions and malicious activities. When versioning is enabled on an S3 bucket, any overwrite or delete operation on an object doesn't remove the previous versions. This allows for easy recovery and provides an additional layer of security.

For those who are already quite familiar with S3 versioning, you might be aware that once enabled, it cannot be disabled – only suspended. This is a crucial consideration for compliance and data retention policies. The cost implications are also non-trivial, as each version of an object is billed separately.

To manage costs and compliance, you can combine versioning with life cycle policies. For instance, you can configure a policy to transition previous versions to cheaper storage classes such as Glacier or even delete them after a certain period. This is particularly useful in regulated industries where data retention policies are stringent.

For added security, enabling MFA Delete on S3 buckets can provide an extra layer of protection against accidental or malicious deletions by requiring MFA credentials for any object deletion activity.

Encryption

S3 offers two primary types of encryption: SSE and CSE. They can both support BYOKs and AWS-managed keys.

SSE

SSE is the most straightforward of the two, where data is encrypted at rest within the S3 bucket. S3 offers different SSE options:

- **SSE-S3**: This uses the default AWS managed key for S3 (`aws/s3`) to encrypt objects stored in S3. While it is the simplest to set up, it does not offer any level of control over the encryption key.

- **SSE-KMS**: This uses your KMS CMK for more granular control over the keys used to encrypt objects stored in S3.

- **DSSE-KMS**: This applies two layers of encryption to encrypt objects stored in S3. It is particularly useful for compliance standards that require multilayer encryption.

- **SSE-C**: This is where you provide the encryption key as part of your API request to S3. While AWS handles the encryption and decryption process, the key management resides with you.

SSE-KMS and DSSE-MKS are often the go-to choices for SSE when compliance requirements dictate a need for key management features like audit trails. They also allow for easy integration with other AWS services that are KMS-aware.

CSE

CSE is when data is encrypted on the client side before being uploaded to S3. This method provides the highest level of control over encryption keys but also places the most responsibility on you to perform encryption and manage those keys securely. AWS provides an S3 Encryption Client, which is a dedicated library that handles encryption on the client side. The AWS S3 Encryption Client is different from the AWS Encryption SDK as it is more integrated with S3. The S3 Encryption Client offers two CSE options:

- **CSE-KMS**: Similar to SSE-KMS but the encryption happens client-side using your KMS CMK

- **CSE-C**: Here, you manage the entire encryption process on the client side, including key management, which provides the highest level of control

CSE is often used in scenarios where there are stringent regulatory requirements around data encryption, or when there is a need for custom encryption algorithms not supported by SSE.

Comparison

The following table (*Table 4.2*) summarizes the different encryption options available in S3:

Option	Type	Key Management	Control Level	Use Case
SSE-S3	Server-side	AWS-managed (aws/s3)	Low	Simplest setup; no key management control
SSE-KMS	Server-side	KMS CMK	Medium	Granular control, audit trails, and integration with KMS-aware services
DSSE-KMS	Server-side	KMS CMK	Medium	Compliance with multi-layer encryption requirements
SSE-C	Server-side	Customer-provided key	High	The customer manages keys, while AWS handles encryption/decryption
CSE-KMS	Client-side	KMS CMK	High	Similar to SSE-KMS but with client-side encryption
CSE-C	Client-side	Customer-managed key	Very High	Full control over encryption and key management; suitable for stringent regulatory requirements

Table 4.2 – S3 encryption options compared

Bucket policy

Bucket policies are resource-based IAM policies that define explicit rules for access to S3 resources. These are essential for implementing fine-grained access control to your S3 buckets and objects. While identity-based IAM policies are attached to principals such as users and roles, bucket policies are attached directly to the bucket, providing a centralized way to manage permissions.

For advanced scenarios, bucket policies can be used in conjunction with other AWS services, such as AWS Organizations and SCPs, for even more granular control. For example, you can restrict S3 bucket access to certain VPCs or even specific IP ranges. This is particularly useful in hybrid cloud scenarios or when you need to enforce strict network segmentation for compliance reasons.

Bucket policies also allow for advanced features such as VPC endpoint policies, which can restrict access to a bucket to requests that come from a specific VPC endpoint. This is a powerful feature for limiting data exfiltration risks.

EBS volumes

While Amazon EBS serves as the go-to block storage service for EC2 instances, offering high performance and durability, this alone doesn't constitute a comprehensive data protection strategy. Let's dive into advanced techniques for securing data stored on EBS volumes.

Snapshots

EBS snapshots provide point-in-time backups of your volumes and are stored in S3, inheriting its durability features. They play a crucial role in data recovery, allowing you to restore your volume to a previous state. Snapshots are incremental, meaning only the blocks that have changed since the last snapshot are stored. This makes it a cost-effective and efficient backup solution.

Snapshots can be triggered manually on-demand from the EC2 console. It is also highly advisable to automate them using Amazon Data Lifecycle Manager. This service automates the creation, retention, and deletion of snapshots, making it easier to adhere to data retention policies and minimizing the risk of human error.

Snapshots can be shared across accounts or even made public. This feature can be both an advantage and a risk. On the one hand, it facilitates data sharing and migration; on the other, it can lead to data exposure if not managed correctly. Therefore, it is crucial to implement proper access controls on your snapshots, similar to how you would manage AMIs.

Encryption

EBS provides robust encryption solutions for both volumes and snapshots to ensure data at rest is secure.

Volumes encryption

EBS offers seamless encryption for volumes that rely on KMS keys for centralized management. Once a volume is encrypted, the data stored on it, the I/O operations, and all snapshots created from it are encrypted.

The process of encrypting an EBS volume is straightforward. When creating a new volume, simply enable encryption. If you don't specify a KMS key, the default AWS-managed key for EBS (`aws/ebs`) is used. However, for more control, you can specify a KMS CMK.

For existing unencrypted volumes, while you can't directly encrypt them, a common workaround is to create a snapshot of the volume, and then create an encrypted copy of that snapshot. From this encrypted snapshot, a new encrypted volume can be created.

It is important to note that incorrect KMS permissions can lead to unexpected issues. For example, a stopped instance with a KMS-protected root volume will fail to start if the entity attempting to start it lacks the necessary permissions to use the KMS key.

Snapshots encryption

When you create a snapshot of an encrypted volume, the snapshot is also encrypted. Moreover, when you copy a snapshot, you have the option to re-encrypt it with a different key. This flexibility is crucial for various scenarios, such as sharing snapshots across accounts where each account has its own set of KMS keys.

EFS filesystems

Amazon EFS is a scalable file storage solution for use with both AWS services and on-premises resources. Given its shared nature and the potential for multiple resources to access it simultaneously, ensuring data protection and security for EFS is essential. Let's explore advanced strategies for safeguarding data stored in EFS filesystems, focusing on backup mechanisms and encryption.

Backup

EFS backups are essential for data durability and recovery. AWS offers native backup solutions for EFS through AWS Backup. AWS Backup integrates seamlessly with EFS, allowing you to centrally manage and automate backups across various AWS services.

Encryption

Data security is critical, and EFS offers robust encryption options to secure data at rest and in transit:

- **Encryption at rest**: EFS features automatic encryption at rest, which can be enabled during filesystem creation or on existing filesystems. This transparently encrypts data before it is written to the storage layer, and decrypts it upon reading. By default, EFS uses the AWS KMS key for EFS (`aws/efs`), but you can use a custom KMS CMK for greater control.

- **Encryption in transit**: EFS supports TLS encryption for data in transit. Ensure encryption by using the TLS mount option when mounting EFS filesystems. It is recommended to enforce this with IAM policies for added security. For a practical demonstration, see the *Filesystem policy* subsection.

- **CSE**: For additional security, especially for highly sensitive data, consider implementing CSE using the AWS Encryption SDK to encrypt data before it reaches EFS and decrypt it client-side after reading. While this offers enhanced security, be mindful of potential latency and management overhead.

Filesystem policy

Filesystem policies are resource-based IAM policies that are directly attached to EFS filesystems. They work the same way as bucket policies work in S3 and can be used for implementing fine-grained access control over the actions users can perform within the mounted filesystem. This is particularly useful for enforcing organization-wide security policies, such as read-only access for certain groups or denying access to specific IP ranges.

Another use case is to restrict mounting actions to only allow encrypted connections. In the following filesystem policy example, the `elasticfilesystem:ClientMount` action is denied if secure transport (TLS) is not used, effectively enforcing encrypted mounts:

```
{
  "Id": "efs-mount-encryption-policy",
  "Statement": [
    {
      "Sid": "DenyUnencryptedMount",
      "Effect": "Deny",
      "Principal": "*",
      "Action": "elasticfilesystem:ClientMount",
      "Resource": "arn:aws:elasticfilesystem:us-east-
1:111111111111:file-system/file-system-id",
      "Condition": {
        "Bool": {
          "aws:SecureTransport": "false"
        }
      }
    }
  ]
}
```

RDS databases

RDS provides robust tools for safeguarding your database, including comprehensive backup options and powerful encryption mechanisms. Let's explore these features to ensure the security and resilience of your data.

Backup

Backups are crucial for data durability and recovery in the event of disruptions. RDS provides two types of backup methods:

- **Automated backups**: These allow you to recover the database instance to any point in time within a retention period of up to 35 days. These backups are triggered during the daily backup window and capture a full daily snapshot of data, as well as transaction logs. This is particularly useful for recovering from accidental user actions, such as deletions or updates.

- **Database snapshots**: These are user-initiated captures of the entire database instance. Unlike automated backups with a set retention period, snapshots are retained indefinitely until manually deleted. This makes them ideal for long-term backup needs or testing migrations before significant application changes.

Encryption

RDS offers extensive encryption capabilities to protect your data at rest:

- **Volume encryption**: RDS supports encryption at rest for all database engines with KMS-managed keys. Enabling this feature upon launching a new database encrypts the underlying storage, automated backups, snapshots, and read replicas. For existing unencrypted RDS instances, it involves creating a snapshot of the unencrypted database, making a copy of that snapshot with encryption enabled, and then restoring an encrypted RDS instance from the encrypted snapshot.

- **Field-level encryption**: This option provides granular protection by encrypting specific data fields within the database. This can be achieved through application-specific logic or database-level features such as Oracle and SQL Server's **transparent data encryption** (**TDE**). TDE automates encryption and key management within the database itself. Notably, while KMS is incompatible with TDE, CloudHSM offers seamless integration with Oracle databases, handling encryption and decryption processes within the HSM.

Volume encryption serves as a robust foundation for RDS security. It protects the entire database if the underlying storage is compromised, which makes it ideal for situations where you need broad protection and compliance.

Field-level encryption adds a powerful, focused layer of security for your most sensitive assets. Consider this option in scenarios with strict compliance requirements or if you have specific concerns about unauthorized access within the database itself (beyond storage-level permissions.) However, keep in mind that field-level encryption may introduce performance impact, additional costs, and management complexity.

DynamoDB tables

Amazon DynamoDB provides a robust foundation, yet data resiliency and security are your responsibility. Let's delve into the backup and encryption features that are essential for safeguarding your valuable DynamoDB assets.

Backup

Data backup in DynamoDB is an essential practice for safeguarding critical data and ensuring business continuity. DynamoDB offers two types of backup options:

- **On-demand backups**: This is a user-initiated action that allows for full backups of tables for long-term retention. On-demand backups do not impact table performance and can be useful for scenarios that require immediate backups, such as before making a significant application change. On-demand backups can be retained indefinitely and are ideal for long-term archival to meet compliance requirements.

- **Continuous backups**: This feature automatically captures changes to data and maintains these backups for 35 days. It allows for point-in-time recovery, making it possible to restore data from any second in the past 35 days. This is particularly useful for safeguarding against accidental writes or deletes.

Encryption

Data security is a non-negotiable aspect of modern databases, and DynamoDB offers robust and straightforward mechanisms to ensure data is encrypted within the table using KMS. When a table is created, the option to enable encryption is available. If this option is selected, all data written on the table, as well as all backups, are encrypted. If a KMS CMK is not specified, DynamoDB will use the default AWS-managed key (`aws/dynamodb`).

Data protection in other AWS services

Data protection is a multi-faceted endeavor that encompasses a range of strategies and techniques, including access control, backups, and encryption mechanisms, to ensure the confidentiality, integrity, and availability of data. In this context, many other AWS services also offer robust data protection features that align well with the strategies discussed for S3, EBS, EFS, RDS, and DynamoDB.

Backup

AWS Backup serves as a centralized backup solution that integrates with various AWS services, allowing for automated and scheduled backups. This is particularly useful for services such as RDS, DynamoDB, and EFS, where data backup is crucial for business continuity and compliance. AWS Backup offers features such as backup vaults, backup plans, and backup selection, which can be configured according to the specific backup requirements of each service. It also supports cross-region and cross-account backup, which is essential for comprehensive disaster recovery planning.

It is crucial to not just implement backup solutions but also to regularly test data recovery processes. This ensures that in the event of data loss or corruption, the recovery mechanisms are effective and meet the organization's **recovery time objective (RTO)** and **recovery point objective (RPO)**.

Encryption

KMS is central in managing encryption across multiple AWS services. For services that support encryption, such as AWS Lambda, Amazon Redshift, Amazon Athena, AWS Glue, and Amazon EMR, KMS can be used to manage the cryptographic keys. Centralized key management simplifies the process of encrypting data at rest and in transit, and also provides additional features such as key rotation, audit trails, and permissions management.

AWS services that support encryption regularly offer both SSE and CSE options. SSE is generally easier to implement and is managed by AWS, while CSE gives you more control but requires you to manage the encryption process using tools such as the AWS Encryption SDK.

Data pipelines introduce complex security considerations as data moves through multiple AWS services, such as S3 for storage, Lambda for processing, and Amazon Kinesis for streaming. For sensitive data, the choice between KMS (for encryption at rest within each service) and CSE is crucial. CSE, applied before data enters the pipeline, adds a persistent encryption layer, ensuring greater control and protection, even if a single component were compromised. However, it can also hinder certain data transformations within the pipeline. Therefore, it is essential to carefully evaluate potential trade-offs before implementing CSE in complex data pipelines.

Access control

For services that support it, resource-based policies can be employed to define who can or cannot perform actions on the respective AWS resources. Similar to S3 bucket policies and EFS filesystem policies, they provide centralized permissions management at the resource level. Resource-based policies can be used in conjunction with identity-based policies for a layered security approach. They are especially valuable for cross-account access, allowing you to grant permissions to principals from other AWS accounts.

Unified data protection strategy

The key takeaway is that AWS offers a unified approach to data protection, making it easier to implement a comprehensive strategy. Whether it is employing resource-based policies for fine-grained access control, using AWS Backup for centralized backup solutions, or leveraging KMS encryption, AWS provides a cohesive and integrated set of tools and services to safeguard your data effectively. By understanding the capabilities and limitations of each service, you can tailor your data protection strategy to meet specific organizational needs and compliance requirements. This holistic approach ensures that data is not only encrypted and backed up but is also accessible only by authorized entities, thereby providing a robust data protection framework across your AWS environment.

Summary

In this chapter, we embarked on a comprehensive journey into the realm of data protection within AWS. This chapter commenced with an exploration of AWS encryption mechanisms, shedding light on the platform's approach to safeguarding data both at rest and in transit. The narrative then transitioned to the pivotal topic of managing cryptographic keys. Here, we gained insights into AWS KMS, with a deep dive into KMS, including the types of keys it manages, their life cycles, policies, and integration with CloudHSM. As we ventured further, the focus shifted to data protection across key AWS services. From S3 buckets to EBS volumes, EFS filesystems, RDS databases, and DynamoDB tables, we learned about the best practices for backup, encryption, access control, and more.

As we transition to the next chapter, we will expand our focus to the vast array of AWS security services, providing an overview of the tools and technologies available to build a robust, enterprise-grade security posture in AWS.

Questions

Answer the following questions to test your knowledge of this chapter:

1. What is the primary purpose of the AWS Encryption SDK, and how does it benefit developers?
2. What is the significance of key rotation in KMS, and how does it work?
3. How does RDS ensure data encryption?
4. Differentiate between SSE and CSE in S3. What are the primary types of each?

Answers

Here are the answers to this chapter's questions:

1. The AWS Encryption SDK is a client-side library that's designed to make encryption more accessible and manageable for developers. It enhances data protection, both at rest and in transit, and can be used across various AWS services and even outside the AWS environment. It offers features such as data key caching, a suite of robust encryption algorithms, and message protection, making it developer-friendly and cost-efficient.
2. Key rotation is crucial for maintaining robust cryptography. KMS supports automatic key rotation for CMKs, where new key material is generated every year. You also have the option to manually rotate keys. When a key is rotated, the key material changes, but the key ID remains the same.
3. RDS supports volume encryption using keys managed through KMS. It also allows for field-level encryption either through application-level logic or native TDE features provided by certain database engines.
4. SSE encrypts data at rest within the S3 bucket, with types including SSE-S3, SSE-KMS, DSSE-KMS, and SSE-C. CSE encrypts data on the client side before uploading to S3, with types being CSE-KMS and CSE-C.

Further reading

To learn more about the topics that were covered in this chapter, take a look at the following resources:

- *Demystifying KMS keys operations, bring your own key (BYOK), custom key store, and ciphertext portability*, by Arthur Mnev (2021): `https://aws.amazon.com/blogs/security/demystifying-kms-keys-operations-bring-your-own-key-byok-custom-key-store-and-ciphertext-portability/`

- *Top 10 security best practices for securing backups in AWS*, by Ibukun Oyewumi (2022): `https://aws.amazon.com/blogs/security/top-10-security-best-practices-for-securing-backups-in-aws/`

- *AWS KMS Encryption: Server-Side Encryption for Data in AWS*, by NetApp (2022): `https://bluexp.netapp.com/blog/aws-cvo-blg-aws-kms-encryption-server-side-encryption-for-data-in-aws`

- *Encryption fundamentals with AWS KMS and CloudHSM*, by Graham Thompson (2021): `https://intrinsecsecurity.com/blog/cloud-security/encryption-fundamentals-with-aws-kms-and-cloudhsm/`

- *NIST FIPS 140-2 Non-Proprietary Security Policy: AWS Key Management Service* (2020): `https://csrc.nist.gov/CSRC/media/projects/cryptographic-module-validation-program/documents/security-policies/140sp3617.pdf`

5

Introduction to AWS Security Services

Welcome to the fifth chapter of our comprehensive guide to AWS security. This chapter serves as a comprehensive guide on using and orchestrating various AWS security services to build a cohesive and strong security posture. We will kick off the chapter by diving into the realm of threat and vulnerability detection, examining the capabilities and real-world applications of AWS services such as Amazon GuardDuty, Amazon Detective, and Amazon Inspector. From there, we will transition into the domain of security governance and compliance, where we will explore the functionalities and best practices associated with AWS Security Hub, AWS Config, AWS Organizations, and AWS Control Tower. As we move forward, we will delve into the crucial aspects of securing secrets and identifying sensitive data, focusing on the roles and capabilities of AWS **Systems Manager** (**SSM**) Parameter Store, AWS Secrets Manager, and Amazon Macie. The chapter will then guide you through the intricacies of orchestrating these services into an integrated security architecture. We will also touch upon important considerations such as cost efficiency, compliance alignment, and incident response, providing you with a holistic view of AWS security orchestration.

By the end of this chapter, you'll have a comprehensive understanding of how to orchestrate AWS security services effectively, align them with governance and compliance requirements, and implement best practices for threat detection, secrets management, and sensitive data protection.

In this chapter, we will cover the following key topics:

- Understanding threat and vulnerability detection
- Managing security governance and compliance
- Handling secrets securely
- Identifying and protecting sensitive data
- Orchestrating AWS security services

Unpacking threat and vulnerability detection

The cybersecurity landscape is an ever-evolving battlefield, rife with emerging threats that surpass traditional attack vectors. This section explores a range of AWS services that are meticulously designed for adaptability and extensive security coverage, tailored to meet these evolving challenges. These services are universally applicable, catering to a wide spectrum of security needs and compliance demands. Their adaptability and scalability make them ideal for various organizations, from agile startups to expansive enterprises and sectors under stringent regulatory compliance.

Collectively, these services constitute a robust, multi-layered ecosystem. They provide a sophisticated approach to threat detection by harnessing the power of **machine learning** (**ML**), integrated threat intelligence, and advanced analytics. This collaborative functionality is key to strengthening your AWS environment against a multitude of security threats.

GuardDuty—your AWS security sentinel

Amazon GuardDuty is more than just a threat detection service; it is an intelligent, fully managed ecosystem designed to safeguard AWS accounts and workloads. It employs a combination of ML, anomaly detection, and integrated threat intelligence to sift through and analyze a vast array of events across your AWS environment.

Key features

GuardDuty has the following key features:

- **Multi-faceted monitoring**: GuardDuty offers an all-encompassing monitoring solution that covers AWS accounts, Amazon S3 buckets, EC2 instances, and even containerized workloads. It analyzes various sources, including VPC flow logs, DNS resolution activities, and other AWS service logs. This provides a comprehensive view of your AWS environment, making it easier to identify and mitigate potential threats.

- **ML-driven analysis**: At its core, GuardDuty leverages ML algorithms to identify suspicious activities based on patterns and trends. This enables the service to detect a wide range of threats, from well-known attack vectors to emerging risks.

- **Enhanced malware detection**: GuardDuty can be used to run on-demand or regular malware scans on EBS volumes. This feature does not require any agent, nor does it need to interact with live volumes since it runs the scan from a snapshot of the target volume.

- **Credentials exfiltration detection**: GuardDuty can identify when EC2 instance credentials are being used from a different AWS account. This feature is crucial for preventing unauthorized access and potential data breaches.

- **Actionable security findings**: When a potential threat is detected, GuardDuty generates detailed and actionable security findings. These can be seamlessly integrated with other AWS services such as Security Hub, Amazon EventBridge, and Detective, facilitating a streamlined investigation and remediation process.

- **Automated remediation**: GuardDuty can be configured to trigger Lambda functions for automated remediation actions, such as isolating compromised instances or revoking IAM credentials.

GuardDuty in the real world

A real-world application of GuardDuty can be exemplified in the following scenario.

Scenario

A financial services company with a complex AWS environment, running workloads on both EC2 instances and Lambda functions, noticed an unusual surge in resource utilization. Traditional security measures were insufficient in identifying the root cause, leading the company to use GuardDuty for a more comprehensive analysis.

Solution

GuardDuty immediately began its investigation by analyzing VPC flow logs and scanning Amazon EBS volumes. The service quickly flagged unauthorized crypto mining activities affecting both EC2 instances and Lambda functions from the following observations:

- **EC2 instances**: GuardDuty's malware scanning feature for EBS volumes detected malware on an EBS volume attached to a compromised EC2 instance

- **Lambda functions**: The analysis of VPC flow logs by GuardDuty revealed unusual network patterns related to the Lambda functions, suggesting they were being manipulated for crypto mining

Outcome

Upon further investigation, it was discovered that the compromised EC2 instance was exfiltrating credentials that were then used from an external AWS account to manipulate the code of a Lambda function for crypto-mining purposes. GuardDuty's EC2 instance credentials exfiltration detection feature played a crucial role in identifying this sophisticated attack vector.

The company took the following immediate action:

- Isolated the compromised EBS volume and initiated a malware removal process

- Terminated the affected Lambda functions and EC2 instances to stop the crypto-mining activities

- Conducted a forensic analysis using VPC flow logs to trace the source and nature of the Lambda function manipulation

It was also found that the IAM role assigned to the EC2 instance was overly permissive, allowing it to modify Lambda functions, which was not a required permission for its operational needs. This led to the following:

- A review and tightening of IAM policies to ensure that EC2 instances had only the permissions they needed, reducing the risk of future incidents

- Implementation of stricter network access controls and monitoring to safeguard against similar threats

This incident underscored the importance of GuardDuty's multi-layered detection capabilities, including its malware scanning for EBS volumes, VPC flow logs analysis, and credentials exfiltration detection, in identifying and mitigating complex threats such as malware involving crypto mining.

Who should use GuardDuty?

GuardDuty is a versatile service that caters to a broad spectrum of organizations, irrespective of their size or industry. Its scalable pricing model makes it accessible and relevant for any business, from startups to large enterprises. Here is a breakdown of who can benefit the most from this service:

- **Highly regulated businesses**: Organizations in sectors such as finance and healthcare can leverage GuardDuty's advanced threat detection capabilities to maintain compliance.

- **Large enterprises**: For organizations with complex and expansive AWS environments, GuardDuty's real-time monitoring of multiple accounts and resources is invaluable.

- **Startups and SMBs**: The service's scalable pricing model is particularly beneficial for smaller organizations with limited security resources. They can take advantage of GuardDuty's automated threat detection and remediation features, which require minimal setup and maintenance.

- **Managed service providers**: Those who manage security services across multiple AWS accounts will find GuardDuty's centralized monitoring and automated remediation capabilities to be a significant asset.

- **Security professionals**: Individuals responsible for maintaining an organization's security posture can use GuardDuty as a proactive tool to identify and mitigate threats before they escalate into serious incidents.

Detective—your AWS security analyst

Amazon Detective serves as a robust analytical engine designed to assist security professionals in dissecting, understanding, and responding to security issues and anomalies. It acts as an extension to other AWS security services such as GuardDuty, offering advanced correlation techniques that go beyond basic alerting. By ingesting and correlating data from a multitude of AWS services, Detective provides a more nuanced and comprehensive view of your security landscape. This is particularly beneficial for complex environments where multiple AWS services are in use and the security signals are often too noisy or too subtle to catch.

Key features

Detective has the following key features:

- **Data aggregation and correlation**: Detective is adept at pulling in data from various AWS services, including GuardDuty, AWS CloudTrail, and VPC flow logs. It then employs advanced algorithms to correlate this data, offering a unified view of security events across your AWS environment.

- **ML algorithms**: The service uses ML to analyze data and identify patterns that could indicate a security incident. This is particularly useful for detecting sophisticated threats that might not trigger traditional security mechanisms.

- **Graphical visualization**: One of the standout features is its ability to provide graphical representations of correlated data. This helps in understanding the relationships between different AWS resources and activities, which is crucial for incident investigation.

- **Grouping of related findings**: A recent addition to Detective is its capability to automatically group related GuardDuty findings that may appear unrelated but can indicate a multi-stage attack when analyzed together.

- **MITRE ATT&CK framework integration**: Detective also maps its findings to the **tactics, techniques, and procedures** (**TTPs**) outlined in the MITRE ATT&CK framework, providing a structured approach to threat detection and response.

Detective in the real world

To understand the practical application of Detective, let's consider its use in the following scenario.

Scenario

Imagine a global media company that streams content to millions of users worldwide using AWS for its content delivery network, user authentication, and analytics. Suddenly, they started noticing an abnormal spike in failed login attempts and a simultaneous increase in data transfer costs. Concerned about a potential security breach, they turn to Detective for deeper insights.

Solution

Upon activation, Detective started its data correlation process, pulling in information from GuardDuty, CloudTrail, and VPC flow logs. The service's ML algorithms quickly identified that the failed login attempts were part of a coordinated effort originating from multiple geographic locations. It also detected the abnormal data transfer to the suspicious S3 bucket. Detective grouped these findings and mapped them to the MITRE ATT&CK framework, providing the security team with a comprehensive view of the threat landscape.

Outcome

Armed with this information, the security team took several immediate actions:

- Multi-factor authentication was enforced for all high-profile content creators
- The suspicious S3 bucket was isolated, and its access permissions were revoked
- Network access controls were tightened to block the IP ranges from which the failed login attempts originated

Detective's advanced correlation techniques were instrumental in identifying the complex attack pattern, enabling the media company to thwart a potentially damaging content leak and unauthorized access to creator accounts.

Who should use Detective?

Detective is particularly beneficial for:

- **Large enterprises**: Given its advanced correlation techniques and the depth of analysis it offers, Detective is well-suited for large enterprises with complex AWS environments.

- **E-commerce platforms**: These businesses often have to deal with a high volume of transactions and customer data, making them prime targets for various types of cyberattacks. Detective can help in quickly identifying and mitigating these threats.

- **Managed service providers**: For those who manage multiple AWS accounts, Detective provides a unified view of all security events, making it easier to monitor and respond to incidents.

Inspector—your AWS security auditor

Amazon Inspector is a cloud security service that automates the assessment of applications and servers running on AWS. It is designed to help organizations identify vulnerabilities and deviations from best practices, thereby enhancing their security posture. This robust platform integrates seamlessly with other AWS services, offering a multi-layered approach to securing cloud resources.

Key features

Inspector has the following key features:

- **Automated scans**: Inspector provides continual, automated assessments, eliminating the need for manual, periodic scans.

- **Resource discovery**: Inspector automatically identifies all running EC2 instances, Lambda functions, and Amazon ECR repositories, among other compatible resources, making it ideal for dynamic cloud environments.

- **Container support**: Inspector extends its capabilities to container-based workloads, offering a comprehensive security assessment.

- **Improved risk scoring**: Inspector offers contextualized risk scores for each finding, aiding in vulnerability prioritization.

- **Recommendations**: Inspector also provides actionable recommendations to improve your security posture and ensure compliance with various regulations.

- **Automated remediation**: You can integrate Inspector findings into automated patch management systems. For instance, when Inspector identifies a vulnerability, it can trigger a Lambda function that automatically applies the necessary patches or updates the security group rules to mitigate the risk.

Inspector in the real world

The following example showcases Inspector in action within a global organization.

Scenario

A global e-commerce platform is obligated to adhere to various international data protection regulations. They have a complex architecture that includes EC2 instances for web servers and containerized microservices for payment processing. During peak sales events such as Black Friday, their resources dynamically scale, making manual security assessments impractical.

Solution

The company deployed Inspector to automate their security assessment process. The service continually scanned their dynamically scaling resources, identifying vulnerabilities in real time. Inspector's integration with organizations allowed the security team to manage assessments across multiple accounts, providing a unified view of their security posture.

Outcome

This proactive approach enabled the company to address vulnerabilities before they could be exploited, ensuring a secure and compliant environment during critical business periods. The automated assessments freed up the security team to focus on other strategic tasks, while the contextualized risk scores helped them prioritize remediation efforts effectively.

Who should use Inspector?

Inspector is particularly useful for:

- **Highly regulated businesses**: Organizations in sectors such as finance, healthcare, and government can benefit from Inspector's automated assessments to demonstrate compliance

- **Large enterprises**: Those with complex and dynamic cloud environments can leverage Inspector for automated resource discovery and continual assessments

- **Startups and SMBs**: Smaller teams with limited security expertise can use Inspector as an easy-to-implement, cost-effective security solution

- **Managed service providers**: Firms offering security as a service can integrate Inspector into their portfolio, adding value to their client offerings

CloudTrail Lake and Security Lake—your AWS analytics powerhouses

Before the more recent introduction of AWS CloudTrail Lake and Amazon Security Lake, organizations mostly relied on Amazon Athena for security using AWS native services. While Athena is powerful, it required a more complex setup and longer operational times, making it less efficient for real-time security analytics. In this context, CloudTrail Lake and Security Lake are game-changers. These services are designed to provide a comprehensive solution for managing, storing, and analyzing your AWS activity logs, filling a crucial gap in the AWS security analytics landscape. Whether you are looking to audit your environment for compliance, investigate security incidents, or gain operational insights, these services offer a unified ecosystem to meet your analytics needs.

Key features, differences, and similarities

Let's compare CloudTrail Lake and Security Lake's key features to see how they differ and where they overlap:

- **Unified ecosystem**: Both CloudTrail Lake and Security Lake offer a unified platform for log management and analytics. However, CloudTrail Lake focuses on AWS-specific logs, integrating aggregation, storage, and querying into a single platform.

- **Integrated querying versus custom data pipelines**: CloudTrail Lake provides an in-built SQL experience within the CloudTrail console, while Security Lake allows you to create custom data pipelines using AWS Glue, Athena, and Amazon QuickSight.

- **Real-time alerts**: Both services can be configured to send real-time alerts based on custom queries, enhancing your ability to respond to incidents swiftly.

- **Multi-source data collection**: Security Lake stands out by allowing data collection from a broader range of sources, including third-party applications and on-premises systems.

- **Data enrichment**: Security Lake allows for the enrichment of data with additional metadata, providing more context for analytics.

- **Scalability**: Both services are designed to scale with your needs, but Security Lake offers more flexibility in handling data from multiple sources.

- **User experience**: CloudTrail Lake offers a more streamlined user experience for those who are focused solely on AWS services, while Security Lake provides a more versatile interface for handling diverse data sources.

- **Integration**: Both CloudTrail Lake and Security Lake integrate with Security Hub to provide a comprehensive viewreal-world application of your security posture. Additionally, CloudTrail Lake integrates with QuickSight to enable interactive dashboards and visualizations, while Security Lake integrates with Amazon Elasticsearch Service to enable advanced queries and analysis.

CloudTrail Lake in the real world

Let's explore a scenario where CloudTrail Lake plays a crucial role in monitoring and ensuring compliance in a large AWS setup.

Scenario

A multinational corporation with a complex AWS architecture spanning multiple accounts and regions faces a challenge. They need to ensure compliance with the **General Data Protection Regulation (GDPR)** and other internal security policies. They also suspect that unauthorized changes are being made to their IAM roles and EC2 instances, which could potentially lead to data breaches.

Solution

The corporation employs CloudTrail Lake's advanced features to set up a comprehensive auditing and monitoring system. They use the integrated SQL querying capabilities to create complex queries that track not just user activities but also system-level changes. These queries are designed to flag any unauthorized or suspicious activities, such as IAM role escalations, EC2 instance modifications, and unauthorized S3 bucket access. They also set up real-time alerts that are triggered by these queries, which are subsequently sent to their **security operations center** (**SOC**).

Outcome

By leveraging CloudTrail Lake's features, the corporation successfully automates its compliance auditing process. They generate real-time reports that are used both for internal reviews and for compliance with GDPR and other regulations. The real-time alerts allow them to quickly identify and respond to any unauthorized activities, thereby significantly reducing the risk of a data breach.

Security Lake in the real world

The practical application of Security Lake can be exemplified in the following scenario.

Scenario

A large healthcare organization is required to comply with stringent regulations such as HIPAA in the U.S. and GDPR in Europe. They have a complex architecture that includes AWS services, third-party applications for patient records, and on-premises systems for clinical data. The organization needs a unified security analytics solution that can monitor and analyze this diverse range of data sources.

Solution

The healthcare organization turns to Security Lake to build a comprehensive, centralized security data lake. They use Glue to create custom **extract, transform, and load** (ETL) jobs that pull data from various sources, including AWS services, third-party applications, and their on-premises systems. This data is then enriched with additional metadata for context, making it easier to analyze. They also employ QuickSight to create custom dashboards that visualize key security metrics, and they set up anomaly detection algorithms to flag unusual activities.

Outcome

With Security Lake, the healthcare organization gains a powerful, scalable, and compliant security analytics platform. It can now monitor and analyze security data in real time, enabling it to detect and respond to threats more effectively. The custom dashboards provide it with actionable insights, allowing it to proactively address vulnerabilities and improve its overall security posture. The anomaly detection algorithms further enhance its threat detection capabilities, enabling it to identify and investigate unusual activities that could indicate a security incident.

Who should use CloudTrail Lake or Security Lake?

CloudTrail Lake is interesting for organizations that require a unified platform for log aggregation, auditing, and real-time analytics of AWS activity logs. It is particularly beneficial for:

- **Large enterprises**: Organizations with complex, multi-account AWS architectures will benefit from the centralized logging and querying features

- **Managed service providers**: Those offering centralized auditing and compliance services can leverage CloudTrail Lake's robust features to add value to their offerings

On the other hand, Security Lake is a versatile solution designed for organizations that need to collect and analyze data from a broader range of sources, including third-party applications and on-premises systems. It is particularly beneficial for:

- **Highly regulated industries**: Businesses in sectors such as healthcare and finance can use Security Lake to meet stringent compliance requirements for data collection and analysis

- **Security operation centers** (SOCs): The multi-source data collection capabilities make it ideal for SOCs needing a unified view of security data

- **DevOps teams**: The ability to create custom data pipelines makes it a strong fit for DevOps environments

Both CloudTrail Lake and Security Lake offer unique advantages tailored to specific organizational needs. Whether it is centralized auditing and real-time analytics with CloudTrail Lake or multi-source data collection and advanced analytics with Security Lake, these services collectively serve as a comprehensive solution for organizations aiming to elevate their AWS security analytics and compliance capabilities.

Best practices for threat and vulnerability detection

In an environment where security risks are continually evolving, it is essential to adopt a proactive approach to safeguard your AWS assets. Here are some best practices to consider to enhance your threat and vulnerability detection capabilities:

- **Utilize multi-layered security measures**: Don't rely solely on a single AWS service for your security needs. Employ a combination of GuardDuty, Inspector, and Detective to create a solid defense strategy that covers various aspects of security, from threat detection to vulnerability assessment.

- **Leverage ML**: AWS services such as GuardDuty and Detective employ ML algorithms to analyze extensive data sets generated by other AWS services. Make the most of these capabilities to stay ahead of emerging threats.

- **Implement real-time alerts**: Configure AWS services to send real-time alerts based on custom queries or predefined conditions. Immediate notification allows for swift incident response, minimizing potential damage.

- **Implement automated responses**: Use Lambda functions to automate responses to common threats. For example, if GuardDuty detects unauthorized access, a Lambda function can automatically revoke the permissions or isolate the compromised instance.

- **Monitor user activities**: Keep an eye on user activities within your AWS environment. Unusual behavior, such as multiple failed login attempts or unexpected resource provisioning, can be early indicators of a security issue.

- **Conduct periodic assessments**: Regularly run automated assessments using Inspector to identify vulnerabilities and deviations from best practices. This helps in maintaining a solid security posture over time.

- **Centralize log management**: Use CloudTrail Lake or Security Lake for centralized log management and analytics. This enables you to have a unified view of security events, making it easier to spot anomalies.

- **Third-party integration**: Consider integrating a third-party **security information and event management** (**SIEM**) solution to correlate data from multiple sources and provide a more comprehensive view of your security landscape.

- **Utilize the MITRE ATT&CK framework**: Use this framework to gain insights into the TTPs that an attacker is likely using, enabling you to take proactive measures.

By adhering to these best practices, you can significantly enhance your ability to detect and mitigate threats and vulnerabilities, thereby fortifying your AWS environment against a wide array of security risks. Shifting our lens from threat detection, let's now explore the array of AWS services aimed at enhancing governance and compliance.

Managing security governance and compliance

The dynamic nature of modern cybersecurity challenges calls for a governance model that is equally adaptable. This section focuses on AWS services that offer a holistic approach to security governance, combining automation, compliance monitoring, and best practices to fortify the cloud environment of various organizations, from different industries and sizes.

Security Hub—your AWS security dashboard

AWS Security Hub serves as a unified security and compliance center that simplifies the way you manage security alerts and automate compliance checks within your AWS environment. It aggregates and prioritizes findings from various AWS services and third-party tools, providing a centralized dashboard for a comprehensive view of your security posture.

Key features

Security Hub has the following key features:

- **Aggregated security findings**: Security Hub collects data from a wide array of AWS services such as GuardDuty, Inspector, CloudTrail Lake, and Security Lake, as well as from third-party solutions. This provides a unified view of your security alerts and compliance status.

- **Automated compliance checks**: The service continuously monitors your environment against industry standards and best practices, such as the CIS AWS Foundations Benchmark and PCI DSS.

- **Custom insights**: This feature allows you to create your own customized findings and insights using the Security Hub's powerful query language, enabling tailored security monitoring. You can use custom insights to track specific types of threats or compliance metrics, offering a more focused view of your security landscape.

- **Multi-region analytic pipeline**: For organizations operating globally, Security Hub offers the ability to aggregate findings from multiple AWS regions into a single dashboard.

- **Consolidated controls and findings**: The controls view consolidates various security standards, making it easier to manage and act upon security findings. Controls and findings have specific severity ratings to help prioritize remediation efforts.

- **Automation capabilities**: Security Hub can automate routine tasks such as sending notifications, updating the security configuration of resources, and initiating predefined remediation actions such as isolating compromised instances, allowing security teams to focus on more complex issues.

- **Enhanced visualizations**: Integration with Detective enriches the investigation process by grouping related findings and offering advanced visualizations. You can also use QuickSight or other visualization tools to create customized interactive dashboards and reports.

Security Hub in the real world

The following example illustrates Security Hub's effectiveness in a practical context.

Scenario

A global e-commerce platform experienced a sudden spike in failed login attempts and unauthorized access to customer data. Traditional security measures failed to identify the root cause, leading the company to seek a more comprehensive solution.

Solution

The company activated Security Hub, which immediately began aggregating data from GuardDuty for container monitoring and AWS WAF. Automated compliance checks were initiated to ensure adherence to PCI DSS standards. Real-time alerts were set up to notify the security team of any unauthorized access or suspicious activities.

Outcome

Within hours, Security Hub identified a coordinated brute-force attack targeting customer accounts. The real-time alerts enabled the security team to take immediate action, blocking the malicious IP addresses involved in the attack and enhancing WAF rules to enforce captcha checks. This swift action successfully prevented a potential data breach, thereby protecting the company's reputation and customer trust.

Who should use Security Hub?

Security Hub is particularly useful for:

- **Highly regulated industries**: Organizations in sectors such as finance and government can use Security Hub to maintain compliance with industry-specific regulations.

- **Large enterprises**: For businesses with complex AWS architectures spanning multiple accounts and regions, Security Hub's centralized monitoring and multi-region analytics are invaluable.

- **Startups and SMBs**: With its automated compliance checks and alerting mechanisms, Security Hub provides smaller businesses with robust security monitoring capabilities without requiring a large security team.

- **Managed service providers**: Those offering security services across multiple AWS accounts can leverage Security Hub's centralized monitoring and automated remediation features to add value to their client offerings.

- **SOCs**: Security Hub offers advanced features such as custom insights and enhanced visualizations, making it a powerful tool for SOC teams involved in incident response and investigations.

Config—your AWS compliance watchdog

AWS Config is not merely a configuration management service; it is a sophisticated, fully integrated platform engineered to streamline compliance and enhance security across your AWS ecosystem. Config continuously monitors and records the configuration of your supported AWS resources, but its power truly shines in combination with other services. For example, CloudTrail provides detailed logs of API activity, and when used alongside Config, you gain deep insights for investigations, allowing you to pinpoint not just a resource's current state but how and when it changed. This creates a cohesive framework for managing configurations, ensuring compliance, and strengthening your overall security posture. This is particularly advantageous in complex cloud architectures where the need for real-time compliance monitoring and automated remediation is paramount.

Key features

Config has the following key features:

- **Configuration snapshots and history**: Config continuously records and stores configuration snapshots for your resources. This enables you to audit changes, investigate incidents, and ensure compliance over time.

- **Proactive compliance checks**: Going beyond mere monitoring, Config allows you to define custom rules that automatically evaluate your resources for compliance with specific policies or best practices. This proactive approach helps you maintain a compliant and secure environment.

- **Resource relationships**: Config provides a visual representation of the relationships between resources in your AWS environment. This is invaluable for understanding dependencies and the potential impact of changes or incidents.

- **Config Aggregator**: For organizations operating in multiple AWS accounts and regions, Config Aggregator consolidates all configuration and compliance data into a single view. This centralized approach simplifies governance and compliance management.

- **Automated remediation**: Config can be used to automatically correct non-compliant resources. This feature significantly reduces the manual effort required to maintain compliance.

- **Customizable rules**: With Config, you are not limited to predefined rules. You can create custom rules using Lambda, allowing for tailored compliance checks that suit your specific requirements.

Config in the real world

To illustrate Config's real-world utility, consider the following scenario involving a large organization.

Scenario

A multinational retail corporation with a substantial online presence notices inconsistencies in its AWS resource configurations across multiple accounts and regions. These inconsistencies are causing compliance issues and increasing the risk of security vulnerabilities. Traditional methods of tracking and auditing configurations are proving to be inefficient and error-prone.

Solution

The corporation turns to Config to address these challenges. It sets up Config Aggregator to consolidate configuration and compliance data from multiple accounts and regions into a single view. Custom rules are created using Lambda functions to enforce the corporation's specific compliance requirements. Automated remediation actions are configured to correct non-compliant resources, and real-time alerts are set up to notify the security and governance teams of any configuration changes that violate compliance policies.

Outcome

Within a short period, Config identifies several misconfigured resources and automatically corrects them, bringing them into compliance. The real-time alerts enable the governance team to act swiftly on non-compliant changes, thereby reducing the window of vulnerability. The centralized view offered by Config Aggregator allows for more efficient auditing and reporting, saving the corporation both time and resources. This proactive approach significantly improves the corporation's security posture and compliance status while also aiding in cost optimization by identifying unused or underutilized resources.

Who should use Config?

Config is particularly useful for:

- **Highly regulated industries**: Organizations operating in sectors such as finance, healthcare, and government often have stringent compliance requirements. Config's robust compliance checks and reporting capabilities make it an ideal choice for such industries.

- **Large enterprises**: For businesses with complex AWS architectures that span multiple accounts and regions, the centralized monitoring and multi-region analytics capabilities of Config are particularly valuable.

- **Startups and SMBs**: Even if you don't have a large security team, Config's automated compliance checks and alerting mechanisms provide robust security monitoring capabilities.

- **Managed service providers**: If you are offering security services across multiple AWS accounts, Config's centralized monitoring and automated remediation features can add significant value to your client offerings.

Organizations—your AWS multi-account manager

Managing multiple AWS accounts can quickly become a complex endeavor, especially as your organization grows and diversifies its cloud resources. AWS Organizations emerges as a centralized governance and management service designed to simplify this complexity. It allows you to consolidate multiple AWS accounts into an organizational structure managed through a master account. With Organizations, you can enforce consistent policy implementation, streamline billing, and architect your environment in a way that meets the unique needs of your business units or workloads.

Key features

Organizations has the following key features:

- **Centralized management**: You can manage all AWS accounts from a single master account for simplified policy application, activity monitoring, and billing.

- **Hierarchical structure**: Create **organizational units** (**OUs**) to group AWS accounts, mimicking the functional or business units within your organization for better resource organization and policy application. This hierarchical structure also allows for easier delegation of administrative responsibilities, enabling more efficient management.

- **Service control policies** (**SCPs**): Utilize JSON-based policies to specify allowed or denied services and actions at various organizational levels, offering granular control over AWS resources.

- **Consolidated billing**: Aggregate billing information of all member accounts into one master account, simplifying expense tracking and enabling volume discounts.

- **Tagging policies**: Categorize AWS resources across accounts and OUs using standardized tags, aiding in cost allocation and compliance tracking.

- **Automated account creation**: Use APIs for programmatic account creation, saving time, especially for large enterprises setting up new accounts.

- **Support for Resource Access Manager** (**RAM**): Integration with AWS RAM allows for easy sharing of resources such as subnets or license configurations across accounts.

Organization units structure

OUs in Organizations are like folders that help you categorize and manage your AWS accounts. For instance, you could have an OU for your development environment and another for production. Policies set at an OU level cascade down, meaning if you restrict an S3 bucket policy in a parent OU, all accounts in child OUs inherit that policy. This is a time-saver and ensures uniformity in policy enforcement.

Let's say your organization has different departments, such as finance, HR, and engineering. You could create an OU for each department. If the finance department is only allowed to access billing information but not compute resources, you can set that policy at the finance OU level. This way, any new or existing AWS accounts linked to the finance OU would automatically inherit these restrictions.

The flexibility of OUs also comes in handy during organizational changes. If a project initially in the development OU moves to production, you can easily shift the corresponding AWS account from one OU to another, and it will inherit the new set of policies automatically.

In a nutshell, OUs offer a streamlined way to manage multiple AWS accounts, making it easier to enforce policies, improve security, and simplify auditing.

Service control policies (SCPs) in depth

SCPs are a powerful feature within Organizations that allow you to define permission guardrails. These guardrails can either be permissive, allowing certain actions across all accounts, or restrictive, explicitly denying certain actions. SCPs are applied at the root, OU, or individual account level, providing granular control over your AWS environment.

The beauty of SCPs is that they operate as a boundary, meaning they don't grant permissions but rather set the maximum permissions a user or role can have. For example, you can create an SCP that prevents any AWS account in a specific OU from terminating EC2 instances. Even if an IAM policy grants a user permission to terminate instances, the SCP would override it, ensuring that the instances remain running.

SCPs are particularly useful for enforcing compliance and security best practices. For instance, you could create an SCP that denies any changes to logging configurations, ensuring that all accounts maintain a consistent and auditable history of actions.

As an example, imagine you have an OU for your development teams and another for your production environment. You could apply an SCP to the development OU that allows broad permissions, enabling developers to experiment and innovate. On the other hand, you could apply a restrictive SCP to the production OU that only allows essential services to be modified, thereby safeguarding your live applications from unintended changes.

SCPs also support condition keys, allowing you to create even more nuanced policies. For example, you could set up an SCP that only allows EC2 instances to be launched if they are tagged with a specific cost center code, helping you manage budgets more effectively.

Here is the JSON example of an SCP that denies the launching of EC2 instances without a specific cost center tag while still preventing the termination of any EC2 instances:

```
{
    "Version": "2012-10-17",
    "Statement": [
        {
```

```
      "Sid": "DenyTerminateEC2Instances",
      "Effect": "Deny",
      "Action": "ec2:TerminateInstances",
      "Resource": "*"
    },
    {
      "Sid": "AllowLaunchEC2InstancesWithCostCenterTag",
      "Effect": "Allow",
      "Action": "ec2:RunInstances",
      "Resource": "*",
      "Condition": {
        "StringEquals": {
          "aws:RequestTag/costCenter": "1234"
        }
      }
    },
    {
      "Sid": "DenyAnyOtherLaunchEC2Instances",
      "Effect": "Deny",
      "Action": "ec2:RunInstances",
      "Resource": "*"


    }
  ]
}
```

In essence, SCPs provide a robust mechanism for centralized governance, enabling you to manage permissions efficiently across multiple AWS accounts.

Organizations in the real world

Let's examine a scenario where Organizations plays a pivotal role in a corporation with varied departmental access requirements.

Scenario

Imagine a multinational corporation with various departments, such as HR, finance, and development, each requiring different levels of access to AWS resources. The development team needs to frequently spin up new EC2 instances for testing, while the finance team mostly needs read-only access to billing information. The HR team, on the other hand, should not have access to any AWS resources but needs to manage IAM roles for employee onboarding and offboarding.

Solution

The corporation uses Organizations to create a multi-account structure with separate accounts for HR, finance, and development. They also create OUs to group these accounts based on departmental needs. SCPs are then applied to these OUs to enforce the required permissions.

For example, an SCP is applied to the development OU that allows the launching of EC2 instances only if they are tagged with a specific project code. Another SCP is applied to the finance OU that restricts permissions to read-only access for billing. The HR OU has an SCP that only allows IAM user and group management.

Outcome

By leveraging Organizations and SCPs, the corporation successfully isolates departmental resources and applies granular permissions. This not only enhances security but also aids in cost management, as the development team is now accountable for the resources they spin up, tagged by project codes.

Who should use Organizations?

Organizations is particularly beneficial for:

- **Large enterprises**: With complex structures and multiple departments, large enterprises can benefit from the granular control and isolation that Organizations offers.

- **Startups and SMBs**: Even smaller businesses can take advantage of Organizations to implement best practices from the start, making it easier to scale securely in the future.

- **Managed service providers**: Those who manage multiple AWS accounts for different clients can centralize their management efforts, making operations more efficient.

Control Tower—your AWS governance blueprint

AWS Control Tower serves as a streamlined governance solution that automates the setup and ongoing management and operations of your AWS accounts centralized under the same organization umbrella. Designed to enforce compliance and operational best practices, Control Tower provides a unified console for easier oversight. With its ever-evolving features, such as support for nested OUs and custom guardrails, Control Tower adapts to the unique governance needs of organizations of all sizes and complexities.

Key features

Control Tower has the following key features:

- **Automated landing zone setup**: It quickly sets up a well-architected multi-account environment based on AWS best practices, saving time and reducing the chance of errors.

- **Blueprints**: It provides a set of blueprints for setting up baseline AWS environments. These are essentially design patterns that help in configuring AWS services securely, ensuring best practices are followed from the get-go.

- **Audit account and log archive accounts**: Control Tower sets up these two isolated accounts for security governance when creating a new landing zone. This allows for logs protection and makes it easier to keep track of actions across your environment, aiding in both monitoring and forensic investigations.

- **Guardrails**: There are pre-configured rules for security, operations, and compliance that work in conjunction with Organizations and Config to provide a holistic governance approach across your AWS environment. Guardrails enforce your policies by monitoring for non-compliance and automatically triggering remediation actions. They can be either preventive or detective, and you can customize them to suit your organization's specific needs.

- **Account factory**: It streamlines the process of creating and provisioning new AWS accounts, making it easier to manage multiple accounts under one organization. It uses blueprints to create accounts that are automatically compliant with your organization's guardrails, making it easier to manage multiple accounts securely.

- **Lifecycle events**: Allows for automation and customization during account provisioning and other significant events. For instance, you can set up lifecycle events to automatically apply specific IAM roles and policies when a new account is created, making your governance more dynamic.

Shared accounts for security

Control Tower's shared accounts feature offers a structured approach to security governance by centralizing key functions into specific accounts. These accounts, including the log archive and audit accounts, are housed within the security OU. They are typically accessed by a selected group of security and compliance professionals within the organization, ensuring a controlled environment for sensitive tasks.

Log archive account

The Log Archive account serves as a centralized repository for all logs generated by CloudTrail and Config. While its primary function is to store these specific types of logs, it can also be configured to store additional logs from other AWS services, such as S3 access logs or VPC flow logs, depending on your organization's requirements.

The immutability of logs in the Log Archive account is a critical feature for ensuring data integrity and compliance. AWS employs multiple layers of security, including encryption and access controls, to ensure that once logs are written, they cannot be altered or deleted. This is crucial for compliance with various regulations such as GDPR, HIPAA, and others that require secure, tamper-proof storage of logs.

To ensure that all accounts are sending their logs to the Log Archive account, Control Tower can be configured to trigger alerts or notifications if an account fails to send logs as expected. This can be done through Amazon CloudWatch alarms or custom Lambda functions that monitor for any discrepancies in log delivery.

Audit account

The Audit account in Control Tower provides read-only access to all the resources across your landing zone, facilitating a secure and controlled environment for conducting audits and security reviews. While the account itself doesn't run any specific services, it is often used in conjunction with various AWS and third-party auditing and compliance tools.

AWS recommends using AWS Audit Manager, which automates the collection of evidence for audits, and Security Hub, which aggregates security findings. These tools can be configured to run within the Audit account, providing a comprehensive view of your security posture without the risk of altering configurations or data.

The Audit account can also be integrated with third-party **governance, risk, and compliance (GRC)** platforms. These platforms can pull data from the Audit account to provide additional insights and reporting capabilities, further enhancing your organization's ability to conduct thorough and effective audits.

Guardrails unveiled

Control Tower's guardrails provide a powerful mechanism for automating compliance and best practice enforcement across your AWS environment. Think of them as customizable barriers and monitors ensuring your cloud operations stay within your defined boundaries. Let's break down their types:

- **Preventive guardrails**: These are designed to proactively enforce compliance by disallowing actions that violate policies. For example, a preventive guardrail might restrict the creation of S3 buckets that are publicly accessible. This ensures that sensitive data is not accidentally exposed.

- **Detective guardrails**: These monitor for non-compliance and generate alerts when violations occur. They don't block actions but serve as a monitoring mechanism. For example, if an EC2 instance is launched without the required tags, a detective guardrail would flag this for review.

- **Custom guardrails**: Control Tower allows for the creation of custom guardrails using Config. This enables organizations to define their own set of compliance rules tailored to their specific needs. Custom guardrails can be as simple as checking for specific tags on resources or as complex as ensuring encryption across multiple services.

Control Tower in the real world

Let's explore how Control Tower functions in a complex, real-world setting.

Scenario

Imagine a multinational retail corporation that has recently transitioned its entire inventory management system to AWS. The company operates in multiple countries and has different compliance requirements for data storage and processing in each region. The challenge is to maintain a consistent governance framework across all these regions while adhering to local compliance laws.

Solution

The company decides to implement Control Tower for centralized governance. They set up a landing zone with different OUs for each region. Within these OUs, they apply various guardrails:

- To comply with data residency laws, they set up a preventive guardrail that restricts data storage to S3 buckets located only in the respective regions.

- They also set up detective guardrails to monitor real-time usage of services such as EC2 and RDS. If any resource is spun up without proper tagging, indicating its business unit and compliance category, alerts are sent to the central security team.

- To ensure that only encrypted data is stored in RDS instances, they create a custom guardrail that flags any RDS instances without encryption.

Outcome

Within the first month of implementation, the preventive guardrail blocks several attempts to create S3 buckets in unauthorized regions, thereby avoiding potential legal complications. The detective guardrails flag a handful of resources that were incorrectly tagged or not tagged at all, allowing the security team to rectify the issues before they escalate. The custom guardrail ensures that all RDS instances are encrypted, adding an extra layer of security.

By using Control Tower's guardrails, the company successfully establishes a robust, automated governance framework that adapts to its complex, multi-regional operational structure. This not only saves time but also significantly reduces the risk of human error, ensuring a more secure and compliant environment.

Who should use Control Tower?

Control Tower is particularly beneficial for:

- **Highly regulated industries**: Companies in sectors such as finance, healthcare, and government can benefit significantly from Control Tower's robust compliance features. The pre-configured guardrails and the ability to create custom rules facilitate adherence to industry-specific regulations.

- **Large enterprises**: For corporations with complex AWS architectures across multiple accounts and regions, Control Tower's centralized governance and multi-account management simplify compliance and security oversight. This is especially useful for managing large, distributed teams and resources.

- **Startups and SMBs**: Smaller businesses often lack the resources for a dedicated security and compliance team. Control Tower's automated guardrails and best practices templates offer a low-maintenance, secure, and scalable environment, allowing startups to focus more on growth and less on governance.

- **Managed service provider**: Those offering AWS services to multiple clients can use Control Tower as a centralized platform for managing multiple accounts. Its automation capabilities can enhance the value of MSP offerings by ensuring consistent governance across client accounts.

Best practices for security governance and compliance

In the ever-changing landscape of cybersecurity, effective governance and compliance are not just checkboxes to tick but are integral to a robust security posture. While AWS provides a suite of tools designed to assist with governance and compliance, the onus is on organizations to implement these tools wisely. Here are some best practices to consider:

- **Implement the principle of least privilege**: Limit permissions to the bare minimum required for users to complete their tasks. This reduces the risk of unauthorized access or accidental misconfigurations. IAM and SCPs are excellent tools for this.

- **Implement segregation of duties (SoD)**: Consider implementing SoD to minimize the risk associated with malicious or erroneous activities against sensitive resources. Divide tasks and privileges among multiple people or systems.

- **Regular audits and reviews**: Periodic audits are essential for maintaining a secure and compliant environment. Use AWS Audit Manager and Config to automate the collection of audit evidence and continuously monitor your environment.

- **Use tagging strategically**: Implement a consistent tagging strategy across all AWS resources. Tags can be used for cost allocation, compliance tracking, and security monitoring.

- **Centralize logging and monitoring**: Centralize all logs in a secure, immutable storage account. Control Tower's Log Archive account can serve this purpose. Ensure that logs are encrypted and access is restricted to authorized personnel only.

- **Automated remediation**: Automate the remediation of non-compliant resources using Config's auto-remediation features or custom Lambda functions. This not only saves time but also reduces the window of exposure.

- **Compliance dashboards**: Use Security Hub or third-party solutions to create compliance dashboards that provide real-time insights into your compliance status.

- **Third-party tools**: Consider integrating third-party security solutions that offer additional capabilities. However, ensure that these tools comply with your organization's security policies and are compatible with AWS services.

- **Keep abreast of regulatory changes**: Laws and regulations are continually evolving. Make sure your governance and compliance strategies adapt to these changes. AWS Artifact and AWS Audit Manager are useful services for accessing compliance reports that can help you stay updated.

By adhering to these best practices, organizations can build a resilient, secure, and compliant AWS environment. These practices are not static but should evolve with your organization and the broader cybersecurity landscape. Therefore, continuous improvement and adaptation are key to maintaining robust security governance and compliance. Moving from governance and compliance, let's focus on the AWS services dedicated to the secure handling of secrets.

Handling secrets securely

In today's digital ecosystem, secrets such as API keys, passwords, and other credentials are as critical as the applications that use them. Managing these secrets securely is paramount to safeguarding your infrastructure and data. Whether you are a startup or a large enterprise, the choices you make in how to manage these sensitive pieces of information can have far-reaching implications for your organization's security and compliance posture.

SSM Parameter Store versus Secrets Manager

Navigating the complexities of application configurations and sensitive data requires robust solutions. AWS offers two such services: AWS SSM Parameter Store and AWS Secrets Manager. Both services aim to centralize the management of secrets and application configurations in a secure, scalable, and automated manner. However, they differ in features, use cases, and pricing. Whether you are looking to streamline application deployments, enforce strict compliance standards, or enhance your overall security posture, these services offer a unified platform tailored to meet your secrets management needs.

Key features, differences, and similarities

Let's compare SSM Parameter Store and Secrets Manager's key features to see how they differ and where they overlap:

- **Unified framework**: Both SSM Parameter Store and Secrets Manager offer a centralized platform for secrets management. SSM Parameter Store is particularly geared towards hierarchical storage, which allows you to organize parameters in a tree-like structure. This is useful for segregating configurations based on environments, projects, or AWS accounts, making it easier to manage and locate secrets when needed. On the other hand, Secrets Manager focuses on rotating, managing, and retrieving secrets.

- **Versioning versus secret rotation**: SSM Parameter Store supports versioning of parameters, allowing you to keep track of changes and revert to previous versions if needed. Secrets Manager also supports versioning but extends this with automated rotation capabilities. You can configure Secrets Manager to rotate your secrets automatically using Lambda functions or built-in templates for common databases.

- **Data types**: SSM Parameter Store supports storing strings, lists, and secure strings. Secrets Manager is more focused on storing secrets such as API keys, passwords, and database credentials.

- **Access control**: Both services integrate seamlessly with IAM, providing granular access control. You can use IAM policies to specify who can access, create, modify, or delete your parameters or secrets. However, Secrets Manager offers more detailed audit tracking via CloudTrail.

- **Monitoring and alerts**: Both services can be monitored using CloudWatch, but Secrets Manager allows for more complex alerting scenarios, especially when integrated with CloudTrail for auditing. You can use CloudWatch alarms or events to trigger notifications or actions based on changes in your secrets or their rotation status. For example, you can send an email alert if a secret rotation fails or invoke a Lambda function to remediate a non-compliant secret.

- **Encryption**: Both services offer encryption using AWS KMS. However, Secrets Manager provides more granular control over encryption settings, including the ability to use **customer master keys (CMKs)** for added security.

- **Pricing**: SSM Parameter Store offers a free tier with optional premium features, whereas Secrets Manager does not have one, and there are additional costs for features such as secret rotation.

- **Integration**: Both services can be integrated with other AWS services and third-party applications, but Secrets Manager offers more native third-party integrations. For example, you can use Secrets Manager to store and rotate secrets for GitHub, Jenkins, and more.

SSM Parameter Store in the real world

To understand how SSM Parameter Store functions in actual environments, consider the following scenario.

Scenario

A software development agency with multiple projects and environments faces challenges in securely managing sensitive configuration parameters and database passwords. They operate separate AWS accounts for development, staging, and production to isolate sensitive data and reduce security risks. However, this multi-account structure has led to deployment delays and configuration inconsistencies.

Solution

The agency turns to SSM Parameter Store, capitalizing on its multi-account capabilities to bolster security. They use its hierarchical storage to meticulously organize parameters by project, environment, and AWS account. Importantly, the account containing the most sensitive configuration parameters and database passwords is isolated and given restricted access, minimizing the risk of unauthorized data exposure. Cross-account access is carefully configured to enable secure and seamless parameter sharing between different environments. To further fortify security, they set up CloudWatch alarms and integrate them with Organizations, enabling centralized monitoring for unauthorized changes across all accounts.

Outcome

By adopting SSM Parameter Store, the agency achieves a dual win. They not only streamline their deployment and configuration management processes but also significantly enhance their security posture. The isolation of sensitive data into a restricted account, coupled with robust monitoring mechanisms, substantially reduces the risk of unauthorized access to critical information. This multi-pronged approach accelerates project delivery while elevating the agency's security measures, leading to improved client satisfaction.

Secrets Manager in the real world

The following example provides insight into how Secrets Manager is effectively used in practical settings.

Scenario

An online retail company with a global footprint operates distinct AWS accounts for various aspects of its business: web application, payment processing, and data analytics. Each of these accounts is further segmented by region. The company faces the complex task of regularly updating and rotating encryption keys for its payment processing system to adhere to PCI DSS standards. The challenge is amplified by the need to maintain this compliance across multiple accounts and regions.

Solution

To tackle this, the company turns to Secrets Manager and sets up automatic secret rotation schedules for their payment processing application, ensuring that each AWS account and region is using the most up-to-date and secure encryption keys. To enhance security further, they employ KMS CMKs for encrypting the secrets. Cross-account access is meticulously configured to allow the secure sharing of these encryption keys between the different AWS accounts. This ensures that the development, staging, and production environments in each account are always in sync with the latest encryption standards. Additionally, they integrate CloudTrail with Secrets Manager to keep a detailed audit trail of all secret retrieval and usage. This enables them to monitor who accessed which secret, when, and from where, providing an extra layer of security and accountability.

Outcome

By employing Secrets Manager's comprehensive features, the company not only ensures ongoing compliance with PCI DSS standards but also significantly elevates its security posture. The automatic rotation of encryption keys, managed through KMS, minimizes the risk of unauthorized access and data breaches. The integration with CloudTrail provides an added layer of security, allowing for real-time monitoring and alerting for any suspicious activity related to secret access.

Who should use SSM Parameter Store or Secrets Manager?

SSM Parameter Store is particularly well-suited for those requiring a centralized, hierarchical approach to managing configurations and secrets in a cost-effective way. It is particularly beneficial for:

- **Large enterprises**: For organizations with complex, multi-account AWS architectures, the hierarchical storage capabilities of SSM Parameter Store enable centralized management of configurations across multiple accounts and regions.

- **Startups and SMBs**: For smaller businesses that may not have a large IT staff but still require secure, centralized configuration management, SSM Parameter Store offers a cost-effective and straightforward solution. Its free tier and scalability make it accessible for startups and small to medium-sized businesses.

- **Administrators**: Those responsible for system configurations across multiple environments will find the hierarchical storage and versioning features to be indispensable tools in their arsenal.

On the other hand, Secrets Manager is a versatile solution designed for those who need to focus on the secure management, rotation, and retrieval of secrets. It is particularly beneficial for:

- **Large enterprises**: Organizations with complex AWS architectures will benefit from the automatic secret rotation features, which enable centralized management of secrets across multiple accounts and regions.

- **Highly regulated industries**: Businesses in sectors such as healthcare and finance can leverage Secrets Manager to meet stringent compliance requirements thanks to its fine-grained access control and detailed audit tracking via CloudTrail.

- **SOCs**: The real-time alerting capabilities and CloudTrail integration make Secrets Manager ideal for SOCs needing a unified view of secret access and usage.

- **DevOps teams**: The automatic secret rotation and API integration features make Secrets Manager a strong fit for DevOps environments where secure and rapid application deployment is crucial.

Both SSM Parameter Store and Secrets Manager offer unique advantages tailored to specific organizational needs. Ultimately, the choice between SSM Parameter Store and Secrets Manager will largely hinge on cost considerations and the value you place on the additional features offered by Secrets Manager, such as automatic secret rotation and robust auditing capabilities.

It is worth noting that some organizations may find value in using both SSM Parameter Store and Secrets Manager. For example, you could use SSM Parameter Store for sensitive configuration data and Secrets Manager for more critical secrets.

Best practices for secrets management

Whether you opt for SSM Parameter Store, Secrets Manager, or a combination of both, adhering to best practices is essential for minimizing risks and ensuring the secure handling of sensitive information. The following are some of the best practices to consider:

- **Least privilege access**: Limit access to secrets to only those individuals or systems that absolutely require it. Use IAM policies to enforce granular access controls and regularly review and update these policies to adapt to changing needs.

- **Regular rotation**: Automate the rotation of secrets at regular intervals or after they have been accessed. Secrets Manager offers built-in capabilities for automatic rotation, but you can also implement custom rotation logic in SSM Parameter Store.

- **Audit and monitor**: Utilize CloudTrail to keep a detailed log of all access and modifications to your secrets. Set up alerts for any unauthorized or suspicious activity. This is not only good for security but also aids in compliance with various regulations.

- **Encryption**: Always encrypt sensitive information. Use customer-managed keys in KMS for added control over the encryption and decryption process.

- **Versioning and backup**: Keep versions of your secrets to roll back in case of accidental deletion or corruption. While SSM Parameter Store offers versioning capabilities, ensure you also have a backup strategy in place.

- **Disaster recovery**: Always have a disaster recovery plan in place for your secrets. This should include regular backups and a well-defined process for restoring secrets in case of accidental deletion or corruption. This ensures business continuity for your applications.

- **Use hierarchical structures for organization**: Especially in SSM Parameter Store, make use of the hierarchical storage to organize secrets based on environments, projects, or AWS accounts. This makes it easier to manage and locate secrets when needed.

- **Implement multi-account strategies**: If you are operating in a multi-account AWS environment, consider centralizing secrets in a dedicated account and using cross-account IAM roles to access them. This adds an extra layer of security by isolating sensitive data.

- **Validate and test**: Regularly validate the effectiveness of your secrets management strategy. Perform routine audits and run tests to simulate real-world scenarios, ensuring that your setup is both secure and resilient.

- **Compliance checks**: Ensure that your secrets management practices are in line with industry standards and regulations such as GDPR, HIPAA, or PCI DSS. For instance, Config can be used to continuously monitor compliance and generate alerts if non-compliant changes are made. Additionally, consider using Config's remediation actions to automatically correct non-compliant resources.

By adhering to these best practices, organizations can significantly enhance the security and reliability of their secrets management systems, Having secured our secrets, let's move to examine AWS solutions dedicated to safeguarding sensitive and private data.

Identifying and protecting sensitive data

As the risk of data exposure grows, it is essential to have a strategy for identifying and securing sensitive data. This section delves into solutions for these challenges.

Macie—your AWS data custodian

Amazon Macie specializes in safeguarding sensitive data stored in S3 buckets. It employs ML and pattern matching to identify your sensitive information.

Key features

Macie has the following key features:

- **Automated data discovery**: Macie utilizes ML algorithms to automatically scan and identify a wide range of sensitive data, including personally identifiable information (PII), financial records, credit card numbers, and confidential text within S3 buckets. This comprehensive approach eliminates the need for manual data classification, streamlining the process for greater efficiency and accuracy.

- **Comprehensive risk assessment**: Macie conducts a thorough evaluation of your S3 bucket access controls and policies, generating security findings that highlight potential vulnerabilities. These findings are consolidated in a risk assessment dashboard, offering a unified view of your data security posture and actionable insights for remediation.

- **Enhanced data visibility**: Macie provides an interactive data map that visually represents the location and sensitivity score of your data across S3, allowing you to identify high-risk buckets for deeper investigation. Additionally, Macie's intuitive dashboards can be customized to focus on specific aspects such as data storage and access patterns, offering a granular view of your security landscape.

- **Multi-account oversight**: For organizations operating in complex architectures with multiple AWS accounts, Macie offers centralized data protection, sensitive data discovery, and visibility through Organizations. This enables a unified approach to data security and compliance across various business units or departments.

- **Customizable security findings**: Macie offers the ability to fine-tune data discovery findings through allow-lists and other customization options, enhancing the accuracy of sensitive data identification while reducing false positives. This ensures that the service closely aligns with your specific data governance and compliance requirements.

- **Automated alerts and responses**: Macie's findings can be published to CloudWatch, enabling both real-time alerting and automated responses. This seamless integration with other AWS services and third-party solutions enhances your ability to act swiftly on security findings and integrate Macie into your existing security infrastructure.

- **Granular access control**: Macie integrates with IAM to provide detailed access controls, allowing you to specify who can access, modify, or delete your sensitive data.

Macie in the real world

To illustrate Macie's effectiveness, let's delve into a scenario where it plays a crucial role in a healthcare organization.

Scenario

A healthcare organization uses AWS to store and manage a vast amount of patient data, including medical records, lab results, and billing information. While the bulk of this data is stored in S3 buckets, some real-time patient data is stored in Amazon DynamoDB for quick access by healthcare applications.

Solution

To ensure the security and compliance of their data, the organization employs Macie. Macie scans the S3 buckets to identify any sensitive information, such as PII and medical records. For the DynamoDB component, the organization sets up Lambda functions that are triggered by CloudWatch events. These functions periodically create snapshots of the DynamoDB tables and store them in specific S3 buckets. Macie then scans these snapshots for sensitive data, just as it does for the original S3 buckets. Any security findings are published to CloudWatch, enabling real-time alerts and automated responses to potential security incidents.

Outcome

By leveraging Macie's capabilities across both S3 and DynamoDB, the healthcare organization significantly enhances its data security posture. The Lambda functions ensure that the real-time data in DynamoDB is not left out of the organization's comprehensive security strategy. This multi-faceted approach to data security ensures continuous monitoring and compliance, substantially reducing the risk of unauthorized access or data breaches.

Who should use Macie?

Macie is a versatile service designed to meet the data security and compliance needs of a wide range of organizations. Its capabilities make it particularly beneficial for:

- **Highly regulated industries**: Businesses operating in sectors such as healthcare, finance, and government can leverage Macie to meet stringent compliance requirements. Its detailed dashboards and fine-grained access controls make it easier to adhere to regulations such as HIPAA, GDPR, and PCI DSS.

- **SOCs**: Macie's real-time alerting capabilities and integration with CloudWatch make it ideal for SOCs that require a unified view of data access and usage. The service's customizable findings also allow SOCs to focus on specific types of sensitive data or potential vulnerabilities.

- **DevOps teams**: For teams responsible for rapid application development and deployment, Macie offers automated sensitive data identification and risk assessment features. This enables DevOps teams to integrate data security seamlessly into their CI/CD pipelines.

- **Data analysts and scientists**: Those who handle large datasets can benefit from Macie's automated data classification and risk assessment features. This ensures that sensitive data is appropriately tagged and managed, reducing the risk of accidental exposure.

Best practices for managing sensitive and private data

Before we delve into the recommended practices for managing sensitive and private data, it is important to note that these guidelines are designed to complement the features offered by Macie. Following these practices can significantly enhance your data security measures:

- **Data classification**: Utilize Macie's ML algorithms to automatically classify your data into various sensitivity levels. This not only helps in identifying what data you have but also in determining the appropriate security controls for each data type.

- **Least privilege access**: Use IAM to create roles and permissions that are as restrictive as possible. For instance, if a user only needs read access to a specific S3 bucket, don't grant them write permissions. This minimizes the risk associated with potential security breaches.

- **Data encryption**: Use KMS to manage encryption keys. You can create, rotate, and disable encryption keys through a centralized interface. This ensures that you have full control over who can decrypt your sensitive data.

- **Guardrails**: Macie's guardrails can be customized to suit your organization's specific data governance and compliance requirements. For example, you can set up a guardrail that triggers an alert if unencrypted PII data is uploaded to an S3 bucket.

- **Regular audits and monitoring**: Integrate Macie with CloudTrail to keep a detailed log of all access and modifications to your sensitive data. Use CloudWatch to set up alerts for any unauthorized or suspicious activity, thereby enabling real-time monitoring.

- **Data masking and tokenization**: For extremely sensitive data, consider using data masking or tokenization techniques. This replaces the actual data with a token, adding an extra layer of security.

- **Beyond S3**: Macie's discovery capabilities can be extended to other AWS services such as Amazon RDS or DynamoDB. You can achieve this by using Lambda functions or Glue scripts to temporarily move data to S3, allowing Macie to scan it. This is particularly useful for organizations that store sensitive data across multiple types of data stores.

By adhering to these best practices, you can achieve a comprehensive and adaptable approach to sensitive data protection, making the most of Macie's capabilities to safeguard your digital assets and meet your compliance objectives. Proceeding to our closing section, let's examine how to unify the various AWS security services detailed earlier for comprehensive protection.

Orchestrating AWS security services

In a world where security threats are increasingly sophisticated and pervasive, organizations need more than isolated solutions. They require a cohesive, integrated approach that can adapt to evolving threats and compliance requirements. This section delves into how you can achieve this orchestration, creating a comprehensive, scalable, and flexible security framework that meets your organization's needs.

Building an integrated security architecture

AWS offers a plethora of security services, each designed to address specific aspects of security. However, the real power lies in designing an efficient security architecture that enables those services to work in harmony. Let's explore their combined effectiveness in more detail.

Multi-service synergy

When it comes to AWS security services, the sum is often greater than its parts. For instance, GuardDuty can detect malicious or unauthorized behavior, but its findings become more actionable when integrated with Security Hub, which aggregates these findings and correlates them with other data points. Similarly, Macie can identify sensitive data, but its effectiveness is amplified when used in conjunction with SSM Parameter Store and Secrets Manager to ensure that sensitive data is not only identified but also securely managed.

Organizations and Control Tower can act as the backbone of your security architecture, enabling centralized governance across multiple AWS accounts. These services can enforce guardrails that are aligned with the findings and recommendations from Config, Inspector, and other assessment services. This creates a feedback loop where detection, assessment, and governance services continually inform and enhance each other.

Data flows and security

Data is the lifeblood of any organization, and its secure flow is crucial for operational integrity. AWS services are designed to work in an interconnected manner, often requiring data to move from one service to another. For example, logs from CloudTrail can be ingested into Security Lake for deeper analysis. While this inter-service data flow is generally secure, additional measures such as encryption during transit and at rest, enabled by KMS, can add an extra layer of security. This data flow should also be secured using IAM roles and policies that grant least-privilege access.

Also, consider using VPC endpoints for private connectivity between AWS services. This is especially important when either the source, the destination, or both are located within your VPC. Doing so reduces the exposure of your data to the public internet.

Scalability and flexibility

One of the most compelling advantages of an integrated AWS security architecture is its inherent scalability and flexibility. As your organization grows, so do your security needs. AWS services such as GuardDuty, Security Hub, and Macie offer features that can be easily scaled up or down depending on your requirements.

Organizations allows you to add new accounts to your organization's structure seamlessly, and services such as Control Tower and Config can automatically enforce security policies on these new accounts. This ensures that your security posture remains consistent, irrespective of the size and complexity of your AWS environment.

Cost and efficiency considerations

When it comes to implementing a robust security architecture, organizations often face a delicate balancing act between cost and effectiveness. By carefully evaluating the cost–benefit aspects and employing smart optimization strategies, you can build a strong, scalable AWS security architecture that aligns with your budget constraints.

Cost–benefit analysis

The first step in understanding the financial commitment involved in implementing AWS security services is to conduct a cost-benefit analysis. This involves quantifying the costs associated with each service and weighing them against the benefits they bring in terms of enhanced security, compliance, and operational efficiency.

Here are some key cost items to consider:

- **Initial setup costs**: Services such as GuardDuty, Inspector, and Macie have initial setup costs that can include data ingestion and initial scans. Initial setup may also require important configuration work that could involve consulting or internal labor costs.

- **Operational costs**: Security Hub, Config, and Organizations have ongoing operational costs based on factors such as the number of checks performed, the number of active members, or the amount of data processed.

- **Data transfer costs**: Services such as CloudTrail and Detective may incur costs based on the amount of data transferred, especially if you are aggregating data from multiple regions.

- **Additional features**: Some services offer additional features at extra costs. For example, Secrets Manager's automatic secret rotation feature incurs an additional charge.

Finally, evaluate the **return on investment** (**ROI**) by measuring the effectiveness of each service in preventing security incidents, improving operational efficiency, and ensuring compliance. Keep in mind that enhanced security can provide significant value, reducing the long-term costs associated with data breaches and non-compliance penalties.

Optimization strategies

Optimizing your AWS security services doesn't necessarily mean cutting corners or compromising on security. Here are some strategies to manage costs effectively:

- **Rightsize your services**: AWS offers various pricing options for its services. Make sure you choose the one that aligns with your usage patterns. For example, Inspector offers assessment-based pricing, so you only pay for the assessments you run.

- **Leverage free tiers**: AWS offers free tiers for services such as Config, GuardDuty, and Secrets Manager. Utilize these to your advantage before committing to higher-cost plans, especially during the initial phases.

- **Use VPC endpoints**: As mentioned in the *Data flows and security* section earlier, using VPC endpoints can enhance security by keeping traffic within your AWS environment. While not their primary purpose, they may also help in reducing data transfer costs in certain scenarios.

- **Centralize billing**: By centralizing billing in your organization, you can take advantage of volume discounts and better manage reserved instances across your organization.

- **Monitor and alert**: Set up CloudWatch alarms to notify you when spending exceeds predefined thresholds. This can help you take timely action to prevent cost overruns.

Aligning compliance and governance

Navigating the complex landscape of compliance standards and governance frameworks is a critical aspect of any organization's security strategy. The challenge is even more pronounced in cloud environments, where data and services are often distributed across multiple regions and accounts.

Compliance alignment

AWS offers a suite of security services that can be instrumental in helping organizations meet various compliance standards while making audits less cumbersome and more efficient. Here are a few examples of how key services can contribute to compliance:

- **GuardDuty for GDPR**: GuardDuty's continuous monitoring capabilities can be a cornerstone for GDPR compliance. It helps in identifying unauthorized or anomalous activities that could indicate a data breach, thereby fulfilling GDPR's requirement for timely breach notifications.

- **Macie for HIPAA**: Macie's data classification and discovery features can be invaluable for healthcare organizations that need to comply with HIPAA. It can automatically identify **personal health information (PHI)** stored in S3 buckets and alert administrators to any unauthorized access.

- **Config for PCI DSS**: For organizations that handle credit card transactions, Config can monitor changes to resources and ensure they align with PCI DSS requirements. It can track changes to security groups, **network access control lists (NACLs)**, and VPC settings, providing an audit trail that can be reviewed during compliance checks.

- **Security Hub for multiple standards**: Security Hub aggregates findings from various AWS services and third-party tools, providing a comprehensive view of your security and compliance status. It offers built-in checks for standards such as CIS Benchmarks and NIST, making it easier to align with multiple compliance requirements.

Governance framework

Governance in a cloud environment involves the management and oversight of multiple accounts, services, and data flows. Organizations and Control Tower play pivotal roles in establishing a governance framework that adapts to evolving needs.

- **Organizations for hierarchical management:** Organizations allows you to create a hierarchical structure of AWS accounts, grouped into OUs. This structure enables centralized billing and easier policy enforcement. SCPs can be applied at different levels, offering granular control over service permissions across accounts.

- **Control Tower for guardrails:** Control Tower simplifies the setup of a well-architected multi-account AWS environment. One of its standout features is the implementation of guardrails—pre-configured rules for security, operations, and compliance. These guardrails work in tandem with Organizations and Config to provide a holistic governance approach.

- **Synergy between Organizations and Control Tower**: When used together, they offer a unified governance framework. Organizations provide the structural backbone, while Control Tower offers the guardrails for policy enforcement. This synergy ensures that governance is not just a checkbox but an integrated part of your AWS architecture.

Alerting and incident response

Effective security management is not just about prevention but also about rapid detection and response. AWS provides a range of tools to help you set up real-time monitoring, alerting, and even automatic remediation for security incidents. Let's dive into some of these capabilities in more detail.

Real-time monitoring and alerting

By integrating security services, you can create a comprehensive real-time monitoring and alerting mechanism that covers various aspects of your AWS environment. Here are some examples of how you can set up alerts across key AWS security services:

- **GuardDuty**: Once enabled, GuardDuty will continuously monitor your AWS account for malicious or unauthorized behavior. From CloudWatch, you can set up alarms and notifications to be sent via Amazon SNS to alert your security team.

- **Macie**: Macie's findings can be published to CloudWatch, where you can set up alarms to notify your security team via email or SMS when sensitive data is accessed or moved.

- **Config**: Set up Config rules and associate them with CloudWatch alarms to get alerted on non-compliant resources.

- **Security Hub**: Enable this service to aggregate findings from various AWS services, including GuardDuty, Inspector, and Macie. You can set up custom insights and also configure CloudWatch alarms for aggregated findings that can be sent directly to your team's Slack channel.

Integrated incident response management

An incident response plan outlines the processes to follow when a security incident occurs. AWS security services can be integrated into your existing or new incident response plan in the following ways:

- **Initial detection**: Use GuardDuty or Security Hub for the initial detection of the incident
- **Investigation**: Use Detective to correlate logs and findings for a more in-depth investigation of the incident
- **Containment**: Lambda functions can be triggered to contain affected resources automatically
- **Recovery**: Use Config to audit changes and ensure that all resources are rolled back to a known good state
- **Lessons learned**: Post-incident, use Security Hub to aggregate findings for reviews

Automated remediation

Automation is key to managing the scale and complexity of modern cloud environments. AWS offers several tools for automating the remediation of security incidents. They are as follows:

- **Config**: Set up remediation actions in Config to automatically fix non-compliant resources. For example, if an S3 bucket is found to be public, a Config rule can automatically make it private using pre-built remediation actions.

- **Lambda**: Use custom Lambda functions to perform specific remediation tasks. For example, if GuardDuty detects a compromised EC2 instance, a Lambda function could automatically isolate the instance in a separate security group. Network security capabilities such as AWS WAF and VPC's NACLs can also be used to immediately block malicious IP addresses.

- **Step Functions**: For complex remediation workflows involving multiple steps and services, use Step Functions to orchestrate Lambda functions and other AWS services. This can be particularly useful for automated incident response scenarios that require multiple steps and options.

- **SSM**: Use SSM Automation documents to execute common security remediation and operational tasks such as patch management.

By effectively utilizing AWSw monitoring, alerting, and remediation tools, you can significantly enhance your organization's ability to quickly detect and respond to security incidents.

Orchestrating AWS security in practice

Let's illustrate the effective orchestration of various AWS security services in the following example.

Scenario

A global financial institution with operations in multiple countries faced the complex challenge of complying with the European Union's GDPR. The institution stored a vast array of sensitive customer data, including financial records and PII, across a multifaceted AWS architecture. The financial institution faced challenges such as data fragmentation across multiple AWS accounts and the complexity of GDPR requirements, including data protection and breach notification.

Outcome

The financial institution successfully achieved GDPR compliance within the stipulated timeframe, thus avoiding potential fines that could have amounted to millions of euros. The integrated AWS security architecture provided a robust, scalable, and cost-effective solution that not only met but exceeded regulatory requirements. Real-time monitoring and automated remediation significantly reduced the risk of data breaches, and the institution gained a comprehensive view of its security posture.

Solution

To address this multifaceted challenge, the institution adopted an integrated approach, leveraging multiple AWS security services that worked in synergy.

- **Data classification and protection**: Macie was the first line of defense, automatically identifying and classifying sensitive data in S3 buckets. Macie's findings were then published to CloudWatch for real-time alerting and automated remediation.

- **Continuous monitoring and compliance**: Config continuously monitored configuration changes across AWS resources, while GuardDuty provided intelligent threat detection. Both services fed their findings into Security Hub, which offered a unified view of the security and compliance status.

- **Centralized governance**: Organizations was used to manage multiple AWS accounts centrally. SCPs such as `DenyPublicS3Bucket` were implemented to enforce organization-wide permissions and restrictions. Control Tower was deployed to set up a well-architected multi-account environment based on AWS best practices.

- **Data analytics and forensics**: Security Lake was integrated into the Log Archive account set-up via Control Tower. It was configured to store, search, and analyze security data, receiving events from Security Hub among other sources. This provided an additional layer of analytics to fine-tune AWS WAF rules and helped in forensic investigations.

- **Real-time alerting and automated remediation**: CloudWatch was configured to receive findings from Macie, GuardDuty, and Security Hub. CloudWatch alarms triggered Lambda functions for automated remediation actions, such as modifying security group rules or modifying permissions to access compromised S3 buckets.

- **Cost management**: Billing alarms were set up in CloudWatch to monitor the financial aspects of implementing these security measures, ensuring that the institution remained within budget without compromising security.

The key to the institution's success was the seamless integration of these AWS services, each contributing a unique piece to the puzzle. Lambda served as the glue, automating tasks and responses across services, from alerting to remediation. Organizations and Control Tower, fortified by SCPs, provided the governance framework, ensuring that all services were aligned with the institution's compliance requirements.

Summary

In this chapter, we delved into the orchestration of AWS security services, laying the groundwork for a robust and adaptable security posture. We began by exploring the nuances of threat and vulnerability detection, discussing the capabilities and real-world applications of AWS services such as GuardDuty, Detective, and Inspector. We then transitioned into the realm of security governance and compliance, examining the functionalities of Security Hub, Config, Organizations, and Control Tower. The chapter also covered the critical aspects of securing secrets and identifying sensitive data, emphasizing the roles of SSM Parameter Store, Secrets Manager, and Macie. We rounded off the chapter by discussing the orchestration of these services into an integrated security architecture, touching upon cost considerations, compliance alignment, and incident response. The chapter concluded with a final case study that encapsulated the key takeaways, providing a holistic view of AWS security orchestration.

As we move forward, we are about to embark on the second part of the book, which focuses on architecting and deploying secure AWS environments. The upcoming chapter will take you through the art of creating secure microservices architectures. You will learn to understand the principles and security considerations of microservices, implement secure communication between them, and apply fine-grained access control. This next chapter promises to deepen your understanding of AWS security, particularly in the context of modern architectural patterns such as microservices.

Questions

Answer the following questions to test your knowledge of this chapter:

1. How does Detective enhance the capabilities of GuardDuty?

2. What role do guardrails play in Control Tower?

3. How do the features and use cases of SSM Parameter Store and Secrets Manager differ, and what are the security implications of choosing one over the other?

4. How can Macie's discovery capabilities be extended to AWS services other than S3, such as RDS or DynamoDB?

5. What are the key considerations and optimization strategies for managing the costs of implementing AWS security services?

Answers

Here are the answers to this chapter's questions:

1. Detective acts as an analytical extension to GuardDuty by ingesting and correlating data from various AWS services. It employs ML algorithms for pattern identification and offers graphical visualization for a better understanding of security events. It also groups related GuardDuty findings and maps them to the MITRE ATT&CK framework.

2. Guardrails in Control Tower are pre-packaged governance rules that enforce compliance and security policies across your AWS accounts. They can be either preventive or detective. Preventive guardrails restrict actions that could violate policies, while detective guardrails monitor for non-compliance and report it. This dual approach ensures both proactive and reactive governance. As an example, a preventive guardrail could restrict the creation of S3 buckets that are publicly accessible, while a detective guardrail could flag an EC2 instance launched without required tags.

3. SSM Parameter Store is more cost-effective and is geared toward hierarchical storage, making it more suitable for configuration management. Secrets Manager focuses on rotating, managing, and retrieving secrets, making it ideal for automated secret rotation and robust auditing capabilities. From a security standpoint, choosing Secrets Manager may offer more specialized features for secret management, while Parameter Store is more versatile for general configuration but may lack some of the specialized secret rotation features.

4. Macie's discovery capabilities can be extended by using Lambda functions or Glue scripts to temporarily move data to S3 for scanning. This allows Macie to work in conjunction with services such as RDS or DynamoDB. Additionally, Macie's findings can be published to CloudWatch for real-time alerting and automated remediation, offering a more integrated approach to security.

5. When conducting a cost–benefit analysis, organizations should consider initial setup costs, operational costs, data transfer costs, and additional feature costs. They should also evaluate their ROI by measuring the effectiveness of each service in preventing security incidents, improving operational efficiency, and ensuring compliance. Optimization strategies include rightsizing services to align with usage patterns, leveraging free tiers, using VPC endpoints to reduce data transfer costs, centralizing billing for volume discounts, and setting up CloudWatch alarms for spending thresholds.

Further readings

To learn more about the topics that were covered in this chapter, take a look at the following resources:

- AWS whitepaper—*Organizing Your AWS Environment Using Multiple Accounts*: `https://docs.aws.amazon.com/pdfs/whitepapers/latest/organizing-your-aws-environment/organizing-your-aws-environment.pdf`

- AWS documentation: *AWS Security Reference Architecture (AWS SRA)*: `https://docs.aws.amazon.com/prescriptive-guidance/latest/security-reference-architecture/welcome.html`

- *Best practice rules for AWS Organizations* by TrendMicro: `https://www.trendmicro.com/cloudoneconformity-staging/knowledge-base/aws/Organizations/`

Part 2: Architecting and Deploying Secure AWS Environments

From architecture to action: In this part, you will design and implement secure AWS environments with a focus on microservices architectures, serverless configurations, multi-tenancy practices, and automation for secure and repeatable deployments.

This part contains the following chapters:

Designing Secure Microservices Architectures in AWS

Welcome to the sixth chapter, which also kicks off the second part of our extensive guide to AWS security, titled *Architecting and Deploying Secure AWS Environments*. This part aims to deepen your expertise in designing secure AWS infrastructures, focusing on advanced subjects such as microservices, serverless computing, multi-tenancy, and **infrastructure as code (IaC)**.

This new chapter focuses on the microservices architectural style, which is increasingly becoming the go-to approach for modern software development. We will initiate our discussion by examining why microservices are gaining such traction, and to offer a well-rounded view, we will juxtapose them with traditional monolithic architectures, dissecting the pros and cons of each. As we progress, the chapter will pivot to the specialized security challenges that microservices present. We will explore the shifts in complexity and responsibilities that come with adopting a microservices architecture, underlining the necessity for a revamped approach to access control and security protocols. We will delve into the zero-trust principle and its role in securing inter-service communication, covering both synchronous and asynchronous methods. AWS App Mesh and Amazon API Gateway will be highlighted as indispensable tools for managing and securing such communications. The chapter will culminate with a deep dive into fine-grained access control within a microservices framework. We will discuss IAM's role, explore Amazon Cognito for secure end-user authentication, and introduce the concept of decoupling authorizations via Amazon Verified Permissions.

By the end of this chapter, you will have a comprehensive understanding of microservices architecture, its security implications, and best practices. You will be well equipped to navigate the complex landscape of microservices security, from securing inter-service communication to implementing robust end-user authentication and authorization mechanisms.

In this chapter, we will cover the following key areas:

- The ascent of microservices and their comparison with monolithic architectures
- The unique security challenges in microservices
- Techniques for securing inter-service communication
- Strategies for fine-grained access control in microservices

Why choose microservices today?

In the ever-evolving landscape of software development, the architecture you choose can make or break your application. The decision between a monolithic and a microservices architecture is more than just a technical choice; it is a strategic one that impacts everything from development speed to operational efficiency. This section aims to shed light on why microservices have become the architecture of choice for many organizations, especially those looking to scale efficiently and securely.

The monolithic way

Before we venture into the transformative world of microservices, it is crucial to have a solid grasp of monolithic architecture. This architectural style has been the bedrock of software development for decades. It offers a straightforward approach where all the code necessary for an application is deployed and executed from a single computing platform. This platform often includes the operating system, the database, and other software stacks that are essential for the application to function.

From mono-tier to multi-tier

The journey of monolithic architecture is a tale of evolution. While they are still relevant today, these architectures have undergone several changes over the years. One of the most significant shifts has been the move from a single-layer or **mono-tier** model to a multi-layer or **multi-tier** model. This evolution has been driven by the growing complexity of applications and the myriad benefits that come with layer separation, such as enhanced security, fault tolerance, and resource allocation.

Mono-tier model

In mono-tier architecture, the application is as simple as it gets. All components—be it the user interface, the business logic, or the data storage—run on a single system. This is the architecture you would typically find in mainframe systems or simple desktop applications. While this model offers the advantage of simplicity, it severely lacks scalability and fault tolerance. Any issue in one part of the system can bring down the entire application, making it highly unreliable for complex, modern-day applications.

The following figure (*Figure 6.1*) represents a mono-tier model, where the overall application is contained within a single, self-sufficient system:

Computer

Figure 6.1 – Mono-tier architecture

Two-tier model

The two-tier or **client-server** model is a slight advancement over the mono-tier model. In this setup, a client communicates directly with a server to access data. The client usually contains the application code and is often referred to as a **thick client**. This model introduced the concept of distributed computing but still had its limitations. For instance, if the server went down, the client would lose access to all functionalities tied to that server.

The following figure (*Figure 6.2*) represents a two-tier model where the application works as a client-server:

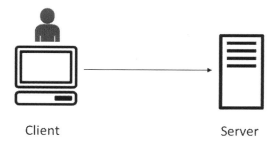

Client   Server

Figure 6.2 – Two-tier architecture

Three-tier model

Three-tier architecture is a more mature evolution of the two-tier model. It relies on a lightweight client, such as a web browser, and separates the code between a frontend and a backend layer. The backend is often called the **business logic layer** or the **application layer**. It handles the application's core functions and communicates between the frontend layer and the data-tier layer. This separation allows for better security, as each layer can only interact with its adjacent layers and offers more straightforward scalability options.

The following figure (*Figure 6.3*) represents an example application deployed as a three-tier model:

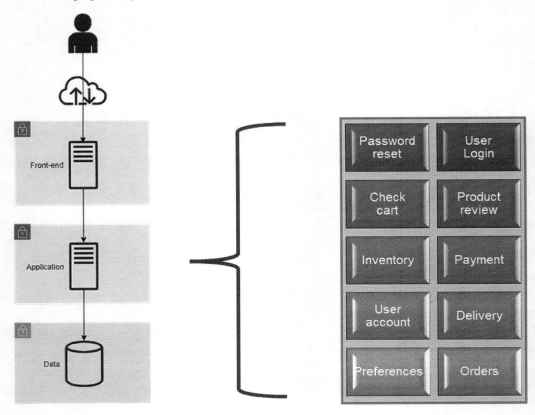

Figure 6.3 – Three-tier architecture example

N-tier model

As applications continue to grow in complexity, they may require additional layers or *tiers* to handle various functionalities such as caching, queuing, and load balancing. This leads to an N-tier architecture, where N can be any number greater than three. Each additional tier can be independently scaled, providing more flexible architecture but also adding complexity in terms of management and monitoring.

Self-contained codebase

In monolithic architecture, the code base is a single, indivisible entity, even though it might be logically structured into different layers, such as the presentation layer (frontend) and the processing layer (backend). This makes version control simpler but poses challenges as the application grows. For example, a small change in one part of the code might necessitate rebuilding and deploying the entire application, which is both time-consuming and risky.

Tightly coupled components

The components in a monolithic architecture are tightly coupled, meaning they are interconnected and dependent on each other. This tight coupling makes the system less flexible and harder to manage as it grows. It also makes it challenging to adopt new technologies or frameworks, as changes in one component can have a ripple effect on others.

The upsides of monolithic

Monolithic architecture has been the go-to approach for software development for many years, and it is not without good reason. Here are some of the key advantages:

- **Simplicity in development**: One of the most significant benefits is the simplicity of the development process. All the code resides in a single codebase, making it easier to manage and navigate.

- **Ease of deployment**: With a single codebase, the deployment process is straightforward. You don't have to worry about deploying multiple services as you would in a microservices architecture.

- **Holistic view for developers**: Developers can easily see how different components interact, which can speed up the development process and make debugging simpler.

- **End-to-end testing**: Testing is often easier to set up and execute because you are dealing with a single, unified codebase. This makes end-to-end testing more straightforward.

- **Shared resources**: All components share the same system resources, which can be an advantage in terms of data consistency and transaction management.

- **Mature technology stack**: Monolithic architectures have been around for a long time, meaning they are well-understood, and there's a wealth of knowledge and tools available for development and troubleshooting.

- **Initial cost efficiency**: For small to medium-sized projects, a monolithic architecture can be more cost-effective initially, both in terms of development time and infrastructure costs.

The downsides of monolithic

Despite its advantages, monolithic architecture has several limitations, especially as applications grow in complexity and scale. Here are some of the key downsides:

- **Limited scalability**: One of the most glaring limitations is the difficulty in scaling specific functionalities. You have to scale the entire application even if only one feature experiences high demand.

- **Codebase complexity**: As the application grows, so does the codebase, making it increasingly challenging to manage and understand.

- **Longer build and deployment cycles**: A larger codebase means longer build times, which can slow down the development process and make continuous deployment challenging.

- **Tight coupling of components**: Components in a monolithic architecture are tightly coupled, making the system less flexible and increasing the risk of a small change affecting multiple areas of the application.

- **Technology lock-in**: The architecture often restricts you to a specific technology stack, making it difficult to adopt new, more efficient technologies over time.

- **Resource inefficiency**: Because you have to scale the entire application, you may end up provisioning resources for components that don't necessarily need it, leading to inefficiency and increased costs.

- **Collaboration challenges**: In a large development team, developers may find it difficult to work on different features simultaneously without stepping on each other's toes due to the tightly coupled nature of the components.

The microservices way

In today's rapidly evolving technological environment, organizations face unprecedented demands for agility, scalability, and rapid deployment. Traditional monolithic architectures are increasingly falling short of meeting these multifaceted challenges. This has led to the emergence of microservices architecture, a decentralized approach that has its roots in **service-oriented architecture** (**SOA**). This modern architectural style is a strategic response to the complex landscape of software development. It aligns seamlessly with agile methodologies, DevOps practices, and cloud-native solutions, offering a robust framework to address contemporary challenges in both deployment and adaptability. In the following sections, we will explore the key features of microservices architecture, examining how it effectively addresses these modern-day requirements.

Small chunks of code

In the world of microservices, the architecture is designed to be as modular as possible. This modularity is achieved by breaking down the application into smaller, more manageable pieces known as microservices. Each of these microservices is highly focused and serves a specific function within the broader application. This focus on single functionality allows for a minimalistic approach to coding, where each microservice contains only the code that is absolutely necessary for it to perform its designated task. This not only makes the code easier to understand and maintain but also facilitates independent deployment, as well as debugging and testing. The independence of each microservice means that it can be updated, scaled, or even completely rewritten without affecting the other parts of the system. This is a significant departure from monolithic architectures, where changes to one part of the codebase can have a ripple effect across the entire application.

Lightweight runtime environment

One of the most compelling features of the microservices architecture is the concept of a lightweight runtime environment. In a monolithic system, the entire application often shares a single runtime environment, which can become quite cumbersome and resource-intensive. In contrast, each microservice in a microservices architecture operates in its own isolated runtime environment. This environment is tailored to the specific needs of the microservice, containing only the essential libraries and dependencies required for that service to function. This results in a much more efficient use of resources and simplifies the deployment process.

Technologies such as containerization, exemplified by Docker, further enhance this by encapsulating the microservice and its lightweight runtime into a single, easily deployable unit. This encapsulation ensures that the microservice is both autonomous and portable qualities that are highly valued in modern software development practices.

The following figure (*Figure 6.4*) shows how a microservice's code and runtime environment are encapsulated together into a container:

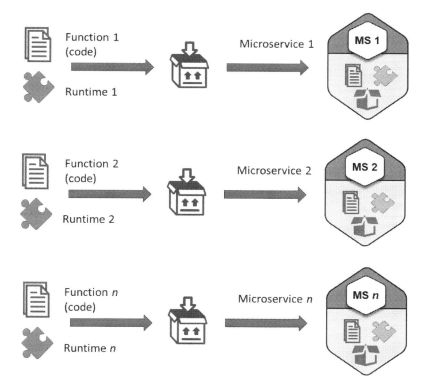

Figure 6.4 – Code and runtime encapsulation into a container

Loosely coupled components

The architecture of microservices is inherently designed to minimize dependencies between the various components of an application. Each microservice is a self-contained unit with its own data model and functions, and it interacts with other services through well-defined APIs. This loose coupling allows for a high degree of flexibility and resilience. For instance, if one service fails, the impact on other services is minimized, ensuring that the entire application doesn't come to a halt. This also facilitates parallel development, as multiple teams can work on different services simultaneously without worrying about creating conflicts or dependencies.

The loosely coupled nature of microservices also extends to technology stacks, allowing different services to be written in different programming languages or use different data storage solutions. This technological agnosticism is a boon for organizations that have diverse skill sets and legacy systems, as it allows them to adopt microservices without being tied down to a single technology stack.

The following figure (*Figure 6.5*) illustrates how the loosely coupled characteristic of microservices differs from tightly coupled monolithic applications:

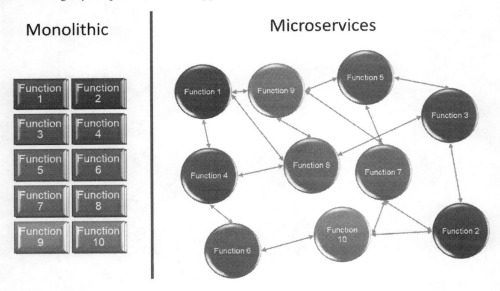

Figure 6.5 – Comparison of tightly coupled (monolithic) and loosely coupled (microservices)

Pros of microservices

The advantages of adopting a microservices architecture are numerous, offering flexibility and scalability, among other benefits:

- **Scalability**: One of the most significant benefits of microservices is the ability to scale individual components independently. If one service experiences high demand, you can allocate more resources to it without affecting the other services.

- **Flexibility in technology choices**: Microservices allow for a polyglot approach, meaning you can use different programming languages, frameworks, and databases for different services. This is particularly useful for leveraging the best tools for specific tasks.

- **Faster time to market**: The modular nature of microservices enables rapid development and deployment. Teams can work on different services simultaneously, making it easier to update features or fix issues without waiting for a complete application overhaul.

- **Fault isolation**: In a microservices architecture, if one service fails, it doesn't bring down the entire application. This isolation improves the system's resilience and availability.

- **Optimized resource utilization**: Because each microservice runs in its own containerized environment, you can optimize the resources it uses, leading to more efficient hardware utilization.

- **DevOps and CI/CD compatibility**: Microservices are a natural fit for DevOps practices and **continuous integration/continuous deployment (CI/CD)** pipelines, allowing for automated testing and deployment, which, in turn, increases operational efficiency.

Cons of microservices

While microservices offer many advantages, they come with their own set of challenges and complexities that need to be carefully managed:

- **Complexity**: The flexibility and independence that make microservices powerful can also make the system complex. Managing multiple services, each with its own database and different scaling requirements can be challenging.

- **Data consistency**: Since each microservice can have its own database, ensuring data consistency across services becomes complicated, often requiring complex coordination.

- **Network latency**: Inter-service communication over a network can introduce latency and risk of network failure, affecting the application's performance and reliability.

- **Operational overhead**: Each service might require its own logging, monitoring, and service discovery, which can significantly increase the operational complexity and overhead.

- **Initial setup cost**: Transitioning from a monolithic architecture to microservices is not trivial and often requires a substantial initial investment in terms of time and resources.

- **Skill set requirements**: The effective implementation and management of microservices require a diverse skill set, including expertise in DevOps practices, containerization technologies, such as Docker, and orchestration tools, such as Kubernetes.

Monolithic versus microservices

The choice between monolithic and microservices architectures is a pivotal decision that can significantly impact the development, deployment, scalability, and security of an application. This section aims to provide a comprehensive comparison between the two, highlighting their respective strengths and weaknesses.

Comparison

The following table (*Table 6.1*) offers a side-by-side comparison of monolithic and microservices architectures across various dimensions:

Criteria	Monolithic architecture	Microservices architecture
Code base	Unified, single code base	Decentralized, multiple code bases
Scalability	Scales as a single unit	Allows for targeted scaling of services
Development speed	Slower due to interdependencies	Faster due to independent services
Fault isolation	A failure can affect the entire system	Failures are generally isolated to single services
Technology stack	Usually a single, unified stack	Allows for a polyglot approach
Operational complexity	Generally simpler but less flexible	More complex but offers greater flexibility

Table 6.1 – Comparison between monolithic and microservices architectures

Let's look into each criteria one by one:

- **Codebase**: Monolithic architectures have a single, unified code base, making it easier to manage but less flexible. Microservices, on the other hand, have multiple, independent code bases, allowing for more agile development and deployment.

- **Scalability**: In monolithic systems, you often have to scale the entire application, even if only one component requires it. Microservices allow you to scale individual services independently, offering more efficient use of resources.

- **Development speed**: The tightly coupled nature of monolithic architectures can slow down development, as changes in one component may require changes in others. Microservices enable faster development by allowing teams to work on different services independently.

- **Fault isolation**: A failure in one component of a monolithic system can bring down the entire application. In microservices, each service operates independently, so a failure in one service usually doesn't affect others.

- **Technology stack**: Monolithic architectures often require a single technology stack, limiting flexibility. Microservices allow you to use different technologies for different services, offering greater adaptability.

- **Operational complexity**: Monolithic architectures are generally easier to manage compared to microservices.

Use cases

Different projects and organizational needs call for different architectural styles. Here, we explore the scenarios where one might be more advantageous than the other:

- **Small to medium projects**: Monolithic architectures are often easier to manage for smaller projects, especially for startups or teams with limited resources. AWS offers services such as Elastic Beanstalk that can simplify the deployment of monolithic applications.

- **Enterprise-level applications**: For complex, large-scale applications requiring high availability and scalability, microservices are generally the better choice. AWS provides a range of services, such as AWS Lambda for serverless architectures and Amazon ECS for container management, that can support the complexities of a microservices architecture.

- **Rapid prototyping**: Monolithic architectures can be advantageous for rapid prototyping and development. However, as the application scales, transitioning to microservices may become inevitable. AWS's suite of development tools can aid in this transition.

- **Highly distributed teams**: Microservices offer the advantage of parallel development, making it ideal for organizations with multiple development teams in diverse locations. AWS's global infrastructure can be a boon in such scenarios, offering low-latency access and data sovereignty.

- **Legacy systems**: For organizations looking to modernize their legacy systems, transitioning to a microservices architecture can be a strategic move. AWS offers services such as AWS Migration Hub to facilitate this transition, but it requires careful planning and a focus on security, given that AWS environments are subject to different kinds of vulnerabilities compared to on-premises setups.

- **Lift-and-shift migration**: This involves moving an application from an on-premises environment to the cloud with minimal modifications. In the context of AWS, a monolithic architecture is often more straightforward to migrate using the lift-and-shift method. AWS services such as Amazon EC2 and Amazon RDS can easily host monolithic applications, allowing organizations to benefit from cloud scalability and flexibility without undergoing a significant architectural overhaul. However, this approach may not fully leverage the cloud's capabilities and may require further optimization post-migration.

- **Refactoring for microservices**: If an organization aims to modernize its application architecture, refactoring to microservices is a strategic move. AWS offers a rich ecosystem of services such as Lambda, ECS, and EKS that are designed to support microservices. Refactoring involves breaking down a monolithic application into smaller, loosely coupled services, each of which can be developed, deployed, and scaled independently. This approach allows organizations to take full advantage of the cloud-native features offered by AWS, such as auto-scaling, serverless computing, and managed databases. However, this is often a complex and time-consuming process that requires careful planning and execution, especially concerning security configurations and data migration.

In conclusion, the architecture you choose plays a pivotal role in shaping your application's scalability, flexibility, and overall performance. Whether it is the simplicity of monolithic architecture or the agility of microservices, AWS offers a range of services to optimize your architectural decisions.

Security considerations in microservices architectures

This section aims to provide a comprehensive understanding of the security implications that come with adopting a microservices approach. We will delve into the complexities introduced by this architectural style, the shift in responsibility domains, especially in cloud environments such as AWS, and the paradox of lightweight components that offer both security benefits and challenges.

Complexity paradigm

In the realm of software architecture, the transition from monolithic to microservices-based systems is akin to a short-term rental company remodeling its single-room studios into multi-room apartments. Imagine a studio with four corners designated for different functionalities: a workout corner, a sleeping area, a storage space, and a workspace area, as shown in *Figure 6.6*. Initially, the studio was simple to manage, with just one door as the entry point and a few windows for natural light. However, to adapt to market demands, the company decides to divide the studio into four separate rooms, each serving a specific function, as shown in *Figure 6.7*. This new layout offers flexibility but also introduces complexity.

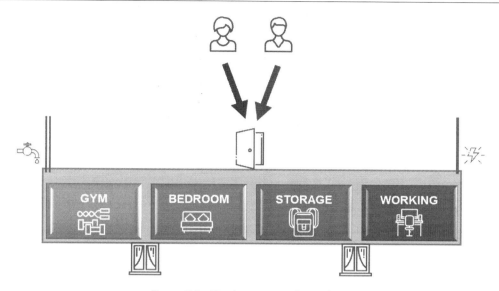

Figure 6.6 – Single-room studio analogy

Now, there are multiple doors, more windows, and additional pipes and wires to manage. Just like this, microservices architecture brings flexibility but at the cost of increased complexity:

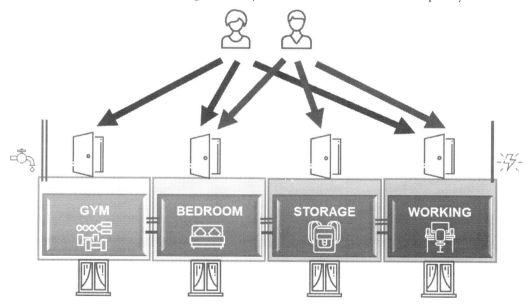

Figure 6.7 – Multi-room apartment analogy

In monolithic architecture, the application is a single entity, much like our initial studio. It is easier to manage, secure, and deploy. However, as the application grows, it becomes increasingly difficult to scale and maintain. Microservices architecture, on the other hand, breaks down the application into smaller, more manageable services, similar to the multi-room apartment. Each service is like a room with a specific function, and they all need to communicate with each other to form a complete application.

While each microservice is simpler and lighter than the entire monolithic application, the overall system complexity increases. This is because each microservice is essentially a subset of an application and needs to communicate with other services through various channels. These channels wouldn't exist in a monolithic model. Therefore, the entire network of microservices and communication channels needs to be managed, orchestrated, and secured, adding layers of complexity and potential security risks.

Complexity of communication channels

In a monolithic system, the components are tightly coupled, and communication happens within the same system memory. However, in a microservices architecture, services often run in different environments, possibly even scattered across multiple servers or clouds. They communicate over the network using APIs or messaging queues. This network-based communication introduces latency and the risk of data breaches if not properly secured. It is like having more doors and windows in our multi-room apartment, each requiring its own lock and security mechanism.

Orchestrating chaos

Managing a microservices architecture is like being a conductor in an orchestra where each musician plays a different instrument. The conductor ensures that everyone plays in harmony. Similarly, in a complex microservices environment, you need an orchestrator such as Kubernetes to manage the services, ensure they communicate correctly, and keep the system running smoothly. Without proper orchestration, the services can fall out of sync, leading to system failures or security vulnerabilities.

Security implications

The complexity of a microservices architecture inherently increases the attack surface. Each service, its communication channel, and the orchestrator itself can be potential points of failure or exploitation. In our multi-room apartment analogy, each room, door, window, pipe, and wire is a potential security risk. They can be exploited to gain unauthorized access or disrupt the service. Therefore, each element needs to be individually secured, requiring complex access control mechanisms.

In summary, while microservices offer numerous advantages in terms of scalability and flexibility, they introduce a new paradigm of complexity, especially concerning security. Each microservice, its communication channels, and the orchestration layer add variables that need to be managed and secured. This complexity is not just an operational challenge but a significant security concern that requires meticulous planning, robust security mechanisms, and continuous monitoring to mitigate risks effectively.

Responsibility domain shift

Building on the foundational understanding of the AWS shared responsibility model discussed in *Chapter 1*; it is crucial to delve deeper into how this model evolves when we transition from monolithic architectures to microservices-based systems. The shift is not merely a technical one; it also involves a significant alteration in the responsibility domain, particularly when these microservices are deployed in cloud environments such as AWS.

Shift in computing models

As we touched upon in *Chapter 1*, different AWS compute services, such as EC2, Fargate, and Lambda, come with varying levels of responsibility for the customer. In traditional EC2-based monolithic applications, you manage everything from the guest OS upwards. However, with microservices often leveraging managed services, such as Fargate or Lambda, the responsibility shifts more towards AWS. This aligns with the trend we noted earlier: modern applications based on microservices are increasingly using managed cloud-native services due to their agility and ease of use, thereby shifting more responsibility toward the **cloud service provider** (**CSP**).

Rethinking access control

Traditional monolithic applications often rely on network-level security controls such as firewalls. However, in a microservices environment running on cloud-native platforms, you lose some of this network-level control. This necessitates a change in how access control is implemented.

Instead of relying solely on network-level security mechanisms, you need to adopt a more granular approach to access control. This involves assigning well-defined roles and policies to different resources and services within your microservices architecture. For example, you might use IAM to define who can access specific services down to the method level in an API. This is crucial because, in a microservices environment, the services often need to communicate with each other, and each interaction is a potential security touchpoint.

Lightweight components

In the world of microservices, there exists an interesting paradox when it comes to security. On the one hand, the overall architecture of an application built on microservices is inherently more complex, thereby increasing the attack surface. On the other hand, each individual microservice is a lightweight component with a minimal attack surface, thanks to its simplicity and ephemeral nature. This duality presents both challenges and opportunities in securing microservices-based applications.

Security benefits

The lightweight and ephemeral nature of these containers offers significant security advantages. With fewer lines of code and fewer dependencies, the attack surface for each individual microservice is reduced. Additionally, the ephemeral nature of containers—often having shorter lifespans compared to traditional monolithic components—means that even if a container is compromised, it is less likely to be a persistent threat.

Balancing complexity and simplicity

While the lightweight nature of individual microservices offers security, it is imperative to keep the broader architectural complexity in view. The overall complexity of the application still exists and requires a comprehensive security strategy. However, understanding the benefits and limitations of lightweight components can help in crafting a more nuanced and effective approach to both security and operations.

In conclusion, the complexity and flexibility inherent in microservices architectures necessitate a rethinking of traditional security models, a task made even more critical when deploying these services in cloud environments such as AWS.

Securing communication between services

Unlike monolithic architectures, where components often reside in the same memory space, microservices communicate over a network, which exposes them to a variety of security risks. Their distributed nature introduces multiple points of interaction, each of which could be a potential security vulnerability. This section aims to provide a deep dive into implementing secure communication methods between microservices.

Zero trust principle

The zero trust model is founded on the principle of **never trust, always verify**, which is especially crucial in microservices architecture. In such an environment, each microservice operates in its own isolated container or virtual machine and often interacts with multiple other services. This distributed nature makes it imperative to ensure that every service is authenticated and authorized before it can communicate with another service.

In the AWS ecosystem, several services and features can be employed to enact zero trust architecture. With IAM, you can specify which services allow communication with each other and what kind of data they can access or modify. Security groups act as virtual firewalls that limit the types of traffic that are allowed to pass through, thereby reducing the attack surface.

By setting up stringent rules using both IAM and security groups, you can create a robust zero-trust environment. This ensures that even if an attacker gains access to one service, they cannot easily move laterally across other services.

Types of communication

In a microservices architecture, the way services communicate with each other is of paramount importance for both functionality and security. Communication between services can be broadly categorized into two types: synchronous and asynchronous.

Synchronous communication

In synchronous communication, a service sends a request to another service and waits for a response before continuing its operation. This is commonly seen in RESTful APIs, where one service calls another via HTTP/HTTPS and waits for the response. While this method is straightforward and easy to implement, it does introduce latency, as the calling service is blocked until it receives a response.

From a security standpoint, synchronous communication often requires robust authentication and authorization mechanisms. In the AWS ecosystem, you can use Amazon API Gateway along with IAM roles to secure your RESTful APIs. API Gateway provides features such as rate limiting, data validation, and API keys, which can be crucial for securing your endpoints.

We will cover APIs and API Gateway in more detail later in this section.

Asynchronous communication

Asynchronous communication, on the other hand, decouples the calling service from the called service using messaging protocols. In this model, the calling service pushes a message and continues its operation without waiting for a response. Asynchronous methods can act as a buffer between microservices components and are particularly useful for operations that are time-consuming and don't require an immediate response.

This mode of communication is often implemented using services such as Amazon SNS and Amazon SQS, among others. Each plays distinct roles, offering different advantages depending on the use case. While SQS is generally used for point-to-point message queuing, SNS excels in a pub-sub messaging pattern using topics, allowing messages to be broadcast to multiple subscribers.

Security in asynchronous communication is often more complex due to the decoupled nature of the services. The message queue (for SQS) or topic (for SNS) itself becomes a critical asset that needs to be secured. Unauthorized access to the queue or topic can lead to data leakage or data manipulation.

However, AWS offers several features to secure your messages and queues. For instance, you can encrypt the messages using AWS KMS and implement IAM role permissions that strictly define which services can publish or subscribe to a particular queue or topic.

Synchronous vs. asynchronous

The choice between synchronous and asynchronous communication depends on various factors such as latency, complexity, and security requirements. Understanding these differences is crucial for designing a secure and efficient microservices architecture.

Comparison

The following table (*Table 6.2*) provides a comprehensive comparison between synchronous and asynchronous communication across various dimensions:

Criteria	Synchronous communication	Asynchronous communication
Communication model	Request-response model	Message sent to a queue or a topic
Coupling	Tightly coupled (coupled downstream services)	Loosely coupled (decoupled components)
Latency	Higher	Lower
Complexity	Lower	Higher
Handling failures	No transmission re-attempt (information is lost if a service crashes)	Allows for failures and retries (message stays in the queue until confirmed)
Security	Requires robust authentication and authorization	More complex due to the decoupled nature

Table 6.2 – Comparison between synchronous and asynchronous communication

Use cases

Here are some common use cases where each type of communication is most advantageous:

- **Real-time operations**: Synchronous communication is often preferred for real-time data fetching, user authentication, and transactional operations where immediate feedback is crucial.

- **Long-running and event-driven tasks**: Asynchronous communication is ideal for long-running processes such as video encoding, event-driven architectures, and batch-processing tasks that don't require an immediate response.

- **Fault tolerance and scalability**: Both synchronous and asynchronous methods have their roles in building fault-tolerant and scalable systems. Synchronous methods are generally used for crucial operations requiring immediate consistency, while asynchronous methods are used for operations that can afford to be retried or delayed.

- **Hybrid systems**: In complex applications that require both real-time user interactions and background processing, a mix of synchronous and asynchronous communication is often employed.

Data in transit encryption

Data in transit encryption is a non-negotiable requirement for securing microservices communication, both synchronous and asynchronous. It plays a pivotal role in ensuring that the data packets transmitted between services are encrypted, thereby safeguarding them from unauthorized interception or tampering. This is especially crucial in a distributed architecture where services are often decoupled and may reside in different network zones.

Transport layer security (TLS)

TLS is a widely adopted protocol for encrypting data in transit. While AWS services such as SQS, SNS, and API Gateway natively enforce TLS, it is important to note that TLS must also be explicitly configured when you are implementing custom data flows between microservices that don't rely on AWS-managed services for communication. This may involve configuring your code to initiate and accept TLS-encrypted connections, which often require additional libraries and dependencies.

While standard TLS provides data encryption with server-side authentication, **mutual TLS (mTLS)** takes it a step further by requiring both the client and the server to authenticate each other. This is particularly useful in scenarios where you need to ensure that both parties in the communication are trustworthy. AWS services such as API Gateway offer native mTLS support, allowing you to enforce strict security policies that require both client and server-side X.509 certificates.

Certificate management

In the context of TLS, managing certificates becomes a critical aspect of security. Certificates are used to authenticate the services and encrypt data in transit. Here are some of the methods used for certificate management in AWS:

- **AWS certificate manager (ACM)**: ACM is a convenient tool for provisioning, managing, and deploying TLS certificates. It offers seamless integration with various AWS services, simplifying the process of setting up and managing certificates for your microservices.

- **ACM private CA**: This is ideal for microservices that require secure communication but are not exposed to the public internet; ACM Private CA allows for the issuance and management of private certificates. These certificates are trusted within your organization, enhancing the security of internal communications.

- **Self-managed alternative**: For organizations with specific compliance requirements, managing their own **public key infrastructure (PKI)** can be a viable option. This approach includes establishing your own CA, issuing certificates, and handling renewals. While it provides greater control, it also involves significant operational overhead, encompassing tasks such as certificate rotation, revocation, and secure storage.

Service mesh

In a microservices architecture, a service mesh serves as a dedicated infrastructure layer that abstracts the complexity of service-to-service communication into a configurable infrastructure layer. It provides a range of functionalities, from load balancing and traffic routing to security and observability. This allows developers to focus on business logic while operators can concentrate on network configuration, security, and observability without altering the application code.

AWS App Mesh works well with container services and platforms such as ECS, EKS, and Kubernetes, providing a unified layer that brings together various AWS services and features. It offers a cohesive approach to securing service-to-service communication across multiple types of computing environments:

- **mTLS support**: Ensures secure service-to-service communication through mutual authentication
- **Fine-grained access control**: Allows the definition of detailed access control policies for enhanced security
- **Circuit breaking**: Implements advanced security measures to prevent cascading failures and gracefully manages overload conditions that could lead to DoS
- **AWS CloudWatch integration**: Provides comprehensive metrics and logs for monitoring the health and performance of services, crucial for auditing and compliance
- **AWS X-Ray integration**: Offers the capability to trace requests across the service mesh, providing valuable insights into latencies and aiding in the optimization of service performance

While AWS App Mesh is a fully managed service mesh that integrates seamlessly with AWS services, there are also alternative solutions for those who may not be entirely within the AWS ecosystem. Istio and Linkerd are alternatives that offer similar functionalities and can be integrated into Kubernetes-based environments. By incorporating a service mesh functionality into your microservices architecture, you gain a powerful tool for enhancing security, simplifying management, and improving observability in service-to-service communication.

Application programming interfaces (APIs)

APIs are the linchpins in a microservices architecture, acting as the front door to your microservices. They serve as the essential connectors that facilitate seamless interactions between different services and external consumers. Their adaptability allows them to be consumed by a diverse array of clients, including web browsers, mobile apps, and third-party services, making them indispensable in modern software architectures.

One of the standout features of APIs is their ability to hide the underlying programming complexity. They offer a simplified interface that allows developers to interact with a system without getting entangled in the intricacies of inter-service communication. This abstraction enables developers to focus more on building features and less on the complexities of network protocols or data serialization.

In addition to their role as facilitators of communication, APIs also serve a vital function in security. They often act as a secure frontend that exposes your backend services to consumers. By functioning as a secure proxy, they ensure that only authorized requests can access the backend services. This is particularly important for maintaining the security and integrity of a microservices architecture. When integrated with AWS services such as API Gateway, they offer additional layers of security such as authentication, rate limiting, and data validation.

The following figure (*Figure 6.8*) shows how an API can be used to allow various types of clients to communicate with a microservice using the HTTP protocol:

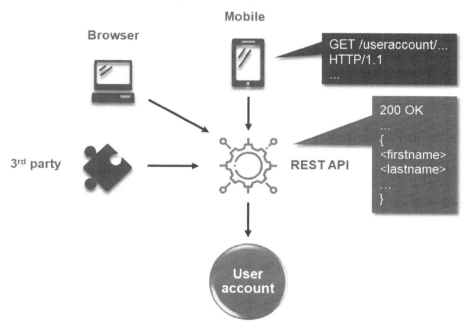

Figure 6.8 – API-enabled communication with microservices

API Gateway

Amazon API Gateway is a comprehensive, fully managed service that streamlines the process of creating, deploying, and managing APIs. In a microservices architecture, it serves as a robust frontend, handling a multitude of tasks associated with processing API calls. These tasks range from traffic management and authorization to access control and monitoring. In the following image, some of the key features and functionalities that make API Gateway indispensable in a secure microservices environment can be seen.

The following diagram (*Figure 6.9*) illustrates API Gateway implementation in a microservices environment:

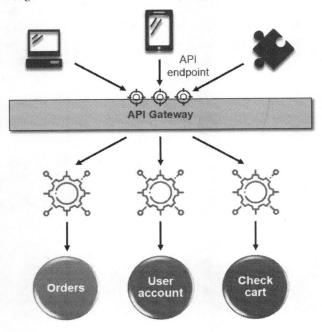

Figure 6.9 – API Gateway implementation

Types of APIs

Several types of APIs can be implemented using API Gateway:

- **RESTful APIs**: These are the most common and are ideal for **Create, Read, Update, and Delete (CRUD)** operations and stateless interactions between services.

- **HTTP APIs**: This is a more cost-effective and optimized option, specifically designed for low-latency communication and serverless workloads.

- **WebSocket APIs**: These facilitate real-time, bidirectional communication between the server and the client, making them useful for applications such as chat services and real-time notifications.

- **Private APIs**: These are restricted within a VPC and are not publicly accessible, making them suitable for secure, internal communications between microservices.

API Gateway security

API Gateway offers a suite of security features that are essential for managing, securing, and optimizing APIs in a microservices architecture. These features include the following:

- **Traffic management**: One of the standout features of API Gateway is its ability to manage traffic effectively. It offers rate limiting and throttling options that help you control the number of requests hitting your backend services. This is particularly useful in a microservices setup where multiple services are publicly exposed. By setting up API keys and usage plans, you can manage the rate at which individual clients can make requests, thereby preventing abuse and ensuring fair usage.

- **Authorization and authentication**: API Gateway integrates seamlessly with IAM, Cognito, and third-party **identity providers (IdPs)**. This allows you to implement robust authentication and authorization layers for your APIs without the need for custom-built solutions. For example, you can use IAM roles to specify who can create, deploy, and manage your APIs or use Cognito to provide user pools for API access. API Gateway also supports mTLS, adding an extra layer of security by ensuring both client and server are authenticated before data exchange. You can use ACM to provision, manage, and deploy these certificates, making the process seamless and integrated.

- **Deployment and versioning**: API Gateway offers the flexibility to deploy APIs in multiple environments, such as development, testing, and production. This is managed through stages, making it easier to introduce new features without affecting existing users. Versioning is also supported, allowing you to maintain different versions of an API simultaneously, which is crucial for backward compatibility.

- **Caching and performance optimization**: The built-in caching capabilities of API Gateway enable you to cache endpoint responses. This reduces the load on your backend services and improves the overall performance of your APIs. You can customize the cache settings, including cache size and **time-to-live** (**TTL**) values, to suit the specific needs of your application.

- **Data validation and transformation**: API Gateway provides various mechanisms for request and response validation. You can validate incoming requests against a predefined schema, ensuring that only well-formed requests are processed. Additionally, you can transform request and response payloads by integrating Lambda functions. This offers an extra layer of flexibility and security, as you can implement custom logic to manipulate the data as it passes through the API Gateway.

By leveraging these features, API Gateway stands out as a versatile tool in securing and optimizing API interactions in a microservices environment.

Implementing fine-grained access control

The decentralized nature of microservices demands a nuanced approach to access control. This section aims to guide you through the advanced techniques and AWS services that can help you achieve a high level of access control.

IAM as the backbone

While the foundational role of IAM in AWS security was extensively covered in *Chapter 3*, its specialized application in a microservices framework deserves a deeper look. Given the distributed and often complex nature of microservices, IAM offers a set of tools that enable the creation of secure, scalable, and finely tuned access control architecture.

Role-based access

In a microservices setup, each service typically performs specialized tasks and requires access to specific AWS resources. By crafting IAM roles with permissions tailored to the unique needs of each microservice, you can adhere to the principle of least privilege. Importantly, long-term credentials such as IAM user access keys should be avoided to minimize security risks.

As an example, consider two microservices `ImageProcessor` and `DataAnalyzer`. The `ImageProcessor` microservice needs to read and write to a specific S3 bucket, while `DataAnalyzer` requires read-only access to a DynamoDB table. You can create two distinct IAM roles: one with `s3:GetObject` and `s3:PutObject` permissions for the S3 bucket, and another with `dynamodb:GetItem` permissions for the DynamoDB table. This nuanced approach ensures that each service has only the permissions it absolutely needs.

Assumed roles

There are scenarios where a microservice may need temporary access to an AWS resource. In such cases, assumed roles are preferable to permanent roles as they offer short-lived privileges, thereby reducing the risk associated with long-lived privileges.

As an example, if a microservice needs to temporarily write data to a DynamoDB table for an ad-hoc batch operation, it can assume a role with the necessary permissions, perform the operation, and then relinquish the role, allowing the assumed role to expire.

Cross-account access

For organizations that have microservices spread across multiple AWS accounts, IAM supports cross-account roles. This enables secure inter-service communication across different accounts.

In some organizations, different microservices may reside in different AWS accounts. IAM allows for cross-account roles, where a service in one account can assume a role in another account, facilitating inter-service communication securely.

As an example, a microservice in a 'Billing' AWS account may need to fetch data from a 'DataLake' AWS account. A cross-account IAM role can facilitate this interaction, with permissions explicitly defining the allowed actions. It is important to restrict the permissions to only what is absolutely necessary for the task at hand.

IAM and API Gateway

When microservices are exposed through API Gateway, IAM roles can be specifically configured to regulate access to these APIs. You can set up resource-based policies in API Gateway that specify which IAM roles are allowed to invoke your API methods. This adds an additional layer of security, ensuring that only specific roles or authorized microservices can invoke the API.

Secure end-user authentication

Securing end-user authentication within a microservices ecosystem is both a challenging and essential task. While IAM is highly effective for managing service-to-service interactions, it falls short when it comes to providing a nuanced, user-centric authentication mechanism tailored for end-users. This is where Cognito comes into play, offering a more specialized approach to end-user authentication.

Amazon Cognito

Cognito is more than just a managed service for end-user authentication and identity management. A microservices architecture can serve as a centralized identity hub that can be accessed by various microservices for tasks ranging from identity verification to role-based access control and beyond.

User pool

User pools in Cognito act as user directories that facilitate sign-in capabilities through Cognito or third-party **IdPs**, such as Google, Facebook, or enterprise SAML-based systems. In a microservices architecture, user pools become the centralized hub for identity storage, offering a unified view of user identities across various services.

Custom attributes in user pools allow you to store application-specific user metadata, such as user roles or department codes. These attributes can be configured to be immutable once set, thereby enhancing the security of user accounts. This is particularly useful in scenarios where a microservice needs to make access decisions based on these custom attributes.

Multi-factor authentication (MFA) is another feature you might want to enable. It is a robust, adaptive system that can challenge users based on a variety of risk factors. For example, if a user attempts to log in from a new device or an unusual geographic location, Cognito can trigger additional authentication challenges, thereby adding an extra layer of security.

Identity pool

Identity pools are particularly useful for granting temporary AWS credentials to end-users for direct access to AWS resources. They can also federate identities from multiple user pools or IdPs.

To achieve a more granular level of access control, you can map federated identities to IAM roles with specific permissions. This is especially useful when you need to segregate access based on the source of federated identity. For example, users authenticated via an IdP might be mapped to a role with more restricted permissions compared to users authenticated via the enterprise's SAML-based IdP.

Identity tokens

Identity tokens, often implemented as **JSON web tokens** (**JWT**), serve as a cornerstone for secure, stateless authentication in a microservices architecture. These tokens encapsulate user information and permissions in a digitally signed payload, making them ideal for transmitting data across services securely.

In a typical microservices setup, an identity token is generated upon successful user authentication. This token is then included in the HTTP header for subsequent API requests, allowing each microservice to validate the user's identity and permissions without needing to query a central database. This is particularly beneficial for scalability and performance, as it reduces the need for repetitive database calls.

OAuth2 framework

OAuth2 is a commonly used authorization framework that complements the use of identity tokens. It provides a standardized way for clients to request and manage tokens, often after the user has authenticated using a separate mechanism such as **OpenID Connect**. OAuth2 defines multiple flows for different types of clients and scenarios, such as authorization code flow for server-side apps and implicit flow for client-side apps.

In the context of Cognito and microservices, OAuth2 can be used to obtain identity tokens and access tokens. The identity tokens can then be used for user identification, while the access tokens can be used to grant permissions to various resources. This separation of concerns between identity and access makes OAuth2 a powerful tool for managing security in a microservices environment.

Identity propagation

One of the key advantages of using identity tokens in a microservices architecture is the ability to propagate identity. This means that once a service receives a token and validates it, the same token can be forwarded to other services in the chain of processing. This is crucial for maintaining a consistent and secure context throughout a multi-step transaction or workflow.

For example, if service A calls service B, which, in turn, calls service C, the identity token can be passed along this chain. Each service can validate and extract the necessary information from the token, ensuring that all actions are performed in the correct user context. This propagation of identity can be invaluable for auditing, logging, and implementing fine-grained access control across multiple services.

Practical workflow with Cognito

The following figure *(Figure 6.10)* shows the different steps involved in using identity tokens across components, as follows:

1. **User authentication and token issuance**: The end user authenticates through Cognito, possibly using MFA for added security. Upon successful authentication, Cognito issues an identity token via its OAuth2 authorization server.

2. **API request**: The client includes the identity token in the HTTP header when making an API request to a microservice.

3. **Token validation**: API Gateway receives the identity token, then validates its signature and scopes to ensure it is issued by Cognito and contains the necessary permissions.

4. **Token propagation**: If the token is valid, it is then passed to the computing layer (here, a Lambda function) running the microservice code.

5. **Exchange for credentials**: The identity token can be exchanged for temporary IAM role-based credentials. These credentials are generated based on the identity context, as defined in the IAM roles assigned to Cognito's identity pool.

6. **Resource access**: These temporary credentials are used to assume the role they are linked to and interact with other services and AWS resources. The credentials allow for fine-grained access control, as they are linked to specific IAM roles with predefined permissions.

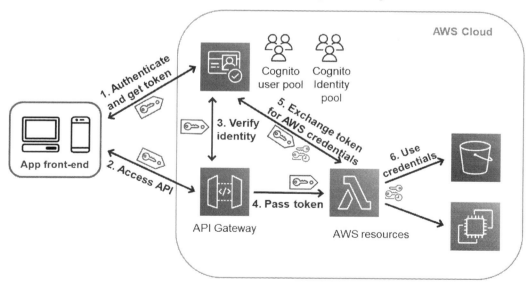

Figure 6.10 – Example using identity tokens and roles to access downstream resources

By integrating identity tokens with OAuth2 and leveraging identity propagation, you can build a robust, secure, and scalable authentication and authorization mechanism tailored for a microservices architecture.

Decoupling authorizations

When deploying microservices on AWS, one of the most intricate challenges is managing application-level authorizations. While IAM is excellent for controlling access to AWS resources, it doesn't extend to the application logic within your microservices. Amazon Verified Permissions and the Cedar policy model can fill this gap by offering a robust and scalable solution for fine-grained, application-level access control.

Amazon Verified Permissions

Verified Permissions is a service designed to provide fine-grained authorizations within applications, operating independently from IAM. It employs Cedar, an open source policy language focused on security, to facilitate **policy-based access control (PBAC)**. This becomes crucial in complex microservices architectures where granular and context-sensitive permissions are essential.

The key features and integrations of Verified Permissions are the following:

- **Schema definition**: At the core of Verified Permissions is the schema definition process. This involves outlining each entity type within your application along with its corresponding attributes. This schema acts as a foundational blueprint, ensuring that your policies are precisely aligned with your application's unique authorization requirements.

- **Policy store**: The service includes a policy store that acts as a central repository for these policies. Its multi-tenancy capabilities allow distinct configurations and schema rules for each tenant. This feature is instrumental in ensuring data isolation and preventing unauthorized access across different tenants.

- **Integration with application logic**: Verified Permissions seamlessly integrate into your application's logic. For example, when a user attempts to perform an action, your application can instantly call the Verified Permissions service to verify the user's authorization for that action. This real-time integration allows for dynamic, context-aware authorization, adapting to the evolving needs of your application.

- **Integration with Cognito**: The service also offers smooth integration with Cognito, enabling the direct transfer of attributes from your IdP into policy evaluation. This integration is especially beneficial for contextualizing authorization decisions. For instance, role information such as 'Admin' and 'User' can be transmitted from Cognito to Verified Permissions. Such integration allows for nuanced access decisions in microservices based on roles and additional contextual data.

Policy-based access control (PBAC)

Before delving into the Cedar policy model, it is important to understand PBAC, which is the broader concept that Verified Permissions leverages. PBAC is more dynamic than **role-based access control** (**RBAC**), allowing for real-time evaluation of contextual information. Unlike RBAC, which is rigid and role-centric, or **attribute-based access control** (**ABAC**), which is flexible but can become complex, PBAC offers a balanced approach. It allows you to manage permissions using high-level policies, making it particularly useful in microservices architectures where you need to manage a multitude of fine-grained permissions across various services.

PBAC provides enhanced flexibility and scalability in your authorization strategy. It allows you to define policies that can be globally applied across multiple services, thereby reducing complexity and administrative overhead.

Verified Permissions is a concrete implementation of PBAC that is designed to work seamlessly in AWS environments.

Cedar policy model

Cedar, is designed to separate business logic from application-level authorization logic. This separation is crucial for enhancing security and simplifying application development. When your microservices receive a request, it can be prefaced with a call to the Cedar authorization engine. This engine evaluates the request in real time, determining whether it should be allowed or denied based on your defined policies.

Before delving into the Cedar policy example, it is worth noting that Cedar's syntax is designed for readability and expressiveness. Each policy statement consists of conditions (when) and permissions (permit or deny), making it intuitive to define complex authorization rules. For instance, let's say you have a policy that allows only Cognito users with a custom attribute `Department` set to the value HR to delete a specific file. In Cedar, this could be represented as the following:

```
permit(
  principal,
  action == Action::"delete",
  resource == File::"payroll.csv"
)
when {principal.custom.department == "HR"};
```

This policy can be evaluated in real time as requests come into your microservices, ensuring that only users with the HR department attribute are allowed to delete the specified file.

By isolating application-level authorization logic from the core business logic, Cedar allows developers to focus on building features and improving the user experience without compromising security.

In conclusion, the combination of IAM, Cognito, and Verified Permissions provides a robust framework for achieving fine-grained access control in a microservices architecture deployed on AWS.

Summary

In this comprehensive chapter, we delved into the world of microservices, starting with a critical evaluation of why they are increasingly becoming the architecture of choice. We contrasted the monolithic and microservices approaches, weighing their respective pros and cons, and provided use cases to help you make an informed decision. The chapter then transitioned into the complex landscape of security considerations unique to microservices. We discussed the paradigm shift in complexity and responsibilities, emphasizing the need for a new approach to access control and security measures. We also explored the zero trust principle and the importance of encryption, along with the types of communication—synchronous and asynchronous. AWS App Mesh and Amazon API Gateway were introduced as essential tools for managing and securing service-to-service communication. The latter part of the chapter focused on implementing fine-grained access control, highlighting the role of IAM and the utilization of Amazon Cognito for end-user authentication. We also discussed the need to decouple authorizations using AWS Verified Permissions.

As we transition to the next chapter, we will build on these foundational principles to focus on the unique security considerations of serverless deployments on AWS, which are commonly used to implement microservices architectures.

Questions

Answer the following questions to test your knowledge of this chapter:

1. What are the security implications of complexity in a microservices architecture?
2. How does the lightweight nature of microservices affect security?
3. What are identity tokens, and how are they used?
4. How do IAM, Cognito, and Verified Permissions work together?

Answers

Here are the answers to this chapter's questions:

1. The complexity increases the attack surface. Each service, its communication channel, and even the orchestrator can be potential points of failure or exploitation. Therefore, each element needs to be individually secured, requiring sophisticated access control mechanisms.
2. Each individual microservice is a lightweight component with a minimal attack surface, thanks to its simplicity. With fewer lines of code and fewer dependencies, the attack surface for each individual microservice is reduced. Additionally, the ephemeral nature of containers means that even if a container is compromised, it is less likely to be a persistent threat.

3. Identity tokens, commonly in the form of JWT, securely represent user information between multiple parties. In a microservices architecture, these tokens are crucial for securely propagating identity and claims between downstream services, aiding in both auditing and fine-grained access control.

4. IAM, Cognito, and Verified Permissions collectively provide a robust framework for achieving fine-grained access control in a microservices architecture. While IAM handles service-to-service interactions, Cognito specializes in end-user authentication, and Verified Permissions focuses on fine-grained, application-level access control.

Further reading

The following resources offer further insights and best practices for VPC security:

- AWS Whitepaper – *Implementing Microservices on AWS*: `https://docs.aws.amazon.com/pdfs/whitepapers/latest/microservices-on-aws/microservices-on-aws.pdf`

- *Security and Microservice Architecture on AWS* by Gaurav Raje (2021). O'Reilly Media, ISBN 1098101464.

- *8 fundamental microservices security best practices* by Joydip Kanjilal (2021): `https://www.techtarget.com/searchapparchitecture/tip/4-fundamental-microservices-security-best-practices`

7

Implementing Security for Serverless Deployments

Welcome to the seventh chapter of our comprehensive guide on AWS security. In this chapter, we will focus on serverless computing and its unique impact on security within AWS environments. We aim to equip you with the knowledge and skills needed to navigate the distinct security landscape presented by serverless architectures. we will begin by demystifying serverless computing, exploring its benefits, challenges, and how it compares to traditional microservices. Next, we will delve into the function-based design paradigm, focusing on the granularity and composition of serverless functions, along with their inherent stateless nature.

As we progress, we will bring the concept of event-driven communication into sharp focus. Understanding this is crucial as we transition into a detailed discussion on event-driven security mechanisms, covering topics from event sources and schema validation to data encryption.

We will then proceed to an in-depth exploration of securing AWS Lambda functions. This section is vital as it covers key security aspects, such as code integrity, environment variables, runtime protection, and effective monitoring and logging strategies.

By the end of this chapter, you will have a well-rounded understanding of the security considerations that are specific to serverless architectures. You will be equipped to design, deploy, and secure serverless applications, appreciating the nuances that differentiate them from traditional cloud architectures.

In this chapter, we will cover the following key areas:

- Introduction to serverless, including its benefits, challenges, and security considerations
- Event-driven security, covering event sources, schema validation, and data encryption
- Securing Lambda functions, with topics such as code integrity, runtime protection, and monitoring

Introduction to serverless security

As we transition from the concept of microservices, which we discussed in the previous chapter, it is essential to understand that serverless architectures are not just an evolution but a specialized form of microservices. While microservices have their own set of security challenges, serverless introduces a new landscape of security considerations that are both unique and complex. This section aims to delve into these aspects before getting more in-depth into specific areas of serverless security.

What is serverless?

First, let's demystify things around serverless. Serverless is a cloud computing execution model where cloud providers automatically manage the infrastructure. In serverless computing, developers write code that is executed in response to events, such as HTTP requests, database modifications, or even changes in system state or periodical execution. Behind the scenes, the cloud provider dynamically allocates resources to run the code. When an event trigger is received, a runtime environment is instantiated, the code is executed, and the output is returned. Once the function execution is complete, the environment is torn down, freeing up resources. This ephemeral, event-driven nature of serverless computing allows for highly efficient resource utilization and simplifies many operational aspects.

Benefits of serverless

Serverless services offer a plethora of advantages that make them an attractive option for modern software development. The following are some of the key benefits of serverless:

- **Efficiency**: Unlike traditional server-based models, where you pay for pre-allocated resources regardless of usage, serverless operates on a *pay-as-you-go* model. This means you only incur costs for the actual amount of resources consumed by your functions during their execution. Additionally, serverless platforms automatically allocate resources as needed, ensuring that each function has just the right amount of computational power and memory to complete its task efficiently. This dual advantage of cost savings and optimal resource utilization makes serverless an economically attractive option, especially for applications with variable or unpredictable workloads.

- **Scalability**: Serverless architectures are inherently scalable. The cloud provider takes on the responsibility of automatically scaling the function instances up or down depending on the incoming traffic or event triggers. This native auto-scaling capability eliminates the need for manual intervention, making it easier to handle varying workloads without worrying about infrastructure limitations.

- **Availability**: Serverless architectures are designed for high availability and fault tolerance. Cloud providers typically distribute serverless function instances across multiple availability zones in a region, ensuring that your application remains operational, even if one zone experiences an outage. This level of redundancy is generally built-in and managed by the cloud provider, so you don't have to configure or manage it yourself. For mission-critical applications where downtime is not an option, the inherent high availability of serverless computing is a significant advantage.

- **Simplicity**: Serverless allows developers to focus solely on their code, abstracting away most of the underlying infrastructure and server management tasks. This leads to quicker development cycles as developers no longer need to spend time on tasks such as server provisioning, patching, and maintenance. The serverless model enables rapid deployment and updating, allowing businesses to react faster to market changes or customer needs.

Challenges in serverless architectures

While serverless offers numerous advantages, it also presents its own set of challenges that developers and architects should be aware of. These challenges often require a new paradigm and way of thinking when deploying serverless architectures as they differ significantly from traditional server-based models. The following are some of the key challenges in serverless architectures:

- **Cold starts**: One of the most talked-about challenges in serverless is the *cold start* phenomenon. When a function is invoked after being idle, it may take a noticeable amount of time to start up, affecting the latency of the application. This is particularly problematic for latency-sensitive applications.

- **State management**: Serverless functions are stateless by design, which means they do not retain any internal state between invocations. While this is advantageous for scalability, it complicates state management and may require external services to manage the state, adding complexity and potential latency. Various strategies, such as provisioned concurrency, can be employed to mitigate this issue, but it remains a concern.

- **Debugging and monitoring**: Serverless architectures can make traditional debugging and monitoring approaches less straightforward. The ephemeral nature of serverless functions means they come into existence only when invoked and disappear afterward, making it challenging to trace issues and collect metrics. Moreover, the distributed nature of serverless functions, often running in isolated, stateless containers, adds another layer of complexity to debugging and monitoring. Tools specifically designed for serverless monitoring are often required.

- **Vendor lock-in**: Serverless architectures are often closely tied to the capabilities and limitations of the cloud provider. This can make it difficult to migrate serverless applications between different cloud providers without significant modifications.

- **Resource limits**: Serverless functions have limitations on resources such as memory, execution time, and package size. These constraints can be a challenge for certain types of applications that require long-running processes or large amounts of memory. However, these limitations can often be addressed by re-architecting applications. For example, functionalities can be split into multiple functions to better fit within the resource constraints, thereby optimizing performance and resource utilization.

Comparison with microservices

Serverless architecture can be considered a specialized form of microservices architecture. In a traditional microservices setup, each service is designed to perform a specific function or process and can be deployed, scaled, and managed independently. However, serverless takes this concept a step further by breaking down services into even smaller, more granular components – functions. These functions are event-driven, meaning they are invoked only in response to specific triggers or events, and they are managed entirely by the cloud provider.

In serverless, the level of abstraction is higher, and the granularity is finer compared to traditional microservices. While a microservice might be responsible for an entire business capability, a serverless function could be responsible for just a single, specific task within that capability. This allows for even more flexibility and scalability but also introduces unique challenges in terms of state management and resource allocation, as discussed earlier.

Therefore, the serverless model offers a more extreme form of decoupling, allowing each function to be developed, deployed, and scaled independently. This makes serverless architecture incredibly agile and cost-effective, but it also requires a different approach to design, monitoring, and security compared to traditional microservices.

Use cases for serverless

Serverless architectures are incredibly versatile, catering to a wide range of use cases across various industries and applications. Here are some common scenarios where serverless shines:

- **Extract, transform, load** (**ETL**): ETL processes can be efficiently handled by serverless functions. They can be triggered by changes in data within databases such as DynamoDB tables, transforming and loading the data into other systems or analytics platforms.

- **Internet of things** (**IoT**) **applications**: The event-driven nature of serverless is well-suited for IoT applications. Serverless functions can process and analyze data from IoT devices in real time, enabling quick decision-making and automation.

- **Microservices**: Serverless is often used to implement individual microservices within a larger architecture. Each function acts as a self-contained unit of deployment, making it easier to manage, scale, and update.

- **Mobile back-ends**: Serverless is popular for mobile application backends, where its auto-scaling capabilities can easily accommodate the variable workloads typical of consumer-facing apps.

Function-based design

In serverless architectures, the primary unit of deployment and execution is the function. This function-based design paradigm offers a high degree of modularity, allowing developers to break down complex applications into smaller, more manageable pieces. This approach contrasts with traditional monolithic or even non-serverless microservices architectures, where the unit of deployment is often much larger. Each function is designed to perform a specific task and can be invoked independently, making it easier to develop, test, and deploy individual components. This approach also facilitates code reuse, as functions can be shared across different services or even different applications. This leads us to consider two key aspects of function-based design: granularity in function composition and state management.

Granularity and function composition

Granularity refers to the size and scope of a function in terms of its responsibilities and the resources it consumes. In serverless, the aim is often to make functions as granular as possible, focusing each on a specific task or operation. This granularity allows for more efficient scaling and better resource utilization.

Function composition involves combining multiple granular functions to perform more complex tasks. This can be done sequentially or in parallel, depending on the application's needs. For example, one function could handle user authentication, another could retrieve data from a database, and a third could perform some form of data transformation. When composed together, these functions could provide a complete end-to-end service.

Stateless versus stateful functions

Serverless functions are stateless, meaning they do not maintain any internal state between invocations. Each function invocation is independent, and any required state must be passed in as input parameters or managed externally. Stateless functions are easier to scale and manage as they can be freely instantiated and terminated without affecting other instances.

However, there are scenarios where stateful behavior is required, such as multi-step workflows or long-running transactions. In such cases, a state can be managed using external data stores such as Amazon DynamoDB or Amazon S3, or through orchestration with AWS Step Functions, which allows Lambda functions to pass data between each other via the state machine definition. It is worth noting that using external data stores for stateful behavior introduces security considerations, such as the need for secure data storage and transmission.

Event-driven communication

In serverless architectures, the concept of event-driven communication plays a pivotal role. Unlike traditional request-response models, serverless functions are often invoked by events – these could be anything from a new file being uploaded to a cloud storage service, a new record being inserted into a database, or a message being posted to a message queue. This event-driven, asynchronous model aligns perfectly with the serverless paradigm, enabling highly responsive, scalable, and efficient applications.

Events act as triggers that initiate function execution. Once an event occurs, the cloud provider's serverless platform takes care of instantiating the runtime environment, executing the function, and then tearing it down. This seamless orchestration of events and functions is what makes serverless architectures so powerful for building real-time, dynamic applications.

Event-driven communication in serverless architectures extends beyond merely triggering functions; it also encompasses function-to-function and inter-service communication. Functions can publish events to message queues, event buses, or directly to other services, fostering loosely coupled, highly cohesive architectures. In this context, Amazon EventBridge serves as a pivotal event bus, routing events from various sources to the appropriate services and functions.

Security considerations

In the realm of serverless architectures, security takes on a unique set of challenges and opportunities. While serverless eliminates certain traditional security concerns, such as patching and server maintenance, it introduces new areas that require attention. The following are some of the key security considerations specific to serverless computing:

- **Responsibility domain**: As discussed in *Chapter 1*, the responsibility domain outlines who is responsible for what in a cloud environment. In serverless architectures, the cloud provider takes on a significant portion of the security responsibilities, such as physical security, runtime environment isolation, and network traffic encryption. However, the application logic, data protection, and permissions remain the responsibility of the developers and administrators. Misconfigurations are a common pitfall, and understanding this division of responsibility is crucial for maintaining a secure serverless architecture.

- **Zero-trust architecture**: In line with the zero-trust model, serverless architectures should inherently not trust any entity – inside or outside the network. Each function invocation, data access, or inter-service communication should be authenticated and authorized. Implementing zero-trust in serverless requires a strong IAM strategy, network segmentation, and continuous monitoring to ensure that trust is never assumed and is always verified.

- **Permissions management**: The granularity of permissions allows for a high level of specificity in controlling access to resources, aligning well with the zero trust model. Each function can have its own IAM role, defining what it can and cannot do. Overly permissive functions can be a significant security risk, and the principle of least privilege should be applied. While this granularity is advantageous, it also increases the administrative burden and the potential for misconfigurations, which falls under the customer's responsibility domain.

- **Data encryption and storage**: Serverless functions often interact with various data stores, both for state management and data processing. Ensuring that data is encrypted at rest and in transit is vital. In addition, access to these data stores should be restricted to only the necessary functions or services.

- **Event data integrity**: As serverless architectures are heavily event-driven, ensuring the integrity of event data is crucial. This involves validating the sources of events and possibly implementing cryptographic methods to verify the integrity of the data being passed through events.

- **API security**: Serverless functions are often exposed via APIs, making API security a significant concern. This includes implementing proper authentication and authorization mechanisms, rate limiting, and protection against common web vulnerabilities such as SQL injection and **cross-site scripting (XSS)**. These attacks can have severe consequences. For instance, a SQL injection attack could compromise the function's access to a connected database, leading to data breaches or unauthorized data manipulation.

- **Third-party dependencies**: Serverless functions often rely on third-party libraries and services. These dependencies can introduce vulnerabilities if they are not kept up to date or if they originate from untrusted sources. Regular vulnerability scanning for third-party libraries is essential, and dependency management should be approached with caution.

- **Isolation and sandboxing**: Serverless functions run in isolated, ephemeral containers. While this provides a level of isolation, it is important to understand the limitations of this isolation in serverless environments and how that impacts the security posture. For instance, functions running in the same environment may have access to shared resources, posing a potential security risk.

- **Monitoring and logging**: Monitoring and logging are crucial aspects of security, especially in a serverless environment. Effective logging can help in identifying malicious activities, while monitoring can provide real-time alerts. Tools specifically designed for serverless monitoring should be employed to gain insights into function behavior, performance, and security incidents.

- **Compliance**: Serverless architectures often align well with compliance requirements such as GDPR, HIPAA, and other regulatory standards. The cloud provider takes on a significant portion of the compliance burden, such as ensuring the physical security of data centers and the underlying infrastructure. This offloading of responsibilities can simplify the compliance process for organizations. While the cloud provider may handle certain aspects, due diligence is required on the part of the organization to ensure that data handling, storage, and processing practices meet the necessary compliance standards. Regular audits and assessments of serverless deployments are essential to maintain a compliant serverless architecture.

In conclusion, the serverless paradigm shifts the focus from infrastructure management to code, requiring a new set of security considerations that align with its ephemeral and event-driven nature.

Event-driven security

Event-driven architectures have emerged as the bedrock of contemporary cloud-native applications, especially those leveraging serverless platforms. While these architectures offer many benefits, such as scalability and decoupling, they also present unique security challenges. This section aims to offer an in-depth exploration of these challenges, focusing on strategies for mitigation, with a specific emphasis on EventBridge.

Event sources

First and foremost, it is essential to identify and secure the event sources. These could range from API requests and message queues to cloud storage and databases. Ensuring that only authorized entities can generate events is the first line of defense in event-driven security. This often involves implementing proper authentication and authorization mechanisms, both at the event source and destination levels.

Event schema validation

EventBridge's schema registry allows event schemas to be defined, which serve as a blueprint for incoming events. This ensures that events conform to expected formats, thereby adding an extra layer of security. The schema registry can validate the structure of incoming events, ensuring they meet predefined criteria before they are processed, thereby reducing the risk of malformed or malicious data entering the system. For instance, you could set up a schema that requires all incoming events to have certain fields, and any event not meeting these criteria could be dropped and flagged for further investigation.

Event data encryption

EventBridge offers multiple avenues for encrypting event data. You can employ an AWS KMS **customer master key** (**CMK**) to encrypt both the event payloads and metadata that are stored by EventBridge. Simultaneously, you can also take advantage of AWS services that inherently support encryption, such as Amazon SNS topics or Amazon SQS queues, when configuring them as targets. In addition to this, data in transit is natively encrypted through AWS API communication, which relies on TLS protocols between the EventBridge bus, event sources, and destinations. This adds an extra layer of security to the data as it moves between components. These combined encryption measures not only protect sensitive data but also help in meeting compliance requirements.

Access control

Access control in an event-driven environment can be particularly complex due to the dynamic nature of these architectures. As always, the principle of least privilege should be thoroughly applied. EventBridge elevates this approach by allowing for granular assignment of IAM roles and policies to specific events. This ensures that events are authorized to trigger only those functions for which they have explicit permissions. This level of granularity is crucial for maintaining a secure and well-ordered system, particularly when dealing with a multitude of events and associated services. In addition, it is essential to configure IAM at both the source and the destination levels in such a way that each function or service has only the permissions it needs to perform its tasks and nothing more.

Moreover, API destinations in EventBridge can be used to send events to external HTTP endpoints requiring authentication, such as APIs or webhooks. When setting up an API destination, you have the flexibility to choose the type of authorization mechanism that suits your needs, be it basic authentication, OAuth client credentials, or API keys.

Monitoring

Monitoring is integral to the security of event-driven architectures. EventBridge seamlessly integrates with Amazon CloudWatch, offering real-time monitoring and alerting capabilities, which are invaluable for promptly identifying and addressing security issues. For example, you might closely monitor `InvocationFailureCount`, which records the number of times a rule failed to invoke a target. A spike in this metric could signify underlying issues that warrant immediate investigation. Similarly, the `MatchedEventCount` metric counts the number of events that matched a rule. An unexpected increase in this metric could signal that unauthorized or unexpected events are being generated and processed.

By selectively focusing on key metrics like these in CloudWatch, you can gain critical insights into system activity, helping you to quickly identify and address potential security issues. CloudWatch alarms can also be set to trigger notifications or automated responses, providing an additional layer of security to your event-driven architecture.

Dead-letter queues (DLQs)

DLQs serve as a safety net, capturing events that fail to reach their intended targets. These queues can be monitored to provide additional security insights, such as identifying patterns of failed deliveries that could indicate a security issue. For example, a sudden increase in the number of failed events could be a red flag for a potential DDoS attack or data store compromise.

EventBridge's support for DLQs ensures that events are not lost due to delivery failures, thereby enhancing both the reliability and security of event-driven applications. This feature is crucial for both debugging and forensic analysis in the event of security incidents, allowing investigators to examine the failed events for signs of malicious activity or vulnerabilities.

Event sourcing

Event sourcing is a pattern that can significantly bolster security by creating an immutable audit trail of events. In the context of EventBridge, this involves capturing a series of events that represent state changes in an application. For instance, consider a banking application that needs to keep track of all deposit and withdrawal events to provide a detailed account activity history. Using EventBridge, this application could capture such events from its core services and route them to a Lambda function, which then stores these events in a database for future retrieval and analysis. This creates a comprehensive log of all the events or *commands* that have altered the application's state.

By storing these events chronologically, the application can reconstruct the exact state of entities at any given point in time. This is invaluable for security analysts who may need to *rewind* the system state to analyze past security incidents. This immutable event log acts as a single source of truth, thereby strengthening the integrity and non-repudiation of security-sensitive operations.

Command query responsibility segregation (CQRS)

CQRS is an architectural pattern that significantly enhances both performance and security by distinctly segregating read and write operations into separate models. EventBridge is exceptionally well-suited for implementing CQRS patterns, serving as a centralized hub for both publishing and consuming events.

On the write side, EventBridge allows you to define rules that target AWS resources such as Lambda functions or Step Functions state machines. These rules are triggered by command events originating from various sources, such as API requests or application events. The targeted AWS resources execute the necessary business logic to process these commands and update data stores such as DynamoDB.

On the read side, you can set up separate EventBridge rules that target query or reporting functions and services. These rules are triggered by events generated from data store updates rather than command events. The targets then query these data stores to generate read models or projections that are used for reporting purposes, without interfering with the write operations.

This clear-cut segregation not only facilitates optimized and independent scaling of read and write models but also substantially reduces the attack surface area. By isolating read and write operations, you eliminate the need for read permissions to have write access and vice versa, thereby minimizing the potential for permission misuse. This focused approach to access control further enhances the overall security posture of your event-driven architecture.

In conclusion, the security challenges that are inherent in event-driven architectures are mitigated through EventBridge's features, providing a comprehensive toolkit from event sourcing to fine-grained access control.

Securing Lambda functions

Securing Lambda functions is a critical aspect of cloud-native applications running in serverless architectures. Lambda functions can be triggered by various services and external sources. This makes them a potential entry point for malicious activities. This section aims to provide a comprehensive guide to securing Lambda functions, focusing on best practices and AWS-specific features.

Code integrity

Code integrity is the foundation of any secure application. Ensuring that the code running in your Lambda functions is exactly what you expect it to be is crucial for preventing unauthorized modifications and injections. Here, we will delve into several methods to ensure the integrity of your Lambda function code.

Code signing

Code signing is a crucial method for verifying the integrity of your Lambda function code. By attaching a digital signature, Lambda ensures that only signed and authorized code packages are deployed. This process adds a robust layer of security by confirming that the code has not been altered since it was signed. Lambda allows you to configure your functions to alert or reject any deployments of unsigned code or code that is signed by unauthorized entities.

To achieve this level of security, AWS Signer is the go-to service within the AWS ecosystem. It allows you to create a signing profile by specifying the code signing configurations and certificates. Once your Lambda function code is packaged into a ZIP file and uploaded to an S3 bucket, AWS Signer takes over. It signs the code package based on the specified signing profile and returns the signed package to the designated S3 location. Finally, when deploying the function in Lambda, the service validates the signature, ensuring it aligns with the approved signing profile.

Lambda layers

Lambda layers are a distribution mechanism for libraries, custom runtimes, and other function dependencies. Layers are versioned and can be shared across multiple functions. Ensuring the integrity of these layers is equally important, as they can be a vector for malicious code. Hence, it is essential to always ensure that you are using layers from trusted sources. When using layers, make sure you apply the same level of scrutiny and security controls as you would for your primary function code. This includes code reviews, package scanning, and code signing.

Package scanning

Before deploying any code to Lambda, it is advisable to scan the code package for vulnerabilities. Various tools are available for this purpose, including AWS-native and third-party solutions. These tools can identify known security vulnerabilities in the libraries and dependencies your function uses. Regularly scanning your code packages can help you catch potential security issues before they become a problem in a live environment. This proactive approach can save time and reduce the risk associated with deploying insecure code. This topic will be covered in more detail in *Chapter 12*.

Secure environment variables

Environment variables in Lambda functions often hold sensitive information, such as API keys, database credentials, or other secrets. While Lambda encrypts these variables at rest and during function execution, additional steps can be taken to enhance the security of environment variables.

Encryption

By default, Lambda encrypts environment variables using a KMS AWS-managed key. However, for greater control, you can specify a CMK. Enabling encryption helpers can further secure these variables by encrypting them client-side before transmission. This adds an additional layer of protection against unauthorized access. To restrict access to these environment variables, you can deny access to KMS CMKs using IAM policies. It is advisable to store only non-sensitive configuration data in environment variables and use more secure options for sensitive information.

Secrets management

For a more secure approach to managing sensitive information, consider integrating AWS Systems Manager (SSM) Parameter Store and AWS Secrets Manager into your Lambda functions. Both services allow you to securely store, retrieve, and manage sensitive data. Rather than hardcoding these values into your Lambda function or storing them as plaintext in environment variables, you can reference them directly from either SSM Parameter Store or Secrets Manager. This approach allows for a separation of duties; developers can configure Lambda functions without needing direct access to the sensitive environment variables they use.

Runtime protection

Runtime protection involves safeguarding your Lambda functions while they are executing. This is crucial for preventing unauthorized activities, data leaks, and other security vulnerabilities during the function's life cycle.

Filesystem

Lambda functions operate in a read-only filesystem. However, the /tmp directory is an exception and is writable. Its read-only nature serves as a security feature by reducing the attack surface. However, the writable /tmp directory comes with its own set of security considerations.

First, it is important to note that the /tmp directory is not encrypted and is shared across invocations in the same execution environment. Given this, sensitive data should never be stored in this directory. If your function requires sensitive files to be stored temporarily, consider using encrypted S3 buckets instead.

When writing temporary data, such as session tokens or files, exercise caution. Always validate the data before writing it to the filesystem and adhere to the principle of least privilege when setting file permissions. Use secure, random generators for any temporary tokens and set them to expire after a short period. If you must use temporary files, consider encrypting them before writing and ensure they are securely deleted, or even securely wiped, as soon as they are no longer needed.

In-memory data

Lambda functions can retain state in memory between invocations, a feature commonly referred to as *warm starts*. While this can offer performance benefits, it also introduces security risks, especially if sensitive data is stored in memory. To mitigate these risks, it is crucial to clear sensitive variables from memory as soon as they are no longer needed. This action minimizes the potential for memory leaks or unauthorized memory access. Moreover, avoid using global or static variables for storing sensitive information, as these can persist across multiple invocations.

Error handling

Errors can be a significant security risk if they are not handled correctly. For instance, revealing too much information in error messages can expose your system to attackers. Lambda functions should be designed to handle errors gracefully, logging the necessary information for debugging without exposing sensitive system details. DLQs can also be used to capture unprocessed events, which can then be analyzed for security implications.

Lambda function versioning and aliases

Lambda function versioning and aliases are essential features that contribute significantly to the security, manageability, and operational excellence of your serverless architecture. Understanding how to effectively use these features can help you maintain a robust security posture, simplify deployments, and facilitate rollbacks in case of issues.

The importance of versioning

Versioning in Lambda allows you to publish one or more versions of your Lambda function. As you make changes to your function, you can publish a new version, which becomes immutable. This immutability is a security feature as it ensures that a particular version of the function cannot be altered once it is published. This is crucial for auditing and compliance as it provides a clear history of what code was running at any given time. Therefore, it is a best practice to always publish a new version for production use, rather than relying on the mutable $LATEST version.

How versioning works

When you publish a new version of a Lambda function, AWS automatically assigns it a new version number. The latest version is always mutable and is referred to as $LATEST. However, once you publish a version, it becomes immutable. This means that the code, environment variables, and other settings are locked for that version. You can still execute it, but you can't change it. This is particularly useful for maintaining a stable environment, especially when your Lambda functions are part of critical workflows. To ensure that only trusted individuals or systems can create, update, or delete versions, you should use IAM policies to restrict these permissions.

Aliases as pointers

Aliases in Lambda act like pointers to specific function versions. An alias enables you to redirect function traffic from one version to another without changing all the places where your function is invoked. This is particularly useful for implementing blue-green deployments, canary releases, or any other strategy that requires routing traffic to different versions of your function. Descriptive alias names such as production, staging, or testing make it clear what each alias is used for, aiding in both manageability and security.

Security benefits of aliases

Using aliases can enhance your security posture in several ways. For instance, you can have an alias that points to a version of the function that has undergone rigorous security testing. Before updating the alias so that it points to a new version, you can ensure that the new version meets all your security requirements. This makes it easier to manage security at scale as you don't have to update every single function invocation – just the alias. Lambda supports weighted aliases, allowing you to route a percentage of your function invocation requests to one version and the rest to another, which is useful for gradually shifting traffic to new versions.

Rollback and audit trail

The immutability of versions and the flexibility of aliases make it easier to roll back to a previous version in case of a security incident or other issues. This is invaluable for incident response and forensic analysis. The ability to quickly switch back to a known, secure version of your function can be a lifesaver in emergencies. Additionally, the history of versions and aliases provides a clear audit trail, which is often required for compliance with various security standards. Monitoring both versions and aliases through CloudWatch and setting up alerts for unusual activity is also a key part of maintaining security.

Access control

Access control is a pivotal aspect of Lambda security as it serves a dual purpose: it regulates both who can access your Lambda functions and what resources your Lambda functions can access. Let's dive deeper into the practical applications of these principles.

Role assignment

Every Lambda function runs with an IAM role known as the execution role. This role grants the function the permissions it needs to interact with other AWS services and resources. AWS provides a default execution role with basic permissions, but it is highly recommended to customize this role according to the specific needs of your function.

The principle of least privilege should be rigorously applied when assigning roles to Lambda functions. This means that a function should only have the permissions it needs to perform its tasks and no more. Over-permissive roles can expose your system to unnecessary risks. For instance, if a function only needs to read from an S3 bucket and write to a DynamoDB table, then its role should only have those permissions.

In addition, IAM policy variables offer a way to create more dynamic policies. These variables can be used to grant a Lambda function permission to access only certain S3 buckets or prefixes. For instance, you can include the function's **Amazon Resource Name** (**ARN**) as a variable within the policy. This allows the policy to dynamically adapt permissions based on the specific ARN of the function that assumes the role. This feature enables you to reuse the same role across multiple functions with similar behaviors, each with its own set of permissions, thereby reducing the management overhead.

Resource-based policies

Resource-based policies are attached directly to AWS resources. This contrasts with identity-based policies, which are attached to IAM roles. Lambda functions support resource-based policies so that they can control who can invoke them. These policies are useful for granting cross-account access or allowing other services to invoke the function.

Resource-based policies can be more granular, specifying conditions under which the policy is applicable. For example, you can restrict function invocation to specific times of the day. This adds an additional layer of security by narrowing down the circumstances under which the function can be invoked.

Long-term access keys

Storing long-term credentials, such as access keys, in Lambda functions is a common yet perilous practice that should be strictly avoided. Even if encrypted or managed through Secrets Manager, these credentials pose a risk of exposure or misuse. Instead, Lambda functions should utilize IAM roles – specifically, execution roles – to gain the necessary permissions. When a function is invoked, Lambda assumes the designated execution role, providing the function with automatically rotated, temporary security credentials. This approach minimizes the risk of credential exposure and unauthorized usage.

Networking

Networking is a complex but crucial aspect of Lambda function configuration. Whether you stick with the default settings or opt for a VPC, understanding the right networking options and their implications is essential for both security and performance.

Default configuration

By default, Lambda functions are not launched within a VPC and can access the internet without traffic filtering, as well as other AWS services, via their public endpoints. Having limited network control is typical for a serverless service. While this setup is sufficient for simple, stateless functions, it may not meet the security or functional requirements for more complex applications. Following are the reasons why:

- **Lack of network isolation**: In the default configuration, Lambda functions do not have the network isolation that a VPC provides. This lack of isolation can be a security risk for applications that handle sensitive data or require strict compliance with regulatory standards such as HIPAA or GDPR.

- **Limited network access control**: Without a VPC, you miss out on the granular control over network traffic that VPC settings provide. This includes security features such as **network access control lists** (**NACLs**) and security groups, which allow you to define inbound and outbound rules at both the subnet and the **elastic network interface** (**ENI**) levels.

- **No private access to internal resources**: Serverless services such as Lambda often need to interact with databases, cache stores, or other services that cannot work without VPC attachment. The default Lambda configuration doesn't provide a straightforward way to privately access these internal resources.

- **Inability to implement advanced networking**: Features such as VPC peering, VPN connections, and transit gateways are not available in the default configuration. These features can be essential for complex applications that require secure and efficient communication with other VPCs or external networks.

- **No support for VPC endpoints**: In a VPC, you can create VPC endpoints to privately connect your VPC to supported AWS services. This is a crucial feature for enhancing security and reducing data transfer costs, which is not available in the default Lambda configuration.

- **Limited monitoring and logging**: While AWS provides some level of monitoring for Lambda, integrating with a VPC allows you to leverage VPC flow logs for more detailed monitoring and auditing of the network traffic.

- **Operational complexity**: As your application grows, you may find that you need to migrate your Lambda functions into a VPC to meet new requirements. This migration can be operationally complex and time-consuming if not planned originally.

VPC configuration

When you need more control over the networking capabilities of your Lambda functions, placing them inside your VPC is often the best approach. A VPC offers network isolation, more granular control over traffic, and the ability to connect to resources that are not publicly accessible. The following are some key considerations for Lambda VPC configuration.

Subnet placement and NAT gateways

Subnet placement and the use of NAT gateways are critical considerations for both functionality and security. Lambda functions can be connected to either public or private subnets within a VPC. If your Lambda function needs to access resources that should not be exposed to the internet, such as a private Amazon RDS instance, you should connect your function to a private subnet. Contrary to what you might assume, connecting a Lambda function to a public subnet does not grant it internet access or a public IP address.

If your Lambda function in a subnet requires internet access, a NAT gateway becomes necessary. It enables your function to initiate outbound internet traffic while effectively blocking unsolicited inbound traffic from the internet. However, it is crucial to emphasize that NAT gateways should be used only when necessary. Avoiding their use when not required not only simplifies your network architecture and saves costs, but also minimizes the potential attack surface, thereby enhancing security.

When configuring subnets, careful consideration of subnet sizing is imperative. Proper subnet sizing is not just a matter of efficient IP address utilization but also a crucial security measure. Incorrectly sized subnets, especially those that are too small, can unintentionally open the door to **denial of service (DoS)** attacks by making it easier to exhaust available IP addresses. By configuring subnet size judiciously and actively tracking IP usage, administrators can mitigate the risk of such attacks, ensuring that the network remains both functional and secure.

For high availability, it is recommended to distribute your Lambda functions across multiple subnets in different **availability zones (AZs)**. This ensures that if one AZ experiences an outage, your function can still operate in another AZ, providing a more resilient system.

VPC endpoints

VPC endpoints enable private connections between your VPC and supported AWS services. By using VPC endpoints, you can ensure that traffic between your Lambda function and other services does not traverse the public internet, thereby enhancing security. This is particularly useful for accessing services such as S3 or DynamoDB, which your Lambda function may need to interact with frequently.

Additionally, VPC endpoints can sometimes eliminate the need for NAT gateways. If your Lambda function only needs to access AWS services that support VPC endpoints, you can configure these endpoints to allow the function to access the services directly without requiring a NAT gateway. This can simplify your architecture, reduce costs, and further tighten security by minimizing the number of components that can access the public internet.

Traffic filtering

Traffic filtering is an essential aspect of Lambda function security within a VPC. This is typically achieved through NACLs and security groups, but it can also be augmented with the usage of AWS Network Firewall. When properly configured, these tools can significantly enhance the security of your Lambda functions.

For outbound traffic, it is vital to be restrictive to prevent potential security risks. A compromised function could be used to exfiltrate data, download malicious content, or perform other unauthorized activities. Therefore, it is important to only allow outbound traffic to the necessary ports and nothing more. Whenever possible, whitelisting destination public IP addresses is recommended to further tighten security. Domain names can also be used when using the more advanced functionalities offered by AWS Network Firewall. This ensures that the function can only communicate with known, trusted services, reducing the risk of data leakage or other forms of compromise.

For inbound traffic, the focus should be on disallowing access to your Lambda functions via the network stack. Given that Lambda functions are event-driven, they generally do not require inbound network access. Therefore, it is a best practice to disable inbound network access altogether.

VPC flow logs

VPC flow logs captures information about the network traffic going to and from ENIs in your VPC. This data can be invaluable for monitoring and troubleshooting network behavior, as well as for conducting security audits and forensic analysis. Flow logs can be sent to CloudWatch logs or S3 buckets for storage and analysis. It is a good practice to enable VPC flow logs to have visibility into the traffic that is leaving and reaching your Lambda functions, as well as denied connection attempts that could be an indicator of malicious activity or misconfigurations. However, it is essential to balance security needs with cost considerations, as enabling flow logs can incur additional costs.

Execution limits

Managing timeouts, throttling, concurrency limits, and reserved concurrency is instrumental in safeguarding and optimizing Lambda functions. These settings help you control how your functions behave under various conditions, including high traffic, long-running processes, and potential abuse or attacks. Understanding and properly configuring these aspects can significantly improve the resilience and security of your Lambda functions.

Timeouts

Lambda functions have a maximum execution timeout, which you can set anywhere from 1 second to 15 minutes. The timeout setting acts as a safeguard against runaway functions that consume excessive resources or get stuck in an infinite loop. When a function reaches its timeout limit, Lambda terminates it automatically.

From a security perspective, setting an appropriate timeout is crucial. A function that runs indefinitely could be exploited in DoS attacks, consuming resources and incurring unnecessary costs. Therefore, always set your timeouts based on the expected behavior of your function. As an example, if a function is expected to complete its task in 10 to 30 seconds, setting a timeout of 1 minute provides a reasonable buffer time to account for occasional network or dependency delays while still protecting against abuse.

Throttling

Lambda functions are subject to throttling as a means to manage resource allocation and prevent abuse effectively. AWS sets both soft and hard concurrency limits per region, which can be increased upon request. When a function exceeds these limits, additional invocations are throttled. By capping the rate at which a function can be invoked, throttling helps mitigate the risk of DoS attacks and ensures fair sharing of compute resources across multiple customers.

When throttling is in effect, it helps maintain the system's overall stability and isolation. Non-critical requests may either be queued or errored out gracefully, preventing them from disrupting other functions or services. This is particularly important in a multi-tenant environment, where excessive usage by one customer can impact others. By staying within their provisioned concurrency limits, customers can avoid unintentional overages that could not only inflate costs but also strain resources on the shared infrastructure.

AWS actively monitors throttling metrics and may automatically adjust provisioned concurrency limits over time based on observed usage patterns. This proactive approach allows your Lambda functions to scale efficiently without requiring manual intervention, making it easier to manage workloads effectively. For those who expect high levels of legitimate traffic, AWS allows you to request limit increases. However, it is crucial to continuously monitor for any unusual activity that could signify a security issue. Utilizing CloudWatch to keep an eye on the throttling metrics of your Lambda functions is a recommended practice. Setting up alerts for unusual spikes in activity can provide early warnings, enabling you to take corrective action promptly.

Concurrency limits

Concurrency in Lambda refers to the number of function invocations happening simultaneously. Lambda automatically scales the function execution in response to the rate of incoming events. However, you can set a concurrency limit on individual functions to reserve a specific number of concurrent executions.

Setting a concurrency limit can be particularly useful for functions that access other resources, such as databases or APIs. Too many simultaneous connections can overwhelm these resources, leading to performance issues or even outages. From a security standpoint, setting a concurrency limit can also prevent a function from being exploited to overload or attack other systems.

Reserved concurrency

In addition to setting overall concurrency limits, Lambda allows you to set reserved concurrency for individual functions. This ensures that a specific number of concurrent executions are always available for a particular function, preventing it from being starved of resources by other functions in the same account.

Reserved concurrency is especially important for critical functions that must be available at all times. However, be cautious when setting this value, as reserving too much concurrency for one function could starve other functions, creating a different kind of vulnerability. Use this feature sparingly and only for critical functions.

Monitoring and logging

In serverless architectures such as Lambda functions, monitoring and logging become especially important. Unlike traditional server-based environments, where you have access to the underlying system to gather metrics and analyze system logs, serverless functions abstract away the infrastructure layer. This means you don't have direct access to the operating system or filesystem to collect logs or metrics. Therefore, monitoring and logging become indispensable components of a robust security posture for Lambda. They not only help in identifying performance bottlenecks but also play a crucial role in detecting and mitigating security threats in real time.

CloudWatch integration

CloudWatch provides essential metrics and logging capabilities for Lambda and acts as a first line of defense in understanding the behavior and performance of your functions.

Logging

CloudWatch logs capture vital information about Lambda function invocations, errors, and other runtime details. These logs serve dual purposes: they are essential for debugging and equally crucial for security monitoring. For example, you can configure log filters to flag specific patterns such as repeated failed login attempts or unauthorized access to sensitive resources. These flagged patterns can then be used to trigger alerts, enabling rapid response to potential security incidents.

CloudWatch Logs Insights allows you to run queries against logs for specific time ranges, which is invaluable for forensic analysis and incident response. This feature enables you to dig deep into log data to identify patterns or anomalies that could indicate a security issue.

Log filters can also be employed to create custom metrics, which can be used to track specific security-related events. For instance, you could create a custom metric that counts the number of times a particular error message appears in the logs, and then set an alarm if that count exceeds a certain threshold within a given time frame.

When developing Lambda functions, it is important to make effective use of the logging capabilities offered by CloudWatch logs. Developers should include meaningful log statements in their code that can aid in debugging, as well as in identifying suspicious activities. However, care should be taken to avoid logging sensitive information such as passwords or API keys, as logs are often accessible to multiple team members and could be a target for attackers.

Regarding log retention and encryption, AWS allows you to specify the retention period for your logs and supports KMS-based encryption to protect data. It is advisable to set a reasonable retention period based on compliance requirements and operational needs. Additionally, you should enable encryption to protect the logs from unauthorized access, especially if they contain sensitive or regulated information.

Metrics and alarms

Lambda automatically monitors functions on various metrics and reports them through CloudWatch. These metrics include the number of requests, concurrency usage, latency, errors, and throttling. This built-in monitoring provides a level of visibility into your Lambda functions' performance and security posture without incurring additional costs.

Beyond these default metrics, CloudWatch offers the flexibility to create custom metrics tailored to your specific monitoring needs. For instance, you might want to closely monitor a sensitive Lambda function that accesses confidential data. You could set up a custom metric to track the number of times this particular function is invoked. Then, you can configure an alarm that triggers if the invocation count exceeds a certain threshold within a specified time frame. This allows you to proactively manage potential security risks.

CloudWatch alarms are not just passive monitoring tools; they can be configured to take automated actions. For example, if an alarm detects an unusually high number of Lambda function invocations, which could be indicative of a security issue such as a DoS attack, it could automatically trigger another Lambda function designed to restrict access to the resource in question. This provides an automated incident response mechanism, enabling you to react swiftly to potential security threats.

Errors and invocation errors are metrics that should be monitored closely. Invocation errors can prevent a Lambda function from running and are often caused by configuration or permission errors. These errors are not just operational concerns; they can also be security red flags. For example, repeated permission errors could indicate an attempt to gain unauthorized access to a resource. By setting up CloudWatch alarms for these specific types of errors, you can be alerted immediately, allowing for quick investigation and resolution.

Events tracing with X-Ray

CloudWatch and AWS X-Ray logs serve complementary but distinct roles in monitoring and securing Lambda functions. While CloudWatch logs capture discrete events and metrics such as function invocations and errors, X-Ray provides a more holistic, end-to-end view of requests as they traverse through various components of your application. This enables you to visualize the entire journey of a request, from the moment it hits your Lambda function to its interactions with databases, other AWS services, and external APIs.

X-Ray's ability to trace requests across multiple functions and services in a serverless application sets it apart from CloudWatch logs. For example, consider a serverless application that involves multiple Lambda functions, each responsible for a specific task like authentication, data processing, and database interaction. If you notice an unexpected spike in database read operations, CloudWatch logs might show you that a particular function is being invoked more frequently, but it may not show you how that function's behavior is related to the other functions in your application. With X-Ray, you can trace the request path across all involved functions to identify the root cause, such as an authentication function that is erroneously validating multiple times, thereby triggering excessive database reads.

From a security perspective, this capability of X-Ray to correlate logs and behaviors across multiple functions can be invaluable. It allows you to spot complex attack patterns that might be missed when looking at individual functions in isolation. For instance, if an attacker is exploiting a vulnerability in one function to trigger a cascade of actions in another, X-Ray would help you visualize this chain of events, enabling you to take targeted security measures.

As for developer responsibilities, it is crucial to enable X-Ray tracing in your Lambda function configurations. This is typically a straightforward process but requires thoughtful consideration of what services and resources you want to trace. Additionally, developers should regularly review X-Ray traces and set up alerts for anomalous patterns that could indicate security issues. Keep in mind that while X-Ray provides valuable data, it also adds a slight overhead to your function invocations, so use it judiciously to balance performance and observability.

Lambda destinations

Lambda destinations offer a powerful mechanism for routing the results of asynchronous function executions to specific AWS services, such as SNS topics, SQS queues, or even other Lambda functions. This feature is not just about workflow automation; it is also a vital tool for enhancing security, particularly in the realms of incident response and forensics.

For example, suppose you have a Lambda function that's responsible for processing uploaded files. If the function detects a file that contains malicious code, it could automatically route this information to a **security incident and event management** (**SIEM**) system for immediate analysis and action. The SIEM system could then correlate this event with other data points to assess the severity of the threat.

Lambda destinations can also be leveraged to create automated incident response workflows. Imagine a scenario where a Lambda function is monitoring for unauthorized access to a sensitive S3 bucket. If such an event is detected, the function could trigger another Lambda function via Lambda destinations. This second function could then automatically quarantine the compromised S3 bucket, revoke the permissions of the suspected user, and send an alert to the security team for further investigation. This level of automation not only speeds up incident response but also minimizes the window of opportunity for an attacker to cause further damage.

In conclusion, the serverless paradigm of Lambda functions introduces a unique set of security considerations, all of which were comprehensively addressed in this section.

Summary

In this chapter, we delved into the world of serverless computing, a paradigm shift that brings both opportunities and challenges to cloud architecture. We kicked things off by introducing the concept of serverless, its benefits and challenges, and how it compares to traditional microservices. We then discussed the security considerations that are unique to serverless architectures, covering a wide range of topics from responsibility domains and zero-trust architecture to data encryption and compliance. We also explored event-driven security mechanisms, diving into event sources, schema validation, and data encryption. This chapter concluded with a deep dive into securing Lambda functions, discussing code integrity, environment variables, runtime protection, and monitoring, among other key security aspects.

As we move on to the next chapter, we will explore the complex yet crucial topic of multi-tenancy in shared environments, focusing on secure design patterns and techniques for data isolation and resource allocation between tenants.

Questions

Answer the following questions to test your knowledge of this chapter:

1. What is event sourcing and how does it bolster security?

2. How does code signing enhance Lambda security?

3. How does versioning contribute to Lambda security?

4. What are the risks and limitations of the default Lambda network configuration?

Answers

Here are the answers to this chapter's questions:

1. Event sourcing involves capturing a series of events that represent state changes in an application, creating an immutable audit trail. This is invaluable for security analysts who may need to *rewind* the system state to analyze past security incidents.

2. Code signing verifies the integrity of your Lambda function code by attaching a digital signature. AWS Signer is used to create a signing profile, and Lambda validates the signature during deployment. This ensures that only authorized and unaltered code is deployed.

3. Versioning allows you to publish immutable versions of your Lambda function, providing a clear history of what code was running at any given time. This is crucial for auditing and compliance.

4. The default network settings for Lambda functions come with certain limitations, such as the absence of network isolation and limited access control options. They also lack support for advanced networking capabilities such as VPC peering, VPN connections, and VPC flow logs for monitoring network traffic. These shortcomings could pose security risks and may not meet the security requirements for critical applications in organizations that want to maintain control of the network.

Further reading

The following resources offer further insights and best practices for serverless security:

- *AWS Whitepaper – AWS Serverless Multi-Tier Architectures with Amazon API Gateway and AWS Lambda*: `https://docs.aws.amazon.com/pdfs/whitepapers/latest/serverless-multi-tier-architectures-api-gateway-lambda/serverless-multi-tier-architectures-api-gateway-lambda.pdf`

- *AWS Whitepaper – Security Overview of AWS Lambda*: `https://docs.aws.amazon.com/pdfs/whitepapers/latest/security-overview-aws-lambda/security-overview-aws-lambda.pdf`

- *Serverless Security Challenges and Countermeasures*, by Abdirahman Mohamed (2021): `https://towardsaws.com/serverless-security-challenges-and-countermeasures-8a94f7d7babe`

8

Secure Design Patterns for Multi-Tenancy in Shared Environments

Welcome to the eighth chapter of our comprehensive guide to AWS security, where we delve into the intricate world of **multi-tenancy** in shared environments. As cloud computing continues to evolve, the concept of multi-tenancy has become increasingly important, bringing with it a unique set of challenges and opportunities. In this chapter, we will start by demystifying what multi-tenancy is and why it holds such significance in the cloud ecosystem. We will then explore the various challenges it presents, including data isolation, resource allocation, and compliance concerns.

As we move forward, the chapter will introduce you to different multi-tenancy design patterns such as the **silo**, **pool**, and **bridge** models. Each of these patterns offers unique levels of isolation and is suited for specific use cases. To help you make an informed decision, we will provide a comprehensive guide on how to choose the right design pattern based on a variety of factors, including security requirements and resource constraints.

The latter part of this chapter will focus on implementing secure data isolation techniques at multiple levels—network, database, compute, application, and even encryption. We will discuss how to achieve this isolation in various AWS services such as Amazon DynamoDB, Amazon RDS, Amazon EC2, and AWS Lambda. Finally, we will round off the chapter by examining how to manage access control for tenants, diving deep into both role-based and attribute-based access control methods, as well as the concept of tenant-managed access control.

By the end of this chapter, you will have a well-rounded understanding of multi-tenancy in AWS, its associated security challenges, and best practices for implementing secure design patterns. You will be equipped with the knowledge to design and manage secure multi-tenant environments effectively.

In this chapter, we will cover the following key areas:

- Understanding the fundamentals and challenges of multi-tenancy
- Exploring multi-tenancy design patterns – silo, pool, and bridge models
- Implementing secure data isolation techniques at various levels
- Managing tenant access control through role-based and attribute-based methods

Understanding multi-tenancy concepts and challenges

Multi-tenancy is a foundational concept in cloud computing, particularly relevant in environments such as AWS. As organizations strive for operational efficiency and scalability, understanding the nuances of multi-tenancy becomes increasingly important.

Definition and importance of multi-tenancy

Multi-tenancy is not just a technical term; it's a strategic approach that can significantly impact both operational efficiency and security. While particularly relevant in **software-as-a-service (SaaS)** applications, its importance extends across various cloud services and models.

What is multi-tenancy?

Multi-tenancy refers to an architectural design where a single instance of a software application serves multiple customers, known as **tenants**. Each tenant's data and configurations are logically isolated, yet they share common resources such as compute, storage, and network infrastructure. This architecture can be likened to living in an apartment building: each tenant has their own secure space but shares common facilities.

Why is multi-tenancy important in cloud computing?

The significance of multi-tenancy in cloud computing lies in its ability to optimize resource utilization, thereby reducing operational costs. By sharing underlying resources, you can maximize utilization, which is particularly beneficial for scaling operations. Furthermore, updates and maintenance become more streamlined, as a single update can serve all tenants.

Types of segregation in multi-tenancy

Segregation in multi-tenancy can take various forms, each with its own set of advantages and challenges:

- **Physical segregation**: Here, each tenant has its own set of dedicated resources. While this is the most secure form of segregation, it is also the most costly.

- **Logical segregation**: In this model, tenants share resources but their data and configurations are logically isolated. This form of segregation is common in cloud environments and offers a balance between cost and security. However, logical segregation comes with its own set of nuances, such as varying levels of data isolation achievable through techniques such as encryption and tokenization.

- **No segregation**: This is the least secure form, where all tenants share both resources and data. It is generally not recommended for most applications due to the inherent security risks.

The cost versus security equilibrium

Striking the right balance between cost and security is a critical challenge in multi-tenancy. On one hand, sharing resources is cost effective; on the other, it can introduce security vulnerabilities. Achieving this equilibrium involves implementing robust security measures, such as data encryption and stringent access control, while optimizing resource allocation.

The following diagram (*Figure 8.1*) illustrates this concept:

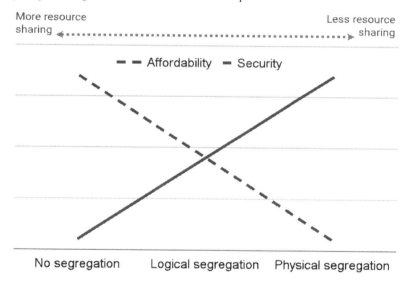

Figure 8.1 – The cost versus security equilibrium

It is important to keep in mind that this equilibrium is not static; it is a dynamic state that requires continuous monitoring and adjustment. As new security threats emerge or as business needs evolve, the balance between cost and security will need to be re-evaluated and recalibrated.

Challenges in multi-tenancy

While multi-tenancy offers a plethora of benefits, it is not without challenges. The following challenges are key considerations for organizations aiming for an efficient and secure multi-tenant architecture:

- **Data isolation**: One of the most critical challenges in a multi-tenant environment is ensuring data isolation among tenants. Logical segregation is the most commonly used method, but it has its complexities. For example, how do you ensure that Tenant A cannot access Tenant B's data when both use the same database instance? To navigate these complexities, a strong governance approach is vital. This involves clearly defined policies, procedures, and controls to manage data access. Techniques such as encryption and tokenization can add layers of security. However, they also introduce complexity and can also impact performance.

- **Resource allocation**: Resource allocation in a multi-tenant environment is a double-edged sword. On one side, sharing resources is cost-effective and allows for better utilization. On the other side, it can lead to resource contention. This is commonly referred to as the *noisy neighbor* issue, in which multiple tenants compete for the same resources, causing performance degradation for others. Solving this issue requires sophisticated resource allocation strategies that can dynamically adjust based on real-time usage data. Fixed allocation strategies can be too rigid, while dynamic allocation strategies require advanced monitoring and automation tools to be effective.

- **Security concerns**: Security is a top concern in multi-tenancy, especially given the shared nature of resources. The risk of data breaches, unauthorized access, and other security incidents is magnified in a multi-tenant environment. Implementing robust access control mechanisms such as **role-based access control** (**RBAC**) and **attribute-based access control** (**ABAC**) becomes essential. Additionally, continuous monitoring and regular security audits are necessary to identify and mitigate vulnerabilities.

- **Compliance concerns**: Last but not least, compliance can pose a real challenge in multi-tenant architectures. When multiple tenants share the same resources, ensuring each tenant's data handling practices comply with regulations becomes complex. This complexity is further exacerbated if tenants operate in different jurisdictions. Moreover, the challenge extends to demonstrating this compliance to auditors. In a complex multi-tenant environment, providing clear, auditable records can be challenging. Therefore, robust internal processes are essential to ensure that compliance is not just achieved but also demonstrable to auditors.

- **Metering and billing**: Multi-tenancy platforms often require mechanisms for metering resource usage and billing tenants accordingly. This involves tracking metrics such as compute time, storage usage, or data transfer, and generating accurate billing statements for each tenant based on their usage. Effective metering and billing systems are essential for ensuring fair and transparent cost allocation among tenants.

In conclusion, the complexities of multi-tenancy should not be underestimated, as they directly influence an organization's ability to scale, secure data, and comply with regulations.

Multi-tenancy design patterns

This section delves into three primary multi-tenancy design patterns—silo, pool, and bridge models—each with its unique advantages, challenges, and use cases. These patterns not only influence the operational efficiency and scalability of the service but also have a profound impact on security and compliance. We will explore the various levels of isolation these models offer, their applicability in different scenarios, and the factors to consider when choosing the right pattern for your organization.

The silo model

The silo model is one of the most straightforward designs for implementing multi-tenancy. In this model, each tenant is assigned to a separate set of resources, effectively creating isolated *silos*. While this approach offers the highest level of security and isolation, it often comes at the cost of resource efficiency.

The following diagram (*Figure 8.2*) illustrates the silo model:

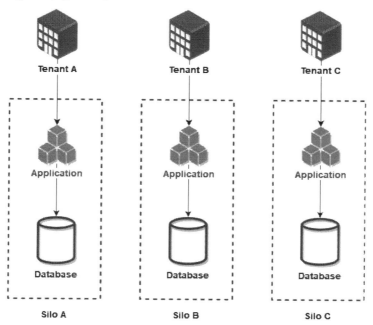

Figure 8.2 – The silo model

Levels of isolation

The silo model can be implemented at various levels of isolation, each offering a different balance between security and resource utilization:

- **Account segregation**: At the most isolated level, each tenant can have a separate AWS account. This not only isolates resources such as compute, storage, and networking but also segregates governance aspects such as IAM. It can even allow tenants some level of control and visibility over their resources. However, this approach can lead to increased operational overhead due to the complexity of managing multiple accounts.

- **VPC segregation**: A more balanced approach is to segregate tenants at the VPC level. Each tenant gets its own VPC within a single AWS account, offering a good balance between isolation and manageability.

- **Subnet segregation**: For finer-grained control, tenants can be segregated at the subnet level within a VPC. This allows for more flexible resource allocation but requires careful network planning and management involving complex routing and security configurations. Therefore, this approach is generally not recommended due to the increased risk of configuration errors, especially as the number of tenants grows.

- **Individual resource segregation**: At the most granular level, individual resources can be segregated for each tenant. This is particularly relevant for non-VPC attached serverless components where segregation cannot be achieved at the network level using VPCs and subnets. While this offers the most flexibility, it can become complex to manage and increase the risk of configuration errors, especially as the number of tenants grows.

Use cases

The silo model is best suited for scenarios requiring strict data isolation, such as in highly regulated industries such as healthcare or financial services. It is also well suited for organizations with a limited number of tenants who require complete isolation.

The pool model

The pool model is a prevalent design approach for implementing multi-tenancy, particularly favored for its resource efficiency. In this model, multiple tenants share the same resources, such as compute and storage, while their data and configurations remain logically isolated. The approach is akin to a public swimming pool where everyone shares the water but has their own designated lane to swim in. The key advantage is the efficient use of resources, which translates into cost savings. However, the challenge lies in maintaining data isolation and security in this shared space.

The following diagram (*Figure 8.3*) illustrates the pool model:

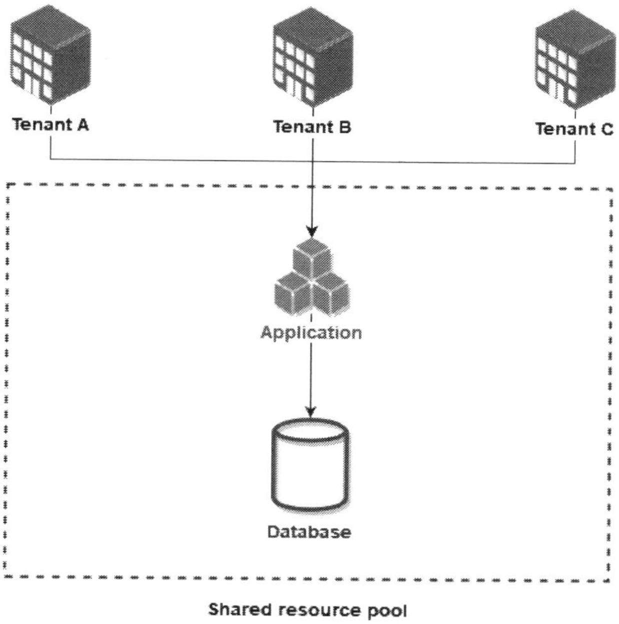

Figure 8.3 – The pool model

Levels of isolation

The pool model offers nuanced levels of isolation due to the shared nature of resources, each balancing resource utilization and data isolation while incorporating robust security measures such as encryption and strict access control policies:

- **Database segregation**: Database segregation can occur at various levels, including the schema, table, or even record level. Each tenant's data can be isolated within the same database instance, offering a balance between resource utilization and data isolation.

- **Namespace segregation**: Another approach is to use namespaces to isolate tenants within the same application or service. This is particularly useful in Kubernetes environments where each tenant can have its own namespace, allowing for logical isolation while sharing the underlying cluster resources.

- **Attribute-based segregation**: This approach focuses on isolating resources and data by using distinct attributes such as tags or identifiers that are specific to each tenant. These attributes can be integrated with ABAC mechanisms to achieve an effective layer of isolation where fine-grained permissions are defined based on the attributes attached to the underlying resources and data. For example, consider a cloud storage service where multiple tenants share the same storage infrastructure. Each file uploaded by a tenant could be tagged with a unique tenant identifier. When a tenant tries to access a file, the ABAC mechanism checks the tag against the tenant's identifier to ensure they are authorized to view or modify the file. This way, even though the storage resources are shared, each tenant's data remains logically isolated and secure.

Use cases

The pool model is highly versatile and can be applied in various scenarios. It is particularly useful for SaaS providers who have a large number of tenants with similar needs but varying scales. This model is also beneficial for start-ups and SMBs who are SaaS customers looking for cost-effective multi-tenancy solutions.

The bridge model

The bridge model stands out as an advanced and adaptable design strategy for achieving multi-tenancy, ingeniously merging the best elements of both the silo and pool models. This hybrid approach is crafted to harmonize the strict isolation attributes of the silo model with the resource-efficient aspects of the pool model. The true strength of the bridge model lies in its flexibility; it provides a highly customizable multi-tenant environment tailored to a wide array of use cases, security standards, and compliance requirements.

The following diagram (*Figure 8.4*) illustrates the bridge model:

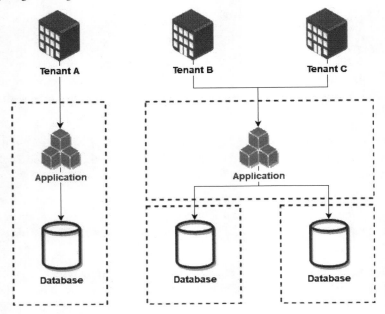

Figure 8.4 – The bridge model

Levels of Isolation

The bridge model offers a spectrum of isolation levels, empowering organizations to customize the multi-tenant environment to meet specific use cases and compliance needs:

- **Service-based segregation**: One of the remarkable features of the bridge model is its capacity to offer diverse resource allocation variations within a unified architectural framework. For example, premium tenants might operate with dedicated resources, enjoying a high level of isolation and control similar to what the silo model offers. At the same time, other tenants could share resources in a way that aligns with the pool model, reaping the benefits of cost-efficiency and scalability. This flexibility is especially beneficial for SaaS providers who offer tiered services where premium customers may demand dedicated resources.

- **Layer-based segregation**: The bridge model takes it a step further by enabling tenants to employ a nuanced blend of both shared and dedicated resources. For instance, a tenant could have dedicated database storage while sharing compute resources with other tenants. This approach allows for a high degree of customization, letting organizations fine-tune their resource allocation based on specific needs, performance, and compliance requirements. It also takes into account the technical limitations and cost concerns associated with each technology layer that comes with using dedicated resources.

- **Layer-based and service-based segregation combined**: In this advanced combination of both layer-based and service-based segregations, standard tenants could share application servers but have isolated databases. In contrast, premium tenants could have an entirely separate set of resources, including both the application servers and the database, ensuring the highest level of isolation and reserved capacity.

Use cases

The bridge model is incredibly versatile, making it suitable for a wide range of scenarios. It is particularly useful for SaaS providers who serve a diverse tenant base with varying needs in terms of security, performance, and data isolation. This adaptability makes the bridge model a compelling choice for businesses aiming to balance cost efficiency with stringent security and compliance requirements.

Choosing the right design pattern

Selecting the appropriate multi-tenancy design pattern is a nuanced decision that requires a deep understanding of various aspects ranging from security and compliance to cost and scalability.

Factors to consider

Several factors come into play that can significantly influence the decision. These factors can be broadly categorized into the following:

- **Security and compliance requirements**: Different industries have varying levels of security and compliance needs. For instance, healthcare and financial sectors often require stringent data isolation, making the silo model a more suitable choice.

- **Costs and efficiency**: If cost-effectiveness and scalability are primary concerns, the pool model may be more appropriate. This model allows for better resource utilization but may compromise data isolation.

- **Customization and flexibility**: Organizations that require a balance between isolation and resource efficiency should consider the bridge model. This model offers a range of isolation levels and can be tailored to meet specific use cases.

- **Scalability**: The ability to handle a growing amount of work or an expanding tenant base is crucial. While the pool model is generally more scalable due to shared resources, the silo model may face challenges in scaling due to its isolated nature. The bridge model offers a balanced approach, allowing for scalability while maintaining some level of isolation.

- **Operational complexity**: Managing multiple accounts or VPCs in the silo model can be operationally challenging and may require more administrative effort.

- **Tenant diversity**: If you have a diverse tenant base with varying needs, the bridge model's flexibility can be a significant advantage.

- **Technical constraints**: The choice may also be influenced by the technical limitations of your infrastructure. For example, some resources may not be easily shareable, or the cost of dedicated resources may be prohibitive.

- **Model variants**: It is worth noting that each model comes in different flavors, offering additional customization options. For example, the silo model can be implemented with varying degrees of resource isolation, from account level down to individual resources.

Comparison

The following table (*Table 8.1*) offers a quick comparative view of the three multi-tenancy design patterns based on various factors:

Criteria	Silo model	Pool model	Bridge model
Security and compliance	High	Low	Medium
Costs and efficiency	Low	High	Medium
Customization and flexibility	Low	Medium	High

Criteria	Silo model	Pool model	Bridge model
Scalability	Low	High	Medium
Operational complexity	High	Low	Medium

Table 8.1 – Comparison between multi-tenancy design patterns

Final thoughts

Choosing the right multi-tenancy design pattern is a critical decision that can have long-term implications on your application's scalability, security, and operational efficiency. While the silo model is often perceived as the most secure due to its inherent design for data isolation, this sense of security can sometimes lead to overlooking other essential security measures such as encryption or access controls. Conversely, the pool model is generally more resource efficient and cost effective but may require additional security layers to meet specific compliance standards. The bridge model serves as a middle ground, offering a blend of customization options and varying degrees of isolation.

Each of these models also comes in different flavors, allowing for further customization based on your specific requirements. By carefully considering the factors outlined previously and using the decision matrix as a guide, organizations can make a more informed choice that aligns with their strategic objectives and operational constraints.

Implementing secure data isolation techniques

Data isolation is a cornerstone of multi-tenancy, ensuring that each tenant's data remains secure and inaccessible to other tenants. This section explores various techniques to achieve secure data isolation across different layers of your AWS infrastructure.

Network-level isolation

Network isolation serves as an initial safeguard in a multi-tenant environment, focusing on the segregation of network traffic to ensure that each tenant's data flows remain separate from one another. However, It is crucial to note that the effectiveness of network-level isolation is contingent on the nature of the resources being used. Specifically, network isolation is most applicable when resources are dedicated to individual tenants and are VPC-attached.

For shared resources that don't have separate network configurations for each tenant, or AWS services that are not attached to a VPC, network-based isolation is not feasible. In these instances, alternative isolation mechanisms become essential. These could include IAM policies that restrict access based on tenant identifiers or service-specific features designed to ensure data isolation and security.

Database-level Isolation

Database-level isolation is a critical aspect of multi-tenancy, ensuring that tenants cannot access or interfere with each other's stored data. Most common database engines in AWS offer a variety of features that support fine-grained access control to achieve this level of security in a shared database environment.

DynamoDB tables

In Amazon DynamoDB, fine-grained access control is a powerful feature that allows for **row-level security** (**RLS**). By leveraging IAM, you can natively create policies that restrict access to individual items and attributes within a table. This is particularly useful for isolating data based on attributes such as tenant IDs. For example, you could set up a policy that allows a user to only access and modify records related to its associated tenant within a multi-tenant table. This ensures that each tenant's data remains logically isolated within the same table, even if the table itself is shared among multiple tenants.

The IAM policies can be as specific as needed, allowing for complex scenarios. For instance, you could restrict a user's access to only certain attributes of an item, such as viewing their account balance but not their transaction history. This level of granularity is invaluable for maintaining strict access controls in a multi-tenant environment.

RDS databases

Implementing fine-grained access control and data isolation in Amazon RDS databases is generally more complex than in DynamoDB. This complexity often arises from the need to leverage the specific capabilities offered by the database engine itself, alongside AWS IAM for identity and permissions. Let's dive into the specifics of each database engine:

- **PostgreSQL**: PostgreSQL is notable for its robust support of RLS, a feature that enables the definition of access controls at the individual row level within a database table. In PostgreSQL, RLS policies can be set up to specify which rows can be accessed, modified, or deleted on a per-user basis. IAM roles can be used for authentication, and these IAM identities can then be mapped to PostgreSQL users, allowing for a seamless transition from AWS-level to database-level access control.

- **SQL Server**: Microsoft SQL Server also supports RLS, which allows you to control access to rows based on group membership or the specific conditions under which a query is executed. IAM roles can be used for authentication to the RDS SQL Server instance. Once authenticated, SQL Server's internal mechanisms enforce RLS based on the IAM identity.

- **MySQL**: MySQL does not natively support RLS within tables. However, a workaround is available: you can create views using the MySQL `CREATE VIEW` statement and define conditions for row visibility. Access can then be granted solely to these views. IAM roles can be used for authentication to the RDS MySQL instance, and once connected, users can be restricted to specific views, thereby achieving a form of row-level isolation.

- **Oracle**: For Oracle databases on RDS, Oracle Label Security is available in the Enterprise Edition. Unlike traditional database security, which operates at the object level, Oracle Label Security provides fine-grained control down to the level of individual table rows. This makes it a strong choice for Oracle environments that require detailed access controls.

- **MariaDB**: MariaDB lacks native support for RLS. In such cases, RLS can be emulated at the application layer. This approach, while functional, could introduce additional points of failure or misconfiguration and is heavily reliant on the application's correct enforcement of these controls, posing a risk if the application has vulnerabilities.

- **Aurora**: Amazon Aurora does not have native support for RLS but offers alternative mechanisms for data isolation. Specifically, you can grant users the privilege to query specific tables or schemas. While not as granular as true RLS, this method does provide a level of data isolation. IAM roles can be used for authentication to the Aurora instance, and once authenticated, Aurora's internal access controls, separate from IAM, can be applied to further restrict table or schema access based on the authenticated IAM identity.

Compute-level Isolation

Compute-level isolation is another critical aspect of ensuring data security and integrity in a multi-tenant environment. Unlike database-level isolation, which focuses on the segregation of data at rest, compute-level isolation is concerned with isolating the computational resources that process this data. This involves leveraging various AWS services and features to ensure that each tenant's computational activities are isolated from one another. AWS offers multiple services for achieving compute-level isolation, including Amazon EC2 instances, managed containers, and AWS Lambda functions. Each of these services has its unique characteristics and capabilities for ensuring resource isolation at different levels.

EC2 instances

EC2 instances are launched within a VPC, providing a foundation for network-level isolation. Beyond that, further security can be applied through IAM roles that the instances can assume. This dual-layered approach serves to restrict not only which AWS services the instances can interact with but also the specific actions they are permitted to perform.

EC2 instances can function as silos, with each instance being dedicated to a specific tenant. This setup ensures a clear separation, confining each tenant's computational resources to their designated boundaries.

Alternatively, EC2 instances can be shared among multiple tenants. However, this approach offers limited segregation. All invocations from different tenants share the same runtime environment. This could potentially lead to unintended data access or leakage between tenants, especially if there are vulnerabilities in the application stack.

Containers

Containers offer a lightweight and portable solution for application deployment and are supported by AWS services such as Amazon ECS and Amazon EKS. Containers can run either on EC2 instances or AWS Fargate and allow for the separation of runtime environments within a shared virtual machine.

Isolation can be achieved at multiple levels, including at the task-definition level in ECS or the pod level in EKS. IAM roles can be assigned to individual tasks or pods, providing fine-grained control over AWS resources.

Network isolation can also be implemented at the container level. This can be implemented in ECS using the `awsvpc` network mode where each task is allocated its own **elastic network interface (ENI)** and IP address, enabling you to assign security groups and isolate container network traffic.

Lambda functions

Lambda offers a serverless compute environment, eliminating the need for server provisioning. Each function runs in its own isolated environment, defined via IAM permissions, ensuring robust security and isolation.

Lambda manages and scales concurrent function invocations across multiple runtime environments, which are like individual instances of a function. In some cases, these runtime environments may be reused to optimize performance, introducing the risk of data leakage or unintended access between tenants. To mitigate this, functions should be designed to be stateless and idempotent. Data should be stored in temporary local variables to prevent exposure to subsequent invocations. Initialization code should be designed to handle both reused and freshly started environments.

Lambda also supports VPC integration, adding an extra layer of network-level isolation, which is especially useful when separate functions are implemented for each tenant.

Application-level isolation

Application-level isolation serves as the last line of defense in ensuring that data and operations are securely segregated among different tenants. This form of isolation is often the most intricate to implement as it involves a blend of coding practices, middleware solutions, and configuration settings that work in harmony to create a secure environment. Let's uncover the key practices that enable application-level isolation.

Session management

Session management is crucial for maintaining a secure multi-tenant environment. By assigning unique session IDs to each user and validating these IDs for each request, the application can ensure that tenants are properly isolated. This can be implemented using **JSON Web Tokens (JWTs)** or OAuth tokens that are designed to carry claims between parties, in this case, the user and the application.

Data filtering

Data filtering serves as a mechanism to ensure that tenants can only access data that they are authorized to. This is often implemented at the Amazon API Gateway level. Each API request made by a tenant is usually accompanied by a unique identifier, often the tenant ID, which is verified and validated by the application.

Once the tenant ID is validated, it is used as a parameter to filter database queries and object access requests. For example, if a tenant makes a request to fetch data from a multi-tenant database, the application logic appends the tenant ID to the SQL query, ensuring that only records associated with that tenant ID are returned. This form of data filtering is often implemented using parameterized queries to prevent SQL injection attacks.

Middleware for data segregation

Middleware can be employed to automate the process of data filtering. This middleware can be a part of the application's backend logic and can be designed to automatically append the tenant ID to every database query or API request. By doing so, the middleware ensures that the application logic remains clean and focused on business requirements, while it takes care of the data segregation. This not only makes the code base easier to manage but also reduces the likelihood of errors that could compromise data isolation.

Caching strategies

Caching is commonly used to improve performance. However, in a multi-tenant environment, it is crucial to ensure that cached data is also tenant specific to prevent data leakage. This can be achieved by appending tenant IDs to cache keys or by using tenant-specific cache partitions. By doing so, the application ensures that each tenant's cached data is isolated, reducing the risk of one tenant inadvertently accessing another's cached information.

Challenging and testing

Ensuring robust application-level isolation is not a *set-it-and-forget-it* task. It requires continuous monitoring and regular testing to ensure that as new features are added or existing ones are modified, the isolation between tenants remains uncompromised. Automated testing frameworks can simulate multiple tenants accessing the system concurrently, trying to probe for data leakage or unauthorized access. Security audits, code reviews, and penetration testing are other techniques that can help ensure that the application-level isolation mechanisms are robust and secure.

Encryption-level isolation

Encryption-level isolation serves as a robust and often indispensable layer of security in a multi-tenant architecture. While other forms of isolation such as network-, database-, and application-level isolation focus on segregating data and computational resources, encryption-level isolation aims to secure the data itself. This is particularly crucial when dealing with sensitive information that, if compromised, could have severe repercussions for both the tenants and the service provider. In this context, encryption becomes not just a feature but a necessity. Key approaches for encryption-level isolation are explained in the following sections.

Unique keys for each tenant

One of the most effective ways to implement encryption-level isolation is through the use of AWS KMS. What sets KMS apart in a multi-tenant environment is the ability to use different keys for different tenants. This adds an additional layer of isolation, as each tenant's data is encrypted using a unique key, making it virtually impossible for one tenant to decrypt another's data.

The use of tenant-specific keys also facilitates easier management and rotation of keys. If a key needs to be revoked or rotated, it can be done without affecting other tenants. This is particularly useful in scenarios where a tenant leaves the service or is found to be in violation of terms, as their specific key can be revoked without disrupting the encryption for other tenants.

Encryption for shared resources

In a multi-tenant environment, there are often shared resources that multiple tenants might access. These could be shared databases, file storage systems, or even cache layers. In such scenarios, using different tenant-specific KMS keys for encrypting different sets of data within these shared resources can provide an additional layer of security.

For instance, in a shared database, each tenant's data could be encrypted using their unique KMS key. Even though the data resides in the same physical database, the encryption ensures that only the respective tenant, who has the correct key, can decrypt and access their data. This method effectively isolates each tenant's data within a shared resource, ensuring that even if one tenant's key is compromised, the data of other tenants remains secure.

Hierarchical keyring

The concept of a **hierarchical keyring** offered by KMS adds another layer of sophistication and structure to ensure robust encryption practices in a scalable multi-tenant environment. In this model, a master key is used to encrypt tenant-specific keys. These tenant-specific keys are then used to encrypt the data keys that secure individual pieces of data.

This hierarchical approach simplifies key management by allowing lower-level keys to be changed or rotated without affecting the master key. It also enables granular access control by allowing IAM policies to be tailored to control access to different levels of keys. For example, you could configure an IAM policy that allows only database administrators to access the master key, while another policy might allow application-level services to access only the tenant-specific keys. Yet another policy could be set up to allow end users to access only the data keys that are relevant to their specific tenant. This ensures that only authorized entities have access to specific keys.

Additionally, the hierarchical nature of the keys makes the rotation and auditing processes more straightforward. Keys can be rotated at different levels without affecting the entire system, as you can change tenant-specific or data keys without needing to modify the master key. Each level of the key hierarchy can have its own set of logging and monitoring rules, simplifying compliance and enhancing security.

In conclusion, achieving secure data isolation in a multi-tenant environment is a multi-layered challenge that demands a holistic approach. From network-level safeguards to application-level mechanisms and encryption strategies, every layer plays a pivotal role in ensuring that each tenant's data remains isolated and secure.

Managing access control for tenants

Access control is a cornerstone of multi-tenancy, ensuring that each tenant's data and resources are only accessed by authorized parties, even when running in a shared component. In a multi-tenant environment, this involves a combination of authentication and authorization strategies that can be tailored to each tenant's needs, as will be explored further in the following parts.

Tenant authentication

Tenant authentication is not just a security measure but a foundational element that proves that users are who they claim to be. Once authenticated, the system can then apply the appropriate access controls based on the tenant to which a user belongs.

Amazon Cognito excels in offering robust authentication capabilities, and it also provides the flexibility for tenants to integrate their own identity providers for even more customized and isolated authentication experiences. By allowing tenants to use separate identity providers or user pools, the system ensures that each tenant's user base remains distinct and isolated, starting from the authentication phase.

Each of these identity providers or user pools can be configured with unique settings for user registration, login, and access control, offering an extra layer of customization and security tailored to each tenant's specific needs. Custom attributes or tenant identifiers can be employed to associate users with the appropriate tenant-specific identity provider, reinforcing the isolation between different tenants.

To further streamline tenant onboarding and management, automation techniques can be applied. This automates the creation and configuration of new identity resources, whether they are Cognito user pools or external identity providers, each time a new tenant is integrated into the service. This ensures that each tenant's authentication mechanism is set up in a way that maintains a strong boundary between different tenants while also meeting their individual authentication requirements.

Implementing access control

Once tenants are authenticated, the next crucial step is to enforce appropriate access controls based on their identities. Cognito identities can be integrated with IAM to create a seamless and secure access control framework. By associating Cognito identities with IAM roles, you can define what actions a tenant is allowed to perform and which resources they can access.

RBAC

RBAC is a widely used model for enforcing access controls in a multi-tenant environment. In AWS, you can create separate IAM roles for each tenant, each with its own set of permissions. This not only isolates each tenant but also makes it easier to manage and audit, as each role's activities can be tracked independently.

Storing tenant-to-role mappings in an external database is a best practice that enhances security by keeping this sensitive mapping information out of IAM. Automation can be employed to handle the provisioning of new IAM roles and policies whenever a new tenant is onboarded, reducing administrative overhead. IAM role tagging can be used to further categorize and isolate roles, making it easier to manage roles across multiple tenants.

ABAC

ABAC offers a more flexible and granular approach to access control compared to RBAC. Instead of relying solely on roles, ABAC uses attributes—such as tenant ID or other tags—to dynamically enforce access policies. This makes ABAC particularly useful for multi-tenant architectures.

Shared IAM policies

One of the key advantages of using ABAC in a multi-tenant environment is the ability to create shared IAM policies that can be applied across multiple tenants. This is particularly beneficial for scalability, as there is no need to rewrite IAM permissions for every new tenant that comes on board. By using attributes, you can create a single IAM policy that dynamically adjusts its permissions based on the tenant making the request. This not only simplifies management but also ensures that the principle of least privilege is enforced, as permissions are granted based on specific attributes tied to end-user identities.

The following diagram (*Figure 8.5*) illustrates an example of ABAC implementation based on tags assigned to both users and resources. In this example, only users tagged with `Tenant` and assigned the value `A` can access resources tagged with the same value. This access control is facilitated through a single IAM policy shared among tenants. Within this policy, IAM conditions are utilized to match user tags with resource tags:

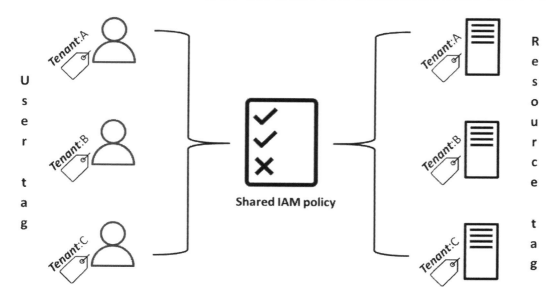

Figure 8.5 – ABAC example based on tags to isolate tenant access

Advantages of ABAC with shared resources

ABAC is not only scalable and secure but also cost effective, especially when dealing with shared resources in a pool model. By using attributes to control access, you can securely share resources such as databases or storage buckets among multiple tenants. Each tenant's access is restricted based on their specific attributes, ensuring that they can only interact with the portions of the shared resource that they are authorized to access.

Identity propagation

In a multi-tenant environment, the seamless transfer of tenant identities is crucial for maintaining robust access control and tenant isolation. One effective way to achieve this is by leveraging Cognito with JWTs to propagate tenant identifiers throughout the system. Specifically, the following steps can be followed as illustrated in *Figure 8.6*:

1. The user first authenticates via Cognito.

2. Cognito triggers a `PreTokenGeneration` Lambda function post-authentication. This function is invoked right after a user is authenticated and its purpose is to enrich the JWT token with additional claims, specifically those related to tenant identification.

3. The `PreTokenGeneration` Lambda function parses the user's attributes stored in Cognito to determine which tenant the user belongs to. The identified tenant ID is then added to the JWT as a custom claim, making it part of the token that will be used for subsequent interactions.

4. After adding the necessary claims, the enriched JWT is signed and returned by Cognito to the user. It will serve as the user's credential for subsequent interactions with the application.

5. The authenticated user then sends a request to the API Gateway.

6. Upon receiving the request, the API Gateway uses a Cognito user pools authorizer to validate the enriched JWT.

7. Once validated, the API Gateway passes the enriched JWT to the application layer together with the request payload.

8. Every component of the application receiving the payload from the request will also validate the enriched JWT token. This token can be verified by calling Cognito's API to ensure its validity and the integrity of the tenant information it carries. The application then will authorize or decline the request depending on the verified tenant information.

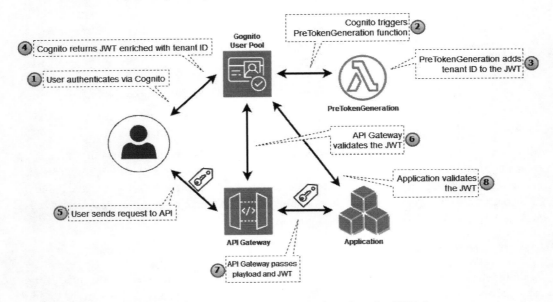

Figure 8.6 – Identity propagation process based on the JWT token

This approach to identity propagation is highly effective in ensuring that each tenant's users can only access the resources and data they are authorized to. It also allows for tenant-aware authorization as the JWT, enriched with tenant-specific claims, navigates through requests between different services.

Role assumption

Role assumption can add an extra layer of security by ensuring that tenant isolation is not solely performed at the application layer. The following steps can be taken to implement role assumption:

1. Before assuming any role, the application must ensure that the received enriched JWT token is valid and extract the tenant ID from it.

2. The application can assume an IAM role that is specifically tied to the tenant ID extracted from the JWT. AWS STS is used to request temporary security credentials for the assumed role, providing the permissions to access tenant-specific resources.

3. The temporary credentials are then used to perform operations that are restricted to the tenant, such as reading from a tenant-specific record in a shared DynamoDB table.

This mechanism ensures that even automated services within the AWS ecosystem adhere to the principles of least privilege and tenant isolation. By assuming roles based on the end user's tenant identity, the application ensures that each shared component can only access resources that are explicitly tied to the tenant from which the request originated. The requested service or function must have received a valid JWT token to assume the role that allows access to a specific tenant's data. This mitigates the impact of a potential service or function compromise, as even if it is compromised, it cannot access data across tenants without a valid token.

Tenant-managed access control

Tenant-managed access control introduces a layer of autonomy that allows tenants to have more control over their own security configurations within the multi-tenant architecture. This is particularly beneficial for tenants who have specific compliance requirements or unique security needs that may not be fully addressed by the provider's default settings.

A prime area for this self-governance is user administration via Cognito. Tenants have the freedom to set up their own user pools, replete with custom attributes and security settings that align with their specific requirements. This allows tenants to establish their own mechanisms for user registration, authentication, and authorization, all while ensuring they remain isolated from other tenants.

Furthermore, tenants can also define their own roles and permissions within their realm. For example, a tenant could create roles for administrators, developers, and different types of end users, each with a different set of permissions and access levels. These roles can be mapped to Cognito identities, allowing for a seamless integration between user management and access control.

By giving tenants the ability to manage their own users and roles, the system empowers them to implement security measures that are most relevant to their specific use cases. This not only enhances the overall security posture but also provides tenants with the flexibility to adapt to changing security requirements without having to wait for the service provider to make global changes.

This tenant-managed approach also has the added benefit of reducing the administrative burden on the service provider. Since tenants can handle many aspects of user and role management themselves, the provider is freed from the complexities of managing diverse security requirements across multiple tenants.

In conclusion, the key to secure multi-tenancy lies in robust access control mechanisms. By integrating Cognito for authentication and ABAC-based IAM policies for authorization, you can build a secure and scalable multi-tenant architecture.

Summary

In this chapter, we delved into the crucial topic of secure design patterns for multi-tenancy in shared AWS environments. We kicked off by defining what multi-tenancy is and why it is pivotal in cloud computing, followed by an in-depth discussion on the challenges it poses, such as data isolation, resource allocation, and compliance. The chapter then transitioned into various multi-tenancy design patterns, including the silo, pool, and bridge models, each with its own levels of isolation and suitable use cases. We also provided a guide on choosing the right design pattern based on various factors. The focus then shifted to implementing secure data isolation techniques at different levels—network, database, compute, application, and encryption. The chapter rounded off with an in-depth look at managing access control for tenants, covering both role-based and attribute-based access control methods. We also touched upon the concept of tenant-managed access control, providing a holistic view of multi-tenancy security.

As we transition to the next chapter, we will focus on the automation of resource management in AWS using **infrastructure as code (IaC)**, and how it can be leveraged to improve security and reduce risks.

Questions

Answer the following questions to test your knowledge of this chapter:

1. What is the *noisy neighbor* issue in resource allocation?
2. What are the three primary multi-tenancy models and how do they differ?
3. How does encryption-level isolation enhance security in a multi-tenant environment?
4. How does Cognito contribute to identity isolation among tenants?
5. How does identity propagation work in a multi-tenant environment?

Answers

Here are the answers to this chapter's questions:

1. The *noisy neighbor* issue refers to the problem of resource contention in a multi-tenant environment. When multiple tenants compete for the same resources, it can lead to performance degradation for others. Solving this issue requires sophisticated resource allocation strategies that can dynamically adjust based on real-time usage data.

2. The three primary multi-tenancy design patterns are as follows:

    - **The silo model**: Offers the highest level of security and isolation but is often less resource efficient.

    - **The pool model**: Multiple tenants share the same resources while their data remains logically isolated. It is resource-efficient but may compromise data isolation.

    - **The bridge model**: A hybrid approach that combines elements of both the silo and pool models, offering a customizable multi-tenant environment tailored to various use cases, security standards, and compliance requirements.

3. Encryption-level isolation focuses on securing the data itself, making it a crucial layer of security in a multi-tenant architecture. KMS allows for the use of different keys for different tenants, adding an extra layer of isolation. Hierarchical keyring structures can also be implemented, allowing for granular access control and simplified key management. This ensures that even if one tenant's key is compromised, the data of other tenants remains secure.

4. Cognito provides robust authentication capabilities and allows tenants to integrate their own identity providers for more customized experiences. It enables the use of separate identity providers or user pools for each tenant, ensuring that each tenant's user base remains distinct and isolated. This isolation starts from the authentication phase and is crucial for maintaining secure boundaries between different tenants.

5. Identity propagation in a multi-tenant environment can be achieved by leveraging Cognito in conjunction with JWT tokens. After a user is authenticated via Cognito, a `PreTokenGeneration` Lambda function enriches the JWT token with tenant-specific claims. This enriched JWT is then used in subsequent interactions with the system, allowing for tenant-aware authorization as it navigates through requests between different services.

Further readings

The following readings offer further insights and best practices for serverless security:

- *AWS Whitepaper – SaaS Architecture Fundamentals*: `https://docs.aws.amazon.com/pdfs/whitepapers/latest/saas-architecture-fundamentals/saas-architecture-fundamentals.pdf#saas-architecture-fundamentals`

- *Security practices in AWS multi-tenant SaaS environments* by Keith P and Andy Powell (2022): `https://aws.amazon.com/blogs/security/security-practices-in-aws-multi-tenant-saas-environments/`

- *Multi-Tenant Architecture for Designing a SaaS Application* by Anna Dziuba (2023): `https://relevant.software/blog/multi-tenant-architecture/`

9

Automate Everything to Build Immutable and Ephemeral Resources

Welcome to the ninth chapter of our advanced exploration of AWS security, where we will transition from the traditional manual management of resources to the cutting-edge realm of programmatic infrastructure. This chapter is a deep dive into the philosophy of *Automate-Everything*, a mantra that champions the creation of immutable and ephemeral resources as the bedrock of a secure and resilient cloud environment.

we will commence our journey by dissecting the limitations and risks that are inherent in manual resource management while highlighting the pitfalls, such as human error and configuration drift, that can compromise security and efficiency. As we move forward, we will illuminate the transformative shift to programmatic management, showcasing how it not only fortifies security but also streamlines compliance and governance across the cloud landscape.

Delving into the heart of **infrastructure as code (IaC)**, we will navigate the landscape of IaC frameworks, such as AWS CloudFormation, AWS **cloud development kit (CDK)**, **serverless application model (SAM)**, and Terraform, and articulate the profound benefits they bring to the table, including enhanced security and operational agility.

This chapter will underscore the *Automate-Everything* philosophy as we progress, advocating for a cultural and procedural shift toward an automation-centric mindset. This approach is critical for enforcing programmatic management and maintaining the integrity and security of cloud resources at scale.

By the end of this chapter, you will have gained a deep understanding of the transformative impact of automation in cloud resource management and how it serves as a bedrock for secure, compliant, and efficient cloud operations. You will be ready to apply these principles to foster a more resilient and responsive cloud infrastructure.

In this chapter, we will cover the following topics:

- The transition from manual to programmatic resource management and its impact on security and compliance
- The implementation of automated security testing in the IaC life cycle
- Best practices for automated security and compliance in IaC

From manual to programmatic management

The evolution of cloud computing has necessitated a paradigm shift from manual to programmatic management of resources. This transition is not merely a change in how resources are handled but a strategic move to enhance security, compliance, and operational efficiency in cloud environments, particularly within AWS.

Manual and programmatic management defined

In the realm of AWS, manual management entails the hands-on operation of services via the AWS Management Console or command-line interactions using the AWS CLI. This traditional approach allows for direct control but can be labor-intensive and prone to human error. In contrast, programmatic management represents a modern methodology where AWS resources are managed through code and automation. This method leverages AWS API requests, SDKs, and CLI commands, encapsulated in scripts or templates, to perform tasks such as deployment, configuration, and operations. It shifts the focus from manual, one-off interventions to systematic, repeatable, and reliable processes.

Risks of manual resource management

In the manual management of resources, the human element is both a strength and a weakness. While human control can be priceless in providing critical judgment and contextual understanding in certain contexts, it also introduces a range of risks. The following subsections cover some of these risks so that we can better recognize them before mitigating them.

Human error

Human error remains one of the most significant security vulnerabilities in IT management. Simple mistakes, such as misconfigurations or the improper handling of credentials, can lead to severe security breaches. In manual systems, where administrators directly interact with the cloud environment, the risk is compounded by the complexity and the repetitive nature of tasks. For instance, consider an administrator who inadvertently opens a security group to the internet. This action exposes sensitive systems to potential attackers.

Moreover, manual processes are often not repeatable or documented, leading to ad hoc fixes that are not well understood or maintained. This lack of standardization can create hidden vulnerabilities in the system as undocumented changes are difficult to track and review.

Configuration drift

Configuration drift occurs when the actual state of the environment diverges from the intended state over time. In manual environments, with each ad hoc change, the drift becomes more pronounced, leading to environments where the security posture is unknown. This drift is not only a security risk but also a compliance nightmare. For organizations subject to regulatory requirements, proving compliance becomes increasingly difficult as the environment's state becomes more uncertain. This can also lead to situations where some resources are not adequately secured or monitored, increasing the risk of non-compliance and the potential for undetected security incidents.

Shift to programmatic management

Shifting to programmatic management via automation addresses many of the risks associated with manual processes. As we embrace automation's potential, the next subsections will delve deeper into how programmatic management reshapes AWS operations, focusing on specific areas where automation can bring significant improvements.

Enhancing security posture

Programmatic management, often implemented through IaC, enhances an organization's security posture by embedding security directly into the deployment process. With IaC, every aspect of the infrastructure – from network configurations to access controls – is defined in code. This approach allows for the implementation of security best practices as standard templates that are applied consistently across all deployments.

IaC templates can be designed to create a baseline security posture that includes pre-configured security groups, role-based access controls, and encryption settings. These templates can be version-controlled, peer-reviewed, and automatically tested before deployment, reducing the risk of human error significantly. Once defined, IaC templates can be used to deploy and redeploy environments with the same settings, ensuring that security configurations are not only consistent but also immutable.

Streamlining compliance and governance

With programmatic management, compliance and governance are integrated into the deployment process. IaC allows for the codification of compliance policies, which can be automatically enforced every time infrastructure is provisioned or updated. This means that compliance checks are no longer a separate, manual process but an integral part of the deployment pipeline.

CloudFormation, for example, can integrate with AWS Config to continuously monitor and record compliance of AWS resource configurations, allowing for automated responses when non-compliant resources are detected. This integration streamlines governance by providing a clear, auditable trail of compliance and non-compliance, which is essential for meeting regulatory requirements.

Moreover, programmatic management enables organizations to implement a governance framework that is proactive rather than reactive. By using tools such as AWS IAM in conjunction with IaC, governance policies can be enforced programmatically, ensuring that only the necessary permissions are granted and that they are granted as per the principle of least privilege.

By embracing IaC and the tools AWS provides, organizations can mitigate the risks associated with manual resource management, enhance their security posture, and streamline compliance and governance processes. This shift is a cornerstone in building a robust security framework in the cloud, where automation and codification become the primary tools in the security professional's arsenal.

Snowflake versus Phoenix systems

The terms *Snowflake* and *Phoenix* refer to two different approaches to managing infrastructure, each with its own security implications.

Security implications of unique Snowflake configurations

Snowflake systems are unique configurations that are often the result of manual setups and ad hoc changes. They are called *Snowflakes* because, like snowflakes, no two are exactly alike. This uniqueness can be a significant security liability. Snowflake systems are difficult to replicate, hard to manage, and often lack proper documentation, making security auditing and compliance verification challenging. They are also more prone to configuration drift, which can lead to security vulnerabilities.

Standardization of predictable Phoenix configurations

Phoenix systems, on the other hand, are designed to be ephemeral and immutable – they can be destroyed and recreated at any moment, with the assurance that they will be configured exactly as intended. This approach ensures a predictable security posture as the environments are defined as code, which includes security configurations. Any changes to the environment are made through code revisions, which can be reviewed and tested before being applied, reducing the risk of introducing security flaws.

IaC frameworks

IaC is a key practice in the realm of DevOps, which involves managing and provisioning infrastructure through machine-readable definition files, rather than physical hardware configuration or interactive configuration tools. IaC is a cornerstone of the programmatic management approach, turning manual, script-based, or ad hoc processes into automated, repeatable, and consistent operations.

AWS supports a variety of IaC frameworks, each with its own set of features and advantages, to meet the diverse requirements of developers and cloud administrators. Here is a breakdown of the most common frameworks used in AWS environments:

- **CloudFormation**: An AWS-native service that simplifies creating and managing AWS resources within *stacks* representing IaC templates. Critical components such as security groups, resource settings, and IAM roles are encapsulated within these stacks, allowing them to be templated and version-controlled. This ensures that each stack deployment is in strict alignment with the organization's security policies.

- **SAM**: An open source framework specifically for building serverless applications on AWS. It extends CloudFormation by providing a simplified way of defining serverless resources, such as AWS Lambda functions and Amazon API Gateway's APIs. It streamlines their deployment and management, incorporating best practices and enabling easy debugging and testing.

- **CDK**: Provided by AWS, this service lets developers define and provision cloud infrastructure using familiar programming languages such as TypeScript, Python, and Java through CloudFormation. It integrates security practices directly into the development life cycle.

- **Terraform**: An open source IaC tool by HashiCorp that's compatible with multiple cloud providers, including AWS. It provisions AWS resources either by generating CloudFormation stacks or interacting directly with the AWS API, supporting a consistent CLI workflow for multi-cloud strategies and security configurations.

The use of IaC for managing AWS resources is a significant step forward in securing cloud environments. By codifying infrastructure, AWS users can ensure that security is not an afterthought but an integral part of the deployment process. IaC frameworks such as CloudFormation, SAM, CDK, and Terraform enable the creation of standardized, repeatable, and secure deployment processes. These tools help in avoiding the pitfalls of Snowflake systems and embrace the predictability of Phoenix systems, where security configurations are consistent, and environments are ephemeral and immutable.

Benefits of adopting IaC

The adoption of IaC brings a transformative approach to infrastructure management, aligning it closely with software development practices. Here are the key benefits of integrating IaC into AWS security strategies:

- **Consistency and standardization**: IaC ensures that every deployment is consistent, which is crucial for maintaining security standards

- **Enhanced security posture**: Security controls and policies are codified, allowing for audit trails of all changes and ensuring that security measures are always in place and up to date

- **Speed and efficiency**: IaC enables rapid provisioning and de-provisioning of resources, facilitating quick rollouts of security patches and updates

- **Error reduction**: By reducing the potential for human error, IaC minimizes the risk of security breaches associated with manual configurations

- **Cost savings**: Automating infrastructure setup reduces labor costs and supports efficient resource scaling, leading to potential cost savings

- **Documentation**: The code base serves as a detailed record of the infrastructure setup, aiding in security audits and compliance

- **Disaster recovery**: IaC enables quick recreation of infrastructure from the code base, which is vital for business continuity in the event of a security incident

- **Scalability**: IaC simplifies scaling infrastructure to meet growing needs, managing complexity with fewer errors

- **Compliance and governance**: Codifying compliance standards into deployment processes ensures infrastructure meets regulatory requirements from the outset

In conclusion, the transformation from manual to programmatic management within AWS is a strategic evolution that enhances security and efficiency through automated, code-driven operations. This strategic shift paves the way for the upcoming sections, where we will expand on how programmatic management can be effectively integrated into broader security strategies and compliance frameworks.

Automated security testing

In the realm of cloud security, automated security testing stands as a bulwark against the ever-evolving threat landscape. As organizations migrate to cloud-native architectures, the need for robust security testing mechanisms that can keep pace with continuous integration and deployment practices has become paramount. This section delves into the critical role of security testing and its integration within IaC pipelines – a series of automated processes that compile, build, and deploy infrastructure code to cloud environments.

Treating infrastructure as software

The concept of IaC revolutionizes the way we think about infrastructure. No longer is it seen as a collection of physical assets to be managed manually, but as code that can be developed, tested, and maintained with the same rigor as application software. This paradigm shift necessitates a corresponding evolution in security testing methodologies.

Treating infrastructure as software means applying software development practices to infrastructure management, including version control, peer reviews, and continuous testing. Security testing, in this context, becomes a matter of analyzing and validating the code that defines the infrastructure to ensure it adheres to security best practices and policies. The benefits of treating IaC as software in the context of security are manifold:

- **Repository management**: Utilizing a repository for IaC allows for centralized management of infrastructure definitions, akin to source code, which facilitates better control, collaboration, and security oversight. Repositories can serve as critical checkpoints in the security process, where automated scans are triggered upon each commit or pull request, acting as an early detection system for potential security issues.

- **Version control**: Every change to the infrastructure can be tracked, reviewed, and audited, providing a clear history of security-related changes. This ensures that any alterations to the infrastructure are documented, allowing for rollback in case of issues and a clear audit trail for compliance purposes.

- **Automated testing**: Security tests can be automated and integrated into the deployment pipeline, allowing for early detection and remediation of potential security issues. This includes unit tests, integration tests, and security-specific tests that are run automatically as part of the IaC life cycle.

- **Repeatability**: Security tests can be run repeatedly, ensuring consistent enforcement of security standards. This repeatability also allows for the testing process to be refined and improved over time, allowing you to learn from past experiences to better detect and prevent future security vulnerabilities.

Security testing in IaC pipelines

Integrating security testing into IaC pipelines is a practice that aligns with the DevSecOps philosophy, where security is integrated into the CI/CD pipeline. This will be covered in more detail in *Chapter 12*. This integration ensures that security is not a separate, siloed process but a continuous and integral part of infrastructure provisioning and management.

The process of integrating security testing into IaC pipelines typically involves the following steps:

1. **Static code analysis**: The IaC code is scanned statically for patterns that indicate potential security issues, such as open security groups or overly permissive IAM roles. This analysis also includes checking for hard-coded secrets and deprecated functions while ensuring that best practices for security are followed.

2. **Change impact analysis**: Any changes in the IaC code are analyzed to determine their impact on the security posture of the infrastructure. This involves risk assessments and the potential for cascading effects due to changes in interdependent resources.

3. **Policy-as-code**: The IaC template is checked against policy-as-code rules that represent regulatory and organizational security requirements. This ensures that the infrastructure is compliant with security requirements and industry standards such as PCI-DSS, HIPAA, or GDPR from the outset.

4. **Dynamic analysis**: Once the infrastructure has been provisioned in a non-production environment, dynamic security tests are run to validate the security of the deployed resources before they are rolled out to production. Importantly, dynamic analysis is also crucial in production environments, where continuous security testing can be facilitated through strategies such as canary deployments or blue/green deployments.

5. **Monitoring and feedback**: The results of the security tests are monitored, and feedback is provided to the development team to fix any issues before the code is promoted to production. This feedback loop is crucial for continuous improvement and helps foster a culture of security within the organization.

Tools for automated security scanning

A variety of AWS native and third-party tools are available to facilitate automated security scanning in IaC pipelines. These tools can be categorized based on their primary function:

*   **Static analysis tools** (**SATs**): Tools such as Checkov, Terraform Lint, CFN-Nag, and AWS CodeGuru Security analyze IaC templates for security misconfigurations and vulnerabilities without executing the code.

*   **Policy-as-code tools**: Tools like **Open Policy Agent** (**OPA**) and AWS CloudFormation Guard allow teams to define and enforce policy-as-code rules.

*   **Dynamic analysis tools** (**DATs**): Tools such as Nessus and Amazon Inspector offer dynamic scanning, which actively assesses a provisioned infrastructure to detect vulnerabilities. These tools can be used for both non-production and production environments.

*   **Integrated security platforms**: Solutions such as Prisma Cloud and Aqua Security provide comprehensive security scanning capabilities across the entire pipeline.

Each of these tools plays a role in ensuring that IaC deployments are secure by default. For instance, SATs are critical for the early detection of potential security issues, while DATs are essential for validating the security of the infrastructure once it is live.

When selecting tools for automated security scanning, it is important to consider the following factors:

*   **Compatibility with IaC frameworks**: The tool should seamlessly integrate with the IaC frameworks in use, such as CloudFormation or Terraform

*   **Comprehensiveness**: The tool should cover a wide range of security checks, from basic misconfigurations to complex compliance requirements

*   **Ease of integration**: The tool should easily integrate into existing IaC pipelines, providing automated scanning without manual intervention

*   **Feedback mechanisms**: It should provide clear, actionable feedback that developers can use to improve the security of the IaC

- **Scalability**: As the infrastructure grows, the tool should be able to scale its scanning capabilities accordingly

By incorporating these tools into the IaC life cycle, organizations can ensure that their AWS environments are not only secure from the start but also maintain that security as they evolve. This proactive approach to security testing is essential in an era where infrastructure changes are frequent and the cost of security breaches is high.

In conclusion, automated security testing in the context of IaC is a fundamental aspect of securing AWS environments. Integrating rigorous security testing into IaC pipelines ensures a high level of security for organizations.. The use of specialized tools for automated security scanning further enhances this process, providing a robust framework for maintaining secure and compliant infrastructure. As AWS environments become increasingly dynamic and complex, the role of automated security testing will only grow in importance, making it an indispensable part of any AWS security strategy.

Security best practices for IaC

The agility afforded by IaC can also introduce security risks if best practices are not applied diligently. This section will explore the security best practices that are essential for maintaining robust IaC frameworks.

Apply least privileges

The principle of least privilege is a cornerstone of security, dictating that permissions are tightly controlled and granted only as necessary for specific roles and tasks. In the context of IaC, this principle is even more critical as the automated scripts and templates define and control vast swathes of cloud resources.

Control access to CloudFormation

Controlling access to CloudFormation is about defining who can interact with the service and to what extent. This control is achieved through precise management of IAM permissions. Each user or entity (principal) must only have access to the CloudFormation actions necessary for their role. For example, developers may require permissions to create and manage stacks, while auditors might only need read-only access to review configurations and compliance. IAM policies are used to grant the appropriate level of access. These policies should be tuned to allow specific actions, such as `CreateStack`, `UpdateStack`, or `DeleteStack`, to specific resources, and can be further restricted to specific stacks through the use of a policy's conditions, thus mitigating the risk of unintentional or deliberate alterations to the cloud infrastructure.

CloudFormation permissions have a unique aspect: principals interacting with CloudFormation may be able to create, modify, or delete resources within a stack, even if they lack direct permissions to those resources outside the CloudFormation context. This design minimizes the need for extensive individual IAM permissions, following the principle of least privilege.

While this approach enhances security, it is crucial to carefully consider the permissions granted to principals for CloudFormation stacks themselves. Controlling access to CloudFormation and understanding the impact of stack-based permissions ensures principals can only perform their necessary tasks. This is essential to reduce the risk of accidental or malicious changes to your cloud environment.

Guard against privilege escalation

Privilege escalation represents a significant security risk, especially in scenarios where permissions are not adequately controlled. Within CloudFormation, it is imperative to architect the system in such a way that each task is associated with its own distinct role rather than inheriting permissions associated with the principal executing the task. This approach ensures that permissions are precisely aligned with the task's requirements, preventing excessive access.

When implementing task-specific roles, it is crucial to establish a governance mechanism that prevents developers from modifying the IAM roles assigned to these tasks. This is to ensure that developers cannot extend their permissions boundaries by manipulating CloudFormation to perform actions that are beyond their authorized scope. For example, a developer should be able to initiate a stack update, but the execution of that update should be performed by a predefined service role with the exact permissions necessary to carry out the task. This service role is assumed by CloudFormation during the stack operation, which effectively separates the user's permissions from the stack's execution context.

By enforcing such a policy, organizations can significantly reduce the risk of privilege escalation. Developers can work within the permissions that are granted to them without the ability to alter the IAM roles that govern the tasks. This approach not only secures the environment against unauthorized access but also aligns with the best practices of least privilege by ensuring that permissions are not just minimized but are also unalterable by those without the authority to do so.

Implement stack policies for resource protection

Stack policies are a means of protecting specific resources within a stack from being unintentionally updated or deleted. These policies provide a layer of governance over stack operations, allowing administrators to define which resources can be modified and under what circumstances.

For example, a stack policy can be crafted to prevent the deletion of an Amazon RDS database instance while allowing updates to its read replica configuration. This ensures that critical components of the infrastructure remain intact and operational, even as other aspects of the stack are iteratively improved. By defining such policies, organizations can safeguard their most sensitive and critical infrastructure elements from disruptive changes.

Concluding our discussion on applying key least privilege principles, let's transition to the equally vital task of securely managing secrets in IaC.

Handle secrets securely

Secrets can include API keys, passwords, and certificates, are essential for authenticating and authorizing actions within cloud services and applications. However, if not managed with stringent security measures, they can become weaknesses that lead to significant breaches.

Secure storage of secrets

The first step in handling secrets securely is to ensure their secure storage. Secrets should never be hard-coded in IaC templates or scripts as this exposes them to unauthorized access, particularly when code repositories are public or shared among team members. Instead, secrets should be stored in a centralized and secure secrets management system, such as AWS Secrets Manager or AWS Systems Manager (SSM) Parameter Store. These systems are designed to securely store and manage secrets according to best practices, as discussed previously in *Chapter 5*.

Secret scanning and detection

Implement automated tools that scan repositories and codebases for hard-coded secrets. These tools can alert teams to potential security risks before the code is deployed. By integrating secret scanning into the continuous integration pipeline, organizations can catch and remediate issues early in the development cycle.

Tools such as GitGuardian, TruffleHog, and Amazon CodeGuru Security are adept at scanning code to identify embedded secrets and can be easily integrated into your IaC pipelines.

Access control and auditing

Access to secrets should be tightly controlled using fine-grained permissions. Only principles that require access to a specific secret for their operation should be granted access, and even then, only for the minimum period necessary. This is where IAM policies play a crucial role. They allow administrators to define who can retrieve which secrets under what conditions, often with the ability to set expiration times for temporary access.

Auditing is another critical aspect of secure secrets management. Every access or change to a secret should be logged and monitored, including calls made by CloudFormation, as well as regular IAM principals. This includes tracking who accessed a secret, when it was accessed, and what operation was performed. Such auditing capabilities are built into AWS secrets management systems and are vital for detecting unusual patterns that may indicate a security incident. Regular monitoring and alerting should be implemented to detect irregular access patterns.

Secret injection at runtime

To utilize secrets within IaC, they should be injected at runtime rather than being embedded in the code. This can be achieved through the use of environment variables or by retrieving the secrets directly from the secrets management system at the time they are needed. For example, CloudFormation stacks can reference secrets stored in Secrets Manager, ensuring that the secrets are only exposed to the resources that require them and only for the duration of their necessity.

Injecting secrets at runtime minimizes the risk of accidental exposure and provides an additional layer of security by keeping the secrets out of the code base. It also simplifies the process of updating secrets as they can be rotated or changed within the secrets management system without the need to update and redeploy IaC templates or scripts.

Ensure compliance

Ensuring and automating compliance within IaC environments is not just a matter of convenience but a strategic imperative. It ensures that compliance is an inherent part of the infrastructure life cycle, from development to deployment and operations.

Embedded compliance standards

Embedding compliance standards directly into IaC templates ensures that every piece of infrastructure is provisioned as per regulatory and security best practices. This method, often referred to as **compliance as code**, allows for the automatic enforcement of compliance policies during the deployment process. For instance, using CloudFormation, you can define stacks that inherently comply with standards such as HIPAA or PCI DSS by including configurations for encryption, logging, and access controls. When these stacks are used to provision resources, they inherently comply with the defined standards, streamlining the compliance process.

Continuous compliance validation

Continuous compliance validation involves integrating automated compliance checks into the IaC pipeline. This integration ensures that every update or change to the infrastructure is evaluated against compliance policies before it is deployed. Tools such as Config rules can be programmed to automatically assess and report on the compliance status of AWS resources in real time. If a resource configuration drifts from the defined compliance standards, Config can flag the issue for review or automatically remediate the configuration to align with the compliance requirements.

Proactive compliance monitoring

Beyond the deployment phase, proactive compliance monitoring involves setting up systems that continuously scan the cloud environment for compliance with the defined policies. This includes monitoring for configuration changes, ensuring encryption standards are maintained, and verifying that access controls are in place. CloudTrail, for instance, can be used to log and monitor all actions taken on AWS resources, providing an audit trail that can be used for compliance reporting and forensic analysis.

Automated remediation strategies

When a compliance violation is detected, the system should not only alert the relevant stakeholders but also take predefined actions to remediate the issue. This could involve rolling back changes to a known compliant state or automatically applying patches to address security vulnerabilities. Lambda functions can be triggered in response to compliance events to execute remediation actions defined in the IaC templates. This level of automation ensures that compliance is maintained without manual intervention, reducing the time and effort required to manage compliance.

Integrating policy as code

Policy-as-code is about defining and managing security policies in a format that can be understood and enforced by automated systems. CloudFormation Guard is one of the tools that allow you to write policies that reflect your organization's security guidelines and automatically enforce those policies during the CloudFormation stack creation process. This ensures that all resources comply with the organization's security policies from the start.

For example, a retail company leveraged CloudFormation Guard to enforce PCI DSS standards across its cloud infrastructure. By setting up policies that required all payment data within RDS instances to be encrypted at rest, they could automatically validate their CloudFormation stacks against these standards, ensuring that no new database resources were provisioned without the necessary encryption configurations. The following code snippet illustrates the corresponding CloudFormation Guard rule, as implemented by the company:

```
rule ensure_payment_RDS_encrypted {
    when %resource.Type == "AWS::RDS::DBInstance" {
        {"Key": "payment", "Value": "true"} in %resource.Properties.
Tags implies %resource.Properties.StorageEncrypted == true
    }
}
```

This rule states that for a resource of the `AWS::RDS::DBInstance` type, if the tags include a tag with a key of `payment` and a value of `true`, then the `StorageEncrypted` property must be `true`. This means that if the `payment` tag is present, then the database is classified as handling payment data and requires encryption to be enabled.

The Automate-Everything approach

The Automate-Everything approach is a transformative strategy that reshapes how organizations manage their cloud infrastructure. It is a philosophy that champions automation at every turn, reducing manual intervention to enhance efficiency, consistency, and security.

Cultural shifts and automation mindset

Adopting the Automate-Everything approach requires a significant cultural shift within an organization. It demands a mindset that prioritizes automation for all repeatable processes. This shift begins with leadership buy-in and must permeate through all levels of the technology and development teams. It involves training and empowering teams to think *automation-first* and to recognize the value of automating tasks. This cultural evolution leads to a more agile organization that can respond quickly to changes and challenges, with the added benefits of reducing human error and freeing up valuable resources to focus on innovation rather than routine tasks.

Infrastructure management via Git

Within the Automate-Everything mindset, managing infrastructure through Git – commonly known as GitOps – stands out as a pivotal practice. In this model, Git serves as the authoritative repository for all infrastructure and application configurations. Changes to the infrastructure are meticulously tracked in the version control system, initiating automated workflows to transpose those changes onto the operational environment. This method not only simplifies the management and deployment processes but also bolsters teamwork and visibility across the board. It facilitates comprehensive tracking of changes, straightforward reversions to previous states, and transparent visibility into the infrastructure's status at any given moment.

Force programmatic management

Forcing programmatic management within the IaC paradigm is a strategic approach that ensures all changes and deployments are executed through code, rather than manual processes. This method is integral to maintaining the integrity, consistency, and traceability of the cloud environment. Here's how it can be implemented in practice:

- **Force exclusive management via IaC**: To enforce compliance and security within the IaC deployment workflow, the process must be automated end-to-end. This means that from the moment a developer commits code to the version control system, to the deployment of infrastructure changes, every step is automated. Tools such as CloudFormation or Terraform are used to define the infrastructure in code, and IaC pipelines are set up to handle the testing, approval, and deployment phases.

- **Monitor non-programmatic changes**: Even with strict automation policies, it is essential to monitor for any changes that might occur outside the automated workflows. AWS CloudTrail is an invaluable service for this as it logs all actions taken in the AWS environment. By setting up alerts for CloudTrail events, organizations can be notified of any manual changes, enabling quick response to potential policy violations.

- **Drift detection**: AWS Config and CloudFormation drift detection are powerful features that help identify discrepancies between the actual state of the cloud environment and the state defined in IaC. Drift detection can automatically report on resources that have been modified, added, or deleted outside of the IaC processes, providing an opportunity for remediation or enforcement actions.

- **Restrict manual changes**: To ensure that changes are made only through IaC, IAM policies and **service control policies** (**SCPs**) can be put in place to explicitly deny manual changes. These policies can be configured to allow only CloudFormation to perform actions on AWS resources, effectively preventing users from making direct changes.

- **Implement an emergency change protocol**: In an automated IaC environment, a *red button* protocol allows for manual emergency changes under strict control. Special IAM accounts, created for such emergencies, are tightly regulated and used only with senior approval. These accounts need to be closely monitored. Once the emergency has been resolved, permissions are automatically scaled back, and a detailed review is conducted to evaluate the response's appropriateness and security impact. This approach ensures a balance between rapid response and security compliance.

To illustrate how manual changes can be restricted, consider the following IAM policy example:

```
{
    "Version": "2012-10-17",
    "Statement": [
        {
            "Effect": "Deny",
            "Action": [
                "ec2:RunInstances",
                "ec2:TerminateInstances",
                "ec2:StopInstances"
            ],
            "Resource": "*",
            "Condition": {
                "StringNotLike": {
                    "aws:CalledVia": "cloudformation.amazonaws.com"
                }
            }
        }
    ]
}
```

In this IAM policy example, we deny the ability to run, terminate, or stop Amazon EC2 instances unless the request is made through CloudFormation. The `Condition` block, with the `StringNotLike` operator and the `aws:CalledVia` key, ensures that if the service principal making the request is not CloudFormation, the action is denied. This policy enforces programmatic management by requiring that all specified actions must be performed via CloudFormation, aligning with the Automate-Everything approach and minimizing the risk of configuration drift and unauthorized changes.

In conclusion, the security measures detailed herein are critical for any organization seeking to leverage IaC while maintaining a strong security posture.

Summary

In this chapter, we journeyed through the paradigm shift from manual to programmatic management of cloud resources, underscoring the transition as a pivotal step toward building immutable and ephemeral resources. We dissected the inherent risks of manual resource management, such as human error and configuration drift, and how programmatic management via IaC frameworks such as CloudFormation, SAM, CDK, and Terraform mitigates these risks. This chapter illuminated the security and efficiency benefits of adopting IaC, detailing how it streamlines compliance and governance while enforcing best practices for security, such as the principle of least privilege and secure secrets management.

We also explored the Automate-Everything approach, which advocates for a cultural shift toward an automation mindset, emphasizing the importance of managing infrastructure through Git and enforcing programmatic management to maintain the integrity of cloud environments. By integrating automated security testing and compliance checks into the IaC pipeline, this chapter provided a blueprint for securing cloud infrastructure in a scalable and sustainable manner.

As we pivot to the next chapter, we will delve into the sophisticated realm of logging, auditing, and monitoring with CloudTrail and CloudWatch among other AWS services, equipping you with the advanced skills needed to configure these services for robust security oversight and proactive incident response.

Questions

Answer the following questions to test your knowledge of this chapter:

1. How does repository management contribute to the security of IaC?
2. What is static code analysis in the context of IaC, and why is it important?
3. How does dynamic analysis differ from static analysis in IaC security testing?
4. How can organizations guard against privilege escalation in CloudFormation?

Answers

Here are the answers to this chapter's questions:

1. Repository management centralizes the control of IaC templates, akin to source code management. It facilitates collaboration, version control, and automated security scanning upon each commit, serving as an early detection system for potential security issues.

2. Static code analysis involves scanning the IaC code for patterns that could lead to security issues, such as open security groups or hard-coded secrets. It is crucial for early detection of vulnerabilities and ensuring adherence to security best practices.

3. Dynamic analysis is performed on the actual provisioned infrastructure, as opposed to the static code. It validates the security of deployed resources in a live environment, which is essential for catching issues that static analysis might miss.

4. To prevent privilege escalation, organizations should architect their systems so that tasks are associated with distinct roles and not the permissions of the IAM principal executing the task. For example, a stack update should be executed by a service role with the exact permissions necessary for the task, not by inheriting the developer's permissions.

Further reading

The following resources offer further insights and best practices for IaC security:

- *Infrastructure as Code Security Cheatsheet*, by OWASP: `https://cheatsheetseries.owasp.org/cheatsheets/Infrastructure_as_Code_Security_Cheat_Sheet.html`

- *Continuous Compliance Workflow for Infrastructure as Code*, by Sumit Mishra and Damodar Shenvi Wagle (2021): `https://aws.amazon.com/blogs/devops/continuous-compliance-workflow-for-infrastructure-as-code-part-1/`

- *AWS Cloud Quest: Security – Infrastructure as Code* (Youtube video), by Hands-On With Digital Den (2023): `https://www.youtube.com/watch?v=6cUdusFptFo`

Part 3: Monitoring, Automation and Continuous Improvement

Proactive defense and continuous evolution: In this part, you will enhance visibility with AWS monitoring tools, achieve compliance, automate for efficiency, embed security practices into your CI/CD pipelines, and adopt an adaptive approach to security.

This part has the following chapters:

- *Chapter 10, Advanced Logging, Auditing, and Monitoring in AWS*
- *Chapter 11, Security Compliance with AWS Config, AWS Security Hub, and Automated Remediation*
- *Chapter 12, DevSecOps - Integrating Security into CI/CD Pipelines*
- *Chapter 13, Keeping Up with Evolving AWS Security Best Practices and Threat Landscape*
- *Closing Note*

10
Advanced Logging, Auditing, and Monitoring in AWS

Welcome to the tenth chapter of our comprehensive guide to AWS security. In this chapter, we will delve into the realms of advanced logging, auditing, and monitoring within AWS, a crucial aspect for ensuring robust security in cloud environments.

We will begin with an in-depth examination of AWS CloudTrail, unraveling its advanced features for meticulous tracking of API usage and detailed user activity analysis. This section aims to provide you with the knowledge to leverage CloudTrail for enhanced visibility and accountability within your AWS environment.

We will then shift our focus to Amazon CloudWatch, examining its vital role in application security monitoring and the creation of sophisticated security dashboards. Here, you will learn how to effectively utilize CloudWatch for real-time threat detection and response, ensuring the ongoing security of your applications.

Our journey will continue with a discussion on Amazon Security Lake, where we will highlight its capabilities in centralized storage and management of diverse security logs. This segment aims to demonstrate how Security Lake can simplify your log management process, ensuring efficient and consistent data formatting.

Lastly, we will explore the powerful log analytics offered by Amazon Athena, providing insights into its usage for complex security data interrogation. This final section will guide you through utilizing Athena for deep and meaningful analysis of your security data.

By the end of this chapter, you will be equipped with advanced strategies and practical knowledge to enhance your AWS security monitoring and auditing capabilities.

In this chapter, we will cover the following key areas:

- Using CloudTrail's advanced tracking and analysis capabilities
- Leveraging CloudWatch for comprehensive application security monitoring
- Centralizing security logs using Security Lake
- Security Lake's centralized log storage and management
- Utilizing Athena for in-depth log analytics and security data interrogation

Strengthening security through logging and monitoring

In the dynamic environment of cloud computing, logging and monitoring stand as critical pillars of a robust security framework. These processes are not just tools for compliance and operational efficiency but are fundamental to ensuring the integrity and security of AWS-based infrastructures.

Importance in cloud security

Logging and monitoring in AWS play a pivotal role in several key areas:

- **Threat detection and response**: The ability to detect anomalies, unusual patterns, or potential security threats hinges on comprehensive logging and real-time monitoring. For instance, detecting a sudden spike in traffic from an unusual geographic location can indicate a potential DDoS attack. Proactive surveillance enables swift identification and mitigation of such incidents, safeguarding the integrity of cloud operations.

- **Compliance and auditing**: Regulatory compliance demands a thorough audit trail of activities within the cloud environment. Logging and monitoring facilitate this by providing detailed records of user activities, resource usage, and access patterns, which are essential for meeting regulatory requirements and conducting effective audits. An example of this is using logs to track access to sensitive data, ensuring compliance with standards such as HIPAA.

- **Operational efficiency**: Beyond security implications, logging and monitoring contribute significantly to operational efficiency. They offer insights into system performance, resource utilization, and application behavior, enabling optimization and informed decision-making.

Now that we have emphasized the importance of logging and monitoring, let's explore the most relevant tools from the AWS services portfolio.

Evolution of AWS services for logging and monitoring

AWS has continuously evolved its offerings to address the growing complexity of cloud operations that require more and more advanced logging and monitoring capabilities. The services that are offered are diverse, each addressing specific aspects of security and operations:

- **CloudTrail**: This service is instrumental in auditing AWS account activities. CloudTrail's detailed logs of AWS API calls and user activities offer a granular view of the operations within the AWS environment, making it an invaluable asset for security analysis and operational troubleshooting.

- **CloudWatch**: As a monitoring service, CloudWatch goes beyond mere logging. It provides real-time monitoring of AWS resources, delivering insights into operational health and system performance. CloudWatch's capabilities in logging, metric collection, and real-time alerting make it a cornerstone for operational monitoring and security vigilance.

- **Athena**: Contrary to being a traditional logging tool, Athena is an interactive query service that's primarily used for analytics. It allows users to analyze extensive datasets, including logs stored in Amazon S3. Athena's powerful SQL querying capabilities make it an excellent tool for extracting actionable insights from large volumes of log data.

- **Security Lake**: More recently introduced, Security Lake centralizes security data from various AWS sources and third-party applications. It is designed to aggregate, manage, and analyze security data at scale, enhancing the ability to gain comprehensive security insights across the AWS environment.

As we have seen, AWS offers a range of specialized services for logging and monitoring. The next step is to explore how combining these services into an integrated approach can amplify their effectiveness and provide a robust framework.

Integrated approach

Integrating AWS logging and monitoring services creates a robust framework, which offers several advantages:

- **Holistic security analysis**: Integrating CloudTrail and CloudWatch data provides organizations with a comprehensive view of their security posture. An example of this is using CloudTrail to track changes in IAM role permissions or configurations and correlating this with CloudWatch metrics showing unexpected spikes in resource utilization. This correlation can highlight potential security breaches or misuse of permissions.

- **Enhanced incident detection and response**: Integrating these tools enables advanced incident detection and facilitates quicker response times. For instance, an anomaly detected through real-time monitoring in CloudWatch can be cross-referenced with detailed CloudTrail logs to pinpoint the source of the issue. Further, deep analytics provided by Athena and the centralized security data from Security Lake can be leveraged to identify subtle and complex security threats, ensuring a rapid and informed response to safeguard AWS resources.

- **Streamlined compliance reporting**: The combination of logging, monitoring, and analytical capabilities from these integrated services streamlines the process of compliance reporting. Organizations can efficiently aggregate diverse data points, such as user access patterns from CloudTrail and system performance metrics from CloudWatch, to demonstrate compliance with various regulatory requirements. This integration not only simplifies the creation of comprehensive compliance reports but also ensures that they are backed by thorough and accurate data analysis.

Key considerations for unified logging and monitoring

To successfully integrate these services, it is essential to consider the following aspects:

- **Strategic data correlation**: Effective integration hinges on a well-thought-out strategy for data correlation. Identifying how data from each service complements and enhances the other is key to creating a unified logging and monitoring solution. For instance, correlating login attempts logged in CloudTrail with network traffic patterns in CloudWatch can help detect potential brute force attacks.

- **Customization and scalability**: Tailoring the configuration of each service to meet specific needs is crucial. This includes setting up customized metrics in CloudWatch, configuring targeted logging in CloudTrail, crafting complex queries in Athena, and efficiently managing security data in Security Lake.

- **Automated alerting and proactive monitoring**: Leveraging automation capabilities enhances real-time security monitoring. Setting up automated alerts based on specific triggers or anomalies detected across services can significantly improve the efficiency and effectiveness of the security response.

In conclusion, this holistic integration of monitoring capabilities provides deeper insights into security incidents, accelerates response times for potential threats, and efficiently consolidates compliance data, significantly strengthening cloud security management.

Beyond basic auditing with CloudTrail

In this section, we will delve deeper into the advanced auditing features offered by CloudTrail, moving beyond basic logging capabilities to explore sophisticated monitoring and troubleshooting techniques. CloudTrail, renowned for its comprehensive logging capabilities, provides a detailed record of API calls, user activities, and other interactions within AWS services, answering the crucial question, *Who did what, where, and when?*

Best practices for configuring CloudTrail trails

Configuring CloudTrail trails effectively is a first step, yet it is essential to maximize the benefits of AWS auditing. The following best practices should be considered when setting up CloudTrail:

- **Comprehensive event logging**: Configure trails to log all management and data events across all AWS regions, ensuring a complete audit trail for every activity and providing a broad view of operations and security incidents.

- **Selective event logging for efficiency**: Consider using multiple trails tailored to specific needs—one trail for all management events, such as API calls for overall security monitoring, and separate trails for data events related to critical resources, enabling targeted analysis and efficient log management.

- **Avoid redundant logging**: Carefully plan your trails' configuration to minimize logging overlaps. Redundant trails can lead to increased costs without adding security value.

- **Trail encryption and security**: Encrypt CloudTrail logs using AWS KMS and securely store them in S3 buckets while implementing robust access controls and bucket policies.

- **Log file integrity validation**: Use this feature to guarantee the reliability and security of your log files, which are essential for compliance and forensic analysis. Additionally, consider enabling versioning in the S3 bucket storing log files. This helps safeguard against tampering by allowing you to recover previous versions of log files if necessary.

- **Integration with AWS services**: Integrate CloudTrail with services such as CloudWatch for real-time monitoring and Lambda for automated event responses, enhancing security capabilities.

- **Centralized log storage**: Direct CloudTrail events to a dedicated S3 bucket for centralized storage, ensuring proper configuration and protection against unauthorized access.

- **Account baselines**: In a multi-account environment, it is crucial to ensure CloudTrail activation across all regions and accounts by default. This practice establishes a consistent security baseline from the start, ensuring comprehensive monitoring and logging within your entire organization.

Anomaly detection with CloudTrail Insights

Transitioning from the proper configuration of CloudTrail trails, we will now focus on the advanced capabilities of CloudTrail Insights. This feature plays a critical role in enhancing AWS security through sophisticated anomaly detection and behavioral analysis.

Anomaly detection and behavioral analysis

CloudTrail Insights is designed to automatically detect unusual operational activities within an AWS environment. It does this by continuously analyzing CloudTrail management events and establishing a normative baseline for user and resource behavior. Any significant deviations from this baseline are flagged as Insights events, which can indicate potential security issues, such as unauthorized resource access or configuration changes.

Automated monitoring for compliance and security

Insights extends the capabilities of CloudTrail by providing an automated solution for monitoring and identifying potential compliance violations or security threats. This proactive monitoring is crucial for maintaining compliance with various regulatory requirements and ensuring a strong security posture in the rapidly evolving cloud environment.

Practical use cases

In practical terms, CloudTrail Insights can be used to monitor for anomalies such as the following:

- **Unusual API call rates**: This involves detecting spikes in API calls that are not consistent with the established pattern. For instance, an abnormal increase in `TerminateInstances` API calls could indicate a potential breach.

- **Irregular resource provisioning**: Insights can flag unexpected increases in resource provisioning activities, such as the sudden creation of multiple instances, which might suggest unauthorized access or misuse of resources.

Through these advanced features, CloudTrail Insights provides a deeper layer of security, offering invaluable insights into the operational and security aspects of the AWS environment.

Advanced data analysis with CloudTrail Lake

As we delve into the advanced features of CloudTrail, CloudTrail Lake emerges as a pivotal tool, offering sophisticated data analysis capabilities. This managed data lake solution is designed for in-depth analysis and investigation, extending beyond the traditional logging functions of CloudTrail.

Features of CloudTrail Lake

CloudTrail Lake is a managed audit and security data lake, enabling aggregation, storage, and in-depth analysis of AWS activities. It captures detailed API activity and user actions, providing a comprehensive view of interactions within AWS services. Here are some of CloudTrail Lake's features:

- Long-term retention of event data, allowing historical analysis over extended periods
- Advanced query capabilities, supporting complex SQL queries across various event fields
- Integration with multiple AWS accounts and regions, offering a unified view of activities

Real-time alerts and analytics with CloudTrail Lake

CloudTrail Lake enhances real-time security monitoring and incident response. It allows for the creation of sophisticated queries and alerting mechanisms based on specific patterns or anomalies in the data, facilitating immediate action and in-depth investigation of security incidents.

For example, the following query helps identify failed login attempts, providing insights into potential unauthorized access attempts:

```
SELECT user_identity.arn, event_time, event_name
FROM cloudtrail_logs
WHERE event_name = 'ConsoleLogin' AND response_elements.ConsoleLogin =
'Failure';
```

This other example counts the number of API calls since a specific date, grouped by `eventName` and `eventSource`. This can help in understanding the usage pattern of different AWS services and can flag unusual activity levels:

```
SELECT
    eventSource,
    eventName,
    COUNT(*) AS apiCount
FROM
    event_data_store_ID
WHERE
    eventTime > '2023-01-01 00:00:00'
GROUP BY
    eventSource, eventName
ORDER BY
    apiCount DESC
```

In conclusion, CloudTrail offers advanced tools that go beyond basic logging, providing in-depth insights into AWS operations. These capabilities allow organizations to conduct intricate security analyses, streamline compliance efforts, and respond effectively to evolving threats.

Advanced security monitoring with CloudWatch

CloudWatch is a multifaceted monitoring service in AWS that provides real-time insights into the operational health and security of AWS resources. This section expands on CloudWatch's role in security monitoring, demonstrating its application in monitoring applications, setting up security-focused metrics and dashboards, and its interaction with CloudTrail for enhanced security vigilance.

Enhancing application security monitoring with CloudWatch

CloudWatch provides detailed insights into application performance and security, making it a vital tool for developers and security teams. By monitoring application logs and metrics, it helps in identifying and mitigating security risks.

Application logs management

CloudWatch facilitates extensive log collection from various AWS services, including system and application logs, alongside Lambda function logs. This comprehensive collection allows for a holistic view of application security and performance. Real-time log analysis, a key feature of CloudWatch logs, provides immediate insights into application behavior and potential security issues. Organizing logs into meaningful groups based on application components or environment types streamlines analysis, enhancing the speed and accuracy of identifying security-relevant data. Moreover, the persistent storage and accessibility of logs in CloudWatch are vital for in-depth post-incident investigations and meeting compliance requirements.

Custom metrics for security

CloudWatch's ability to create custom security metrics is a key asset in monitoring specific security aspects of applications. These metrics can originate from direct instrumentation within the application code or be derived from log data. They can be utilized to highlight specific security incidents such as sudden spikes in error rates or unusual patterns in user behavior.

For example, a web application can push custom metrics to CloudWatch whenever a login attempt occurs, recording both successes and failures. Similarly, metrics can be extracted from CloudWatch logs using metric filters. This could involve parsing application logs to count occurrences of specific error messages or failed access attempts. By utilizing both methods, teams gain a multi-faceted view of security events, allowing for more accurate and comprehensive monitoring.

Continuous monitoring with advanced queries

For more sophisticated analysis, especially with structured logs such as Apache server logs, CloudWatch Logs Insights can be utilized. Consider the following complex query example for an Apache log:

```
fields @timestamp, @message
| parse @message '* - - [*] "* * *" * * "-" "*"' as ip, datetime,
request, statusCode, bytes, referrer, userAgent
| filter statusCode >= 400
| stats count(*) as errorCount by bin(1h), ip, request, statusCode
| sort errorCount desc
```

This query parses the Apache log entries, extracts relevant fields such as IP address, request details, and status codes, and then filters for entries with status codes indicating errors (400 and above). It aggregates these into hourly bins, counts the errors, and sorts them by the count in descending order. This can help identify patterns such as frequent error codes from specific IP addresses or unusual request patterns, which could indicate security threats.

Alerts for security events

In CloudWatch, creating alerts based on specific conditions in the logs or metrics is crucial for timely response to potential security threats. For instance, the advanced log analysis in CloudWatch can also be the basis for creating effective security alerts. Using Apache's log analysis as an example, you can set up an alert to trigger when there's an unusually high count of error responses (status codes 400 and above) from the same IP address within a short period. This could indicate a brute-force attack or a web scraping attempt. The alert can then be configured to notify the security team and can trigger automated response actions using Lambda, such as blocking the suspicious IP address.

Building security dashboards in CloudWatch

CloudWatch dashboards provide an intuitive interface for visualizing and interacting with security data These dashboards can be customized to display a variety of security-related information, facilitating quick detection, analysis, and response to potential security issues.

Harnessing dashboards for effective security visualization

Creating security-focused dashboards in CloudWatch involves selecting and organizing relevant metrics and logs that pertain to an application's security. The process includes integrating various data points, such as API call logs from CloudTrail, application-specific metrics, and system-level indicators such as CPU and network usage. This integration allows for a comprehensive view of the security landscape, encompassing everything from user access patterns to system performance anomalies.

The customizable nature of CloudWatch dashboards empowers teams to tailor their security views according to specific needs or focus areas. For instance, a dashboard could be set up to highlight metrics related to network traffic, including the number of inbound and outbound requests, which could indicate potential security breaches such as DDoS attacks or data exfiltration.

By aligning dashboards with an organization's security framework and best practices, teams can proactively manage their security posture. Regularly reviewing and updating dashboards ensures that they remain relevant and effective, adapting to the continuously evolving landscape of cloud security.

Key components of security dashboards

To construct a CloudWatch dashboard that effectively monitors and manages security, several key components should be included. These components not only offer a real-time overview of security status, but also enable in-depth analysis of historical data and rapid response to emerging threats:

- **Real-time monitoring**: Incorporate widgets that display real-time data, such as current active connections or recent unauthorized access attempts. This immediate visibility aids in rapid detection and response to potential security incidents.

- **Historical data analysis**: Include widgets that showcase historical data trends, offering insights into long-term security patterns and helping identify slow-building threats that might not be evident in day-to-day operations.

- **Alert summaries**: Integrate summaries of recent alarms and notifications, ensuring that the latest security issues are prominently displayed and can be acted upon swiftly.

- **Custom visualizations**: Utilize CloudWatch's capabilities to create custom visualizations that cater to specific security needs, such as geographic maps for visualizing the source of network traffic or custom graphs to track specific application behavior anomalies.

Practical use cases

An example of a CloudWatch dashboard for security might focus on network monitoring, featuring widgets that display metrics such as unusual spikes in inbound/outbound network traffic, a summary of **Network Access Control Lists** (**NACLs**) changes, and recent security group modifications. This setup provides a quick overview of network security status, alerting teams to potential external threats or internal misconfigurations.

A more complex example could involve creating a dashboard to monitor and analyze user behavior and access patterns. This dashboard could include the following:

- Widgets for tracking login attempts, both successful and failed, across different applications, highlighting potential brute-force attacks.

- A geographical map widget showing login attempts' origins. This is useful for identifying unauthorized access from unexpected regions.

- A line graph depicting API call frequency over time, with the ability to drill down into specific, user-executed actions. This is useful for spotting anomalies in user behavior or privilege escalation attempts.

- An integration widget with Lambda, triggering automated responses or deeper investigations based on specific alarm conditions.

Integration with diverse log sources for comprehensive monitoring

CloudWatch serves as a centralized monitoring solution that's adept at integrating with a wide array of log sources from various AWS services. This integrative capability is crucial for comprehensive monitoring and analysis, offering a more centralized and cohesive approach to log management compared to alternatives such as log centralization in S3.

Bringing logs from different sources into CloudWatch has several benefits:

- **Unified monitoring experience**: Centralized log analysis simplifies the monitoring process, enabling cross-service correlation and comprehensive security analysis

- **Streamlined log management**: Centralization reduces complexities associated with handling logs in disparate locations, offering a more efficient log management workflow

- **Improved alerting and troubleshooting**: Centralized logs enhance the ability to set up effective alerts and simplify troubleshooting as cross-service patterns and anomalies can be identified more easily

Now, let's examine various AWS services that can commonly be used as data sources for CloudWatch logging and security monitoring.

Integration with AWS services

CloudWatch is commonly used with the following sources:

- **EC2**: Logs from EC2 instances are pivotal for understanding virtual server operations and crucial for performance tracking and identifying security events.

- **Lambda**: Function execution logs provide insights into serverless application behavior, including performance metrics and potential security issues.

- **S3**: Monitoring access logs from S3 buckets is vital for detecting unusual data access or modification activities, thus bolstering data security for critical objects stored in S3.

- **RDS**: Database logs offer a window into database operations, helping in pinpointing potential security breaches or performance bottlenecks.

- **CloudFront**: Content distribution logs are essential for analyzing content distribution patterns and monitoring for abnormal requests that might indicate a security concern.

- **API Gateway**: Access logs offer details of API requests, usage patterns, authentication errors, and potential malicious activity targeting your APIs.

- **Elastic Load Balancer** (**ELB**): Access logs contain information about incoming requests to the ELB and their processing, assisting in security audits and troubleshooting by tracking how requests are routed to the targets.

- **CloudTrail**: This service's integration is vital for auditing API calls and user activities, offering a detailed perspective for security analysis.

- **VPC flow logs**: These logs are instrumental in monitoring network traffic. They help in detecting anomalous traffic patterns or unauthorized network access attempts within the VPC, enhancing network security.

Comparison with centralization in S3

Using S3 for log centralization contrasts with CloudWatch in essential ways:

- **Primary focus**: S3 is mainly a storage solution, which makes it best suited for long-term log retention. In contrast, CloudWatch provides real-time analysis and monitoring capabilities.

- **Access patterns and use cases**: Logs in S3 are typically accessed less frequently and used mainly for compliance or historical analysis. CloudWatch, however, is designed for ongoing, active monitoring and rapid incident response.

- **Integration capabilities**: CloudWatch offers superior integration with AWS's monitoring and automated response tools, providing a more dynamic and responsive logging solution compared to S3.

Having compared CloudWatch with S3 capabilities for logs centralization, let's shift to developer best practices for security monitoring, emphasizing the role of CloudWatch in these practices.

Developer best practices for security monitoring

In the AWS ecosystem, developers are pivotal in embedding robust security monitoring within applications. Utilizing CloudWatch effectively requires adherence to best practices that integrate security monitoring seamlessly into the development life cycle:

- **Embed monitoring from the start**: Design applications with built-in CloudWatch logging and metric collection, making security monitoring an integral part of application architecture

- **Define custom security metrics**: Create custom CloudWatch metrics specific to the application's security requirements, such as tracking failed login attempts or unusual database activity

- **Automate security alerts**: Use CloudWatch alarms to set up automatic alerts for specific security conditions and integrate these alerts into development and operational workflows, such as messaging platforms or issue-tracking systems

- **Organize log groups strategically**: Classify logs into meaningful groups based on application components, environments, or security levels for efficient management and quick identification during investigations

- **Set appropriate log retention and access controls**: Implement retention policies for log data that are in line with compliance and operational needs, and maintain strict access controls to safeguard log integrity

- **Leverage CloudWatch Logs Insights for advanced analysis**: Utilize the advanced query capabilities of CloudWatch Logs Insights to perform in-depth analysis of log data, uncovering patterns and trends indicative of security threats

- **Conduct regular log audits**: Regularly review log data to identify unusual activities or trends, and adjust security strategies accordingly based on these findings

- **Design informative security dashboards**: Create custom CloudWatch dashboards that visually represent security metrics and logs, including a mix of high-level overviews and detailed event drill-downs

- **Combine data from multiple sources**: Integrate data from various AWS services, such as CloudTrail and VPC flow logs, with application-specific metrics for a comprehensive view of the security landscape

- **Stay informed and adapt monitoring strategies**: Keep updated with the latest security threats and AWS features, and continually refine monitoring approaches to incorporate new security practices

- **Implement a feedback loop**: Establish a process where insights from security monitoring inform and enhance future development efforts, continuously improving security features and monitoring effectiveness

Practical use cases

CloudWatch's versatility extends to advanced security scenarios, offering solutions for complex challenges in AWS environments. In this section, we'll look at two practical examples showcasing its capability.

Use case 1 – real-time threat detection in a microservices architecture

In a microservices architecture, where applications are broken down into smaller, independent services, monitoring each component becomes crucial for security. Imagine an eCommerce platform with various microservices for user authentication, payment processing, and inventory management. By leveraging CloudWatch, you can set up a real-time threat detection system that monitors each microservice for signs of security breaches or anomalies:

- **Setup**: Configure CloudWatch to collect logs and metrics from each microservice. This might include API call logs, function execution times in Lambda, and data access patterns in DynamoDB.

- **Custom metrics**: Define custom metrics that are indicative of security issues, such as a high rate of failed login attempts in the authentication service or unusual spikes in payment transaction volumes.

- **Alerts and automation**: Create CloudWatch alarms based on these custom metrics. For instance, if the number of failed login attempts exceeds a certain threshold within a short time frame, it triggers an alarm. This alarm can automatically notify the security team or even trigger a Lambda function to temporarily lock down the affected service, preventing further unauthorized access attempts.

- **Dashboards**: Develop comprehensive CloudWatch dashboards that provide a real-time view of the security status of each microservice. These dashboards can be used to monitor ongoing activities and respond quickly to potential threats.

This use case demonstrates how CloudWatch can be effectively utilized to provide real-time security monitoring in a complex microservices architecture, enabling rapid detection and response to potential threats.

Use case 2 – automated compliance monitoring for sensitive data storage

For businesses handling sensitive data, ensuring compliance with regulatory standards such as GDPR or HIPAA is critical. CloudWatch can be utilized to automate compliance monitoring, particularly for sensitive data stored in AWS services such as S3 or RDS:

- **Setup**: Implement CloudWatch to monitor access and modification logs of S3 buckets and RDS instances that store sensitive data.

- **Compliance rules**: Define specific compliance rules in CloudWatch based on regulatory requirements. For example, you can create a rule to alert if any sensitive data is accessed from outside the approved geographic region, which could indicate a potential compliance violation.

- **Automated reporting**: Set up CloudWatch to generate regular compliance reports by analyzing logs and metrics. These reports can be automatically sent to compliance officers or relevant stakeholders, providing them with ongoing assurance that the data is being handled in compliance with regulatory standards.

- **Incident response**: In case of a detected compliance violation, configure CloudWatch to automatically initiate predefined response actions. This might include notifying the compliance team, revoking access to the data, or starting an automated workflow to investigate and remediate the issue.

This use case exemplifies how CloudWatch can be leveraged for automated compliance monitoring, ensuring that sensitive data is handled as per regulatory standards and reducing the burden of manual compliance checks.

In conclusion, CloudWatch serves as a powerful tool in the AWS security arsenal. By leveraging its advanced features, developers and security professionals can achieve a proactive stance in detecting and mitigating security threats, ensuring the integrity and reliability of AWS-based applications and infrastructure. With CloudWatch's capabilities outlined, let's turn our attention to advanced tools such as Security Lake and Athena for deeper security logs integration and analytics.

Empowering security logs integration and analytics

In advanced scenarios, AWS offers robust tools such as Security Lake and Athena to enhance security log management beyond the capabilities of CloudTrail and CloudWatch. These services are vital for situations demanding a deeper approach to security log integration and analytics. Together, they offer a comprehensive approach to managing and analyzing security logs, which is ideal for complex environments needing a refined analysis of security data.

Understanding Security Lake

Security Lake offers a comprehensive solution for aggregating, categorizing, and managing vast volumes of security data from various sources, going beyond CloudWatch and CloudTrail's log storage capabilities. Its key features are as follows:

- **Centralized security data storage**: Security Lake centralizes storage for security logs in multi-account AWS environments. It aggregates logs from diverse sources, such as CloudTrail, GuardDuty, and custom application logs, creating a cohesive data repository. This is particularly relevant for organizations dealing with diverse log sources and dispersed account structures as it streamlines log access and analysis.

- **Simplified log management**: Security Lake simplifies the complexity associated with managing disparate security logs format. It provides tools for automated log ingestion, normalization, and categorization using the **open cybersecurity schema framework (OCSF)**, ensuring that data is consistently formatted and easily retrievable. This standardization is key for efficient analysis, removing the complexities that arise from disparate and inconsistent log sources, and reducing the time and resources needed for log management.

- **Enterprise-wide threat detection**: Perhaps the greatest strength of Security Lake in a multi-account setup is the ability to correlate security events across the entire organization. This means detecting attacks that exploit resources in multiple accounts or pinpointing suspicious behavior patterns that might otherwise go unnoticed. Consider a scenario where a compromised EC2 instance in one account is used to exfiltrate data to an S3 bucket in another – a coordinated attack that only becomes apparent through centralized analysis.

- **Enhanced security data analysis**: The integration of Security Lake with analytical tools such as Athena enables powerful data analysis capabilities. Its structured repository enhances the efficiency of querying and analyzing security data, enabling organizations to uncover insights and patterns that might otherwise be overlooked.

Leveraging Athena for log analytics

Athena is an interactive query service that allows users to execute complex SQL queries across vast datasets, enabling a depth of analysis beyond basic monitoring. Athena's ability to query security logs from various sources, including Security Lake, is invaluable for identifying complex patterns and correlations indicative of sophisticated security threats.

With Athena, organizations can perform real-time analysis of their security data, which is crucial for timely detection and response to potential security threats. Athena also facilitates the creation of comprehensive security reports, which are useful for internal audits, compliance verification, or incident response documentation.

As an example, consider the following SQL query in Athena, which combines data from CloudTrail and VPC flow logs to detect unusual patterns indicative of a potential security threat:

```
WITH cloudtrail_events AS (
  SELECT
    eventTime,
    eventName,
    awsRegion,
    sourceIPAddress,
    userAgent,
    eventSource,
    recipientAccountId
  FROM cloudtrail_logs
  WHERE eventName IN ('StartInstances', 'StopInstances')
),
vpc_flow AS (
  SELECT
    interfaceId,
    startTime,
    endTime,
    sourceAddress,
    destinationAddress,
    action
  FROM vpc_flow_logs
  WHERE action = 'REJECT'
)
SELECT
  ct.eventTime AS apiEventTime,
  ct.eventName AS apiEventName,
  ct.awsRegion AS apiRegion,
  ct.sourceIPAddress AS apiSourceIP,
  vpc.startTime AS flowStartTime,
```

```
  vpc.endTime AS flowEndTime,
  vpc.sourceAddress AS flowSourceIP,
  vpc.destinationAddress AS flowDestIP,
  vpc.action AS networkAction
FROM
  cloudtrail_events ct
JOIN
  vpc_flow vpc
ON
  ct.sourceIPAddress = vpc.sourceAddress
WHERE
  ct.eventTime BETWEEN vpc.startTime AND vpc.endTime
ORDER BY
  ct.eventTime;
```

The preceding query does the following:

- It creates two **common table expressions (CTEs)**: `cloudtrail_events` for CloudTrail logs and `vpc_flow` for VPC flow logs.

- In `cloudtrail_events`, it selects relevant fields from CloudTrail logs, filtering for specific events such as `StartInstances` or `StopInstances`, which could indicate unauthorized instance manipulation.

- In `vpc_flow`, it selects data from VPC flow logs where network traffic was rejected, which could signal blocked attempts to access resources.

- The main `SELECT` statement joins these two datasets on the condition that the source IP address in the CloudTrail log matches the source address in the VPC flow logs. Additionally, it ensures the CloudTrail event time falls within the start and end times of the VPC flow logs entry.

- The query then orders the results by the event time from CloudTrail, providing a chronological view of potentially related API and network activities.

By correlating CloudTrail and VPC flow logs, this query helps identify instances where API calls to control AWS resources coincide with rejected network traffic from the same IP address. This pattern could suggest a targeted attack, where an adversary is attempting to manipulate AWS resources while simultaneously probing the network for vulnerabilities or attempting unauthorized access. This insight allows security teams to conduct a focused investigation, check for compromised credentials, or identify the need for tighter security controls.

Best practices for integrating Security Lake and Athena

To maximize the benefits of Security Lake and Athena, the following best practices can be followed:

- **Comprehensive data aggregation**: Collect logs from diverse services such as CloudTrail, VPC flow logs, application logs, and custom logs for thorough security analysis

- **Structured data organization**: Categorize and tag logs within Security Lake for efficient retrieval, using consistent naming conventions for ease of analysis

- **Efficient query design**: Develop specific, performance-optimized SQL queries in Athena to address key security concerns, reducing execution time and cost

- **Regular data auditing and cleanup**: Implement a data retention policy in Security Lake to periodically review and purge outdated logs, optimizing storage costs

- **Real-time analysis and alerting**: Utilize Athena for immediate detection and response to security incidents, setting up automated alerts and actions

- **Security dashboard integration**: Combine data from Athena in CloudWatch custom dashboards or Quicksight for comprehensive visualization of query results

- **Advanced data analysis techniques**: Invoke your SageMaker machine learning models into your Athena query for deeper insights and threat identification

- **Continuous security posture assessment**: Continually update security strategies based on insights from log analysis, adapting to evolving threats and models

- **Compliance and regulatory adherence**: Generate compliance reports and ensure log storage and analysis practices meet relevant standards and regulations

Security Lake and Athena offer powerful tools for enhancing security log integration and analytics. By understanding their features, setting up effective integrations, and adopting advanced analytical techniques, organizations can significantly improve their security operations, ensuring a robust defense against evolving cyber threats.

Summary

In this chapter, we explored advanced logging, auditing, and monitoring in AWS, emphasizing their importance in cloud security. We discussed the evolution and integration of AWS services such as CloudTrail, CloudWatch, Security Lake, and Athena, highlighting their roles in threat detection, compliance, and operational efficiency. This chapter provided best practices for configuring CloudTrail trails, utilizing CloudTrail Insights for anomaly detection, and leveraging CloudTrail Lake for in-depth analysis. We also examined CloudWatch's capabilities in application security monitoring, building security dashboards, and integrating with diverse log sources. Finally, we delved into using Security Lake and Athena for enhanced security log integration and analytics, offering practical use cases and best practices for effective implementation.

The next chapter will focus on achieving and maintaining security compliance in your AWS environment using tools such as AWS Config and AWS Security Hub, combined with auto-remediation capabilities.

Questions

Answer the following questions to test your knowledge of this chapter:

1. In what ways can CloudTrail Insights assist in preempting security breaches?
2. What are the strategic benefits of using Security Lake for log management?
3. Can Athena be employed for time-sensitive security threat detection?
4. How can the integration of CloudTrail and VPC flow logs in Athena uncover hidden security threats?

Answers

Here are the answers to this chapter's questions:

1. CloudTrail Insights is adept at detecting anomalies in AWS resource usage and management activities. It can preempt security breaches by alerting administrators about unusual patterns such as mass resource deletion or unexpected geographical access, providing an opportunity to investigate and respond before a full-scale breach occurs.
2. Security Lake centralizes log management, which is beneficial for handling diverse and large-scale log data efficiently. It allows organizations to aggregate logs from various AWS services and applications into a single repository, making it easier to manage and analyze data. For example, a company can combine VPC flow logs, CloudTrail, and custom application logs for a comprehensive security analysis.
3. Yes, Athena's capacity for real-time analysis makes it an excellent tool for quick threat detection. In scenarios where swift response is critical, such as detecting and stopping a DDoS attack in progress, Athena's real-time analysis can provide the immediate insights needed to take prompt action.
4. Integrating CloudTrail and VPC flow logs in Athena allows for correlating AWS account activities with VPC's network traffic, revealing hidden security threats. For example, unusual calls to AWS APIs from an IP address combined with suspicious network traffic patterns from the same IP address can indicate a coordinated attack attempt.

Further reading

The following resources offer further insights and best practices for advanced security logging and monitoring in AWS:

- *Logging strategies for security incident response*, by Anna McAbee, Ciarán Carragher, and Pratima Singh (2023): `https://aws.amazon.com/blogs/security/logging-strategies-for-security-incident-response/`

- *Getting Started with Collecting and Managing AWS Logs*, by Ayooluwa Isaiah (2023): `https://betterstack.com/community/guides/logging/aws-logging/`

11

Security Compliance with AWS Config, AWS Security Hub, and Automated Remediation

Welcome to the eleventh chapter of our detailed journey through AWS security, where we will build on the foundations laid in *Chapter 5*, particularly focusing on AWS Config and AWS Security Hub. In this chapter, we will take a closer look at the crucial practices of continuous compliance monitoring, automated remediation, and centralized compliance management. As the complexity of cloud environments and regulatory demands continue to escalate, mastering these aspects becomes vital for any robust AWS security strategy. We will begin by unraveling the intricate process of continuous compliance monitoring, emphasizing the role of Config as a cornerstone tool. We will then move to a practical exploration of automated remediation, showcasing its application through a real-world case study centered on common AWS security challenges. The chapter will culminate with an in-depth discussion on centralized compliance management, highlighting the synergistic integration of Config with Security Hub to create a more cohesive and efficient compliance management system.

By the end of this chapter, you will possess a thorough understanding of how to effectively monitor, remediate, and manage compliance in AWS environments. This knowledge will prepare you to address complex compliance challenges in today's dynamic cloud security landscape.

In this chapter, we will cover the following key areas:

- Implementing and managing continuous compliance monitoring strategies
- Understanding and applying automated remediation techniques
- Developing a centralized approach to compliance management

Continuous compliance monitoring and assessment

Ensuring continuous compliance and monitoring is a cornerstone of a robust security and compliance management framework. This ongoing process involves the meticulous monitoring and evaluation of an organization's cloud resources to ensure they adhere to established compliance standards and best practices. The dynamic nature of cloud resources, coupled with the complexity and scale of AWS environments, demands a vigilant approach to compliance. This section will delve into mechanisms and strategies to establish and maintain compliance, focusing on Config as a pivotal tool in this endeavor.

Overview of compliance with Config

AWS Config is a service designed to offer a comprehensive view of your AWS resource configuration and compliance. It functions by continuously monitoring and recording your AWS resource configurations, enabling you to automate the evaluation of these configurations against desired guidelines. This service is not just a means to an end for compliance but an essential part of a proactive security posture in AWS. Regular updates to Config rules are crucial to adapt to evolving compliance requirements and ensure continued alignment with organizational and regulatory standards.

Config plays a crucial role in compliance by providing the ability to do the following:

- **Track changes**: It tracks changes in the configurations of AWS resources, capturing details such as resource creation, modification, and deletion. This tracking is vital for understanding the evolution of the AWS environment and for auditing purposes.

- **Evaluate configurations**: It evaluates configurations against compliance rules, which can be either predefined by AWS or custom-defined by users. This evaluation helps in identifying resources that do not comply with organizational standards and policies.

- **Provide detailed insights**: It offers detailed insights into relationships between AWS resources, which assists in security analysis and risk assessment.

- **Automate remediation**: It can trigger automated remediation actions based on defined rules, thereby reducing the manual effort required to maintain compliance.

The integration of Config into a compliance strategy ensures that organizations have a proactive stance on their AWS resource configurations, maintaining an optimal security and compliance posture and swiftly responding to any deviations from the desired state.

Setting up Config

The setup of Config is a crucial step in leveraging its full capabilities for continuous compliance monitoring. The process involves several stages, from enabling the service to defining the necessary configurations and rules.

Initial configuration

The initial setup of Config involves the following steps:

1. **Enable recording**: The first step is to enable Config in the management console.

2. **Select resources**: Determine which AWS resources need monitoring. Config can monitor most types of AWS resource, including EC2 instances, VPC subnets, S3 buckets, and more.

3. **Define the recording scope**: Configure the recording of all resources within your AWS environment or select specific resource types for monitoring.

4. **Set up a delivery channel**: Configure where configuration and compliance data will be stored and how it will be delivered. This typically involves setting up an S3 bucket for storage and an SNS topic for notifications.

After the initial configuration, Config will begin collecting data and recording the configuration history of your AWS resources. You can then use this inventory for auditing, security, and compliance purposes. It is important to regularly review and update Config settings to align with organizational changes and AWS updates.

Defining compliance rules

After setting up Config, the next critical step is to define compliance rules that align with your organization's policies and regulatory standards. These rules are used by Config to evaluate if AWS resources deployed in an environment comply with best practices, as well as your specific compliance requirements.

Types of rules

Config's compliance rules can be classified into two main types:

- **AWS managed rules**: AWS provides a set of pre-built, managed rules that can be readily implemented. These rules cover common compliance scenarios and best practices. Some examples include rules to check for **AWS Certificate Manager** (**ACM**) certificate expiration, SSH access restrictions, and S3 bucket public access.

- **Custom rules**: Organizations can also define custom rules tailored to their specific compliance requirements. This involves writing Lambda functions or Guard rules that evaluate the configuration of AWS resources. For instance, a custom rule might require that all S3 buckets have logging enabled or that EC2 instances are tagged appropriately according to organizational standards.

Rule configuration and management

Once a rule is selected, several settings can be adjusted to define the way it will be evaluated:

- **Rule parameters**: Most AWS-managed and custom rules can be configured with specific parameters that define their behaviors and the conditions under which they evaluate resources. For example, the AWS-managed rule checking for ACM certificate expiration can be set with a specific number of days after which a certificate will be considered expired.

- **Rule triggers**: All rules can be configured as either proactive, change-triggered, or periodic. Proactive rules are deployed when a new resource is about to be deployed. Change-triggered rules are evaluated when a configuration change affecting an existing resource is detected. Periodic rules run on a defined schedule such as every hour to check compliance.

- **Rule scope**: Similar to the recording scope of the initial setup but operating at a distinct level, the rule scope determines the specific resources each rule assesses for compliance. It can target certain resource types or resources with specific tags. This targeted approach ensures compliance checks are both relevant and efficient, focusing on appropriate resources for each rule.

- **Remediation**: Config can take various remediation actions when a resource is found to be non-compliant with a rule. This can include fully automated remediation or manual remediation that still requires human intervention.

Crafting rules using Guard

AWS **CloudFormation Guard** (**cfn-guard**) allows the creation of custom rules using a **Domain-Specific Language** (**DSL**), enabling you to define compliance policies in a more intuitive and readable format. Unlike traditional methods requiring complex scripting or Lambda functions, Guard simplifies the process by allowing **Policy-as-Code** (**PaC**) definitions that can be embedded directly within the rule without the need to use a separate Lambda function. This approach streamlines the creation of custom rules, making them easier to manage and understand.

To ensure the reliability and safety of these rules, it is critical to test them in a non-production environment before deployment. This precautionary step verifies their functionality and confirms they will not disrupt normal operations when implemented in a live setting.

Consider a scenario where you want to ensure that all your EC2 instances are not only using specific instance types but also have encrypted EBS volumes and specific security group settings. A Guard policy for this could be as follows:

```
rule secure_ec2_compliance {
    let applicable_instances = %configuration where resourceType ==
'AWS::EC2::Instance'
    applicable_instances {
        configuration.instanceType in ['t2.micro', 't2.small']
        configuration.blockDeviceMappings[*].ebs.encrypted == true
```

```
            configuration.securityGroups[*].any { sg => sg.groupName ==
'secure-communication' }
        }
}
```

In this example, the policy checks for the following:

1. EC2 instances being of type `t2.micro` or `t2.small` for cost optimization.

2. All EBS volumes attached to these instances are encrypted, ensuring data security.

3. Instances are associated with a security group named `secure-communication`, indicating a specific configuration for secure data transmission.

Working with the Rule Development Kit

The Config's **Rule Development Kit (RDK)** is an open-source command-line utility designed to simplify the development, deployment, and management of custom rules in Config. It aids in the rapid creation and testing of Lambda-based rules, accommodating various AWS resource types. It supports the full life cycle of rule development, from initial setup to testing and deployment. The RDK is particularly useful for integrating custom rules into DevSecOps workflows, allowing for automated and scalable compliance checks within AWS environments.

As an example, consider a scenario where we aim to prevent public accessibility of subnets. The following RDK command can be executed to create a skeleton for a Lambda function that will support a new Config rule named `SubnetNotPublic` targeting subnet resources:

```
rdk create SubnetNotPublic --runtime python3.11 --resource-types
AWS::VPC::Subnet
```

The `evaluate_compliance()` function can then be tailored to perform the necessary subnet compliance checks:

```
def evaluate_compliance(subnet):
    # Check if the subnet has a default route to an internet gateway
    for route in subnet['configuration']['routeTable']['routes']:
        if '0.0.0.0/0' in route['destinationCidrBlock'] and
'gatewayId' in route:
            return 'NON_COMPLIANT'
        return 'COMPLIANT'
```

In this example, the function checks each subnet's route table for routes that allow public internet access. If such a route is found, the subnet is marked as NON_COMPLIANT. Following these modifications, the `rdk create` command automatically sets up both the Lambda function and the Config rule, along with all necessary dependencies.

This example underscores RDK's utility in swift custom rules development for Config, transitioning us next to the domain of compliance monitoring.

Monitoring compliance

Monitoring compliance is an integral part of managing AWS resources, ensuring they adhere to specified compliance standards. This process involves a combination of real-time monitoring, scheduled assessments, and analytical insights from Config dashboards.

Real-time monitoring

Real-time monitoring in Config involves continuously tracking resource configurations and changes, providing instant visibility into the compliance status of AWS resources. This proactive approach enables immediate detection of non-compliance events, allowing for swift remedial actions. The integration of real-time notifications plays a crucial role, where any deviation from established compliance rules triggers an immediate alert to the relevant teams or can also trigger auto-remediation actions. Additionally, leveraging Amazon CloudWatch in conjunction with Config can further enhance real-time monitoring capabilities, offering advanced alerting and metric analysis for more comprehensive oversight of compliance status.

Scheduled assessments

Scheduled assessments are periodic evaluations of resources against compliance rules. Unlike real-time monitoring, these assessments occur at predefined intervals—for instance, daily, weekly, or monthly—depending on the organization's needs and the nature of the resources. These assessments provide a regular, systematic review of the compliance posture. They are particularly useful for less dynamic environments or for compliance checks that do not require immediate action upon deviation.

For example, a weekly scheduled assessment might be used to verify that all IAM users have **MFA** enabled, ensuring ongoing adherence to security best practices.

Config dashboards

Config provides dashboards that offer a visual representation of the compliance status of AWS resources. These dashboards aggregate and display compliance data in an easily interpretable format, providing a bird's-eye view of an organization's AWS environment. For instance, a dashboard could display the compliance status of all EC2 instances with specific security configurations, such as those requiring certain types of encryption or network settings. By customizing these dashboards, organizations can focus on key metrics and trends that are most relevant to their compliance requirements, enabling efficient tracking and management of their AWS resource compliance.

Compliance reporting

Config facilitates compliance reporting and audit preparation by providing detailed reports of configuration changes and compliance history. Key reports include configuration history, showcasing changes over time, compliance reports from Config rules, and relationship mapping for understanding resource connections. Configuration drift analysis is available to detect deviations from expected setups. Additionally, Config allows exporting this wealth of data to S3, supporting long-term retention and external analysis. These comprehensive reports are vital for demonstrating adherence to both internal and regulatory standards, providing essential evidence during audits, and facilitating thorough change management and security analysis.

Compliance trend analysis

Compliance trend analysis focuses on evaluating historical compliance data to uncover evolving patterns or recurring issues. For example, an organization might want to analyze the trend of unauthorized security group changes over several months. By observing the frequency and nature of these changes, they can identify specific areas where security policies might be frequently misunderstood or bypassed. This practical approach to trend analysis not only aids in pinpointing systemic issues but also helps in evaluating the effectiveness of current compliance measures and in formulating strategies for enhancing overall compliance in the future.

These analyses can be performed using the advanced query functionality within Config. It offers an SQL-based interface for retrieving AWS resource configuration metadata and assessing resource compliance across single or multi-account setups. A more recently introduced feature is the generative AI-powered **natural language** querying feature, enabling users to interrogate AWS resources, configurations, or compliance status using simple commands or questions in everyday language. This innovation minimizes the necessity for SQL proficiency or a deep understanding of resource configurations, simplifying the query process significantly.

Alternatively, organizations can combine Config data with other operational datasets using Amazon Athena to gain more comprehensive insights. For example, by combining Config data on security group changes with VPC flow logs, an organization can analyze the correlation between security group modifications and network traffic patterns. This combined analysis can reveal whether certain security group changes lead to unexpected network traffic spikes or breaches, providing valuable insights for enhancing security measures and compliance strategies.

Managing multi-account compliance

Managing compliance across multiple AWS accounts presents a complex challenge, especially for large organizations. It involves overseeing and ensuring consistent adherence to compliance standards across various accounts, often spread across different regions. We now turn to methods of addressing these challenges, focusing on centralized monitoring, compliance standards, and the use of conformance packs.

Centralized compliance monitoring

Centralized monitoring through Config involves the use of a configuration aggregator, crucial for gathering compliance details from various accounts into a unified view. Integration with AWS Organizations allows for the aggregation of this data into a master account, providing a comprehensive overview and ensuring uniform compliance standards across all accounts. This setup is enhanced by cross-account data aggregation, which offers a consolidated view of compliance, crucial for a holistic understanding of the organization's compliance posture.

Compliance standards with Config rules

Config rules are instrumental in establishing and enforcing compliance requirements across multiple accounts. They ensure that resources in different accounts adhere to consistent standards. Centralized monitoring of these rules allows tracking of compliance statuses and changes across accounts, offering a holistic view of the organization's compliance health. This process is further streamlined by automated policy enforcement, where automated scripts or AWS services enforce compliance policies across accounts, ensuring consistent rule application and immediate rectification of deviations. For instance, if a Config rule detects that a certain resource in an account does not meet predefined compliance standards, automated remediation actions can swiftly enforce the necessary changes, bringing the resource back into compliance.

Leveraging conformance packs

Conformance packs serve as a critical tool for implementing and maintaining consistent compliance standards across multiple AWS accounts. These packs bundle together a group of Config rules and remediation actions, providing a unified approach to enforce compliance and security rules at scale. This capability is especially beneficial in multi-account environments, where managing the diversity and complexity of resources is a significant challenge.

Conformance packs simplify compliance management by automatically checking and remediating each account according to predefined rules and standards. For instance, the *Operational Best Practices for CIS Top 20* conformance pack is a prime example of how organizations can use these packs effectively. Designed for compliance with the **CIS** *Top 20 Critical Security Controls*, it includes rules that ensure secure configurations, stringent access controls, and monitoring for unusual activities. When deployed across various accounts, it ensures uniform enforcement of these critical security controls, aligning every account with high cybersecurity standards.

The flexibility of conformance packs is a key advantage. Organizations can customize existing packs or create new ones to meet specific compliance needs, including organization-specific rules and actions. This customization ensures that the conformance pack fully aligns with internal policies and regulatory requirements.

Transitioning from multi-account compliance, let's now consider the best practices for maximizing Config's potential.

Best practices for Config

Incorporating Config for continuous compliance monitoring and assessment in AWS environments is a multi-faceted endeavor. Here are best practices to ensure a comprehensive and efficient approach:

- **Prioritize critical resources and configurations**: Focus on key resources and configurations that have the most significant impact on security and compliance. Prioritizing these elements ensures efficient use of resources without compromising on critical compliance needs.

- **Effective rule management**: Implement Config rules strategically, targeting essential compliance and security requirements. Avoid overloading the system with unnecessary rules to maintain clarity and manageability.

- **Cost-effective monitoring**: While ensuring comprehensive compliance monitoring, also consider the cost implications. Optimize monitoring strategies to balance thoroughness with cost efficiency, focusing on high-impact areas.

- **Optimize data storage and retention**: Manage data storage and retention policies effectively to reduce unnecessary data accumulation and associated costs.

- **Utilize conformance packs**: Implement conformance packs for standardized and automated compliance checks across accounts. This approach can offer a more efficient solution compared to managing multiple individual rules.

- **Incorporate cost management tools**: Use tools such as Budgets to monitor and manage costs associated with compliance monitoring. Keeping an eye on expenses ensures that the compliance strategy remains within budgetary constraints.

- **Review and adjust compliance costs**: Regularly evaluate costs associated with compliance monitoring and make necessary adjustments. Ensure that spending is justified by the security and compliance benefits it offers.

- **Stay informed and agile**: Keep abreast of the latest AWS updates and best practices in compliance monitoring. Be ready to adapt your strategies to leverage new features or respond to changing compliance requirements.

Config's continuous monitoring of compliance and configurations is central to cloud security. We now end this discussion and look toward automated remediation.

Automated remediation

In the dynamic nature of cloud environments, where configurations and deployments can change rapidly, maintaining and enforcing compliance is a critical challenge. Automated remediation becomes a key strategy in ensuring continuous compliance and security. This section explores the concept of automated remediation in-depth, examining how it can be effectively designed and implemented using various AWS tools.

Understanding automated remediation

At the heart of automated remediation is the principle of proactive security management. Instead of reacting to compliance issues after they occur, automated remediation aims to address these issues as they arise by automatically correcting non-compliant resources within an AWS environment. It involves identifying non-compliant resources, triggering appropriate remediation actions, and applying these actions to bring resources back into compliance. Automated remediation not only saves time and resources but also significantly reduces the window of exposure to security vulnerabilities.

Designing automated remediation strategies

Effective automated remediation requires a well-thought-out strategy that aligns with the organization's compliance goals and security policies. This strategy is crucial in addressing compliance issues as they emerge, ensuring a prompt and appropriate response. Putting it into practice starts with the identification of trigger events, essential for the quick and effective handling of compliance challenges, and then progresses to the definition of suitable remediation actions that align with these issues. Now, let's explore these two critical stages in more detail.

Identifying trigger events

Trigger events are specific conditions or changes in the AWS environment that initiate an automated remediation process. Defining the right triggers is crucial for the effective implementation of automated remediation. To do so effectively, organizations must have a deep understanding of their AWS environment and the compliance rules they need to enforce. Examples of common trigger events could include the following:

- **Security group modifications**: A common trigger event is unauthorized changes in security group settings, such as opening up a port to the public internet. For instance, if a security group is altered to allow unrestricted SSH access, this could trigger an automated process to revert the security group to its secure state.

- **Configuration drift in critical resources**: Any deviation from standard configurations in critical resources, such as changes in IAM role permissions or alterations in the network configuration of a production VPC, can be set as a trigger. For example, if an IAM role unexpectedly gains full access to S3, it can trigger an immediate review or a reversal action.

- **Non-compliance with tagging policies**: Organizations often enforce specific tagging strategies for cost allocation, security, or management purposes. Changes or omissions in the tagging of resources such as EC2 instances or S3 buckets that violate these policies can be set as triggers for remediation actions.

Defining remediation actions

Once trigger events are identified, the next step is to define remediation actions that should be executed in response. These actions vary depending on the nature of the compliance issue but generally include modifying resource configurations, revoking permissions, or even terminating non-compliant resources. The design of these actions should be aligned with the organization's risk appetite and compliance requirements. It is important to ensure that remediation actions do not disrupt legitimate business operations or lead to unintended consequences. For example, an overly aggressive remediation action, such as immediately terminating instances for minor security group changes, could disrupt legitimate operations and lead to service downtime. Therefore, remediation actions should be precise, targeted, and, where possible, reversible to allow for quick recovery in case of false positives or errors in automation logic.

Tools for automation

AWS offers a diverse range of tools to automate remediation tasks, each suited for different scenarios based on the complexity and requirements of the task. AWS **Systems Manager** (**SSM**) documents, Lambda functions, and AWS Step Functions state machines are key components in this toolkit, offering flexibility and power in automating responses to compliance and security events.

SSM documents for streamlined operations

SSM documents are ideal for performing routine operations and remediation tasks on AWS resources, including EC2 instances, RDS instances, or Lambda functions, among others. These documents, essentially scripts or command sequences, are highly effective for straightforward tasks such as software patching, configuration adjustments, and resource state changes. An SSM document can be invoked directly in response to a compliance event. For example, consider a scenario where an EC2 instance becomes non-compliant due to misconfigured software. An SSM document could be designed to automatically stop a web server running on an EC2 instance if that instance does not meet specific compliance standards. A sample snippet of an SSM document for this purpose might look like this:

```
{
  "schemaVersion": "2.2",
  "description": "Restart a service",
  "mainSteps": [
    {
      "action": "aws:runShellScript",
      "name": "stopService",
      "inputs": {
        "runCommand": [
          "sudo systemctl stop nginx"
        ]
      }
    }
  ]
}
```

```
    ]
  }
```

In this document, the `aws:runShellScript` action is used to execute commands that stop the `nginx` service on a Linux-based instance.

Lambda functions for complex logic

Lambda functions are powerful for handling more complex remediation scenarios that require the execution of custom code in response to various events. They are particularly adept at tasks that involve multiple conditional checks, data transformations, or interactions with various AWS services. They shine in situations where specific conditions must be evaluated before taking action or where the remediation action involves multiple steps that are not linear. For instance, a Lambda function could assess whether an S3 bucket's public access is due to a legitimate business need before changing its permissions, ensuring no disruption to intended workflows.

Step Functions state machines for multi-step workflows

Step Functions state machines are best suited for orchestrating multiple AWS services into a coherent, multi-step workflow. This is particularly useful for automated remediation processes that involve several stages, such as approval requests, execution of remediation actions, and post-remediation verification.

Imagine a scenario where an IAM policy change needs to be reverted, but only after specific conditions are met. Step Functions state machines can orchestrate this workflow, starting with a Lambda function to evaluate the change, proceeding to an SSM document to revert the policy, and concluding with another Lambda function to verify and log the remediation. This ensures a comprehensive, controlled approach to remediation, crucial in complex environments.

In conclusion, choosing the right tool for automation in AWS depends on the complexity and specifics of the remediation task. SSM documents offer simplicity and direct action, Lambda functions provide flexibility for complex logic, and Step Functions orchestrate multi-step remediation workflows. Understanding these tools and their best use cases is key to implementing effective and efficient automated remediation strategies in AWS environments.

Tips for effective automated remediation

Automated remediation in AWS environments can significantly streamline compliance and security processes. However, to ensure its effectiveness, certain practices and considerations should be kept in mind:

- **Clearly define remediation goals**: Begin by clearly defining what you want to achieve with automated remediation. This could range from enforcing security best practices to ensuring compliance with regulatory standards. A well-defined goal helps in crafting precise remediation actions.

- **Understand the impact of remediation actions**: Before implementing any remediation action, understand its potential impact on the environment. Some actions might have unintended side effects, such as service downtime or loss of data. Thoroughly test remediation scripts in a controlled environment to assess their impact.

- **Implement conditional logic**: Use conditional logic in remediation scripts to handle different scenarios judiciously. For instance, if a security group is misconfigured, the script should consider whether to simply alert an administrator or to revert to a known good configuration based on the severity of the misconfiguration.

- **Integrate approval workflows**: For critical actions, integrate approval workflows into the remediation process. This can be done using Step Functions, whereby a manual approval step can be included before executing significant changes.

- **Monitor and log remediation actions**: Implement comprehensive logging and monitoring of all remediation actions. This not only aids in troubleshooting but also provides an audit trail for compliance purposes. CloudWatch and CloudTrail can be utilized for this purpose.

- **Regularly update and review remediation scripts**: As the AWS environment evolves, so should your remediation scripts. Regularly review and update these scripts to accommodate changes in the environment or compliance requirements.

- **Implement rollback mechanisms**: Always have a rollback mechanism in case a remediation action does not go as planned. This could be as simple as taking a snapshot before making changes or having a script ready to revert changes.

- **Balance automation with oversight**: While automation can significantly enhance efficiency, it should be balanced with human oversight, especially for complex or high-impact changes. This helps in mitigating risks associated with fully automated processes.

Case study – automated remediation scenario

A global retail corporation leveraging AWS for its e-commerce platform faces a significant challenge in ensuring data security, especially for S3 buckets. These buckets are often prone to misconfigurations, leading to potential data exposure. The company frequently encounters issues with S3 buckets being inadvertently set to public access, necessitating an effective solution for automated detection and remediation of these misconfigurations. The key objective is to implement an automated system capable of identifying S3 buckets with public access and executing appropriate actions based on their tagging, thereby ensuring data security and compliance.

The steps for implementing this automated remediation are as follows:

1. **Initial detection**: This stage involves the establishment of a Config rule that continuously monitors S3 bucket policies to identify instances of public access. Upon detection of any public access, this rule triggers a Step Functions state machine designed for more detailed analysis.

2. **Step Functions for advanced remediation**: The triggered Step Functions state machine begins by executing a Lambda function that evaluates tags associated with the S3 bucket. The process of assessment categorizes buckets based on their tagging: buckets tagged with `public-marketing` are acknowledged as legitimate public access, indicating a justified situation; those tagged with `review-required` or other tags are flagged as unjustified but potentially legitimate; and buckets without any relevant tags are considered non-controlled situations.

3. **For justified situations**: When the `public-marketing` tag is identified, the system acknowledges this as a valid public access scenario and refrains from initiating any remediation actions, recognizing the legitimacy of the bucket's public accessibility.

4. **Handling unjustified but potentially legitimate cases**: In cases where buckets are flagged as unjustified but potentially legitimate, the system maintains their public access. However, it escalates the issue to the compliance team for manual review. Concurrently, it activates S3 server access logging for these buckets, ensuring close monitoring of all access activities.

5. **Addressing non-controlled situations**: For buckets that are identified without any relevant or justifying tags, indicative of non-controlled situations, the Lambda function steps in to modify the bucket policy, thereby restricting public access. This modification is communicated to relevant teams to maintain awareness and enable follow-up actions if necessary.

6. **Testing and deployment**: Before full-scale deployment, the Step Functions state machine undergoes thorough testing in a controlled environment, ensuring that all pathways and scenarios are accurately addressed. Following successful testing, the Step Functions state machine is deployed with continuous monitoring by CloudWatch to track its operation and efficiency and to log any errors that might occur.

7. **Compliance and monitoring**: Regular audits are conducted to evaluate the effectiveness of the automated remediation process. Metrics such as the number of detected public buckets, frequency of escalations, and the rate of successful automated remediation are tracked to gauge the success of the implemented strategy. Tools such as CloudTrail and CloudWatch are used extensively to log and monitor activities related to the Step Functions state machine, providing insights into its performance and compliance.

8. **Documentation and reporting**: To maintain compliance, detailed documentation of the entire automated remediation process is kept. Regular reports generated from S3 access logs and Config data provide critical information for auditing purposes and facilitate trend analysis, helping in the continuous improvement of the remediation strategy.

This implementation effectively resolves the issue of S3 bucket misconfigurations, adopting a nuanced approach that differentiates between various scenarios and applies appropriate remediation actions. This ensures data security while accommodating operational needs.

Here are some key takeaways from this case study:

- **Granular remediation logic**: The use of Step Functions enabled the development of a sophisticated remediation logic, handling different scenarios based on bucket tagging.

- **Balanced approach**: The solution balanced between security needs and operational requirements, ensuring that legitimate public access is not hindered while enhancing security monitoring.

- **Effective tagging strategy**: The importance of a clear and consistent tagging strategy was highlighted, as it played a crucial role in the decision-making process of automated remediation.

- **Continuous monitoring and adjustment**: Regular monitoring and adjustments were necessary to refine the process, ensuring that it remained effective and aligned with evolving security policies and compliance requirements.

- **Future trends in automated remediation**: As cloud environments continue to evolve, the practice of automated remediation is expected to become more advanced, incorporating AI and **Machine Learning (ML)** for more predictive and proactive security measures. Organizations will likely see more sophisticated integration with other AWS services and third-party tools, enhancing the scope and accuracy of automated responses to security incidents.

In conclusion, automated remediation is a key strategy in AWS for rapid response and effective management of security and compliance challenges.

Centralized compliance management and integration

In today's fast-evolving cloud ecosystem, centralized compliance management has become pivotal for organizations leveraging AWS services. As they navigate through complex regulatory landscapes, integrating various AWS tools such as Config and Security Hub provides a streamlined approach to compliance monitoring and security posture management. This section delves into the integration of these services and their roles in enhancing compliance benchmarking and managing security standards.

Integrating Config with Security Hub

While enabling the integration of Config with Security Hub is very straightforward, it offers a robust solution for consolidated compliance monitoring and management across AWS environments. Config primarily deals with the status of configuration items, categorizing them as compliant or non-compliant, while Security Hub focuses on the broader aspect of findings derived from these and other sources. This integration brings forth several key benefits:

- **Enhanced insight with contextual information**: When Config findings are ingested into Security Hub, they are enriched with additional context. This context includes detailed information about the resources involved, their relationships, and historical data, allowing for a more profound understanding of the compliance status. This enriched insight aids in identifying not just the *what* but the *why* behind compliance issues, providing valuable clues for resolving them effectively.

- **Unified security and compliance view**: Security Hub aggregates findings from Config alongside other data, creating a singular, centralized view of the organization's compliance and security posture. This unified view eliminates the need to navigate through multiple consoles, simplifying the monitoring process and enhancing the efficiency of security teams. It provides a comprehensive snapshot, making it easier to identify patterns, trends, and areas requiring immediate attention.

- **Security standards for compliance benchmarking**: Security Hub allows organizations to benchmark their AWS environment against well-known security standards, such as the *CIS AWS Foundations Benchmark*. These standards offer structured guidelines and best practices to ensure a robust compliance posture.

- **Streamlined remediation**: Security Hub's automation capabilities can expedite the remediation of compliance issues identified by Config. By setting up specific rules and actions, such as automatic ticket creation in **IT service management** (**ITSM**) tooling or triggering Lambda functions for immediate rectification, organizations can respond swiftly and effectively to compliance deviations. This automation reduces response times and enhances the overall security resilience of AWS environments.

Utilizing Security Hub for compliance benchmarking

Security Hub plays a crucial role in compliance benchmarking within AWS environments. It offers a structured approach to evaluate and measure an organization's adherence to established security standards and best practices. Compliance benchmarking in Security Hub involves several key aspects:

- **Adoption of industry standards and best practices**: Security Hub provides access to a range of industry benchmarks that represent a consolidation of best practices and standards widely recognized in the industry. By aligning with these benchmarks, organizations can ensure that their AWS environment adheres to proven security practices.

- **Customizable frameworks**: Recognizing diversity in organizational needs and regulatory requirements, Security Hub allows for the customization of compliance frameworks. Organizations can tailor these frameworks to align with their specific security policies, regulatory mandates, and business objectives. This customization ensures that benchmarks remain relevant and effective in addressing unique compliance needs.

- **Continuous compliance assessment**: Security Hub continuously assesses the environment against selected benchmarks. It automatically checks AWS resources and configurations to ensure they comply with defined standards. This ongoing assessment provides real-time visibility into the compliance status, enabling organizations to promptly address non-compliance issues.

- **Scoring system for compliance levels**: Security Hub includes a scoring system that quantifies compliance levels, helping organizations to gauge their security posture numerically, track their progress, and identify areas needing improvement.

- **Detailed compliance reporting**: Security Hub offers comprehensive reporting capabilities, providing detailed insights into compliance status. These reports include information on compliant and non-compliant resources, specific compliance checks that have failed, and recommendations for remediation. These reports are invaluable for internal audits, regulatory compliance assessments, and continuous improvement efforts.

Managing security standards

Managing security standards in Security Hub is a critical process involving the selection and customization of controls—specific rules or requirements within each standard. These controls form the backbone of an organization's security and compliance strategy, addressing various aspects from data encryption to user authentication. Each control comes with an assigned severity rating ranging from *Low* to *Critical*.

The choice of standards and controls should reflect the organization's unique operational needs and compliance requirements. For example, a healthcare provider might focus on data protection-related controls with an emphasis on higher severity ratings for patient data protection, while an online retailer would generally emphasize PCI DSS standards. This relevance and severity-based prioritization ensure that security standards and controls are not merely generic guidelines but are integral to the organization's security infrastructure, addressing the most critical areas of risk first.

In addition, some controls support further customization so that their parameters can be tailored to the organization's specific environment. This might involve modifying sensitivity levels, defining compliance parameters, or setting exceptions aligned with business processes. Such customization makes controls more applicable and effective in the specific operational context of the organization.

With AWS's evolving security landscape, it is vital to stay updated. The automatic enabling of new controls in Security Hub as AWS updates its standards ensures that the organization's security measures remain current and robust against emerging threats. Regular review and adaptation of these standards and controls are necessary for maintaining an effective and relevant security posture. This dynamic approach to managing security standards in Security Hub, with its focus on customization and continuous updating, forms a crucial part of an adaptive and proactive security strategy.

Creating custom insights

Creating custom insights in Security Hub is a strategic approach to enhance your organization's monitoring and compliance. By tailoring these insights to specific areas of concern, such as tracking frequently non-compliant resources or focusing on critical AWS services with recurring issues, targeted monitoring ensures awareness of critical vulnerabilities. These custom insights can be integral to your broader security **Incident Response (IR)** plans, providing timely and relevant data that enhances overall readiness and resilience against potential security threats.

Prioritizing high-severity issues through grouping findings based on severity is another effective tactic. Addressing the most pressing vulnerabilities first streamlines your remediation efforts. Further, applying resource-type filtering provides a clear understanding of which areas are more prone to compliance issues, be they related to EC2 instances, IAM roles, or S3 buckets.

Integrating insights with compliance reporting is key to supporting internal audits and regulatory assessments. Regularly generate detailed reports to evaluate compliance status and the effectiveness of your controls. This not only aids in maintaining compliance but also highlights areas for continuous improvement. Finally, ensuring that insights are actionable is essential. They should identify issues and offer recommendations or solutions, turning data into practical steps for enhancing your security posture. This approach transforms insights into valuable tools for maintaining a vigilant and responsive security and compliance stance in your AWS environment.

In conclusion, the seamless integration of Config with Security Hub offers a centralized solution for compliance management, bolstering overall security effectiveness in line with industry best practices and security benchmarks.

Summary

In this chapter, we delved into the essential practices of continuous compliance monitoring, automated remediation, and centralized compliance management in AWS. It began by exploring the critical role of AWS Config in providing a comprehensive view of resource configuration and compliance, detailing the process of setting up Config, defining compliance rules, and integrating it with other AWS services for a holistic approach. The chapter then transitioned to a case study on automated remediation, illustrating its application in a real-world scenario involving S3 bucket misconfigurations, and highlighting the importance of granular remediation logic and effective tagging strategies. The final section discussed the integration of Config with AWS Security Hub, emphasizing their combined strengths in enhanced insight, unified security views, and streamlined remediation. This chapter equipped readers with practical knowledge and insights into managing and automating compliance in complex AWS landscapes, preparing them for the sophisticated challenges of cloud security.

As we move to the next chapter, we will shift our focus to incorporating security into the development life cycle, adopting DevSecOps principles. We will discuss best practices, strategies, and tools to achieve a secure and agile development environment in AWS.

Questions

Answer the following questions to test your knowledge of this chapter:

1. How do conformance packs aid in managing multi-account compliance?

2. How does tagging help in automated remediation strategies?

3. How does Security Hub facilitate compliance benchmarking?

Answers

Here are the answers to this chapter's questions:

1. Conformance packs bundle together a group of Config rules and remediation actions, providing a unified approach to enforce compliance and security rules across multiple AWS accounts.

2. Tags categorize resources for specific remediation actions based on their purpose or sensitivity. For instance, resources tagged as *Critical* might trigger immediate escalated responses, while those tagged as *Non-essential* may follow a standard remediation process.

3. Security Hub facilitates compliance benchmarking by providing access to industry benchmarks, customizable frameworks for compliance assessment, a scoring system for compliance levels, and detailed compliance reporting.

Further reading

The following readings offer further insights and best practices for continuous compliance and remediation management:

*   *Optimize AWS Config for AWS Security Hub to effectively manage your cloud security posture* by Nicholas Jaeger and Dora Karali (2023): `https://aws.amazon.com/blogs/security/optimize-aws-config-for-aws-security-hub-to-effectively-manage-your-cloud-security-posture`

*   *Automate continuous compliance at scale in AWS* by Kanishk Mahajan (2022): `https://aws.amazon.com/blogs/mt/automate-cloud-foundational-services-for-compliance-in-aws`

*   *AWS Cloud Security & Compliance* (YouTube video) by Ron Gerber with Angelbeat Seminars (2021): `https://www.youtube.com/watch?v=gHM5aItFdrc`

12

DevSecOps – Integrating Security into CI/CD Pipelines

Welcome to the twelfth chapter of our in-depth exploration into AWS security, where we will align the principles of DevSecOps with the complexities of the modern software supply chain. This chapter marks a significant shift in our journey, as we dive into integrating robust security practices within the continuous flow of software development and delivery. Our focus will be on how DevSecOps, a methodology that embeds security into every stage of the software life cycle, is crucial in managing the myriad components that constitute today's software supply chains.

We will start by exploring the transformative impact of DevSecOps on the software supply chain. We will examine how the shift from traditional security practices to a more integrated approach not only enhances security but also aligns with the agile nature of modern software development. This shift is vital for addressing the unique challenges and security risks inherent in today's software supply chains, such as dependency vulnerabilities and supply chain attacks.

As we progress, we will delve into the specifics of implementing a secure **Continuous Integration/Continuous Deployment** (**CI/CD**) pipeline in AWS. We will showcase how AWS services and tools can be effectively utilized to build secure CI/CD workflows, ensuring that security is a continuous and integral part of the development process.

In the latter part of the chapter, we will then turn our attention to the various security tools that can be integrated into the CI/CD pipeline, both AWS native and third-party ones. This discussion will include strategies and best practices to optimize their integration and enhance your overall security posture.

By the end of this chapter, you will have gained the skills to strategically apply DevSecOps practices within the software supply chain, enhancing your ability to manage security risks effectively and maintain an agile development environment in AWS.

In this chapter, we will cover the following key areas:

- Understanding software supply chain security in the age of DevSecOps
- Strategies for embedding security into CI/CD pipelines
- Best practices for integrating security tools

DevSecOps in the modern software supply chain

In the rapidly evolving world of the **Software Development Life Cycle** (**SDLC**), the integration of security into its processes has never been more critical. As the first section of this chapter is about DevSecOps, it is imperative to understand its role in modern software development, especially before delving into the specifics related to AWS.

Understanding DevSecOps

First, let's demystify the concept of DevSecOps. DevSecOps marks a significant evolution in software development methodologies. In traditional frameworks, security tended to be an afterthought, often relegated to the later stages of the SDLC. This delay frequently resulted in extended project timelines and escalated costs, stemming from belatedly identified security vulnerabilities. DevSecOps addresses this inefficiency by embedding security practices and tools throughout every phase of the software development process. It is not just about automation; DevSecOps also enhances the DevOps model by reshaping team dynamics. It fosters a culture where security is an integral and shared responsibility, ensuring that every member is an active participant in developing and maintaining a secure environment.

Benefits of DevSecOps

Integrating DevSecOps into the SDLC offers several advantages:

- **Improved security posture**: By incorporating security practices and tools from the beginning, potential vulnerabilities are identified and mitigated early. This approach significantly diminishes the risk of security breaches and the leakage of sensitive data.

- **Streamlined process**: DevSecOps facilitates a more continuous process by integrating security as part of every step of the workflow. This leads to faster detection and resolution of security issues, reducing delays in deployment.

- **Improved compliance and risk management**: With increasing regulatory requirements, compliance becomes a significant concern for businesses. DevSecOps helps in meeting these compliance needs by embedding compliance checks into the workflow, thus maintaining a consistent compliance posture.

- **Collaboration and cultural shift**: DevSecOps fosters a culture of collaboration between development, security, and operations teams. This collaborative approach breaks down silos, enhances communication, and leads to better overall outcomes.

Challenges and common pitfalls

While the benefits of DevSecOps are substantial, its implementation is not without challenges:

- **Cultural resistance**: Shifting to DevSecOps requires a cultural change within the organization. It demands a mindset where security is a shared responsibility, which can be a significant hurdle in organizations used to traditional siloed approaches.

- **Tooling integration**: Implementing DevSecOps requires the integration of various AWS and other security tools into the development pipeline. Selecting the right tools that seamlessly integrate and do not disrupt existing workflows can be challenging.

- **Skills gap**: DevSecOps requires professionals who not only understand development and operations but are also proficient in security. This multidisciplinary requirement can lead to a skills gap, making it challenging to implement DevSecOps effectively.

- **Continuous monitoring and adaptation**: DevSecOps requires continuous monitoring and quick adaptation to emerging security threats. Keeping up with fast-paced changes and integrating them into the SDLC can be challenging.

Building on our introduction to DevSecOps, we now turn our attention to the shift in software development paradigms. This shift moves us from the structured phases of traditional models to more adaptable and responsive agile methods, a transformation that is integral to the DevOps philosophy and forms the basis for embedding security within these methodologies.

Evolution from traditional to agile methods

Let's take a brief journey through the evolution of methodologies, from traditional SDLC to agile methods.

Traditional SDLC

Emerging from the engineering world, the **waterfall** model is the most common traditional SDLC model. It is based on linear sequential stages, generally described as follows:

1. Planning
2. Analysis
3. Design
4. Development
5. Testing
6. Deployment and maintenance

The waterfall model relies on rigorous sequencing of the different stages. Each stage requires several tasks and deliverables to be completed before moving forward to the next phase. This rigid approach can be burdensome and make the SDLC process less adaptable to changes. This is because the complete execution of the overall life cycle can take a long time, and it is difficult to go backward when the original requirements for the software product need to be changed. In this situation, it is often necessary to wait for the end of the ongoing life cycle before taking these changes into account for the next release. However, these situations are becoming more and more common in the current world as it is crucial to have a short **Time-To-Market** (**TTM**) delay and to be able to adapt to frequent changes.

Agile methods

Due to the inherent rigidity of traditional SDLC models, agile software development methods have emerged as a more flexible and iterative model. These methods, integral to the DevOps culture, allow better coping with unplanned and frequent changes. Agile methods have shorter release cycles compared to traditional SDLC, adapt better to changes and increase software deployment frequency by working on smaller increments of code. Frequent small increments are preferable to occasional big changes, and a **Minimum Viable Product** (**MVP**) can be made available rapidly to the customer so that it creates value earlier while capturing user feedback as soon as possible in order to adjust to new requirements.

CI/CD

The demand for shorter and more frequent release cycles in agile development, a core principle of DevOps, has led to the widespread adoption of CI/CD practices. CI/CD, often considered the backbone of DevOps, automates software releases, streamlining software integration and deployment into a continuous flow. CI involves integrating code changes quickly and frequently, while CD manages the entire software release process, often automated to ensure swift and efficient deployments.

CI

CI is the practice of integrating code changes as quickly and as often as possible using automated build and testing tooling. Developers integrate code into a shared repository multiple times per day or week so that they can quickly obtain feedback on code changes. This allows for faster software updates and improved quality by finding and addressing bugs very early in the life cycle. There are two main stages in the CI process:

- **Commit**: The code is integrated into the shared repository
- **Build**: The code is compiled into an executable component

CD

CD starts when CI ends. Once the code is committed and built, CD takes care of the overall software release activities until it runs into the production environment. The entire flow can be automated, although the final decision to deploy changes in production can also be triggered manually as an approval gate. This allows for automated deployment in a staging environment, testing, and rapid deployment in production. There are two main stages in the CD process:

- **Test**: The code is deployed and tested into a staging environment

- **Deploy**: The code is deployed into the production environment

CI/CD pipeline

A **CI/CD pipeline** consists of a set of tools that are used to automate both CI and CD activities. It is referred to as a *pipeline* because its objective is to allow for a constant flow of software integration and delivery, just as if software were a fluid flowing into a pipeline.

A CI/CD pipeline consists of two types of tools:

- A workflow management tool that orchestrates all stages and activities of both CI and CD

- Various automated tools specific to each stage that can be set up and customized to fit the organization's requirements

Figure 12.1 represents the different stages and the usual underlying activities that can be found in a CI/CD pipeline:

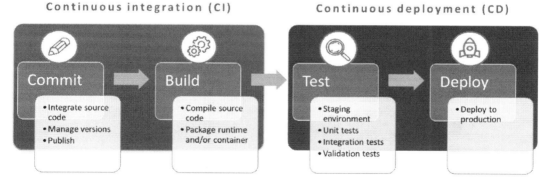

Figure 12.1 – Stages and activities of a CI/CD pipeline

Here, CI/CD emerges as a key component of agile and DevOps approaches, and it naturally sets the stage for our next topic—the integration of advanced security practices within the development process.

Embedding security

While security needs to be embedded within the different SDLC stages, it also needs to evolve as software development practices move toward agile methods. Let's explore how the continuous and rapid delivery models of agile influence the security landscape.

Security in the traditional SDLC

Traditionally, security in the SDLC was a sequential process, aligning with the structured phases of the development model. This approach entails separate, distinct security activities at each stage of the SDLC, constituting what is commonly referred to as the **Secure SDLC** (**SSDLC**) model. The following security activities are commonly included in the SSDLC flow:

- **Planning stage**: Security resource allocation is a key activity, setting the groundwork for subsequent phases
- **Analysis stage**: Involves data classification based on **Confidentiality, Integrity, and Availability** (**CIA**) requirements, risk profile analysis, and security requirements gathering
- **Design stage**: Focuses on threat modeling and risk assessment to preemptively identify potential security issues
- **Development stage**: Includes activities such as source code review (static testing) and scanning for vulnerabilities in libraries and dependencies
- **Testing stage**: Entails vulnerability assessment and dynamic testing, such as penetration testing, to identify and mitigate security risks
- **Deployment and maintenance stage**: Focuses on fixing vulnerabilities, ongoing security monitoring, and addressing residual risks

While this method provided a comprehensive security framework, it was often rigid and slow to adapt to changes, posing challenges in dynamic development environments.

Shifting security to the left

In agile software development, aligning security with rapid development cycles presents a significant challenge. Traditionally, the SSDLC relied on specialized security teams, leading to extended timelines and potential friction with development teams focused on speed and cost-effectiveness. This conflict is pronounced in agile methodologies where intensive security processes can hinder the swift progression of development sprints.

To resolve this, a shift-left approach in security is gaining traction. The term derives from the usual graphical representation of a process in the form of stages arranged in chronological order from left to right. As can be seen in *Figure 12.2*, it involves integrating security early in the development cycle, particularly during the design phase. This strategy enables developers to incorporate secure coding practices from the outset and utilize automated tools for code auditing, enhancing the overall security quality. Shifting security left aligns with the agile model's smaller, iterative changes, reducing the need for extensive security checks at every update. While not eliminating the need for rigorous security assessments, this approach allows for their strategic scheduling, decoupling them from the development cycle's pace:

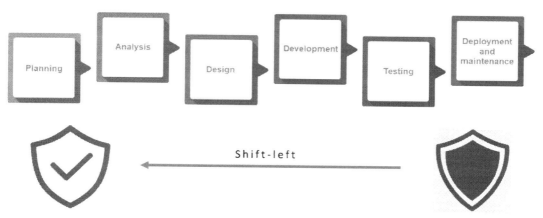

Figure 12.2 – Shift-left security principle

By adopting this shift-left approach, organizations can maintain high security standards while embracing the agility and speed of modern software development. It offers a balanced solution where security is a continuous, integrated element of the development process, tailored to an organization's risk tolerance and maturity level.

Integrating security into CI/CD pipelines

A fundamental aspect of this automation is its role in the *shift-left* approach to security—it is not only about introducing security earlier in the development process but also about harnessing the power of automation to make this integration seamless and effective.

In the realm of agile and DevOps, the CI/CD pipeline becomes a robust platform for embedding automated security tools within each stage of software development. This integration allows for the early detection and resolution of security issues, paralleling and complementing other automated processes in the pipeline. The beauty of this approach lies in its ability to suspend the CI/CD flow when potential security risks are detected, ensuring that code is not just rapidly developed and deployed but also secure. Here is how various automated security tools play a pivotal role at different stages of the CI/CD pipeline:

- **Code repository scanning**: Scans committed code for exposed secrets, such as hardcoded credentials, preventing accidental leaks of sensitive information.

- **Software Composition Analysis (SCA)**: Scrutinizes third-party dependencies in the code, identifying vulnerabilities that could pose risks to the application

- **Static Application Security Testing (SAST)**: Assesses the source code for potential security flaws without needing to execute the code, acting as an automated *white-box* testing tool within the development stage

- **Runtime and container scanning**: Evaluates the execution environment and container images for risky components or unnecessary elements that might increase vulnerability

- **Dynamic Application Security Testing (DAST)**: Performs automated *black-box* testing, dynamically analyzing running code to detect security issues, ideally in a staging environment before production deployment

This extensive integration of automated security tools within the CI/CD pipeline embodies the essence of the shift-left approach. It ensures that security is not an isolated phase but a continuous, integral part of the different stages. The following diagram (*Figure 12.3*) illustrates how those tools integrate with the CI/CD pipeline's stages:

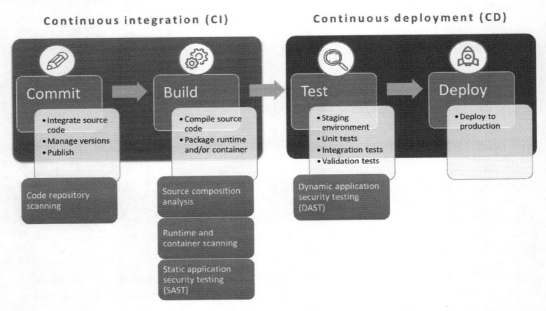

Figure 12.3 – Automated security tools' integration into the CI/CD pipeline

Now that we have familiarized ourselves with the integration of security in software development on a broader scale, let's pivot to AWS-specific practices, focusing on designing CI/CD workflows where security is a primary concern.

Building secure CI/CD pipelines with AWS services

AWS services provide a comprehensive toolkit for building CI/CD pipelines that prioritize security at each stage of the development and deployment process. The following sections delve deeper into designing these workflows, focusing on security-first principles and utilizing AWS services effectively.

Key services for CI/CD

Several AWS services play a crucial role in constructing a secure and efficient CI/CD pipeline. These services include the following:

- **AWS CodeCommit**: Securely stores and manages assets from source code to binaries. It supports Git functionalities such as branching, commits, and tagging.

- **AWS CodeArtifact**: Artifact repository that makes it easy for organizations to securely store, publish, and share software build outputs, dependencies, and packages generated throughout the pipeline.

- **AWS CodeBuild**: Compiles source code, runs tests, and produces ready-to-deploy software packages.

- **AWS CodeDeploy**: Automates code deployments to diverse platforms such as **EC2** instances and on-premises servers, reducing deployment downtime and managing application update complexities.

- **AWS CodePipeline**: Continuous delivery service that models, visualizes, and orchestrates the steps needed to release software through various tools in a CI/CD workflow.

Next, let's integrate these key AWS CI/CD services into designing security-first workflows.

Designing security-first CI/CD workflows

Incorporating security into CI/CD pipelines is not just about adding tools; it is about designing workflows with security as a primary focus. This subsection explores how to implement security-first principles in CI/CD pipelines using AWS services.

Implementing least-privilege access

In the DevOps realm, where collaboration and rapid deployment are key, implementing the **Principle of Least Privilege** (**PoLP**) is a critical security measure. It involves carefully allocating access rights and permissions to ensure that every individual and service has just enough privileges to perform their required tasks and no more. This approach minimizes potential vulnerabilities without hindering the efficiency of the CI/CD pipeline.

Role-Based Access Control (RBAC)

RBAC allows for granular management of permissions. Different roles within the CI/CD pipeline, such as developers, operations, and **Quality Assurance (QA)** teams, are granted access rights tailored to their specific job functions:

- **Developers**: Primarily given permissions to commit code, initiate build processes, and access results in pre-production environments. This level of access supports their need for rapid iteration and testing without exposing production environments to undue risk.

- **Operations teams**: Retain control over production environments. They manage deployment processes and have the authority to apply final changes to the production systems, ensuring that all deployments meet strict compliance and security standards.

- **QA**: Granted permissions to access both the development and staging environments for testing purposes, but typically restricted from making changes in the production environment.

Least privilege in automated processes

Often underestimated for automated processes, applying PoLP is just as crucial as it is for human users. By granting specific permissions tailored to the operational requirements of automated tasks such as code scanning, build, or deployment, we ensure these processes operate within a tightly controlled security boundary. This approach minimizes the attack surface by ensuring that automated tasks cannot perform actions beyond their intended scope, thereby significantly reducing the risk of exploitation by malicious actors. Consider revisiting *Chapter 3* for further guidance and best practices on utilizing **IAM** to enforce the least privilege principle effectively.

Secure repository and artifact access

Securing access to code repositories and artifacts is a critical aspect of maintaining the integrity and security of the CI/CD pipeline:

- **Code repositories**: Implement IAM permissions to regulate access to code repositories such as CodeCommit. Create granular IAM policies to control access, attaching these custom policies to IAM identities such as users and roles instead of using managed CodeCommit policies. This approach allows for more specific control, such as using resource-level permissions in IAM to specify who can perform actions such as `git push` and `git pull`. For instance, you can create a read-only user allowing `git pull` but not `git push`. These measures prevent unauthorized code modifications and maintain code base consistency.

- **Artifact storage**: Managing access to build artifacts and dependencies is equally important. Services such as CodeArtifact should be employed to control who can access and manage these artifacts. This includes setting permissions for uploading artifacts, fetching dependencies, and version management. Granular IAM policies can be used to control access to artifacts at the repository or package level. Proper control over artifact storage prevents unauthorized modifications and ensures that only secure, verified components are used in the build process.

Managing secrets

Handling sensitive data such as API keys, third-party credentials, and secrets is crucial in CI/CD pipelines. AWS Secrets Manager securely stores, manages, and retrieves database credentials, API keys, and other secrets. As discussed in *Chapter 5*, while Secrets Manager is specifically designed for handling secrets, AWS **Systems Manager** (**SSM**) Parameter Store can also provide a broader solution for managing configuration data and secrets. The integration of these tools ensures that sensitive data is not hardcoded in the source code, thereby maintaining security and compliance. Moreover, AWS **KMS** can add an extra layer of encryption and access control to your secrets.

Ensuring compliance

Adhering to compliance standards and security best practices is a critical aspect of building CI/CD pipelines. As discussed in *Chapter 11*, AWS provides services such as AWS Config, which helps you assess, audit, and evaluate the configurations of your AWS resources. In the context of your CI/CD pipelines, you can leverage Config to do the following:

- **Automate compliance checks**: Design custom Config rules to automatically assess and ensure that your CI/CD resources comply with specific standards and best practices. For instance, you can use Config to monitor changes in Lambda functions or EC2 instances used in the build and deployment process, ensuring they adhere to specific security configurations such as network settings, IAM role bindings, and environment variables.

- **Cross-service compliance**: Implement cross-service rules whereby Config can check the compliance status of core services used in the CI/CD pipeline. For instance, ensure that IAM roles used by CodeBuild projects have least-privilege access or that CodePipeline adheres to specific encryption and logging standards.

- **Compliance monitoring**: Config continuously monitors and records your AWS resource configurations, allowing you to evaluate your CI/CD pipeline's compliance status in real time. This ongoing monitoring is crucial for identifying and rectifying any deviations from compliance standards promptly.

Incorporating IaC

IaC is a key practice in DevOps. As discussed in *Chapter 8*, it allows teams to automatically manage and provision their infrastructure through code.

Integrating IaC into a CI/CD pipeline offers the advantage of aligning infrastructure deployment closely with application updates for smoother, more synchronized operations. When considering the structure of CI/CD pipelines, especially regarding IaC and application code, the options boil down to either combining them into a unique pipeline or maintaining them separately. Let's discuss both approaches:

- **Complexity of the infrastructure**: If the infrastructure is relatively simple, it may be easier to manage a unique pipeline that handles both application code and IaC. However, if the infrastructure is more complex, it may be beneficial to have separate pipelines to avoid confusion and ensure that changes are properly tested and deployed.

- **Team structure**: If the development and operations teams are separate, it may make sense to have separate pipelines for application code and IaC. This can help ensure that each team has the necessary control and visibility over their respective areas.

- **Deployment frequency**: If the application code and infrastructure changes are deployed at different frequencies, it may be beneficial to have separate pipelines. This can help ensure that changes are tested and deployed at the appropriate times.

- **Tools and technologies**: The tools and technologies used can also impact the decision. For example, if different tools are used for application code and IaC, it may be easier to have separate pipelines.

There are also some security considerations to keep in mind when choosing between both options:

- **Risk of cross-contamination**: In combined pipelines, a security breach in one part can potentially affect both application and infrastructure, necessitating robust isolation mechanisms

- **Dedicated security focus**: Separate pipelines allow for specialized security measures, reducing the chances of threats slipping through due to a generalized security approach

Choosing between unique or separate CI/CD pipelines for IaC and the application code is a decision that should be guided not only by operational factors but also by a thorough assessment of security implications. If the infrastructure is relatively simple and the team structure favors integrated operations, a combined pipeline could be more efficient. However, in scenarios where application code and infrastructure changes occur at different frequencies or are significantly complex, separate pipelines might provide better control and reduce the likelihood of cascading issues. Ultimately, this choice should be made after a careful evaluation of the organization's operational structure, deployment schedules, and the specific complexities involved in the infrastructure and application development processes, as well as the overarching security strategy.

Continuous monitoring

Implementing continuous monitoring and feedback within CI/CD pipelines is a key practice for maintaining the security and integrity of the deployment process. Leveraging CloudWatch and CloudTrail, organizations can implement a comprehensive monitoring strategy, aligning with the best practices outlined in *Chapter 10* regarding logging, monitoring, and auditing. This ensures not only operational efficiency but also robust security compliance. Here are some examples of metrics and alarms to integrate into your CI/CD pipeline for enhanced security:

- **Failed deployment counts**: Track the number of failed deployments. Frequent failures might indicate potential security issues or misconfigurations in the pipeline.

- **Change frequency**: Monitor the rate of changes or deployments, as a sudden spike may signal unauthorized activity.

- **Duration of pipeline stages**: Excessive time spent in specific pipeline stages could indicate performance issues or security breaches.

- **Access patterns**: Keep an eye on access patterns to resources such as CodeCommit or CodeBuild. Unusual patterns might suggest unauthorized access attempts.

- **Error rates and types**: Track error rates and types in different stages of the pipeline. Specific error types, especially in security scans or deployment stages, can highlight vulnerabilities.

Deployment and rollback strategies

Finally, effective CI/CD pipelines require robust deployment and rollback strategies that also consider security. CodeDeploy supports various deployment methods, each offering unique advantages in terms of security and operational continuity:

- **Blue/green deployments**: This strategy, involving parallel running of the new (*green*) and old (*blue*) versions, allows for testing the new version in a live environment without fully committing to it. If a security issue or operational failure is detected in the green environment, a quick rollback to the blue environment ensures minimal disruption and risk exposure.

- **Canary deployments**: By rolling out the new version to a small subset of users or servers first, canary deployments offer a cautious approach. This gradual rollout allows for monitoring the new version's performance and security in a controlled manner, enabling quick rollback if issues are detected, thus minimizing potential impact.

- **A/B testing**: This strategy is useful for gauging user response to new features, but it also has a place in security testing. By directing a portion of traffic to a new feature, teams can assess its security impact in a real-world scenario, with the option to quickly revert if issues arise.

CodeDeploy enhances these strategies with automated rollback capabilities, ensuring that if a deployment introduces unforeseen issues or vulnerabilities, a swift and efficient reversion to a previous stable state is possible. This approach provides a balance between rapid deployment and maintaining a secure, stable environment.

By carefully integrating these components and practices, you can build a secure, efficient, and compliant CI/CD pipeline using AWS services, thus ensuring that security is a core part of your software development and delivery process. This approach aligns with the evolving landscape of software development, where agility and security are not mutually exclusive but rather complementary facets of a sophisticated CI/CD strategy.

The next step in this journey is to integrate specific security tools throughout the different stages of your CI/CD pipeline, enriching the entire development and deployment process with layers of security checks and balances.

Integrating security tooling into the pipeline

Integrating security tooling directly into the CI/CD workflow is essential for ensuring that each release is not only functional but also secure. This integration involves a combination of AWS native and third-party tools, each offering unique capabilities to enhance the security posture of your deployment processes. Let's delve into the process of selecting and integrating these essential tools.

AWS native and third-party tools

AWS offers Amazon CodeGuru, an automated code review service that utilizes **Machine Learning (ML)** to detect critical issues and potential security vulnerabilities in code. This tool is instrumental in identifying performance degradation risks and security weaknesses, thus significantly contributing to maintaining high code quality and robust security standards.

However, CodeGuru, while powerful, may not fully address all diverse security requirements and cover every relevant stage of the workflow. Consequently, the integration of third-party security tools into your CI/CD pipeline is crucial for achieving a comprehensive security landscape. Tools such as SonarQube for code quality, Snyk for vulnerability scanning in open source dependencies, and Aqua Security for container security not only offer additional layers of security but also complement AWS native offerings. These third-party tools often come with advanced features tailored to specific aspects such as SAST, DAST, or other types of security scanning, providing more comprehensive security coverage.

Leveraging CodeGuru Security

CodeGuru Security, a crucial component of CodeGuru, can significantly enhance security aspects of software development, especially when integrated within CodePipeline. Its primary function involves conducting comprehensive SAST by leveraging advanced ML models and automated reasoning. This meticulous analysis of the source code aims to identify a range of common security vulnerabilities, including issues such as improper handling of sensitive data, unsecured API calls, and potential data breaches.

Integrating CodeGuru Security within CodePipeline guarantees that every piece of code submitted undergoes a detailed security review, ensuring adherence to best practices and compliance standards. One of the key functionalities of CodeGuru Security lies in its proactive vulnerability identification. As the code is being written and submitted, CodeGuru Security scrutinizes it to pinpoint potential security flaws that might otherwise go unnoticed. This proactive approach is instrumental in preventing future security breaches and diminishing the costs and complexities associated with rectifying issues at later stages.

Another significant strength of CodeGuru Security is its capacity to provide in-depth, actionable recommendations. These recommendations are more than mere alerts; they are accompanied by insights and potential solutions, thus enabling developers to not only identify but also effectively rectify security vulnerabilities. This feature of CodeGuru Security plays a crucial role in empowering developers with the necessary knowledge and tools to enhance the security of their code.

To effectively integrate CodeGuru Security into the CI/CD pipeline, consider these recommendations:

- **Pull request scanning**: Configure CodeGuru Security to analyze pull requests in your **Version Control System** (**VCS**), enabling it to provide instant feedback on code changes.

- **Code repository scanning**: Beyond pull requests, configure CodeGuru Security to periodically scan the entire code repository. This helps in identifying any latent vulnerabilities that might not be part of recent changes but still pose a security risk.

- **Code review policy enforcement**: Implement policies that require resolving all critical security findings identified by CodeGuru Security before code merges are allowed. This policy enforcement ensures that security concerns are addressed promptly.

- **Real-time security alerts**: Configure real-time alerts to notify the development team immediately when CodeGuru Security identifies significant security risks. Quick notifications enable swift action to mitigate potential vulnerabilities.

- **Continuous feedback loop**: Establishing a process where developers regularly review and act upon recommendations provided by CodeGuru Security ensures a continuous improvement in the security and overall quality of the code.

- **Security metrics tracking**: Implement a system to track and report on security metrics derived from CodeGuru Security findings. Tracking metrics such as the number of vulnerabilities detected, time to fix, and recurrence of specific issues can provide valuable insights for improving security practices.

With a focus on CodeGuru Security and its integration, we have explored how this native AWS tool can elevate software security. Now, let's discuss third-party tools that can further bolster security in the CI/CD pipeline.

Exploring popular third-party security tools

Numerous third-party security tools can be combined and integrated into CI/CD pipelines for robust application security. Popular tools include the following:

- **SonarQube**: SAST tool that excels in detecting bugs, vulnerabilities, and code smells in your source code
- **Checkmarx**: Another SAST tool that specializes in scanning source code and identifying security vulnerabilities, providing actionable insights
- **OWASP Dependency-Check**: SCA tool that identifies publicly disclosed vulnerabilities in project dependencies
- **Snyk**: SCA tool focusing on dependencies and container vulnerabilities
- **Clair**: SCA tool for vulnerabilities in application containers.
- **Grype**: SCA tool for container images and filesystems
- **OWASP Zed Attack Proxy (ZAP)**: DAST tool that identifies security vulnerabilities in web applications in test or production environments
- **Trivy**: Comprehensive vulnerability scanner for containers and other artifacts capable of detecting vulnerabilities within operating systems, application dependencies, and misconfigurations

While some of these tools may appear to have overlapping functionalities, it can be advantageous to combine different tools, even of the same type, within your pipeline. This approach allows for leveraging the strengths and compensating for the limitations or weaknesses of each tool, ensuring a more robust security posture overall.

Now, let's delve into the specifics of SonarQube and OWASP ZAP integrations, as they are among the most commonly used third-party tools in both the SAST and DAST categories.

SonarQube integration

SonarQube is a leading SAST tool that can significantly enhance code quality and security, particularly when integrated into CI/CD pipelines. Its capabilities extend from continuous code analysis to identifying bugs, vulnerabilities, and code smells, ensuring adherence to high-quality coding practices. SonarQube offers both a self-managed and a **software-as-a-service** (**SaaS**) option.

In a CI/CD pipeline, SonarQube integrates into VCSs, offering automated reviews for every pull request. This integration provides developers with immediate feedback on potential security vulnerabilities and code quality issues, fostering a culture of high-quality coding standards and proactive security practices. Teams can also customize quality gates in SonarQube, setting specific criteria that code must meet before merging or deployment, thus ensuring compliance with established coding standards and security best practices.

Furthermore, when specific criteria set in quality gates are not met, it triggers a crucial process of review and revision. Developers are prompted to revisit their code, address the identified issues, and enhance the overall code quality. This iterative process not only improves the immediate code base but also contributes to long-term skill development among the development team. Developers become more adept at writing cleaner, more secure code from the outset, reducing the frequency of revisions in future projects.

OWASP ZAP integration

As a free open source SAST solution, OWASP ZAP can be used to actively test web applications for vulnerabilities during runtime, offering an effective complement to SAST. This dynamic assessment is crucial for uncovering runtime issues such as authentication and session management flaws, **Cross-Site Scripting** (**XSS**), and SQL injection, among other vulnerabilities. The tool's ability to simulate real-world attack scenarios gives a realistic assessment of how applications might fare against actual security threats. This includes performing authenticated scans to test both public and private aspects of applications.

When embedded in CI/CD pipelines, OWASP ZAP automates security testing as part of the deployment process. This integration ensures that each new release undergoes thorough security assessments, thereby identifying and addressing vulnerabilities at the build stage in a test environment. The tool's customizable scanning capabilities allow teams to tailor security tests to their specific application architecture and security needs, ensuring effectiveness across different application types.

OWASP ZAP's integration also includes generating detailed reports after each scan. These reports are crucial for providing developers and security teams with actionable insights into potential security risks. Immediate feedback facilitates prompt remediation efforts, enhancing the overall security posture of the application.

As we move forward, we will integrate the insights gained from these third-party tools with the centralized capabilities of AWS Security Hub.

Tooling integration with Security Hub

Integrating Security Hub into CI/CD pipelines enhances the security management process by providing a unified platform that aggregates, organizes, and prioritizes security alerts from various AWS services and third-party tools. Thanks to the **AWS security finding format** (**ASFF**), Security Hub ensures that all security findings are standardized, making it simpler to monitor and address potential issues identified by different tools, be it SAST, DAST, or SCA. This standardization is key in allowing for effective cross-tool data analysis and reporting.

Teams can set up custom security alerts in Security Hub tailored to their specific needs and risk profiles, enabling rapid response to critical issues detected by the integrated security tools. Additionally, the integration streamlines the process of managing and remediating security findings. Teams can use Lambda functions or other automated mechanisms for quick and efficient resolution of security issues.

The following diagram (*Figure 12.4*) illustrates how Security Hub can be integrated with both AWS native and third-party tools attached to various stages of the CI/CD pipeline:

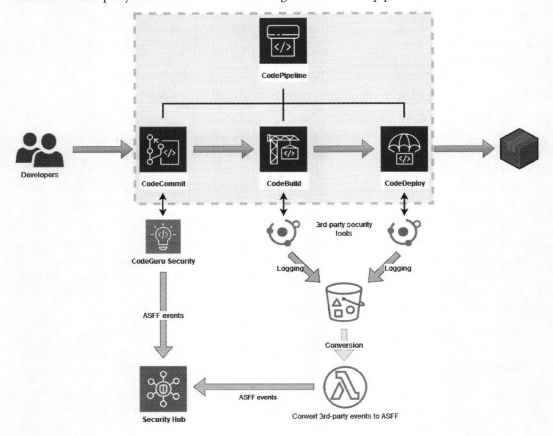

Figure 12.4 – Security Hub integration into the CI/CD pipeline

Next, let's turn our attention from Security Hub to best practices that are key to successfully integrating security tools in the CI/CD landscape.

Best practices for security tooling integration

Integrating security tools into CI/CD pipelines is a critical step for ensuring robust software security. However, the effectiveness of this integration hinges on adhering to best practices that optimize the functionality and impact of these tools. Here are some key strategies:

- **Prioritize seamless integration**: Choose tools that integrate smoothly with your existing CI/CD pipeline. Tools should complement and enhance your workflow, not complicate it.

Look for features such as API compatibility, easy configuration, and support for common development environments.

- **Use a layered approach**: Don't rely on a single tool or type of tool. Use a combination of SAST, DAST, SCA, and container scanning tools to cover different aspects of security. This layered approach ensures more comprehensive security coverage.

- **Customize tool configuration**: Tailor each tool's configuration to suit your specific project needs. This includes setting appropriate scanning thresholds, customizing alert settings, and defining relevant security policies. A one-size-fits-all approach rarely works in security; customization is key.

- **Automate**: Leverage automation to streamline security processes. This can include automating scans at certain stages of the pipeline, such as post-commit or pre-deployment, and using automated responses for identified issues.

- **Balance speed and security**: While it is essential to catch security issues early, it is equally important not to hinder the development process. Striking a balance between thorough security checks and maintaining velocity is crucial.

- **Regularly update and maintain tools**: Security tools need to be regularly updated to detect the latest vulnerabilities. Schedule regular maintenance and updates to ensure your tools are up to date and effective.

- **Establish and monitor security metrics**: Focus on assessing the effectiveness of your security tools by monitoring the types of vulnerabilities detected and their impact, while closely tracking key security metrics such as detection frequency and remediation speed, utilizing CloudWatch for comprehensive analysis.

- **Cultivate a knowledge and security mindset**: Ensure developers are well trained in using security tools and understanding their outputs, and foster a security-conscious culture through ongoing discussions, learning from past incidents, and encouraging proactive security actions.

- **Evaluate and adjust strategies regularly**: Security is an evolving field. Regularly evaluate the effectiveness of your security strategies and make adjustments as needed. This might involve adding new tools, tweaking existing configurations, or changing processes.

By following these best practices, organizations can effectively integrate security tools into their CI/CD pipelines, enhancing their overall security posture while maintaining development efficiency and agility.

Summary

In this chapter, we delved into the integration of security within CI/CD pipelines, a concept central to modern DevSecOps practices. We began by exploring the evolution from traditional to agile methodologies, highlighting the importance of embedding security at every stage of the SDLC. Our focus then shifted to the pivotal role of AWS services in constructing secure CI/CD pipelines, examining key services such as CodeCommit, CodeBuild, CodeDeploy, and CodePipeline, and their roles in enhancing security.

We addressed the challenges of implementing DevSecOps, including cultural resistance, tooling integration, skills gaps, and the need for continuous monitoring and adaptation. Practical solutions and strategies were provided to overcome these hurdles, emphasizing the significance of automated tools for security scanning and the shift-left approach to security. The chapter highlighted the integration of AWS native and third-party security tools, such as CodeGuru, SonarQube, and OWASP ZAP, into CI/CD workflows, demonstrating how they bolster the pipeline's security.

We also discussed best practices for security tool integration, emphasizing the need for seamless integration, a layered security approach, customization, automation, and regular updates. A balanced view was presented on maintaining speed and thoroughness in security checks and the importance of continuous team education and fostering a security-minded culture.

In conclusion, this chapter underscored the criticality of integrating security into CI/CD pipelines, offering insights into using AWS services and tools to build secure, efficient, and compliant software delivery workflows. By following the outlined best practices and leveraging the capabilities of AWS services, organizations can enhance their security posture while maintaining development agility.

Looking ahead to the final chapter of this book, we will focus on the ever-evolving landscape of AWS security best practices and threats. It will focus on resources and strategies for staying informed and adapting to new security challenges, emphasizing the importance of continuous learning and the integration of new security features into AWS environments.

Questions

Answer the following questions to test your knowledge of this chapter:

1. Which AWS services can be used to maintain continuous compliance, especially with frequent changes in CI/CD pipelines?

2. How does Security Hub contribute to managing and improving the software supply chain's security in a DevSecOps framework?

3. How can Lambda be used to automate security tasks in the CI/CD pipeline?

4. Can you explain the process of integrating SSM Parameter Store or Secrets Manager for secure management of credentials and secrets in a DevSecOps pipeline? How does this enhance the security of the software supply chain?

Answers

Here are the answers to this chapter's questions:

1. Leverage Config for ongoing monitoring of AWS resource configurations, coupled with CloudTrail for logging all API calls made by CI/CD pipelines. Set up rules and alerts within these services to promptly identify and react to any deviations from predefined security and configuration standards.

2. Security Hub aggregates and prioritizes security alerts from various AWS services and third-party tools, providing a comprehensive view of the security state of the software supply chain and enabling quicker response to potential threats.

3. Lambda functions can be used to automate security tasks such as vulnerability scanning post-deployment or triggering remediation actions in response to security alerts. This automation is essential for maintaining continuous security in DevSecOps workflows.

4. Both SSM Parameter Store and Secrets Manager can be integrated for dynamic secrets retrieval in the pipeline, eliminating hardcoded credentials. This enhances security by centralizing secret management, enforcing access policies, and automating credential management, thus reducing vulnerabilities in the software supply chain.

Further reading

The following readings offer further insights and best practices regarding DevSecOps in AWS:

- *Building end-to-end AWS DevSecOps CI/CD pipeline with open source SCA, SAST and DAST tools* by Srinivas Manepalli (2021): `https://aws.amazon.com/blogs/devops/building-end-to-end-aws-devsecops-ci-cd-pipeline-with-open-source-sca-sast-and-dast-tools`

- *Use the Snyk CLI to scan Python packages using AWS CodeCommit, AWS CodePipeline, and AWS CodeBuild* by BK Das (2021): `https://aws.amazon.com/blogs/devops/snyk-cli-scan-python-codecommit-codepipeline-codebuild`

- *Integrating and automating security into a DevSecOps model* by Deloitte: `https://www2.deloitte.com/content/dam/Deloitte/us/Documents/risk/us-integrating-and-automating-security-into-a-devsecops-model.pdf`

- *Introduction to DevSecOps with AWS: How to Integrate Security into DevOps* by Apriorit (2022): `https://www.apriorit.com/dev-blog/530-delivering-devsecops-aws`

13

Keeping Up with Evolving AWS Security Best Practices and Threat Landscape

Welcome to the thirteenth and final chapter, where we will focus on equipping you with the knowledge and tools to navigate the ever-evolving AWS security landscape. We will begin by examining emerging threats in cloud environments and how to keep them at bay.

We will then emphasize the importance of continuous education and adaptation. We will delve into the myriad resources AWS offers for enhancing your security acumen, from in-depth training programs to community-driven insights.

To conclude this chapter, we will lay out a roadmap for staying relevant and keeping abreast with AWS security developments, guiding you through the essential practices for maintaining a resilient and forward-looking security posture.

By the end of this chapter, you will be equipped with different strategies to develop your knowledge and keep up with the evolving landscape of AWS security, ensuring you remain at the forefront of technological advancements and security practices.

In this chapter, we will cover the following key areas:

- Identifying and adapting to emerging threats in your cloud environment

- Leveraging resources for ongoing education in AWS security

- Incorporating new security features, services, and tools as they emerge

Identifying and adapting to emerging threats

Cloud computing technologies are continuously evolving at a growing pace, bringing forth a landscape where new threats emerge with increasing sophistication. These emerging threats challenge the foundational security paradigms of organizations globally. As cloud computing has become integral to modern business infrastructure, offering scalability, flexibility, and cost-effectiveness, it also opens the door to unique and complex security risks. Moving forward, let's explore the rise of advanced threats that are reshaping security challenges in the cloud era.

The rise of advanced threats

The digital era has seen significant advancement in technology, which, while empowering organizations, has equally empowered cybercriminals. These threat actors are more sophisticated than ever, employing advanced techniques and tools such as **Artificial Intelligence** (**AI**) and **Machine Learning** (**ML**) to outsmart traditional security defenses. Here are some key examples of these advanced threats:

- **Ransomware attacks**: These involve encrypting critical data by attackers who then demand a ransom for its release. Ransomware attacks can cripple an organization's operations and lead to substantial financial losses.

- **Advanced Persistent Threats (APTs)**: APTs are prolonged and targeted cyberattacks in which an intruder gains access to a network and remains undetected for an extended period. The objective is often to steal data rather than cause immediate damage to the network or organization.

- **Phishing scams and social engineering**: With increasing reliance on cloud services, attackers often use sophisticated phishing scams, targeting employees to gain access to sensitive cloud-stored information.

- **Distributed denial of service (DDoS) attacks**: Cloud services, given their internet-based nature, are susceptible to DDoS attacks, where servers are overwhelmed with traffic, disrupting service.

Understanding these threats sets the stage for a deeper examination of cloud-specific vulnerabilities.

Cloud-specific threats and vulnerabilities

As cloud computing continues to reshape the landscape of modern business infrastructure, it brings with it a complex array of security vulnerabilities and emerging threats. Understanding these challenges is critical for organizations to safeguard their cloud environments effectively:

- **Misconfigurations**: Misconfigurations in cloud settings are a leading cause of security incidents. Simple errors, such as improperly set S3 bucket permissions or misconfigured network settings, can leave sensitive data vulnerable to unauthorized access. These misconfigurations highlight the delicate balance required in cloud security management.

- **Inadequate access control**: IAM roles and policies in cloud platforms such as AWS are crucial for securing access to resources and data. However, the dynamic nature of cloud environments complicates effective access control. Weak authentication processes and insufficient access control strategies can lead to unauthorized access to sensitive cloud resources.

- **Shared responsibility model challenges**: The shared responsibility model in cloud computing divides security obligations between the cloud service provider and the client. Misunderstandings in this model often lead to security gaps, especially regarding data security, application-level controls, and endpoint protections.

- **Concentration risk in cloud services**: The centralization of cloud resources introduces a concentration risk, where a single security incident can have widespread impacts. This risk is magnified when multiple organizations rely heavily on a single cloud service provider, potentially leading to significant disruptions in the event of a major breach.

- **The proliferation of resources**: Infrastructure sprawl, the unchecked proliferation of cloud resources, emerges as a key vulnerability when organizations lack strong policies or controls. This sprawl makes it challenging to grasp the full extent of an organization's cloud infrastructure, leading to potential security and compliance pitfalls.

- **Cryptojacking**: Attackers increasingly exploit cloud resources for cryptojacking, using hijacked computing power to mine cryptocurrency. This not only incurs higher operational costs but also degrades the performance of legitimate workloads in the cloud.

- **API vulnerabilities**: APIs are essential for cloud service integration but have become prime targets for attackers. Vulnerabilities in these APIs can result in data breaches and manipulation of cloud services. Addressing these vulnerabilities requires enhanced security measures such as robust authentication, encryption, and regular security assessments.

- **IoT device security**: The growing integration of IoT devices with cloud networks introduces new vulnerabilities. These devices, often lacking advanced security features, can be exploited to gain access to cloud networks, making stringent security protocols and network segmentation vital.

- **Supply chain attacks**: Sophisticated supply chain attacks target components integrated into cloud environments, potentially breaching the security of multiple organizations simultaneously. These attacks emphasize the need for comprehensive security vetting of third-party vendors and robust encryption throughout the cloud service chain.

- **Serverless computing security**: The shift to serverless computing architectures brings unique challenges, such as managing permissions for serverless functions and securing event-triggered workflows. The transient nature of serverless computing necessitates specialized security tools and application-level security focus.

- **Containerization security**: The adoption of containerized environments has exposed several security issues, including container escape attacks and misconfigurations. Ensuring the security of containerized environments involves comprehensive management practices, regular vulnerability scanning, and strict network policies for container interactions.

With the key cloud-related threats outlined, let's transition to strategies to adapt and respond effectively.

Strategies for adapting to emerging threats

Adapting to these emerging threats requires a multi-layered approach that combines advanced technology, skilled personnel, and robust policies. Here are some key strategies:

- **Developing a strong cloud security architecture**: Essential for risk mitigation, this involves integrating security into every layer of cloud infrastructure. Key elements include implementing secure access controls, using data encryption to protect sensitive information, and establishing comprehensive network protection strategies.

- **Establishing a robust incident response plan**: A well-defined incident response plan is vital for quickly addressing security incidents. This plan should detail procedures for isolating affected systems, eradicating threats, and restoring operations promptly. Regular drills and updates ensure preparedness for various scenarios.

- **Implementing a zero-trust security model**: In this model, trust is never implicitly given and every access request is scrutinized. Continuous validation of user credentials and enforcing least privilege access are crucial components of this strategy.

- **Utilizing threat intelligence feeds**: Staying up-to-date with the latest threat landscape helps anticipate and prepare for potential security breaches. This strategy involves analyzing real-time threat data from both internal and external sources, integrating intelligence insights into security tools, and using this information to inform strategic security decisions.

- **Enhancing threat detection capabilities**: A proactive approach to threat detection is crucial for maintaining a strong security posture in a dynamic cloud environment. This involves employing a variety of advanced tools and techniques, such as continuous monitoring and AI-driven analytics, to identify and address potential threats swiftly.

Next, let's focus on specific tools and techniques that enable threat detection in AWS.

Tools and techniques for threat detection

Effective threat detection is critical and can be significantly enhanced by employing a comprehensive blend of sophisticated tools and techniques. These methods are designed not only to identify potential threats but also to provide actionable insights for timely response. Here's an in-depth look at some key tools and techniques:

- **Cloud Security Posture Management (CSPM)**: CSPM solutions such as AWS Security Hub or Palo Alto Networks Prisma Cloud are essential for continuous monitoring and securing cloud configurations. They help identify misconfigurations, compliance issues, and security risks in real-time by scanning cloud environments against best practices and regulatory standards.

- **Endpoint Detection and Response (EDR)**: EDR solutions such as AWS GuardDuty or CrowdStrike Falcon are vital for protecting critical endpoints from sophisticated threats. These tools operate by continuously monitoring and collecting data from endpoints, using behavioral analytics to identify potential security threats. Upon detecting a threat, they enable rapid response by isolating affected endpoints, analyzing the root cause, and remediating the issue, thereby preventing the spread of the threat.

- **Network Traffic Analysis (NTA)**: Analyzing network traffic is key for detecting anomalies and potential threats. AWS VPC flow logs, for instance, captures information about network traffic in your VPC. It can help to detect unusual patterns, unauthorized data transfers, or other indicators of malicious activity that may indicate security threats, including data exfiltration attempts or unauthorized network access. To fully exploit these logs, integration with other analytical tools is required. Additionally, for serverless components such as AWS Lambda to be monitored by VPC Flow logs, they need to be attached to the VPC, enabling comprehensive traffic visibility.

- **Security Information and Event Management (SIEM)**: SIEM solutions such as Splunk aggregate and analyze data from various sources across both cloud and on-premises environments. They provide real-time analysis of security alerts by correlating events from logs, systems, and applications, facilitating the detection of complex threats and enabling a quick response. Modern SIEM solutions incorporate advanced analytics and **User Behavior Analytics (UBA)** to identify subtle anomalies indicative of sophisticated cyber-attacks.

- **Threat hunting**: Incorporating proactive threat hunting into security strategies can enhance threat detection and response. Tools such as AWS Detective and Elastic Security enable security teams to proactively search through network and application data to identify hidden threats that automated tools might miss. This approach involves actively looking for indicators of compromise or anomalous activities that suggest a breach or an imminent threat.

- **AI and ML**: The integration of AI and ML technologies is revolutionizing threat detection. Solutions such as Amazon Q, Bedrock, and SageMaker can be utilized to analyze large amounts of historical data to predict and identify potential security incidents. They automate the detection and response processes, rapidly identifying threats and initiating responses without human intervention.

Recognizing threats is just the beginning. To effectively defend our infrastructure, we must also understand the attacker's playbook. Let's explore how the MITRE ATT&CK framework can be utilized to tailor our defense mechanisms against those threats.

Threat modeling with MITRE ATT&CK

The MITRE ATT&CK framework has emerged as an interesting tool for organizations using AWS to understand, anticipate, and counteract cyber threats. This globally recognized framework offers a comprehensive matrix of tactics and techniques that are commonly employed by cyber adversaries. The MITRE ATT&CK for Cloud matrix, specifically, is tailored to address cloud environments. It provides insights into potential cloud-specific threats and vulnerabilities, which are particularly useful for AWS users.

Incorporating the MITRE ATT&CK framework into AWS security practices offers numerous benefits as it provides a structured methodology for understanding and anticipating potential threats within your AWS landscape. Here are its key integrations:

- **Mapping to AWS services**: By aligning the ATT&CK framework with AWS services, organizations can gain detailed insights into potential attack vectors. This involves understanding how specific ATT&CK tactics and techniques can be applied to or mitigated by AWS services, such as EC2, S3, or IAM.

- **Utilization in security assessments**: Incorporating the framework into security assessments allows for a more thorough evaluation of AWS environments. It helps in identifying vulnerabilities that could be exploited through known attack methodologies, thus enabling a more targeted approach to securing cloud assets. For instance, organizations can use the framework to simulate attack scenarios, such as a credential access attack, where an attacker might attempt to obtain AWS access keys through phishing or other methods.

- **Enhancing incident response**: The framework can significantly improve incident response strategies. By mapping ongoing attacks to the ATT&CK matrix, incident response teams can more quickly understand the attacker's **Tactics, Techniques, and Procedures (TTPs)**, leading to faster and more effective containment and remediation.

- **Feeding continuous monitoring**: The framework aids in the development of continuous monitoring strategies that are more aligned with the evolving threat landscape. It allows security teams to proactively look for indicators of attack tactics and techniques, enabling early detection of potential threats.

- **Developing customized threat models**: Creating threat models based on ATT&CK scenarios tailored to AWS can significantly enhance defense strategies. For example, building a model around the *exfiltration* techniques can help in preparing defenses against potential data breaches from S3 buckets.

- **Developing red team exercises**: Conducting red team exercises using ATT&CK-based scenarios provides a realistic test of AWS defenses. For example, simulating an attack where a red team uses *lateral movement* techniques to move between EC2 instances can test the effectiveness of network segmentation and access controls.

Building upon our discussion of MITRE ATT&CK and how to handle emerging threats in general, next, we will explore the wealth of resources available for continuous learning in AWS security.

Leveraging resources for ongoing education

The dynamic nature of AWS cloud technology and security necessitates continuous learning and adaptation. With AWS at the forefront of cloud innovation, there exists an extensive array of documentation, training programs, and community resources. This section aims to guide you through the wealth of information available so that you can learn about the latest in security practices and technologies in a way that aligns with your learning objectives. Let's begin by establishing a learning path tailored to your specific goals in AWS security.

Building a personal learning path for AWS security

Developing a personal learning path in AWS security requires a thoughtful assessment of your current skills, career aspirations, and the specific knowledge areas you aim to master. Whether you are just beginning your journey in cybersecurity, aiming to become an AWS expert, or seeking to specialize in AWS security, setting clear career goals is the first step:

- **Identify your career goals**: Determine if your objective is to become a cybersecurity expert with a broad understanding of various platforms, an AWS specialist who masters the intricacies of AWS services, or an AWS security expert focused on navigating the complex security landscape of AWS. For those aiming to excel in multi-cloud environments, understanding how AWS integrates with other cloud technologies will be crucial.

- **Prioritize your learning plan**: Once you have defined your career trajectory, prioritize your learning objectives based on your role and goals. For cybersecurity professionals, gaining a deep understanding of cloud security fundamentals and threat landscapes across multiple platforms may be the starting point. AWS security specialists need to dive deeper into AWS security services, security automation, and compliance. Other AWS experts might seek to deepen their security knowledge to comprehend the security aspects related to their discipline, whether it be development, data science, or architectural design.

- **Resource selection**: Choose resources that align with your learning style and objectives. AWS offers a wide range of learning materials, from documentation and whitepapers to workshops and certification courses, catering to different levels of expertise and areas of interest.

Let's go through the different types of resources that AWS offers to bolster your security expertise.

AWS security knowledge landscape

AWS provides an extensive array of resources that can be leveraged to support your ongoing education in AWS security. These resources are designed to cater to a wide range of learning needs, from foundational knowledge to advanced security techniques. Let's learn more about them:

- **AWS whitepapers**: Dive into AWS whitepapers for comprehensive insights into security best practices, architectural recommendations, and service-specific security advice. They serve as an excellent starting point, laying a solid foundation for understanding the principles behind AWS security measures and how they can be applied in real-world scenarios.

- **AWS security blog**: This dynamic platform is regularly updated with insights from AWS security experts, offering deep dives into new features, security enhancements, and detailed guides on implementing AWS security services. The blog's content is organized by product and by level (100, 200, 300, or 400), making it easy for readers to filter articles based on their expertise and areas of interest. Whether you are a novice in cloud security or an experienced professional, the AWS Security Blog provides valuable knowledge tailored to your learning curve.

- **AWS security announcements**: Staying updated with the latest security announcements from AWS is crucial for maintaining the security integrity of your AWS environment. These updates include information on security patches, vulnerabilities, and compliance issues that may affect your services. Integrating these bulletins into an RSS aggregator is a proactive way to ensure you receive timely updates, enabling you to implement necessary security measures swiftly.

- **AWS documentation**: The official AWS documentation is an indispensable resource for anyone working with AWS services. It covers detailed instructions on configuring and using AWS services, including security protocols and best practices. The documentation is regularly updated to reflect the latest service features and security guidelines, making it an essential reference for day-to-day operations and troubleshooting.

- **AWS Well-Architected Framework**: This framework is pivotal for learning how to design and operate secure, high-performing, and resilient cloud applications. Its so-called Security Pillar in particular focuses on offering guidance for protecting data and systems. Learning through this framework enables you to assess and improve your architecture in alignment with AWS best practices, enhancing your ability to identify and mitigate risks.

- **AWS workshops**: AWS workshops are interactive learning sessions that offer hands-on experience with AWS services, facilitating the practical application of theoretical knowledge. These workshops, categorized by level and topic, allow learners to select sessions that match their current skills and learning objectives. Opt for higher-level (300 or 400) security workshops to gain practical knowledge on implementing AWS security services and features.

- **AWS re:Post**: As a user-driven Q&A community, AWS re:Post is a platform where AWS users can ask questions and share knowledge about AWS services, including security. It is an excellent resource for getting insights from real-world experiences and expert advice on specific security challenges.

- **AWS Q as your virtual mentor**: Tap into AWS Q for an engaging and responsive learning experience, obtaining swift solutions to your AWS security questions. Whether you are addressing a particular challenge or looking for advice on security best practices, AWS Q serves as your on-demand guide, breaking down complex AWS concepts into understandable information. With its comprehensive coverage of AWS knowledge, including the topics discussed earlier, AWS Q is an essential resource for AWS learners of every level.

Incorporating these resources into your learning path allows for a structured and comprehensive approach to mastering AWS security. By staying informed about the latest developments and engaging with AWS security-related content, you can ensure that your skills remain sharp and relevant. Prioritizing your learning based on your career goals—whether you are aiming to be a cybersecurity generalist, an AWS expert, or a specialized AWS security professional—facilitates a focused and rewarding professional development journey in the realm of cloud security.

Formal AWS certification program

AWS certifications encompass a wide range of knowledge areas within AWS. They can be very interesting options for professionals seeking to validate and enhance their expertise. Opinions on the value of certifications in general vary widely and are often debated. I find certifications to be instrumental in setting goals for self-study and invaluable as a freelance AWS security consultant and instructor for demonstrating expertise and commitment to professional development.

Overview of the AWS certification program

AWS offers a series of certifications that can be instrumental for individuals aiming to develop and demonstrate their AWS knowledge. A considerable portion of each certification's curriculum is devoted to security-related topics, accounting for 15% to 30% of the exam content, as outlined in the guide documentation for each specific exam. The exception to this range is the AWS Certified Security—Specialty exam, which is wholly centered on security topics.

For readers of this book embarking on their AWS learning path, the following certifications are particularly pertinent:

- **AWS Certified SysOps Administrator – Associate (SOA)**: This certification validates expertise in deploying, managing, and operating workloads. It also covers operational security to ensure VPCs and systems are secure and compliant.

- **AWS Certified Developer – Associate (DVA)**: Ideal for developers, this certification covers security concepts relevant to developing and maintaining secure applications on AWS throughout the CI/CD pipeline.

- **AWS Certified Solutions Architect – Associate (SAA)**: This certification focuses on designing secure and robust distributed systems using multiple AWS services. It covers aspects of network security, encryption, and access control, among others.

- **AWS Certified DevOps Engineer – Professional (DOP)**: Tailored to professionals involved in DevOps roles, this certification dives deeper into automation and security protocols for continuous delivery and the secure deployment of applications and infrastructures on AWS.

- **AWS Certified Solutions Architect – Professional (SAP)**: For advanced architectural skills, this certification includes designing scalable and secure solutions across diverse AWS projects and services.

- **AWS Certified Security – Specialty (SCS)**: Specifically tailored for security experts, this certification is crucial for those looking to prove their knowledge of AWS security services and best practices. It is highly relevant to you as it offers deep insights into AWS-specific security considerations.

- **AWS Certified Advanced Networking – Specialty (ANS)**: This certificate demonstrates mastery in architecting and operating highly available, secure network solutions on AWS. It's ideal for network engineers and security specialists responsible for robust network infrastructure.

With an understanding of the key AWS certifications to target, let's proceed to examine the wealth of resources and study strategies to ensure your success in these exams.

Resources to prepare for your next exam

Preparing for an AWS certification exam demands a methodical study approach and the right resources:

- **Official exam page**: Start with the official AWS certification web page, where you can find exam guides detailing the content areas covered. Ensure any training material you use is aligned with the correct exam number and version.

- **Online video courses**: Platforms such as Udemy and Coursera offer video courses by highly recognized authors. These courses are very cost-effective and can be valuable for those who like learning from videos. Search for the most reviewed and recently updated courses, avoiding content older than 2 years.

- **Books**: Investing in a well-reviewed book tailored to the targeted AWS certification exam can provide in-depth knowledge to study at your own pace. Note that this book itself, while not an exam guide, can complement your study plan with practical AWS security knowledge, enriching your preparation for any exam.

- **AWS Skill Builder**: This platform is excellent for an official overview and exam preparation questions, although it may not be free.

- **Cloud Academy**: This platform offers structured learning paths for AWS certifications, including hands-on labs and quizzes.

- **Tutorial Dojo**: This platform provides a mix of free and paid content, including practice exams and cheat sheets that are highly regarded for exam preparation.

- **AWS exam preparation webinars**: AWS regularly hosts webinars focusing on exam preparation, offering insights into the exam structure and tips for success.

- **Instructor-led classroom training**: Though often the priciest option, they offer intensive, focused training sessions that can significantly boost your understanding and readiness for the exam. Perform due diligence and prefer official training delivered by AWS-accredited instructors in case of doubt.

- **Mentoring and peering**: Connecting with peers or finding a mentor who has successfully navigated AWS certifications can provide personalized advice and encouragement.

Having explored the key resources that are available for your exam preparation, let's move on to practical advice and strategies that can enhance your study routine and performance.

Personal advice from an experienced exam taker

Having taken more than 20 exams in my career and only failing two on the first attempt, I recommend the following strategies for effective exam preparation:

- **Diversify learning resources**: Use at least two different types of learning resources to cover all bases and limit the risk of bias from specific authors – for example, a Udemy video course and a book, or a video course and a Cloud Academy learning path.

- **Develop a detailed learning plan**: Structure your study time and topics to cover comprehensively. Set achievable goals, regularly assess your progress, and adjust your plan as necessary to stay on track.

- **Schedule your exam date and time**: Booking your exam in advance gives you a clear deadline to work toward. Schedule your exam for when you are most alert and focused. For many like myself, the morning is ideal. Additionally, after booking your exam, consider giving a call or sending an email to the exam center. Some centers are infrequently used, and issues such as no staff presence on the exam day can occur, leading to lengthy rescheduling frustrations.

- **Practice with exam quizzes**: Engage in extensive quiz practice, focusing on retaking failed questions and undertaking full new quizzes to simulate the exam experience and improve time management. Aim to consistently score above 80% on fresh quizzes to gauge your readiness for the real exam day.

- **Manage time**: Always aim to answer all questions as guessing yields a better success rate than leaving answers blank. Calculate the time per question and set easy-to-remember milestones. As an example, the CSC exam requires 65 questions to be answered within 170 minutes, which means you should allocate 2.5 minutes and 37 seconds for each question. Aim to answer 12 questions after the first 30 minutes, 24 questions by the 60-minute mark, and so on.

- **Prefer in-person exams for lengthy tests**: While online proctoring allows for taking an exam from home, it can be overly strict, risking disqualification for minor infractions. My preference is to opt for test centers to avoid these issues.

Moving on from the AWS certification, let's delve into continuous professional development, emphasizing the power of participating in events and networks.

Engaging in continuous professional development

Continuous professional development is essential for staying current in the rapidly evolving field of cloud computing and AWS security. Engaging in such activities ensures that professionals not only maintain their skills and knowledge but also stay ahead of new AWS technologies and security best practices. Let's go through strategies for engaging in continuous learning and professional growth.

Participating in webinars

AWS and other reputable platforms frequently host webinars covering a broad spectrum of topics, from unveiling new services to comprehensive explorations of specific security practices. These sessions, which are often led by field experts, present a prime opportunity to stay abreast of the latest trends and best practices in AWS security. The majority of these webinars are offered free of charge, providing an accessible avenue for broadening your knowledge. Engaging in these webinars not only enhances your expertise but also facilitates interaction with professionals and allows for direct questioning. Here's how to derive maximum benefit from these learning opportunities:

- **Select relevant topics**: Focus on webinars and courses that align with your career goals and areas where you seek improvement or deeper knowledge.

- **Engage with experts**: Most webinars offer Q&A sessions. Take advantage of these opportunities to engage directly with AWS experts and gain insights that are not readily available in written content. It is also common to connect with speakers on LinkedIn post-event. Seize the opportunity to expand your professional network and deepen your understanding.

- **Dedicate time for learning**: Schedule regular slots in your weekly or monthly schedule for attending webinars or progressing through online courses, treating them as essential components of your workweek.

- **Apply learned concepts**: After attending a webinar, look for AWS workshops or consult the AWS Security Blog for posts that offer hands-on applications related to the topics discussed. This approach helps bridge the gap between theoretical knowledge and practical implementation.

- **Become a speaker**: Consider sharing your expertise by becoming a webinar speaker. This not only enhances your visibility within the professional community as a thought leader in AWS security but also deepens your understanding of the subject matter as you prepare your presentation.

The following platforms are known to regularly host webinars related to AWS security:

- **AWS events and webinars**: This page lists all upcoming AWS webinars and events, ensuring access to the latest information directly from the source.

- **Securzy**: A platform dedicated to security professionals, it offers deep-dive sessions into the latest AWS security technologies and challenges. While most webinars are free, replays may require a subscription.

- **BrightTALK and TechTarget**: Both platforms offer a wide range of webinars across various topics, including cloud security and AWS-specific sessions. Note that content is often sponsored by vendors, so a degree of marketing material can be expected, yet they remain valuable for educational content.

- **Cloud Academy**: While primarily known for its comprehensive courses, Cloud Academy also hosts webinars that delve into the latest trends and practices in AWS and cloud security.

- **Cloud Security Alliance (CSA)**: CSA provides webinars focusing on wider cloud security issues, which is ideal for those looking to understand the broader security landscape.

Following webinars, let's dive into the opportunities offered by AWS conferences.

Attending AWS conferences

AWS conferences provide opportunities for deep immersion in the AWS community. Here's how to make the most of these events:

- **Virtual or in-person attendance**: Many AWS conferences are accessible both virtually and in-person, catering to a global audience. Virtual attendance can be a convenient option for those unable to travel, while in-person attendance offers a more immersive experience and direct networking opportunities.

- **Plan your agenda**: With numerous sessions available in parallel and limited seats available, review the agenda in advance and prioritize sessions that are most relevant to your interests and professional needs.

- **Network actively**: Use these gatherings to connect with peers, AWS professionals, and industry leaders. Networking can open doors to new opportunities, insights, and collaborative ventures.

- **Participate in workshops and breakout sessions**: These interactive sessions provide valuable hands-on experience and facilitate deeper discussions on security features and challenges.

- **Stay updated on announcements**: AWS often introduces new services, features, and updates during these events. Keeping up with these announcements can give you a competitive edge.

- **Replay access**: Many conferences offer replay access to sessions post-event. This feature is useful for revisiting content or catching up on sessions you may have missed, ensuring you don't miss out on any learning opportunities.

Here is an overview of key relevant AWS conferences:

- **AWS summits**: These are free events that are hosted around the world, designed to bring the cloud computing community together to connect, collaborate, and learn about AWS. Attending these summits provides insights into new AWS features, networking opportunities with AWS experts and peers from your country, as well as hands-on workshops that can enhance your practical skills.

- **AWS re:Invent**: This is the largest annual AWS cloud conference, offering multiple sessions on cloud strategies, security, and service deep dives. Besides attending AWS re:Invent, look for re:Cap sessions that summarize key takeaways, something that's perfect for those unable to attend every session of interest.

- **AWS re:Inforce**: This is another key event for security professionals and AWS enthusiasts focusing specifically on security. It is ideal for gaining advanced knowledge, discovering new tools and techniques, and networking with industry leaders in that field.

Transitioning from conferences, let's shift our focus to communities and peer networks.

Leveraging communities and peer networks

Continuous professional development thrives on a strong support network. Seek out and engage with communities of like-minded individuals to exchange knowledge, troubleshoot challenges, and stay updated on the evolving AWS landscape. Here are a few ways to get involved:

- **Online forums**: Utilize platforms such as AWS re:Post and Stack Overflow to ask questions, share your expertise, and connect with the broader AWS community.

- **Local meetups and user groups**: Discover AWS user groups in your area. These gatherings foster a sense of community and create valuable opportunities for collaboration and networking with peers.

- **AWS Community Builders**: This program offers a wealth of resources, mentorship, and networking opportunities for those passionate about sharing AWS knowledge. It's a fantastic way to accelerate your learning, grow your professional network, and give back to the AWS community.

- **Conferences and community events**: Actively participate in the various events hosted by AWS, community groups, or third-party organizations. These are excellent avenues to expand your professional network, learn from others' experiences, and stay abreast of the latest trends in AWS security.

- **Find a mentor**: Build relationships with experienced community members for mentorship and guidance. A mentor can help you learn faster, avoid common pitfalls, and become an active contributor to the AWS security community yourself.

In the next and final section, we will review best practices for keeping abreast of AWS security advancements, enabling you to proactively strengthen your knowledge and your AWS environment's security posture.

Keeping abreast with new technologies

The AWS ecosystem is dynamic, with the landscape of cloud technology and security threats constantly evolving. AWS and third-party vendors frequently introduce new security services, features, and tools designed to address these challenges. For AWS professionals, staying updated with these innovations is not just about enhancing security postures—it is also about ensuring their knowledge remains current. This section delves into effective strategies for keeping pace with these developments and seamlessly integrating them into your environment.

Staying informed

Information is power in the realm of security. Security professionals must proactively seek out information on the latest AWS security announcements and security blog posts related to their topics of interest. Regular participation in AWS-specific webinars and workshops provides opportunities to gain firsthand knowledge of the latest updates and how they can be applied in practice. These resources can help you to anticipate and mitigate emerging threats with the latest AWS security technologies.

The next crucial phase involves evaluating and testing these advancements within AWS.

Evaluating and testing

Upon discovering new security technologies, evaluating their potential impact and testing their effectiveness is key. This involves doing the following:

- **Defining security enhancement objectives**: Evaluate how new services or features can bolster your security posture. Establish clear metrics for evaluating new security tools, including performance, compatibility with existing systems, and overall security enhancement.

- **Testing in a controlled environment**: Implement new technologies in a sandbox or development environment first. This allows you to gauge their performance, identify any integration issues, and understand their operational implications without risking production systems.

- **Security testing**: Determine the actual security benefits by simulating attack scenarios or using penetration testing tools. Evaluate how technology improves your defense against these simulated threats.

- **Performance testing**: Measure how the new technology performs under different scenarios. Look at its responsiveness, speed, and resource consumption during peak and off-peak hours.

Following evaluation and testing, let's transition to ensuring compatibility and compliance as our next essential step.

Ensuring compatibility and compliance

As new security technologies are adopted, ensuring compatibility with existing systems and compliance with relevant regulations is essential. This step requires a thorough review of how new tools interact with current architectures and an assessment of compliance implications, especially for industries subject to strict regulatory standards. This requires doing the following:

- **Mapping the current infrastructure**: Start by creating an updated map or diagram of your current AWS infrastructure and security setup. This will help you pinpoint where new tools will be integrated.

- **Identifying integration points**: Highlight specific areas within your infrastructure where the new security solutions will interact with existing systems. This could include network connections, data flows, APIs, and Lambda functions.

- **Compatibility assessment**: Conduct a detailed analysis of how new security solutions integrate with your current AWS setup. Look for potential conflicts or dependencies that might affect their function.

- **Compliance evaluation**: For organizations subject to industry regulations, it is crucial to ensure that new technologies do not compromise compliance. Review the security and compliance documentation provided by AWS or third-party vendors to understand their implications.

Next, let's discuss how to effectively integrate these solutions into your environment.

Integrating into existing environments

The successful adoption of new security technologies depends on their integration into your existing AWS environment without causing disruptions. This involves doing the following:

- **Incremental deployments**: Gradually introduce new technologies, starting with non-critical systems to minimize disruption and allow for adjustments based on initial observations.

- **Automating where possible**: Leverage automation for the integration process to reduce manual errors and streamline deployment. Automation can also assist in maintaining configuration standards across your environment.

- **Updating security documentation**: Revise your existing security documentation. This update should cover any new **Standard Operating Procedures** (**SOPs**) introduced by the integration.

- **Monitoring and adjusting**: After deployment, continuously monitor for operational and security performance. Be prepared to make adjustments based on the outcome.

Integration lays the groundwork for our final focus—planning for future-proof security.

Planning for future-proof security

Adopting a forward-thinking approach to security can help you stay ahead of threats and leverage innovations in the AWS ecosystem effectively. This includes doing the following:

- **Future trends analysis**: Keep an eye on emerging trends and anticipate technological advancements by leveraging market studies from renowned institutes such as Gartner, Forrester, and the **Cloud Security Alliance** (**CSA**). Such research provides a broad view of the cloud security landscape, helping you predict shifts in threats and technology that could impact your security posture.

- **Engaging with AWS previews**: Participate in AWS beta and preview programs by regularly checking AWS blogs and announcements, engaging with the AWS community, and attending AWS events for early access to upcoming features and services. This engagement not only offers a sneak peek into potential AWS innovations but also allows you to test and adapt these technologies in a controlled manner, giving you a competitive edge in security preparedness.

- **Monitoring AWS roadmaps**: Keep a close watch on AWS product roadmaps and future feature announcements. By staying informed about planned developments, you can better align your security measures and strategies with upcoming AWS enhancements.

- **Adopting an adaptive security framework**: Establish an inherently adaptable security framework, allowing for the seamless integration of new technologies. Such a framework typically involves modular security policies that can be quickly updated, automation to swiftly implement changes, and continuous monitoring to assess the effectiveness of your current security measures.

Employing these strategies will help you stay abreast of new security developments and ensure that your AWS environment remains secure and prepared for the future. Concluding our exploration of future-proof security strategies, let's pivot to a summary of the essential points that were discussed throughout this chapter.

Summary

This final chapter served as a comprehensive guide for AWS professionals aiming to stay at the forefront of AWS security advancements. We delved into the critical importance of staying current with AWS security best practices and the evolving threat landscape. This chapter emphasized the necessity of continuous learning and adaptation in the face of rapidly advancing cloud technologies and security threats. We explored how AWS professionals can leverage a wide array of resources, including educational materials, training and certification programs, and community insights to enhance their security knowledge and skills. Through strategic planning, regular engagement with AWS updates, and proactive integration of new security measures, professionals can fortify their AWS environments against current and future vulnerabilities. This chapter serves as a guide to navigating the complex and dynamic field of AWS security, providing the tools and strategies needed to maintain a robust and resilient security posture.

Questions

Answer the following questions to test your knowledge of this chapter:

1. What is cryptojacking and why is it a concern for cloud environments?
2. What role does the MITRE ATT&CK for Cloud matrix play in understanding cloud-specific threats?

Answers

Here are the answers to this chapter's questions:

1. Cryptojacking involves attackers exploiting cloud resources to mine cryptocurrency, leading to higher operational costs and degraded performance for legitimate cloud workloads.
2. The MITRE ATT&CK for Cloud matrix offers a comprehensive matrix of tactics and techniques that are used by cyber adversaries and tailored for cloud environments, helping organizations anticipate and counteract threats. This tool can be used for risk assessment, continuous monitoring, and incident response.

14
Closing Note

Reflecting on the journey we have undertaken together through this book, we see the complexity and the rewards of mastering AWS security. From the foundational principles to the advanced tactics and strategies, this book has been designed as a comprehensive guide to secure your AWS environment effectively. Let's revisit the essence of our exploration, emphasizing the continuous evolution of cloud security and the imperative of lifelong learning and application, and conclude with a forward-looking perspective.

The essence of AWS security mastery

Our journey began with the shared responsibility model, a foundational concept that sets the stage for understanding the balance of security tasks between AWS and its users. We ventured deeper into infrastructure security, IAM, data protection, and the vast arsenal of AWS security services. We dissected VPC design, IAM intricacies, the power of encryption, the nuances of securing microservices, serverless deployments, multi-tenancy, automating security, and many more topics. Each chapter was built upon the last, brick-by-brick, layering knowledge to equip you with a robust framework for AWS security. With practical examples and in-depth discussions, the goal was to illuminate the path toward a comprehensive and resilient security posture.

The continuous evolution of cloud security

In the realms of AWS, cloud computing, and cybersecurity, change is the only constant. New threats emerge with increasing sophistication, prompting AWS to continuously roll out new services and features. These advancements are designed not just to combat emerging threats but also to meet the evolving demands of businesses. This ever-shifting landscape demands a proactive and informed security approach – an approach agile enough to embrace change and integrate cutting-edge technologies.

A significant part of AWS security's future lies in the advancements of **artificial intelligence** (**AI**), **machine learning** (**ML**), and the burgeoning field of generative AI. These technologies are already reshaping our security strategies, from enhancing threat detection and prediction to automating security responses. AWS has begun this transformative journey, integrating AI and ML into services such as Amazon GuardDuty for intelligent threat detection and Amazon SageMaker for building ML models to predict and thwart security vulnerabilities. As AWS continues to innovate, your ability to harness these technologies is crucial for staying ahead in the security domain.

The journey of continuous learning

As the landscape of cloud security continuously evolves, so does the need for perpetual learning and adaptation. True mastery in AWS security transcends theory; it thrives on application. This book has provided the seeds, but the garden of your expertise must be continually cultivated. The vast expanse of cloud security demands relentless curiosity, exploration, and hands-on experience. To refine your skills, actively engage with the vibrant AWS community, dive into forums and workshops, and embark on real-world projects that challenge and expand your knowledge. Remember, the path to proficiency is one of perpetual learning, where each challenge conquered is a stepping stone toward mastery.

In conclusion

This book marks a significant milestone in your journey toward AWS security mastery, but it is merely the beginning. The road ahead is filled with opportunities to expand your knowledge and refine your skills. As you progress, carry the principles and insights from these pages with you. May this knowledge serve as a foundation upon which you will continue to build, innovate, and secure within the ever-evolving AWS ecosystem.

Keep learning, keep exploring, and keep securing your cloud with passion and expertise.

Index

A

www.packtpub.com

Subscribe to our online digital library for full access to over 7,000 books and videos, as well as industry leading tools to help you plan your personal development and advance your career. For more information, please visit our website.

Why subscribe?

- Spend less time learning and more time coding with practical eBooks and Videos from over 4,000 industry professionals

- Improve your learning with Skill Plans built especially for you

- Get a free eBook or video every month

- Fully searchable for easy access to vital information

- Copy and paste, print, and bookmark content

Did you know that Packt offers eBook versions of every book published, with PDF and ePub files available? You can upgrade to the eBook version at packtpub.com and as a print book customer, you are entitled to a discount on the eBook copy. Get in touch with us at customercare@packtpub.com for more details.

At www.packtpub.com, you can also read a collection of free technical articles, sign up for a range of free newsletters, and receive exclusive discounts and offers on Packt books and eBooks.

Other Books You May Enjoy

If you enjoyed this book, you may be interested in these other books by Packt:

Building and Automating Penetration Testing Labs in the Cloud

Joshua Arvin Lat

ISBN: 978-1-83763-239-8

- Build vulnerable-by-design labs that mimic modern cloud environments
- Find out how to manage the risks associated with cloud lab environments
- Use infrastructure as code to automate lab infrastructure deployments
- Validate vulnerabilities present in penetration testing labs
- Find out how to manage the costs of running labs on AWS, Azure, and GCP
- Set up IAM privilege escalation labs for advanced penetration testing
- Use generative AI tools to generate infrastructure as code templates
- Import the Kali Linux Generic Cloud Image to the cloud with ease

Cloud Auditing Best Practices

Shinesa Cambric, Michael Ratemo

ISBN: 978-1-80324-377-1

- Understand the cloud shared responsibility and role of an IT auditor
- Explore change management and integrate it with DevSecOps processes
- Understand the value of performing cloud control assessments
- Learn tips and tricks to perform an advanced and effective auditing program
- Enhance visibility by monitoring and assessing cloud environments
- Examine IAM, network, infrastructure, and logging controls
- Use policy and compliance automation with tools such as Terraform

Packt is searching for authors like you

If you're interested in becoming an author for Packt, please visit `authors.packtpub.com` and apply today. We have worked with thousands of developers and tech professionals, just like you, to help them share their insight with the global tech community. You can make a general application, apply for a specific hot topic that we are recruiting an author for, or submit your own idea.

Share Your Thoughts

Now you've finished *Mastering AWS Security*, we'd love to hear your thoughts! Scan the QR code below to go straight to the Amazon review page for this book and share your feedback or leave a review on the site that you purchased it from.

https://packt.link/r/1805125443

Your review is important to us and the tech community and will help us make sure we're delivering excellent quality content.

Download a free PDF copy of this book

Thanks for purchasing this book!

Do you like to read on the go but are unable to carry your print books everywhere?

Is your eBook purchase not compatible with the device of your choice?

Don't worry, now with every Packt book you get a DRM-free PDF version of that book at no cost.

Read anywhere, any place, on any device. Search, copy, and paste code from your favorite technical books directly into your application.

The perks don't stop there, you can get exclusive access to discounts, newsletters, and great free content in your inbox daily

Follow these simple steps to get the benefits:

1. Scan the QR code or visit the link below

https://packt.link/free-ebook/978-1-80512-544-0

2. Submit your proof of purchase
3. That's it! We'll send your free PDF and other benefits to your email directly

Made in the USA
Middletown, DE
24 September 2024

61375875R00205